DOMESTIC MANNERS

OF THE AMERICANS

PORTRAIT OF

FRANCES TROLLOPE

[FROM THE FIFTH EDITION]

DOMESTIC MANNERS

OF THE

AMERICANS

BY

Frances Trollope

EDITED, WITH A HISTORY OF
MRS. TROLLOPE'S ADVENTURES IN AMERICA,
by DONALD SMALLEY

GLOUCESTER, MASS.

PETER SMITH

1974

155040

PUBLISHED BY VINTAGE BOOKS, INC.

By arrangement with *Alfred A. Knopf, Inc.*

FIRST VINTAGE EDITION

Reprinted, 1974, by Permission of
Alfred A. Knopf, Inc.

ISBN: 0-8446-3090-X

MARK TWAIN, in the suppressed passages of
Life on the Mississippi:

"It was for this sort of photography that poor candid Mrs. Trollope was so handsomely cursed and reviled by this nation. Yet she was merely telling the truth, and this indignant nation knew it. She was painting a state of things which did not disappear at once. It lasted to well along in my youth, and I remember it. . . .

"Of all those tourists I like Dame Trollope best. She found a 'civilization' here which you, reader, could not have endured; and which you would not have regarded as a civilization at all. Mrs. Trollope spoke of this civilization in plain terms — plain and unsugared, but honest and without malice, and without hate. . . .

"She lived three years in this civilization of ours; in the body of it — not on the surface of it, as was the case with most of the foreign tourists of her day. She knew her subject well, and she set it forth fairly and squarely, without any weak ifs and ands and buts. She deserved gratitude — but it is an error to suppose she got it.

"Nearly all the tourists were honest and fair; nearly all felt a sincere kindness for us; nearly all of them glossed us over a little too anxiously . . . but Mrs. Trollope, alone of them all, dealt what the gamblers call a strictly 'square game.' She did not gild us; and neither did she whitewash us."

INTRODUCTION

MRS. TROLLOPE IN AMERICA

BY

DONALD SMALLEY

WHEN Frances Trollope, mother of the novelist Anthony
Trollope, sailed for America late in 1827, she did not intend
to write a book of travels but to found a department store.
At Cincinnati, Ohio, then a pushing frontier town of twenty
thousand inhabitants, she planned and erected her Bazaar, a
huge, fantastic structure that remained for years a marvel of
the community. While the Bazaar was building, Mrs. Trollope looked about her. She was an Englishwoman of refined
sensibilities, and she beheld with intense curiosity and some
alarm the ways of the natives in the youngest section of a
young democracy. The larger meaning of what she saw —
the portentous stir and shaping of Western empire — she was
unfitted by both background and temperament to understand. But nothing in the detail of the raw new life escaped
her. She took notes on it all — the oddities of speech and
dress and politics, of eating and love-making and housekeeping, the curious manners of the parlor, the ballroom, the marketplace, and the camp meeting.

Three years and nine months after she had sailed for
America, she was once again in England. She had undergone
strange and trying adventures. Her Cincinnati speculation
had failed utterly, sweeping away every farthing of her capital; even her household furnishings had been seized. During
her last months in the United States she had lived in humili-
ating poverty, depending for her livelihood upon the charity
of a friend. One asset, and that a doubtful one, she brought

with her from America — the nearly completed manuscript of a book of travels. She had seen much of American life during her three and a half years in America, most of it from the rough side of the cloth; she had few hosts to thank and small cause to soften her remarks for reasons of diplomacy. In her book she set down her experiences with an abundance of lively anecdote and intimate detail that makes the accounts of earlier travelers seem formal and abstruse by comparison.

I

Frances Trollope's *Domestic Manners of the Americans* reached the public on March 19, 1832. It could not have come out at a better time. Agitation for the reform of Parliament along more democratic lines was at its highest pitch. The Tories snatched at her disparaging tale of life in a democracy as potent propaganda. The powerful Tory *Quarterly Review* praised Mrs. Trollope as "an English *lady* of sense and acuteness" and rejoiced that her book on America appeared at a moment "when so much trash and falsehood pass current respecting that 'terrestrial paradise of the west.' " Friends of the Reform Bill damned Mrs. Trollope's two volumes as loudly as the Tories praised them. The Whig *Edinburgh Review* called her an irresponsible caricaturist who drew her sketches not with pen and Indian ink but with vitriol and a blacking brush. Her book, it said, was nothing but four-and-thirty chapters of American scandal.

But Britons of both parties read her book and relished it for the racy genre pictures of American life with which its pages abound. Before the end of the year, *Domestic Manners* had run through four editions, "Yankeeisms" were a conversational fad, and Mrs. Trollope was a literary lion, well launched at the age of fifty-two upon her remarkable career as a writer of novels and travel books. In the next quarter-century she was to publish no less than one hundred and thirteen volumes.

In the United States an outraged citizenry read *Domestic Manners* as they had read no travel book before it. Lieutenant E. T. Coke, a British subaltern who was at New York when Mrs. Trollope's book first appeared there, found the commotion that it created "truly inconceivable."

The Tariff and Bank Bill were alike forgotten, and the tug of war was hard, whether the "Domestic Manners," or the cholera, which burst upon them simultaneously, should be the more engrossing topic of conversation. At every corner of the street, at the door of every petty retailer of information for the people, a large placard met the eye with, "For sale here, with plates, Domestic Manners of the Americans, by Mrs. Trollope." At every table d'hote, on board of every steam-boat, in every stage-coach, and in all societies, the first question was, "Have you read Mrs. Trollope?" And one half of the people would be seen with a red or blue half-bound volume in their hand, which you might vouch for being the odious work; and the more it was abused the more rapidly did the printers issue new editions.

Newspapers in every section of the country made a pastime of reviling Mrs. Trollope, though they also quoted long sections from her book. Even the polished quarterlies denounced her "coarse exaggeration" and "bitter caricature"; a Western editor indexed his review under "Lies of an English lady." American journalists soberly repeated, and probably believed, that "libeling the United States" had netted her "the immense profit of between one hundred and thirty and one hundred and forty thousand dollars."

Frances Trollope was soon one of the best-known of British authors throughout America, and the worst-hated. She was lampooned in prose and poetry and on the stage; she was travestied in cartoons. She became a folk character. A frontiersman named his "hound with a number of whelps" after her. A circus band played "Mrs. Trollope's March" to the roar of a lion. "A Trollope! a Trollope!" became the accustomed cry from the pits of theaters when gentlemen failed to sit properly in the boxes. A German traveler reported viewing a wax figure of Mrs. Trollope in New York. "She appeared in the form of a goblin and the public is given the pleasure to see her in this form for the price of admission." In Maine an English tourist encountered a traveling menagerie which advertised " 'an exact likeness' of the celebrated Mrs. Trollope":

. . . this exact likeness turned out to be the figure of a fat red-faced *trollop*, smoking a short pipe, and dressed in dirty flannel and worsted, and a ragged slouched hat.

"This," said the showman, "is the purty Mrs. Trollope, who was sent over to the United States by the British lords, to write libels against the free-born Americans." The figure excited a good deal of attention, and was abused in no measured terms.

More than one responsible person in England and America feared that behind such smoke there might lurk the sparks of an international "incident." An American writer, Timothy Flint, half-seriously plotted the course by which Mrs. Trollope's book could lead to open war.

We first fight the wordy war of tongue and pen. The emergency comes, and evil passions, and concentrated and long-gathered bitternesses concur with reasons of state, and the passions of a dominant party, to engender a war, and we redden the ocean and the land with human blood, that is spilled because Mrs. Trollope had no letters of recommendation, and was a short dumpling and ill-dressed figure — a war of a frock and a petticoat.

No blood was spilled, but the war of words, kept in motion by the works of other critical British travelers, went on for years and was a serious factor in Anglo-American relations.

To a modern reader, the amount of resentment that Mrs. Trollope raised is apt to seem out of all proportion to the modest pretensions of her book. She carefully disavows at the start any claim to furnish "complete information" about America. Her subject, she insists, is simply "the daily aspect of ordinary life," and she proposes to limit herself to recording her own observations during her three years and six months in the United States. Few travelers, as a matter of fact, have written so intimately of their day-to-day experiences and their thoughts and feelings in a strange land. *Domestic Manners* is essentially the story of Frances Trollope. It neither promises nor affords a rounded view of American society. Because she came to the United States as a threadbare business woman, her tale has a good deal more to do with petty tradesmen and their wives, with trips to market and revival meetings, with cheap travel and cheap boarding-houses, than it has to do with American drawing-rooms. Because her own experiences were not happy, she paints an unflattering picture of life in the New World. And because she wrote of her own adventures and denied any intention of doing more than that, she felt free to criticize everything and everybody in the offhand manner that is a privilege of the personal raconteur. It was this airy irresponsibility of Frances Trollope's that, more than anything else, infuriated American reviewers. She could speak lightly of her "gossipy pages," but thousands on two continents read them. She modestly disclaimed any right to sit upon the judge's bench, and then proceeded, in effect, to pronounce opinion upon all America from a tradesman's front parlor and a stagecoach seat.

There is no good reason, however, to believe the charges of her American reviewers that she willfully distorted her account of what she saw. She was ambitious for detail and for accuracy. She early developed the habit of jotting down particulars and pursued it often at strange times and in strange places. She did not let her sense of propriety keep her from chatting with the wife of a publican or peering beneath the flap of a camp-meeting tent. She describes the mores of the back country with a downright frankness that shocked her bluestocking friends. In the preface to her *Belgium and Western Germany in 1833* she wrote an oblique reply to the charges of her critics.

My little volumes on America have been much read. Many have said that this was owing to their being written with strong party feeling:

but I — who am in the secret — know that such was not the case. The
cause of their success, therefore, must be sought elsewhere; and I attribute it solely to that intuitive power of discerning what is written
with truth, which is possessed, often unconsciously, by every reader.
Be he pleased, or displeased by the pictures brought before him, he
feels that the images portrayed are real; and this will interest, even if
it vex him.

I have an inveterate habit of suffering all I see to make a deep impression on my memory; and the result of this is a sort of mosaic, by
no means very grand in outline or skilful in drawing; but each morsel
of colour has the reality of truth — in which there is ever some value.

While the storm of criticism against her was at its fiercest,
Americans could concede that she had struck truth on many,
or perhaps most, points. Washington Irving, who toured the
West a few months after *Domestic Manners* was published,
took the book along with him and read it "not without acquiescence." With the passage of time, even Cincinnati, which
was her principal subject and had by all odds greatest cause
to complain of the sharpness of her pencil, came to see her in
a fairer light. "Her book," says Charles Anderson, looking
back upon events that he had witnessed as a young man, "was
too just a picture of our people to make her anything in their
opinion than the very opposite of what she was." "That her
book aroused the hot indignation of Cincinnatians was altogether proper," Charles Frederick Goss writes in his history
of the city (1912), "but that she gave a pretty true account of
affairs here is also true." Her scenes of American life, it is now
generally agreed, are as honest as they are sharp-cut and
graphic. Of course they are limited in perspective. They represent America in the age of Jackson as it was seen and felt
by an especially English Englishwoman who had strong personal reasons for viewing the New World with disenchanted
eyes.

These reasons were largely born of Cincinnati. To appreciate the peculiar qualities of *Domestic Manners,* one needs
to know more of certain episodes that occurred during Mrs.

Trollope's two eventful years in that frontier city and of the curious sequence of events that led her there than can be found in the pages of her book.

II

In the fall of 1827 Frances Wright came to Harrow to visit Thomas Anthony Trollope and his wife Frances Trollope, her friends of some years' standing. The visit was not purely social in character. Miss Wright was soon to take ship once more for the United States, the country of her ardent adoption. She was now a dedicated person, and she had returned to Europe the preceding May only to recover from a fever and to enlist new members for the co-operative enterprise that occupied her thoughts, energies, and finances. Her health had improved in Europe, but her recruiting had not gone well. In fact, she arrived at Harrow without having persuaded any of several likely prospects to go with her to the United States. In the Trollopes' household she was to have better luck.

Miss Wright was a tall young woman, handsome in a mannish way, who was given to intense enthusiasms for nearly all advanced causes, including socialism, rationalism, and women's rights. She was a reformer by temperament, and a large inheritance enabled her to satisfy her itch for putting her ideas to the test of practice. Scottish by birth, English by rearing, Fanny Wright had made her first voyage to America in 1818 at the age of twenty-three. She had brought with her a sheaf of manuscript teeming with revolutionary feeling and a scheme for founding a school of republican drama. Failing in this project after stirring up mild commotion, she had returned to England in 1820 to publish a book full of fleers at British institutions and praise for nearly all things American.

The Trollopes had first met her through friends of both soon after her return. Mr. Trollope, according to a family tradition, read her book in manuscript and was influential in getting it published. The Trollopes' friendship with Miss Wright, once formed, improved rapidly. She was soon dating letters from their home. When they visited Paris in 1824, she made their trip memorable by introducing them to her "paternal father," General Lafayette, the venerable hero of the American Revolution, who entertained them splendidly at his château La Grange. Fanny Wright sailed for America a second time in the fall of 1824, and the Trollopes did not see her again until her fateful descent upon their Harrow household in the fall of 1827.

Fanny Wright's talk was now full of her plans for Nashoba, the colony that she had founded during the interval. On the Wolf River, fifteen miles behind Memphis, Tennessee, she had bought several hundred acres of land and set up a model plantation that was to solve the problem of Negro slavery in America. Here slaves would work their way to emancipation while the schools of Nashoba prepared them and their children for leading free and enlightened lives outside the United States. But Nashoba was also to be the seat of a white cooperative community, an improved and more daring New Harmony, where European settlers of good will and advanced thinking could live in communal harmony amid the charms of rustic scenery in a brave new country. The Trollopes were not ready to become members of Fanny Wright's freethinking communal society. Frances Trollope, the more impressible of the two, liked bright company of all sorts, including charming revolutionists; but she had a healthy respect for the conventions and daily put her daughters through the catechism. What she and her husband listened to with eager attention was the glowing account Fanny Wright gave them of Western America.

Both the Trollopes were ripe for visions of the New World as a land rich in opportunity. While Miss Wright's plans and principles had been growing bolder, the Trollopes had been drifting closer and closer to bankruptcy. For the last ten years their finances had been steadily dwindling. Mr. Trollope, a pedantic, irritable man dogged by ill luck and violent headaches, was an able student of the law, but he had ruined his practice by arguing with his clients. Nevertheless, confident of inheriting a fortune from a childless uncle, he had built a large and splendid house near Harrow on leased land and had proceeded to lose more money as a gentleman farmer. When the uncle who had been expected to make all things right married a second time and begot an heir in his old age, the Trollopes found themselves in a desperate situation. The Harrow estate continued to cost far more than it brought in, and they were committed to a long-term lease. Trollope's law practice promised no improvement. They may often have thought of mending their fortunes in America — what English family in difficulties had not? — but now, with the advent of Fanny Wright, there was an immediate spur to action. Here was the turn for which the Trollopes had been waiting.

A business venture in the New World would redress the misfortunes that had brought them perilously low in the Old. Frances Trollope, it was finally decided, would sail for the United States with her friend Miss Wright. She would take three of her five children with her. While Anthony, who was twelve, and Tom, who was seventeen, remained in school at Winchester, her nine- and eleven-year-old daughters, Emily and Cecilia, and Henry, a muscular but ailing boy of sixteen, would accompany her. Henry had rebelled against his studies at Winchester, and he had also failed to make the most of an opportunity to gain a footing in a Parisian counting-house. He was to receive another chance to prove himself in Western America. Mrs. Trollope with her three children would spend some months at Nashoba enjoying the pleasures of Miss Wright's forest colony; then she would continue her journey up the Mississippi and the Ohio to Cincinnati. It was here that the serious business of making a fortune would begin.[1] In Cincinnati, within a few miles of the backwoods, Frances Trollope and her husband planned to establish a glorified department store, an emporium where the citizens could buy fancy goods from London and Paris. Mrs. Trollope was to make the preliminary arrangements; Mr. Trollope was to buy stock and sail later.

This plan was less impracticable than has often been made out; but it is doubtful whether Frances Trollope would have done much better in Cincinnati with the soundest of plans. Certainly few women entered the back country of America with greater handicaps of rearing and circumstance. She was already forty-seven, a middle-aged woman of bluestocking tendencies who loved her daily round of domestic duties and who also was extremely fond of parties and good society and all the amenities of genteel European living. When the evil days had come, she and her husband had taken to reading by two tallow candles, but they still kept a liveried footman. There was a restlessness and an easy optimism about her that made her welcome a new adventure, but nothing in her earlier career had prepared her for the rigors of existence in a raw community of the Western United States. She was innocent of any knowledge of business affairs. She brought with her three children and a pitifully meager stock of money.

---

[1] Cincinnati received a good deal of publicity in and about London during the fall of 1827 through the efforts of William Bullock, English showman, traveler, and lecturer, who was trying to secure settlers for the model town he proposed to build directly opposite Cincinnati on the Kentucky shore of the Ohio River. The Trollopes may well have known about Bullock's recruiting activities. As part of his program to obtain colonists, Bullock published his *Sketch of a Journey through the Western States,* in which he not only detailed his own highly favorable impressions of Cincinnati but reprinted as an appendix the whole of *Cincinnati in 1826,* a thick pamphlet describing this rising Western center and its rapid advancement from a "humble village . . . to the rank and opulence of a city." Bullock's book reached the public in late October or early November, probably too late to figure in the Trollopes' councils; but Bullock quite possibly gave an advance copy to his fellow recruiter, Fanny Wright — or to the Trollopes themselves, for that matter.

III

On November 4 the Nashoba party sailed from London for New Orleans. Besides Frances Wright, Mrs. Trollope, her son Henry, her daughters, Emily and Cecilia, and the Trollope's manservant, there was Auguste Hervieu, thirty-three years old, an exile from monarchist France. As a protégé of the Trollopes and a frequent guest at their home, he had learned about Nashoba from its priestess. He was an artist of some ability, and he was now going out as drawing master for the society. On Christmas Day the party arrived at New Orleans; within a fortnight they were at Nashoba.

Where Frances Trollope had expected a comfortable rustic retreat in which she could spend a few months with pleasure, she now found an appalling scene of misery and desolation. A small clearing in the midst of swamps and forest, six or seven crude log cabins, a few Negro slaves and their children, a malaria-shaken white overseer and his sickly wife — these constituted Nashoba. Nothing was as she had imagined it would be. Even the woman who had led her here seemed to undergo a transformation, like a character in a folk tale, and become a strange person amid these alien surroundings. "The Frances Wright of Nashoba," Mrs. Trollope later wrote in the rough draft of her book, "in dress, looks, and manner, bore no more resemblance to the Miss Wright I had known and admired in London and Paris than did her log cabin to the Tuileries or Buckingham Palace." So absorbed was the imagination of Fanny Wright in the affairs of her community that "all her other faculties were in a manner suspended."

Mrs. Trollope shared a bedroom with her hostess. It was without a ceiling, and the rain dripped through the roughly shingled roof. The floor was of planks laid loosely a few feet above the marshy earth. The chimney, which was built of logs lightly plastered with mud, caught fire "at least a dozen times in a day." The food and drink of Nashoba Mrs. Trollope found even harder to bear than its housing. The community was "without milk, without beverage of any kind except rain water. . . . Wheat bread they used but sparingly, and to us the Indian corn bread was uneatable. They had no vegetables but rice, and some potatoes we brought with us, no meat but pork, no cheese, no butter. . . ." But Miss Wright seemed genuinely surprised that her guests should find anything disagreeable in the arrangements of her colony. She "stood in the midst of all this desolation with the air of a conqueror" and dined upon a bit of corn bread and a draft of rain water, smiling the while with a complacency that made her guest think of Peter the Hermit eating acorns in the wilderness.

Immediately upon his arrival, Auguste Hervieu, eager to start upon his duties as drawing master, had cried out: "Where is the school?" He was told that it had not as yet been formed. "I think I never saw a man in such a rage," Mrs. Trollope wrote home. "He wept with passion and grief mixed." Hervieu determined at once to set off for Memphis. As for Frances Trollope, her dismay soon gave way to fear. She observed a painful contrast between the Camilla Wright whom she had known in Europe and the gaunt and obviously ailing Camilla, now Mrs. Whitby, whom she found at Nashoba. When Mrs. Trollope inquired the cause of her evident bad health, Fanny's sister confessed that it was a result of Nashoba's climate. Alarmed for the health of her children, Mrs. Trollope resolved to leave the spot "with as little delay as possible." So scant, however, were the funds with which she had come to America that for the time being there was no alternative to staying.

On January 23 the trustees of Nashoba recorded "a loan of $300 to Mrs. Trollope to assist her in removing from Nashoba to some place in the western world better suited to her future plans for herself and her children." Four days later the Trollopes had left Fanny Wright's community and its marshy forests and its threat of fever and chills. At Memphis the

Trollopes again picked up Auguste Hervieu. He had found a brisk demand for his brush and palette in the little river town, where an artist of his caliber was a prime novelty; but already he had painted nearly all the tradesmen who could afford the luxury of being done in oils. He seemed glad to join fortunes with the Trollopes once more and push on to a new field.

As the steamboat *Criterion* churned its way up the thousand miles of river between Memphis and Cincinnati, Mrs. Trollope had time to meditate on many things. "I used to give a sort of dreamy acquiescence," she wrote later, "to the reasoning that went to prove each added want an added woe. Those who reason in a comfortable London drawing-room, know little about the matter."

On February 10 Frances Trollope reached the city where she was to spend the next twenty-five eventful months.

IV

The *Cincinnati Chronicle* had greeted the advent of 1828 (a leap year, as two letters to the editor point out) with a pardonable complacency. New and better buildings were cropping up as never before. Immigrants were pouring into the city so rapidly that an addition of three hundred houses during the year could not take care of this vast but welcome multitude. Active capital was increasing, and new manufactories springing into being, commerce was enlarging its sphere; indeed, everything connected with the city presented "an aspect of activity, enterprize and substantial prosperity." In a single quarter of a century Cincinnati had risen "from an inconsiderable village, to an opulent city of 19 or 20,000 inhabitants."

River traffic and manufacturing had made Cincinnati the chief city of a vast territory. Flour, whisky, and pork left its expansive wharfage for remote points in the West Indies and South America. Imports totaled upward of three million dollars annually. Cincinnati claimed to have built more steamboats than any other place in the world. As for further branches of industry, by 1826 there were already fifty-four foundries of various kinds, four steam-engine factories, a powder mill, two paper mills, a woolen factory, a sugar refinery, nine printing establishments, and numerous manufacturers besides of white lead, glass, hats, shoe trees, casks and barrels, cabinet furniture, chairs, and other commodities.

Cincinnati possessed a medical college, a hospital, a theater, circulating libraries and reading-rooms, many churches, several schools, and an Academy of Fine Arts. Including religious publications, there were nine newspapers, two of which were dailies. "The refinements of society," concluded the editor of the *Chronicle*, "both of a social and moral kind, exist in a degree that would justify comparison with the larger and older cities of the East."

Mrs. Trollope beheld this bustling metropolis with less delighted eyes. She had heard much, she says, of the wealth and beauty of Cincinnati. Now she saw an "uninteresting mass of buildings," a crude and noisy town without domes, towers, or steeples, where garbage was dumped in the middle of the streets to be cleared away by wandering hogs. Her book gives us a lively account of her early adventures in Cincinnati — her problems in setting up house, her trials with servants, her explorations of the town. Understandably she passes over one grim fact in silence: the scant supply of money that she had brought with her was soon exhausted. Some expense had at first been saved by sending Henry to the co-operative school founded by the philanthropist William Maclure at New Harmony, Indiana, a school where students earned their way by manual labor between classes. Maclure was now in Mexico (Mrs. Trollope had met him at New Orleans while he was on his way), and Madame Fretageot, who managed the school in his absence, had set Henry to work in the fields during his hours away from his studies. Poor Henry's health was not equal to this rigorous regimen, and Mrs. Trollope had to draw upon the savings of Auguste Hervieu for money to bring the lad to Cincinnati.

Once he was in the city, Henry tried to help as best he could. He had been idle in his years at Winchester and had not done well in his studies. Now he made an effort to put to use what learning he had acquired. In the columns of the *Cincinnati Gazette* for March 28, he announced his willingness to offer his services.

MR. HENRY TROLLOPE, having received a completely classical education, at the royal college of Winchester, (England,) would be happy to give lessons in the Latin language to gentlemen at their own houses. By an improved method of teaching, now getting into general use in Europe, Mr. H. Trollope flatters himself he shall be able to give a competent knowledge of the Latin tongue in a much shorter space of time than has hitherto been considered necessary. Terms: Fifty cents for lessons of one hour. Apply to Mr. H. TROLLOPE, Hollingsworth Row, Race street.

But the young gentlemen of Cincinnati were too busy with the challenge of the present to give much of their time to dead languages. On May 4 Mrs. Trollope dispatched her ninth letter to her husband. She had not received a single line from him, and she was now totally dependent upon Auguste Hervieu. "Our situation here would be dreadful," she wrote to her eldest son Tom on the same day, "were it not for M. Hervieu's grateful, and generous kindness. It is more than a month that we have not had a mouthful of food that he has not paid for."

Already Mrs. Trollope's fortunes in America were closely linked with those of Auguste Hervieu. He was to take part in all her enterprises in Cincinnati and to be her companion throughout her travels in the United States, for long periods her only means of support. He was to share *Domestic Manners* with her as the creator of its twenty-four Hogarthian lithographs of American life and thereafter become a sort of family retainer, going with her on her tours about Europe and illustrating her books.

Most of Auguste Jean Jacques Hervieu's life had been spent in a lonely pursuit of art and revolution, without family, without funds. Now, by a sudden turn of chance, he became the provider for a sizable household. Probably he welcomed his new responsibility; he had good reason to be grateful to the Trollopes for past favors, and he must have been drawn close to these English friends by the strangeness of everyone and everything else surrounding him. Born near Paris in 1794, he had lost his mother when he was three, and had been put out to board while his father followed Napoleon as an officer in the commissary. Auguste soon showed a strong liking for art, but his father ordered his crayons and paper taken from him and enrolled him in a school that would train him for a military career. When his father died in the retreat from Moscow, Auguste returned to the study of art and did so well that he became a favorite pupil of his master, Girodet. In the troubled years that followed Waterloo, however, he entered into secret societies that plotted the overthrow of Louis XVIII, and he carried on his underground activities with such enthusiasm that in 1823 he was exiled by royal mandate. He took refuge in England, but soon re-embarked to join a small band of French revolutionaries who had come to the aid of antimonarchist forces in Spain. When this little army was defeated and captured, Hervieu managed to escape and make his way back to England. There he learned that the French courts had sentenced him to a fine of fifteen thousand francs and five years' imprisonment. He continued his study of art in London, managing to make a meager livelihood by taking pupils. From England he submitted a *Sketch of the Combat of Thermopylæ* to the Royal Academy of Lisle and won a medal and membership in the Academy.

Hervieu first became known to the Trollopes as a drawing master for their children. Mrs. Trollope's letter to Miss

Mitford written in the spring of 1827 shows a good deal regarding her sponsorship of Hervieu while she remained at Harrow:

If I have any knowledge of what is meant by the phrase *a man of genius,* I conceive it to belong to him; but he is totally and entirely *alone,* and unknown. His father, who was a colonel in the emperor's army, died in the retreat from Moscow, and left him no inheritance but debts. His only surviving relative is a rich priest — a Jesuit — whom, as you may well imagine, he has utterly offended. It would make your gentle heart ache if I were to tell you one quarter of what he has endured since he took refuge among us. How he has contrived to live I know not, but he has now a few pupils, and this has enabled him (by sometimes going without his dinner, to buy colors) to paint a picture, which has been received by the committee at Somerset House. It is not *my* judgment alone that I give you, when I say that this picture is *most admirable;* but I well know its merits will never be felt without the aid of the public press. I know you have influence enough with Mr. Walter to get it spoken of in the *Times,* and perhaps in some other publications. All I would ask is to direct attention to it; for I am *quite* sure that, if it is hung where it can be seen, it cannot be looked at without admiration. The picture will be called in the catalogue "Love and Folly," by A. J. J. Hervieu, No. 78 Newman Street. Will you then, dear friend, pardon all this long history, and try to aid by your influence a being who is worthy to call you friend — one day or other I shall hope to make him known to you.

For this French exile and his sponsor, eleven months and a fresh locale had greatly altered conditions; but the spirit of their relationship appears to have remained about the same in America as it had been before. Despite her poverty, she was still the resourceful patron and he the protégé grateful for her ideas and suggestions.

Hervieu soon found opportunities open to him in Cincinnati. On March 15 Frederick Eckstein, a German painter and sculptor who had come to the city a few years earlier, announced that Hervieu had joined him as a second teacher in the Academy of Fine Arts, recently established with high hopes and eighteen directors. Eckstein made the most of the occasion. He advertised that the Western country now had at

its command "the talents of an artist of the first order, even
in the higher branches of the art, and that the school of the
Academy may now compete with any in the United States,
and in proportion to its means does not yield to similar institutions in Europe." Hervieu was already at work upon a
"specimen of his abilities," *The Landing of Lafayette at Cincinnati,* a huge historical canvas that was later to figure prominently in the Trollope Odyssey. Three weeks later, however,
Hervieu broke with the Academy and announced the opening of his own school of drawing "at the same terms as Mr.
Eckstein." The easy-going German had objected to certain
regulations that Hervieu considered necessary if young Cincinnatians were to accomplish anything under his tutelage;
the chief of these was "to induce silence during the lessons."
A few days later Hervieu achieved local celebrity through
his decorations for the Western Museum. Frances Trollope
was responsible for the plan and purpose of these decorations.

V

Frances Trollope's experiences at the Western Museum
were an important part of her life in Cincinnati, but one that
has been largely forgotten. Apparently Mrs. Trollope later
took scant pride in her activities at this institution, for in *Domestic Manners* she allows no hint that she had had anything
to do with it. Yet it was here that she first felt the pulse of
Cincinnati, and she would probably never have built the
Bazaar, and the story of her life might have been much different, if she had met with less encouragement. Almost certainly the remarkable success of her schemes at the museum
was what caused her to go ahead with her plans for a large
building, to buy ground and to let contracts, after she had
had over eleven months in the city to study the populace and
to calculate the risks of such an ambitious project. There is
more than a tinge of irony in Mrs. Trollope's history at Cincinnati. She failed in her own undertakings, but at the West-

ern Museum she became an anonymous dictator of the town's amusement. With the assistance of Auguste Hervieu and a young native sculptor, she contrived a strange form of entertainment that was to draw crowds throughout the months when her own affairs were going from bad to worse and that was to keep on making money for its successive proprietors three decades after she had returned to Europe.

The Western Museum had been founded in 1820 by a group of public-minded citizens for the display of specimens of natural history and archæology. Shortly thereafter Joseph Dorfeuille, a naturalist of some attainments from New Orleans, came to Cincinnati and assumed the curatorship. When the stockholders found after three years that they could no longer meet expenses, they gave Dorfeuille their collections of fossils and minerals and Indian artifacts with the proviso that he continue to allow free admittance to the original subscribers and their families. Dorfeuille still believed that he could make a scientific museum a means of livelihood in Cincinnati and proceeded to buy additional collections. By degrees he came to realize that the people of the town did not care enough for biology and archæology to make frequent visits and that the Ohio River traffic did not bring in enough sightseers of scientific bent to keep his doors open. He took to featuring two-headed pigs, lambs with eight feet, and similar monstrosities, but these, too, soon palled upon his public. To draw customers from Letton's, a rival museum frankly commercial in character, Dorfeuille gradually found it necessary to submerge the scientist in the showman. He resorted to such attractions as "a splendid transparent Painting of the Battle of New Orleans." Letton rose to the challenge with a life-size "Equestrian Statue of Gen. Andrew Jackson" framed by a "Triumphal Arch, with revolving columns, on which are inscribed the emblems of the General's victories."

Dorfeuille likewise took to displaying wax figures. When an assortment of them that he had bought came broken in transit, he hired a young sculptor in the city to repair and alter them. The result was the exhibit that Dorfeuille announced on January 5, 1828, slightly more than a month before Mrs. Trollope entered the city. The advertisement shows how far Dorfeuille had departed from his earlier designs for attracting customers, but it reveals also how limited was the range of his showmanship before Mrs. Trollope gave him the benefit of her talents. Monsters, Indian chiefs, and presidents done in wax were by now rather common fare for this town of two museums.

INTERESTING & RARE ADDITIONS TO THE WESTERN MUSEUM, CORNER OF MAIN AND SECOND STREETS.

1. — The astonishing *Human Monster and Cannibal,* lately caught in Mulgrave's Island, dressed in the real dress of the Mulgrave Islanders.

2. — The celebrated Indian Chief *Tecumseh,* also completely dressed in the Indian garb.

3. — A superb allegorical representation, in wax, of the *Death of George Washington,* consisting of four figures, with appropriate scenery and decorations.

4. — A *Weighing Chair.*

The whole got up in a style of splendor never equalled in the West.

This museum now consists of about *Thirty Wax Figures,* twenty-four optic views and upwards of *sixteen thousand six hundred* articles of curiosity in every department.

Admittance 25 cents — Children, half price.

Good music on an organ. N.B. The two first mentioned figures will be exhibited on the *fifth,* the groupe of Washington on the *eighth,* of January, 1828.

A few days later the *Cincinnati Chronicle* paid its respects to the exhibit. Omitting mention of the Cannibal and the Indian Chief Tecumseh, the *Chronicle* stated that the likeness of Washington was "very well preserved" and that the figures of the allegorical group were *"got up"* in a style "superior to any representations in wax we have ever seen." But the notice ended by scolding the populace for not patronizing Dorfeuille's institution. Dorfeuille, it remarked, had to incur heavy annual expenditures merely to keep his museum in operation. "It is obvious therefore, that if it be increased in a degree corresponding with the progress of our city, it must receive a substantial amount of patronage. — This we fear, is not the fact." Dorfeuille had struck no really new note. What the citizens wanted was novelty.

The following April the citizens got their wish in the form of as strange a mixture of literary allusion, Oriental hocus-pocus, and Georgian beau-monde charade as had been witnessed on land or sea. Almost certainly Mrs. Trollope not only supplied the suggestions but also phrased the advertisements for this as for a later exhibition. Prefaced by a six-line quotation from the verse of Tom Moore, the first advertisement announced that Dorfeuille would soon present the *Invisible Girl*, a philosophical wonder that "a few years since excited the admiration of every portion of Society, attracted crowds of fashion and taste to the *audience* of this mysterious oracle, and employed the pens of the first wits and poets of the day." Frances Trollope, who had formerly delighted in planning dramatic entertainments and staging them in her English drawing-room, had found a new field for her talents:

THE INVISIBLE GIRL, AT THE WESTERN MUSEUM

corner of Main and Columbia Streets, is now ready to deliver her RESPONSES to visiters.

The chamber prepared for the audience is fitted up as one of those theatres of probation in the *Egyptian Mysteries*, in which the candidate for initiation was subjected to her incipient trials. The light is admitted *through transparencies* painted by MR. HERVIEU.

HECATE,
AND THE THREE WEIRD SISTERS,

Are seen passing along the wall, opposite the entrance, on the wall of which are seen the savage countenances of a groupe of BANDITTI, (in wax) who from an inner cave, look out on the

MAGIC CHAMBER.

SPECTRAL FIGURES and curious animals, who are supposed to aid in magic rites are seen traversing the inner apartment.

Parties of twelve persons, and no more, could be admitted at one time to the "presence of the Oracle." Each visitor was allowed to propound three questions. The *"profoundest silence"* was enjoined during the delivering of the responses.

The focus of attraction was the Invisible Girl and her sibylline pronouncements.

The responses of the invisible maiden [said the *Gazette*], are very pertinent and amusing. She answers with great readiness; and the curiosity is increased by the utter inability of the hearer to ascertain whence the sound proceeds. Many have exercised their skill to find out the secret, but in vain.

In the centre, enveloped in clouds [said the *Advertiser*], is suspended the trumpet, by which the INVISIBLE GIRL, the oracle of the cave, delivers her responses. — She promptly answers any questions propounded to her, if it be not an improper or immodest one. To all such a peculiar sound proceeds from the Oracle, indicative of her displeasure and refusal to answer.

Henry Trollope was the Invisible Girl. At the Western Museum his mother had found a use for his stock of learning, which the town had not wanted to buy at face value. This Oracle's modest resources in Latin, Greek, and French made a tremendous impression. "He spoke seven languages," Jose Tosso, a Cincinnati musician, averred many years later, "and under the guise of the invisible woman puzzled the wise-acres of the community for weeks."

The *Invisible Girl* was a success without precedent. Dorfeuille publicly thanked the citizens "for the very liberal encouragement" which had of late been tendered to him and drew the final curtain at the end of eight solid weeks only to make way for a still more spectacular show, conceived in the same fertile mind that had already found him a way to prosperity.

In this second and more memorable undertaking Frances Trollope was to have her schemes carried out by two artists who seem to have taken about equal parts in executing her conception. While Hervieu painted new and more splendid transparencies, Hiram Powers, the young sculptor whom Dorfeuille had hired to mend his broken statues the preceding January, set to shaping an array of wax figures. Powers had probably contrived the "groupe of BANDITTI, (in wax)" that had played a subordinate part in the *Invisible Girl*. In the new exhibit, his figures were to prove to be the most sensational part of the show. Later, when Hervieu's transparencies became dimmed with lamp smoke, Powers was to replace them with mechanical creatures of his designing until the whole show came to be known as his work. Years after Powers had left Cincinnati and had become the most lavishly praised sculptor in Europe, Cincinnatians were fond of reminding visitors to their city that the creator of the *Greek Slave* (wildly hailed in its day as the greatest piece of sculpture known to history) had got his start at the Western Museum and that his early handiwork could still be seen at the *Infernal Regions* of that institution, admittance twenty-five cents.

When Mrs. Trollope first met Powers, says her eldest son, Thomas Adolphus, who became a close friend of Hiram's a few months later, she "at once remarked him as a young man of exceptional talent and promise." Certainly he was among the most striking of her new acquaintances in Cincinnati, a tall, lanky, fierce-eyed young man with a remarkably inventive brain and clever hands, an epitome, in his way, of frontier drive and resourcefulness. To Tom Trollope he seemed "a sort of Adam, a fresh, new and original *man*," yet "an eminently *practical* man — a man whose tendency was not to dream, but to *do*." Powers had come to Ohio with his parents from their native Vermont in 1819. His father had died the next year of the ague and fever, and the fifteen-year-old boy worked first in a provision store and then as the keeper of a reading-room in a Cincinnati hotel. When this scheme failed, he went back to service with a merchant in flour, butter, whisky, and salt pork. Within a few years he found a job collecting bad debts for Luman Watson, a Cincinnati manufacturer of clocks and organs. He soon worked himself into the factory. Once there, he began to show proofs of his ingenuity. He invented a new mechanism for cutting wooden clock wheels, an improvement on the big machines that Watson had had to freight over the mountains from Connecticut. He fashioned a new reed for Watson's organs, so that they could be tuned by the twisting of a screw.

But Powers had small desire to settle down as a prosperous foreman of a clock and organ factory; he was fascinated by his own ability to invent and create and kept putting it to new tests in his off hours. When an itinerant cutter of paper profiles set up in Cincinnati, Powers took the scissors from him and outdid the professional. He tried shaping objects from glass and bone and iron. When Eckstein came to Cincinnati, Powers decided that his proper medium of expression was sculpture and began to take lessons from this molder and caster of busts in his spare hours from Watson's factory.

I formed his acquaintance [Powers later told Henry W. Bellows in Florence] and he taught me all he knew about it. I found a sitter in the little daughter of Mr. John P. Foote, who was willing to come to me at off-hours, often early in the morning, but more commonly after the day's work was over. Knowing that my job would be a long one, I was afraid to begin with clay, which was liable to harden or freeze, and I made my first bust in bees'-wax — here it is — and, so far as the flesh and the likeness are concerned, I don't believe I have done better since.

When Mrs. Trollope and Hervieu arrived in Cincinnati, Powers was exposed to new ideas and new challenges. With Hervieu he formed a relationship that was half friendly and half hostile. Hervieu proposed that he and Powers sit to each other and proceeded to give the young Cincinnatian pointers on the principles of art. He insisted that Powers make his bust without measurements, quoting Michelangelo on the subject, and Powers (who was an extreme literalist all his life) did so under protest. When Hervieu painted Hiram's picture, the pupil took up the calipers and showed triumphantly that his instructor had missed the distance between the eyes. Hervieu insisted that he had altered the measurement to "give effect," but Powers felt that he had won the argument.

With Frances Trollope, however, Powers from the outset was on wholly friendly terms. "When I reached Cincinnati," says Tom, "I found him intimate with my brother [Henry], and a favorite with my mother, who had formed a high opinion of his character and of his talents." Her suggestions for the museum he "never failed to carry into effect, to the great amusement of both parties." Tom goes at length into the origins of the Western Museum's *Infernal Regions*. When, in the spring of 1828, Mrs. Trollope conceived the idea of presenting "some of the more striking scenes of Dante's *Divina Commedia*," the idea "fired the imagination of Powers." Mrs. Trollope "was to draw up the programme, and he undertook, with the materials furnished him by the museum, and with the help of some of his own handiwork, to give scenic reality to her suggestions." [2] Tom quotes the four-page program that his mother had composed for the show; a copy had been preserved in the family.

The beginning promises much for a modest price:

The World to come, as described by Dante, and comprising, Hell, Purgatory, and Paradise, will be exhibited in a room adjoining the Western Museum on the 4th of July, and days following. Admittance, twenty-five cents.

Central to the spectacle was "a grand colossal figure of Minos, the Judge of Hell," holding a two-pronged scepter. On his right appeared a frozen lake from which emerged the heads of doomed earthlings, including Ugolino, pictured "eternally gnawing the head of his enemy." A "BLACK IMP" was "seated

---

[2] Writing many years after the event, Tom does not allow for the substantial part that Hervieu played in the original exhibition.

on a rock dandling a young monster." Throngs of condemned spirits "in all varieties of suffering" crowded about a fountain of flame in the midst of the frozen lake, and birds and animals of hideous form and evil omen fluttered over the heads of the sufferers. On the left of Minos a skeleton ascended a column of icicles, the bright surfaces of which glared red with the reflection of hell-fire, and held aloft a standard with these lines, prepared for the occasion by Mrs. Trollope:

> To this grim form our cherished limbs have come,
> And thus lie mouldering in their earthly home.
> In turf-bound hillock or in sculptured shrine
> The worms alike their cold caresses twine.
> So far we all are equal: but once left
> Our mortal weeds, of vital spark bereft,
> Asunder farther than the poles we're driven —
> Some sunk to deepest Hell, some raised to highest Heaven.

Behind Inferno gleamed Hervieu's transparencies of Purgatorio and Paradiso, bright with symbols of hope and progress upward, in some attempt to counterbalance the threats of hell with the promises of heaven:

Still farther on the left of Minos, and melting into distance behind him, is seen the shadowy region of Purgatory. Four bright stars — the Cardinal Virtues — give a delicate and cheering light amid the gloom. A group of figures loaded with the burthen of their sins are about to plunge into the lake of purgatorial waters, in the hope of depositing them there. A boat wafted by the wings of an Angel is bearing departed souls toward Heaven; and near it is a column of pale light to direct its course. In the distance the departed mistress of Dante, is standing on its summit, encouraging him to proceed with her to Heaven, where his former guide, Virgil, cannot be admitted (being a Pagan). Groups of Pilgrims who have passed through Purgatory are ascending the mountain. Still farther to the left, and opening in unbroken splendor above the head of Beatrice, is seen the Heaven of Heavens. The golden light pours down on the heads of the Pilgrims, and angels are seen floating in the air and encouraging their efforts.

But the emphasis was on Inferno and the terrifying images ("size of life") that Powers fashioned for the foreground.

Later advertisements speak of "unearthly sounds, horrid groans, and terrible shrieks" which seemed to be emitted from "every direction." "At a moment when utter darkness prevails all the sufferers, imps, and monsters are heard shrieking together till the light returns. . . ." It was Inferno that the crowds came to see. They pushed against the grating set across the room to separate them from the scenery and reached out to explore the mysteries of hell with their fingers as well as their eyes. To prevent damage to the figures, Powers put up a card written in flame-colored letters threatening immediate and dire punishment to anyone who dared touch the denizens of the nether world. Adventurers who refused to heed this warning recoiled in fear and astonishment as a sharp electric shock went through their bodies. But this new terror merely heightened the attraction of the *Infernal Regions* for the citizens of Cincinnati.

The show produced one result that Mrs. Trollope or Hervieu or Powers could hardly have looked for. A Bostonian who traveled in Ohio a few months after the *Infernal Regions* opened reported that in Columbus he had heard of a "great and glorious 'revival' " that was under way in Cincinnati.

On arriving at Cincinnati, we were informed by respectable persons, that this *hell*, which I have attempted to describe, had done more toward producing the excitement than either God or his ambassadors. The truth is, great pains had been taken to induce people to visit that place, and there they were *got under conviction!* Indeed, we were informed, that *ministers* had attended the exhibition of this artificial Tophet, and had added their groans and entreaties to the unearthly sounds above mentioned. — To give effect to the whole farce, they were said to have issued from the dark corners of the room, and while the timid and ignorant were viewing this work of man's device, they would exhort them to flee to the ark of safety!

The *Cincinnati Chronicle* denied a part of the report, insisting that "Whatever effects may have been produced by depicting the horrors of that tophet, spoken of in the Bible," the ministers of Cincinnati had not figured in them. There is

no doubt, at least, that the citizens flocked to witness "Dorfeuille's Hell" and that they were tremendously impressed.

The *Infernal Regions* kept on drawing audiences for well
over a quarter of a century; the show continued to be a
notable feature of Cincinnati's cultural life long after the
city had doubled and redoubled in size. When Frederika
Bremer visited Cincinnati in 1850, the *Infernal Regions* were
the property of "a Swede [Frederick Franks]"; he had become "a rich man" by staging the spectacle. It was still running in 1861, when Artemus Ward beheld it with great
delight and declared it "the best show in Cincinnati."

VI

If anyone could have told Mrs. Trollope that her scheme
for the Western Museum was to gather such impetus and
that thousands of Cincinnatians yet unborn were to make this
strange show of her devising a staple of their amusement in
decades to come, she would have been startled, but possibly
not at all pleased. Wax figures she considered a "barbarous
branch of art," and though in *Domestic Manners* she speaks
of "Dorfeuille's Hell" as a very amusing exhibition, there is
condescension in her tone. Nevertheless, in the summer and
fall of 1828 as the *Infernal Regions* went on drawing packed
houses, she must have been greatly impressed by her achieve-
ments at the museum. She had, in effect, tested her powers
over the citizens of Cincinnati in two separate experi-
ments. Both had been remarkable successes. If Cincinnatians
thronged to such simple forms of amusement as the *Invisible Girl* and the *Infernal Regions,* she must have reasoned, surely the more refined among them would respond
eagerly to the splendid attractions that she planned for the
Bazaar.

When her husband and eldest son arrived in Cincinnati
late in November, she was confident that the Bazaar had
only to be built and opened to the public in order to suc-

ceed. Her plans for the Bazaar seem, indeed, to have expanded considerably during the months since her entry into
the city. The prospectus contained in the *Cincinnati Directory for 1829* states that only a "small proportion" of a great
building was to be used for the selling of fancy goods. There
were to be an Exchange Coffee House, an "elegant Saloon"
where ices and other refreshments were to "lend their allure-
ments to the fascinations of architectural novelty," a barroom,
an exhibition gallery, an immense ballroom, and a circular
structure intended for "Panoramic Exhibitions."

Neither Frances Trollope nor her husband planned to remain in Cincinnati. Once the Bazaar was operating smoothly,
Henry was to be placed in charge, and Mrs. Trollope could
then return to England to publish a book upon her adventures. She had been planning such a book for some time. "I
amuse myself by making notes," she had written home in
June, "and hope some day to manufacture them into a volume. This is a remote corner of the world, and but seldom
visited, and I think that if Hervieu could find time to furnish
sketches of scenery, and groups, a very taking little volume
might be produced." When, in the course of the winter, Mrs.
Trollope wrote a long letter to her novelist friend Miss Mitford, she did not exactly confide that she was preparing notes
for such a book — the growing success of *Our Village*, "whole
pages" of which were appearing in the American newspapers,
may have put her a little in awe of her old friend — but she
let out that the thought of writing such a book had crossed
her mind.

Oh, my dear friend, had I but the tenth of an inch of the nib of
your pen, what pictures might I draw of the people here — so very
queer, so very unlike any other thing in heaven above or earth below!
But it may not be. I can look and I can laugh, but the power of describing is not given to above a dozen in a century.

Her mind was chiefly occupied with plans for the future of
her family.

Henry's prospects here are, I think, very good; but eighteen is too young to be left, too young to be judged of fixedly. I believe him to be very steady, but I must watch by him for a year or two longer. I think Mr. Trollope returns to us next year, and I shall then be able to decide whether it will be advisable to continue here or not. My girls have very good masters, and I know that they are not losing their time. *Nothing* shall keep me here after my eldest girl is sixteen — at least, nothing that I can possibly foresee or imagine, as I think I owe it to her to let her see young ladies' daylight in a civilized country.

Even if all had gone as well in Cincinnati as Mrs. Trollope now hoped it would, she would have painted many a droll picture of American manners for her readers; but there are passages in the same letter which strongly suggest she might in that event have dipped far more frequently into brighter colors on her palette. She speaks of Cincinnati as "this remote but very pretty nest, where I am sitting to hatch golden eggs for Henry." Though the weather has been dreary and she has missed fine, full London conversations, "Yet is the country beautiful, and wonderful in its rapid progress towards the wealth and the wisdom, the finery and the folly, of the Old World; and I like it well — the better, certainly, that while Henry is making money I am saving it."

The winter of 1828–9 was the happiest part of Frances Trollope's sojourn in Cincinnati. Except for Anthony, who labored on his studies at Winchester, her family was once more united; the Bazaar, still an insubstantial, golden dream, promised to clear away the threat of bankruptcy that had long hovered over the Trollopes. Her eldest son remembered these months as pleasant ones. The Trollopes lived five or ten minutes' walk from the edge of town in a house "built of wood, and all white with the exception of the green Venetian blinds." There was an air of roominess and brightness about it that delighted Tom. The road from the entrance gate had not been completed, and fragments of boarding and timber still littered the large field in which the house stood, but everything was new and clean-looking. Tom discovered that he liked the "frank and unconstrained" manner with which Cincinnatians talked, and he soon struck up an acquaintance with several of them, including the already wealthy Nicholas Longworth, whom he found very willing to deliver long monologues on his schemes for developing vineyards in the Western states. Mrs. Trollope's eldest son found much to admire in the simple social life of Cincinnati.

There were very few formal meetings among the notabilities of the little Cincinnati world of that time, but there was an amount of homely friendliness that impressed me very favorably; and there was plenty of that generous and abounding hospitality which subsequent experience has taught me to consider an especially American characteristic.

Special friends of the Trollopes were the family of the physician William Price. Dr. Price had come to Cincinnati a few years earlier from New Harmony, where he had been a leader in Owen's Community of Equality. He was a staunch friend of Fanny Wright, who was probably the link between this family and the Trollopes. Tom remembered Dr. Price as an especially clever man:

a very competent physician with a large practice, a foolish, friendly little wife, and a pair of pretty daughters. He was a jovial, florid, rotund little man who professed, more even, as I remember, to my astonishment than my horror, perfect atheism. His wife and daughters used to go to church without apparently producing the slightest interruption of domestic harmony. "La! the doctor don't think anything more of the Bible than of an old newspaper!" Mrs. Price would say; "but then doctors, you know, they have their own opinions!" And the girls used to say, "Papa is an atheist," just as they would have said of the multiform persuasions of their acquaintances, "Mr. This is a Baptist," and "Mrs. That is a Methodist."

The two daughters gave frequent dances at their home, and the Trollope young people were constant and welcome guests. The Prices also staged theatricals in which the Trollopes took part. Tom remembered playing Falstaff in *The Merry Wives of Windsor* "with immense success to an assuredly not very critical audience."

Mrs. Trollope gave parties of her own. Jose Tosso recalled one at which she had entertained "about a hundred guests,"

. . . and a handsome one it was. First we had "Les Deux Amis" in French, and then "The Merry Wives of Windsor." The "Deux Amis" went off very well. Mrs. Trollope spoke excellent French. So did Dr. Price, Mr. Morgan Neville, Mrs. Ameling and Anthony [probably Tom] Trollope. . . . I played first violin; Morgan Neville second fiddle, and John Douglass, 'cello. After the play came supper, and then the dancing till daylight.

Another home to which the Trollopes had entree was that of William Bullock, the English traveler, naturalist, antiquarian, and showman, who had earlier gained celebrity through his exhibitions at Egyptian Hall in London. He and his family were now comfortably settled on a large estate that he had bought on the Kentucky bank of the Ohio directly opposite Cincinnati, though his plan for establishing a model rural town on his property was not prospering. If Charles Anderson's memory served him truly, the Bullocks gave a dinner party at their mansion in honor of Frances Trollope not many months after her arrival in Cincinnati, with the literati and notables of the city collected for the occasion. Mrs. Trollope speaks in *Domestic Manners* of Mr. Bullock's "truly English hospitality" and of his "enlightened and inquiring mind."

But of all her acquaintances in Cincinnati, Frances Trollope seems to have enjoyed most the family of Timothy Flint. Congregationalist minister, missionary, teacher, novelist, critic, editor, author of a widely read book upon his travels and observations in the Western states during ten years chiefly spent in frontier communities and travel by keelboat, flatboat, and horseback, Flint was at the time working upon his novels and editing the *Western Monthly Review,* which he had established in 1827. Mrs. Trollope found this man of varied experiences and accomplishments a conversationalist of the highest order, the only person she had ever known who displayed "first-rate powers of satire, and even of sarcasm," without injuring the kindness of his nature or his manner. The intelligence and domestic virtues of Emeline Flint, his daughter, also struck Mrs. Trollope favorably, so much so that she put a lengthy eulogy upon this young lady into *Domestic Manners*. An Easterner who paid a visit to Cincinnati in 1829 later wrote of finding Mrs. Trollope at the home of Timothy Flint during one of her many informal visits there:

[Flint] was sitting at a centre-table, overshadowed with reviews, magazines, and pamphlets, seemingly arranging the "last number" for the press, surrounded by his wife and very interesting family. His young and lovely daughter was there, with her scarlet robe and pink slippers, redolent of all those charms and virtues which Mad. Trollope has lavished upon her, in her "Domestic Manners of the Americans"; and in one corner of the room sat the veritable old Trollope herself [few Americans, Eastern or Western, spoke well of Mrs. Trollope for some time after the appearance of her book] — rough-cast and misshapen — of coarse and vulgar expression, and a head, viewed phrenologically, of the very lowest order.

Timothy Flint recorded his own impressions of Mrs. Trollope in a review of *Domestic Manners*. A thousand persons, he was sure, had asked him what sort of person she was. His reply is colored by his reading of her strictures upon America, but it gives us some idea of Frances Trollope as an intimate acquaintance knew her in Cincinnati. In person, Flint says, she was "a short, plump figure, with a ruddy, round, Saxon face of bright complexion." He considered her appearance "singularly unladylike"; she lacked taste in her manner of dressing or perhaps held herself above such considerations. At times, however, "she was as much finer and more expensively dressed than other ladies, as she was ordinarily inferior to them in her costume." She was "robust and masculine" in her habits and took long walks regardless of pouring rain or the fierce noonday sun; she probably owed a severe fever to her contempt for American weather.

Her voice was shrill and piercing in its tones, and she was "voluble as a French woman." She was an accomplished mimic and was often piquant and sarcastic. (Mrs. Trollope considered Timothy Flint a master of satire and sarcasm.) But Flint found her conversation "remarkably amusing"; he was greatly impressed by the range of her subject matter. It seemed to him that she had been everywhere and had seen everybody of importance in Europe. She "knew more about plays, English, French, and Italian, than any person with whom we are acquainted." She was familiar with the language and light literature of both France and Italy, "and was, moreover, acquainted, as we knew from her correspondence, with the most distinguished men and women of genius in England." All in all, she was "a woman of uncommon cleverness, a first rate talker."

Flint was careful to deny that her conduct with Hervieu ("which connexion naturally furnished much tea table conversation") had been anything but exemplary, and he added that her neighbors had reason to remember her with gratitude.

She was amiable in the highest degree in her relations with the people about her in the suburbs of Cincinnati, where she resided, during the greater part of her stay in America, and among whom she was extremely popular, enacting among them *Lady Bountiful*, with a graciousness of distribution, and nursing the sick, which every where gains favor.

VII

When Tom and his father left Cincinnati late in January, the site of the Bazaar had been bought (for $1,655) and contracts had been let. Mr. Trollope was to send a large shipment of goods upon his return to London. Frances Trollope set about supervising the actual building of the Bazaar. Gradually there rose above the shops and warehouses of Cincinnati a structure as grotesque in its design as it was impractical in its purposes. Mrs. Trollope was a child of the romantic movement. The Bazaar came from an imagination steeped in the Oriental fantasies of Lord Byron and Tom Moore. It was *The Giaour* and *Lalla Rookh* mixed with a good deal of sheer personal whimsy and frozen into brick and stone.

While the Bazaar was still under construction, the *Cincinnati Chronicle* gave its readers a description of the building. The Bazaar nearly covered an area thirty-eight by one hundred feet and varied in height from fifty-two to eighty-five feet. The front facing Third Street was "taken, in part from the Mosque of St. Athanase, in Egypt," and was formed of "three large arabesque windows with arches, supported by four Moorish stone pilasters with capitals." Above these were "large and beautifully wrought free stone ornaments," and still above these was a wall that terminated in "gothic battlements, each of which supports a stone sphere." The *Chronicle* considered this front a "rich and tasty compound of ancient and modern architecture," with not so much of either as to forfeit strong claims to orginality. The sides of the Bazaar were of brick wall without openings; they were "castellated at such a height as to give the appearance of a flat roof to the building."

The front facing south toward the Ohio River was, if anything, still more novel in appearance than the front that faced Third Street. Its chief feature was an Egyptian colonnade formed of four massive columns modeled after those "in the temple of Appollinopolis at Etfou, as exhibited in Denon's Egypt." The four great columns rose three stories, and their entablature constituted a fourth story. Above this rose a rotunda twenty-four feet in height to its curvilinear roof, and this was in turn to be topped by a large Turkish crescent!

The interior of the Bazaar was in keeping with the exterior. One entered the basement floor from Third Street by any of three several flights of stone steps and found oneself in a hallway sixty feet long; this hallway terminated at the base of the grand circular staircase, which spiraled through four

stories up to the rotunda. Beyond this staircase on the basement floor were more rooms, which led into an area containing the bases of the four Egyptian columns of the southern
front of the Bazaar. The basement had "several compart-
ments," some of which were to be used for an "Exchange
Coffee House."

The second floor, entered from Third Street by two circular
flights of stone steps, was chiefly occupied by the room that
was to be "appropriated exclusively to the sale of fancy
goods." This room was the breadth of the building and sixty
feet long. Two rows of Doric columns ran the full length,
supporting elliptic arches that formed a "handsome arcade."
Beyond this room was a lobby through which passed the
great circular staircase, and on the far side the lobby opened
upon a balcony "formed by the Egyptian columns supporting
the rotunda." "Immediately in front of this balcony," or so
says the *Chronicle* (the arrangement is hard to visualize),
"stands a separate building designed as an exhibition room
for Mr. Hervieu's large and elegant picture of the landing of
Lafayette in Cincinnati."

On the third floor, immediately above the room designed
for the sale of fancy goods, was the ballroom, its dimensions
also thirty-eight by sixty feet. "The large arabesque windows
in front, the lofty walls, and arched ceiling give a fine effect
to this apartment." At the southern end of the room was an
"elegant orchestra, supported by four Corinthian columns."
The decorations executed by Hervieu for the ballroom were
not only splendid but "the only specimen of the kind in the
United States." The object of the artist had been to follow
as closely as possible "the style of the Alhambra, the celebrated palace of the Moorish kings in Granada." Hervieu
must have had a very busy time with his pencil and brushes.
He had painted the roof to represent masses of granite "decorated at intervals by mosaic designs of a great variety of objects, and by accurate imitations of the brilliantly coloured

tiles of the Alhambra." The windowless side walls of the ballroom he had endowed with the simulacra of a double row
of marble pilasters, and between each pair of false columns
he had painted arabesque windows richly draped with crimson curtains. These blind windows he caused to look out
upon "a variety of Spanish scenery." The *Chronicle* considered the perspective in these picturesque views to be remarkably fine.

Hervieu also exercised the magic of perspective in painting
the music gallery, so that it appeared to lead to an upper
apartment from which it was divided by a damask curtain.
Below the gallery he executed "niches containing the figures
of infant boys, holding standards on which are various patriotic inscriptions." The door to the lobby was painted with
ten allegorical designs representing the triumph of liberty
over despotism, and in the lobby the muses of dancing and
music floated above "a variety of arabesque ornaments in
mosaic work."

The fourth floor contained a hall and five apartments, and
above them, behind the gothic battlements, was a promenade that afforded a wide view of the city, the Ohio River,
and the countryside. As for the interior of the rotunda, one is
not surprised to learn, after the wonders of the ballroom, that
Hervieu had had it covered with canvas and intended to
paint it with fifteen hundred feet of panoramic exhibition.

The Bazaar was to be lighted with gas; tradition says that
it was the first building in Cincinnati to use this means of il-
lumination. The *Chronicle* conjectured that in the ballroom
the effect of this bright light "upon the brilliant decorations
and the no less brilliant assemblage of persons that will occasionally be collected within its walls, cannot but be truly fas-
cinating to the beholder." The *Chronicle* was quite willing to
view this strange new edifice as a fitting emblem of Cincinnati's rise from the wilderness to civic splendor. It ended its
notice with a glowing peroration:

The Bazaar, which when finished, will not have cost less than fifteen thousand dollars, is owned by Thomas A. Trollope, Esq., of London, who deserves much credit for the taste and public spirit that induced the erection of a building so ornamental to our city.

As evincing the march of improvement in the west, we may here remark, that the Bazaar stands upon a part of the ground formerly occupied by Fort Washington, which was built in 1789 to check the incursions of the Indians. . . . Cincinnati . . . contained eleven families. A prediction at that time, that within forty years, the population of the place would be increased to twenty-five thousand inhabitants . . . and that one of its block houses would be substituted by this splendid Bazaar, would have been deemed the wild vagary of a disordered imagination. Yet such is literally the fact. . . .

But long before her fanciful building was completed, Mrs. Trollope had come face to face with an unromantic reality. "Everything from the time you left us," she later wrote Tom, "went wrong, spite of exertions — nay, hard labour, on our part that would pain you to hear of." The funds that her husband had left with her for the erection of the Bazaar were probably not large. Through her guileless fingers they went like water. "In building," says a contemporary editor, "a 'green horn' is snuffed like carrion by every rogue within cheating distance." According to one Cincinnati observer, "every brick in her Babel cost her three prices." She hired one man, "a countryman of her own, by the by," to lay the gas pipes for the Bazaar and paid him his money in advance only to discover too late that he had "evaporated with the cash." She hired another, who actually laid the pipes, but "instead of gas, his apparatus manufactured nothing but smoke."

In August, while the Bazaar was still under construction, Mrs. Trollope was stricken by malaria; for some time her life was in danger. When she recovered, her money had run out, and angry creditors were demanding payment. The ten thousand dollars' worth of goods that her husband sent were scarcely offered for sale when they were taken by the sheriff to satisfy the claims of the contractor. But the goods would not have sold in any event, if we can trust the accounts of eyewitnesses. In the few days that Mrs. Trollope was able to offer her merchandise, "people came in multitudes — to look at it; but buying was another affair; nobody wanted any thing there."

Timothy Flint wrote into his review of *Domestic Manners* a terse obituary of Mrs. Trollope's golden dream:

[At Cincinnati], visited by her husband, who spent one winter with her, she passed two desultory and aimless seasons, rearing the while, a huge building called a bazaar, which was no air castle, but a queer, unique, crescented Turkish Babel, so odd, that no one has seen it since, without wonder and a good humored laugh: a building which cost her twenty-four thousand dollars, on which she actually paid some twelve or thirteen thousand, leaving the remainder minus, spending, probably, four or five thousand dollars more in French articles of finery, which she exposed for sale in stalls in this building; and so injudiciously, owing to her total ignorance of the American market, and of the proper place in which to build her Bazaar, and to her entrusting the sales to irresponsible and probably dishonest foreigners, that the establishment ran her in debt, instead of yielding her a revenue. A fact will explain this utter ignorance. When told, that the market could not be transported from the place where people had been accustomed to purchase, she imagined that her Bazaar would tempt the crowd of fashionables a quarter of a mile from their accustomed haunt. When advised to examine the fancy stores in the city, and furnish herself with such articles, as they had not, she only conformed to this salutary counsel, after her orders had arrived from France. The consequence was, that in eking out the defects of her store, she visited one of the most ample assortments in the country, holding up her hands in undisguised astonishment, to find that such a large and splendid assortment had found its way there, antecedent to the grand findings of the Bazaar, an assortment of twenty times her capital, and far more rich and expensive. How could such things, she exclaimed, have found their way to the United States.

The result of all this is easily seen. As incapable as an infant of such a project in her own country, in America her ruin was more complete than that of infantine folly.

There is a final chapter to Frances Trollope's adventures at the Bazaar that needs to be told; it has long been forgotten. Even after her stock of goods was taken from her, Mrs. Trollope made a valiant attempt to recoup some part of her

losses. Her plan was to stage novel entertainments with the
aid of actors from the local theater. On November 21 the
Cincinnati press carried this advertisement:

MUSICAL FANTASIA

ON THURSDAY ev'g, 26th, the Great room at the Bazaar will be open
for music, songs, and recitation. This species of amusement, so popular, of late years, both in Paris and London, has not hitherto been
introduced in America, and it is hoped the present attempt will be
favorably received. Mr. and Mrs. A. Drake have kindly promised their
services on the occasion. Between the acts tea and coffee will be
served in the saloon.

Doors to be opened at half past six.

Admittance one dollar, tea & coffee included.

Children half price.

For twenty years or more after *Domestic Manners* was
published, the notion was widely circulated that Mrs. Trollope during her stay in Cincinnati had made desperate efforts to improve the manners of the city. It seems to stem in
part from these entertainments, but the poor woman was
probably much more interested in making a few dollars to
stave off total bankruptcy than in elevating the tone of Cincinnati society. So, at least, thought the editor of the *Cincinnati Gazette,* who commented in his editorial columns: "The
enterprising individuals who have spent so much money in
our town in the erection of a splendid building, such as the
Bazaar, ought to be encouraged by receiving back from the
citizens, some portion of it, and this we trust will be the case."
But though the Musical Fantasia was clearly designed for
the elite of Cincinnati who should be taken with the idea of
enjoying what was popular in Paris and London, the elite did
not attend. The first entertainment was "very handsomely *got
up,*" the *Cincinnati Chronicle* reported. "The music, the recitations and the repast, were all in good taste." But the audience had been regrettably small. The editor advised the
proprietors of the Bazaar not to feel discouraged, "for it is

not at all the *fashion* of our *fashionable* to attend the first evening of any public amusement." There was hope for the future:

Since the above was penned, we are informed that another great entertainment of a similar kind will be given on Thursday evening next, at the Bazaar, which is likely to be even more attractive than the last. Mr. Cowell and his son, of the New-York and Philadelphia Theatres, have kindly volunteered their services on the occasion.

Joe Cowell, the star of the evening, wrote his impressions of this second performance in his memoirs. He was a comedian by profession, and he was not the man to deliver an unvarnished tale if he could improve on it; but the evening must have gone somewhat as he describes it. There was a raised platform at one end of the ballroom of the Bazaar, and across the middle of the platform Mrs. Trollope had fastened a green baize curtain. Behind this curtain the entertainers of the evening huddled together, since only one door led into the room and it would have been improper for the artists to "parade through the fashionables" in order to perform. Mrs. Drake, the tragic actress for whom Mrs. Trollope expresses great admiration in *Domestic Manners,* was to deliver "O'Connor's Child," the "Scolding Wife," and "half a hundred more *fashionable* recitations." She and her husband, Alexander Drake, manager of the Cincinnati theater, were to act isolated scenes, including those of Sir Peter and Lady Teazle in *The School for Scandal.* A violin and violoncello constituted the orchestra.

When the audience of about thirty people had entered and seated themselves, Drake rang a little bell. After a minute's shuffling of feet and legs and chairs, he rang the bell again and Mrs. Drake opened the green curtain, "her majestic form and white satin train, which Drake had spread out and placed on the floor at its full extent . . . taking possession entirely of the stage." She gave three queenlike curtsies to the right, left, and center (which was entirely vacant), but there was no response from the audience. "The fact is, it was not fashionable to take notice of anything," and the only general laugh of the evening came when a young lady attempted ineffectually to stifle a fit of sneezing.

At intermission time Mrs. Trollope took Cowell aside and confided to him her hopes for her new enterprise. "A series of entertainments of this kind must become fashionable in time," she told him, and her friend Mrs. Drake was exactly of her way of thinking. "And as to a *regular* theatre, just step this way, and I'll show you what I intend to do."

And away the bustling little lady went, and I at her heels.

"Now you see, Mr. Cowell, I'll have the dais enlarged, and made on a declivity; and then I'll have beautiful scenes painted in oil colours, so that they can be washed every morning and kept clean. I have a wonderfully talented French painter, whom I brought with me, but the people here don't appreciate him, and this will help to bring him into notice. And then I'll have a hole cut here," describing a square on the floor with her toe; "and then a geometrical staircase for the *artistes* to ascend perpendicularly," twirling round and round her finger, "instead of having to walk through the audience part of the area. Or," said she, after a pause, "I'll tell you what will be as well, and not so costly. I'll have some canvass nailed along the ceiling, on this side, to form a passage to lead to the stage; Mr. Hervieu can paint it like damask, with a large gold border, and it would have a fine effect!"

No doubt Mrs. Trollope did outline to Cowell some such plan for turning the Bazaar into a theater. Her friends the Drakes were in bad straits at the regular playhouse and would probably have been glad to move into her building if there was to be no initial payment on account. But the plan would have required money, and Mrs. Trollope was in no better position to carry it through than were the Drakes.

This second social evening at the Bazaar, observed the *Chronicle,* had shown improvement in at least one respect. "The company, though not so large as could have been wished, was fashionable." The whole entertainment was "characterized by the absence of every thing at variance with

propriety and good taste." But music and recitations delivered with propriety, and coffee and tea "handsomely served
up in the saloon adjoining the ball-room" were not enough to
capture the custom of Cincinnati's fashionables; most of them
seem to have had enough of this variety of amusement in
a single evening. On December 19 Hervieu, as master of ceremonies, regretfully announced that the entertainments at the
Bazaar had run their course. It had been his earnest wish, he
said, to offer patrons such an entertainment every Thursday
evening as would have obtained their continued support.
"Painting, Poetry, and Music, were put in requisition at the
great room of the Bazaar, to gratify their taste, and to win
their favor — but it has failed. . . ." On the last Thursday
evening the entire audience had consisted of "half a dozen
gentlemen from a steamboat." He therefore respectfully
withdrew his attempt.

VIII

A week later Hervieu put on exhibition at the Bazaar the
magnum opus of his two years in America, his picture *The
Landing of Lafayette at Cincinnati*. Earlier, when the future
of the Bazaar was a bright prospectus, the picture had been
intended to serve as a permanent exhibit, an incidental attraction; now it was an important possibility for gathering
badly needed funds from Cincinnatians, who might be willing to pay their quarters to see it. Hervieu had chosen his subject adroitly; the event was one still fresh in the imaginations
of the citizens. General Lafayette had visited Cincinnati in
the spring of 1825. He had been rowed across the Ohio River
from Kentucky in an "elegant six-oared barge" while twenty-
four guns roared a "general national salute"; he had been received with wild enthusiasm and ceremonies that lasted for
two days. Hervieu had doubled his chances of success by in-
corporating into his work a portrait of nearly every citizen of

prominence in the community, including a few who had not been present at the historical landing. All together there were over forty likenesses. Timothy Flint, Joseph Dorfeuille, Hiram Powers, Dr. Daniel Drake, physicians, preachers, editors, and statesmen of the city were all there for admiring fellow townsmen to recognize and point out to companions. The picture held other attractions — for example, a "beautiful child, astride of his dog, which is easily imagined by children to loll, and wag its tail." There was little danger of crowding, for the painting took up one hundred and ninety-two feet of canvas, measuring twelve by sixteen feet.

The local press was enthusiastic. The *Chronicle* pronounced Hervieu's picture "the most finished historical painting which has ever been exhibited in the West" and advised readers that it must be seen more than once to be fully appreciated. One caviler did appear, who complained in a letter to the *Chronicle* that the painting failed to represent the actual scene as he had witnessed it: "Pray, what part . . . did that redcoated *darkey* act, who figured so conspicuously on the foreground . . . ? Where was that amazon, whose phiz somewhat resembled the stern of a Dutch coaster . . . ?" Hervieu replied (probably with much help from Mrs. Trollope, for he did not write English very well) that it was not the office of a historical painter to present "every eye, nose, mouth, coat, waistcoat and breeches that were in actual presence at the event" any more than it was the duty of a poet to record them in verse. Both the Negro and the Indian woman with the prominent nose were allegorical figures:

I fear that "X" must be deeply shocked at the violation of truth in the introduction of the female Indian, whose figure is intended as an allegorical symbol of Western America. — *Certes* she was not there, and if she had been, a quiet squaw would assuredly have looked as little like the figure represented as it is well possible to imagine. The dog WATCH too! alas, he cannot even pretend to believe he was there: — All this is allowed, yet the Painter ventures to say, speaking in the terms of art, that the composition is strictly historical. . . .

A month after *The Landing of Lafayette at Cincinnati* had gone on exhibition, Timothy Flint published a highly laudatory eight-page notice of Hervieu and his work in the *Western Monthly Review*. "We know but one place, where this painting, in our judgment, ought to rest," Flint said in closing, "and that is in one of the vacant pannels of the capitol at Washington." There it would help to counterbalance pictures commemorating historical events of the Atlantic states; it would serve as an appropriate "image of the great West."

The painting was so lavishly praised that Mrs. Trollope and Hervieu began to base new hopes upon it. They were persuaded by enthusiastic citizens that a good deal of money could be made by exhibiting the picture in various Eastern cities. "I then hoped," Mrs. Trollope wrote later, "that some of the brilliant prophecies which poor Hervieu heard for his picture would be realized." While Hervieu gathered funds by showing the *Landing of Lafayette* and perhaps ultimately selling it to Congress, Mrs. Trollope with her two daughters planned to seek refuge at the home of a Mrs. Stone, a childhood friend who had migrated to the United States some years earlier and was now, she understood, settled in the city of Washington. At whatever sacrifice, Henry, now in a precarious state of health, must at once be shipped back to England. But even before Henry could leave, a final degradation was visited upon the family. Mrs. Trollope's household effects were seized by the sheriff, and she shared "one small bed" with her daughters at the house of a neighbor while Henry and Hervieu slept on the kitchen floor.

Early in March 1830 Frances Trollope boarded the steamboat *Lady Franklin* to put Cincinnati forever behind her. The Bazaar towered above her departure, a huge, grotesque monument to her hopes and failures. It was also, in a way, her revenge upon the city; for she had fashioned her temple so curiously that Yankee ingenuity itself could not hit upon a

means of putting the building to profitable use. The natives
soon rechristened it "Trollope's Folly." In the years that followed, it became, among other things, an inn, a dancing
school, a Presbyterian church, a theater, a mechanic's institute, and a military hospital. When Anthony Trollope visited
Cincinnati thirty years after his mother had left, the Bazaar
was a "Physico-medical Institute":

It was under the dominion of a quack doctor on one side, and of a college of rights-of-women female medical professors on the other. "I believe, sir [the proprietor said], no man or woman ever yet made a dollar
in that building; and as for rent, I don't even expect it."

IX

Three days after leaving Cincinnati, Mrs. Trollope and
her party disembarked from the *Lady Franklin* at Wheeling,
now in West Virginia. There, after an enforced stay of two
days due to a scarcity of stagecoach accommodations, they
began their journey toward and over the Alleghenies. It was
a rough journey; it is vividly described with all its amusing mishaps in *Domestic Manners*. At Baltimore, Hervieu
probably exhibited his historical painting, though evidence
is lacking, and Mrs. Trollope spent a fortnight making notes
on the city. From Baltimore they again took passage on a
steamboat and reached Washington by way of Chesapeake
Bay.

At Washington, on March 27, Hervieu unrolled and set up
The Landing of Lafayette at Cincinnati in the gallery of
Charles King, the American artist, on Twelfth Street. The
Daily National Journal gave Hervieu's picture favorable notice. The composition was "spirited and admirable. All seems
to be animation and life; and though the characters are numerous, they are not injudiciously huddled together. . . ."
The writer considered the subject "interesting and striking"
and hoped that Hervieu would meet with the encourage-

ment he deserved. But the people of Washington seem to have been reluctant to pay twenty-five cents' admission to see this depiction of "the flourishing city of the West"; nor did Congress show any eagerness to buy Hervieu's picture to adorn the Capitol.

The plans that Hervieu and Mrs. Trollope had laid in Cincinnati received another disappointment, one which as their slender funds dwindled must have seemed serious indeed. For some time Mrs. Trollope boarded in Washington while she searched fruitlessly to find the residence of Mrs. Stone. Eventually she discovered that her old friend did not live in Washington but at Stonington, Maryland, ten miles distant. Mrs. Stone was now a widow with a large family to support. She had suffered severe reverses and could not keep Mrs. Trollope and her two daughters except as paying guests.

Toward the end of April the Trollopes moved to Stonington. The faithful Hervieu, by taking pupils and securing commissions for an occasional portrait, was able to pay their board. "I wish with all my soul that you could see and hear poor Hervieu!" Mrs. Trollope wrote Tom during the course of the summer. "He seems only to live in the hope of helping us. He has set his heart on getting us home without drawing on your father's diminished purse." But they were desperately poor. Cecilia was "literally without shoes," and Mrs. Trollope intended to sell one or two small articles to buy some for her and also for Emily. "As to other articles of dress, we should any of us as soon think of buying diamonds!" The one great hope was her book. "If it *should* succeed, a second would bring money." She had already begun to put her materials into better shape, piecing together her notes and her memories. "I sit still," she told Tom, "and write, write, write. . . ."

The copybooks in which she first began to gather and expand her scattered notes tell us something of how she set to her task, in what moods and under what difficulties. The first

had been Henry's notebook.³ In her need for paper that she
could hardly afford to buy, she ignored the boyish warnings
"Private" and *"Noli me tangere"* and *"Nemo me Impune
lacessit"* on the cover and wrote around his letters in French
to one Adolphe Barzaine, the poems that he had composed in
Cincinnati, and the lists of his modest expenditures for books
and for a "Collection" (two mammoth bones, three Indian axes,
four arrows, and other similar items). On the flyleaf is her
record "1830 April 24 board begun at Stonington 8/25 per
week." Beneath this heading is a series of sums starting
with $50.00 but dwindling to one payment of 60¢ and an-
other of 12½¢. There is a three-page glossary of American
phrases — "That's a fact," "right bad," "to fix = to arrange,"
"I calculate," and the like — and immediately thereafter the
brief entries:

> Moving houses & forty oxen.
> Sleighing.
> Strawberries & cream 50 cents.

These brief jottings, which were later to be expanded into
accounts of happenings in Cincinnati, are followed by "Bak-
ery | to tote = to count | ugly = unamiable," and on the next
line begins a short description of the approach to Philadelphia by way of the Delaware River which could have been
written only after Mrs. Trollope's visit to that city late in
June. This does not mean that once she had begun, she set
aside her work until that time, for the passages of the notebooks occur in no discernible order. Well beyond this description there is the very faintly penciled and largely illegible
first draft of a letter dated from Stonington May 26. Passages on the most divergent subjects rub elbows in the notebooks; they vary from brief jottings to several hundred words
in length, but relatively few of them are over two hundred

---

³ Miss Muriel Rose Trollope, great-granddaughter of Frances Trollope,
has kindly allowed the Indiana University Library to purchase the three
notebooks and the rough draft of *Domestic Manners*. These materials are
further described in an appendix to this edition.

words. Some are written in pencil, more are written in ink, some are part ink and part pencil.

There are reminders that Mrs. Trollope's cares as a mother often interrupted her writing. A medicine for dysentery ("Laudenum, and lavender, and spirits of hartshorn in equal quantities — 80 or 100 drops to an adult. To children in proportion. Shake the bottle well!") is followed by "Literary conversation at Mrs. Spencer's [in Cincinnati]. Dryden unknown. Ford and Massenger d[itt]o." A formula to stop bleeding appears directly above a memorandum later worked into a paragraph on American women's passion for modish dress: "Frost-bitten ears from fine bonnets in winter." There are other entries that Mrs. Trollope pretty clearly wrote not so much to furnish possible copy for her book as to disburden her own feelings. "I am certain that no one who has not experienced the suffering produced by American spitting can imagine what it is," she exclaims at one point, " — not one moment's interval! Never can the mind forget that the body is a nasty encumbrance." At another time she is taut with the sort of strain that many an expatriate has felt before and since. "Were it not for the extreme fatigue of listening to their drawling talk — 'helps and no helps,' or 'good negurs' and 'bad negurs,'" she writes, or of hearing them praise their "never to be equalled in time past or present or to come great men,"

I could bear it for a while pretty well; but there is a pain that must be felt to be understood in passing days and weeks and months without once hearing the tones, the expressions, and the accents we have been accustomed to listen to *nel dolce paese dicono* — "*poetry*" and not "poatry," "*chivalry*" and not "*shivalry.*"

Once she entrusted her emotions to verse. Only a part of the lines are now legible (others she erased to make way for a prose passage written in ink), but enough remains to show her mood as she thought back upon her entry into the New World on the waters of the Mississippi:

> now we glide
> Between thy slimy banks; the horrent bear
> And bloated crocodile lie crouching there.
> Thy dark shores breathe miasma! on thy breast
> The uptorn forest droops its leafy crest,
> Thy storm-crushed victims; none her strength can save
> That once hath dipped beneath thy fatal wave.
> This flood contemned of nature let me free —
> Turn here again, my bark, and seek the deep blue sea.

At other times during the course of her writing her mood was whimsical, even puckish. She amused herself by penning an epitaph for an imaginary American whom she named "George Washington Spitchew," and she wrote a dramatic sketch depicting the manners of a frontier family when getting up in the morning that goes beyond anything in her final manuscript for rough, realistic humor. (These and many other passages from the notebooks appear in an appendix to this edition.)

But in the main she worked on passages that were later to go into her book with only minor changes, or set down brief memoranda that would help her to write such passages later. The brief jottings show how often she went over her last two and a half years' experiences to salvage incidents or observations that might be put to use. Those that follow appear at widely scattered places in the notebooks, wedged between longer and more polished passages:

Fire at Cincinnati & reflection on the water.

Funerals. All the friends invited by an advertisement in the newspaper.

A rule was passed at Cincinnati that no gentleman should enter the ball room without having his hair combed.

Theatre at Washington. Vomiting in the pit, beer, chewing tobacco.

Negro men and women will not dine together. I never could get accustomed to the manner in which ALL *Americans talk of the blacks in their presence.*

A pic nic gives the idea of too great familiarity.

If a distinguished man is at table, he is helped before the ladies.

Conversation at Table respecting Wilson & Porter's execution.

I met with none but were of literary habits who did not drink whisky.

The American parties remind me of my earliest childhood at the house of a great aunt, or like a visit to a religious family on a Sunday.

Queer effect of hearing that one's friend's cousin is a shoemaker or a baker or a sailmaker.

She gave much thought to the plan and tone of her book. Not far into the first notebook she wrote down: "Chapter 1st. 'Is this freedom?' — St. Paul. Voyage from London to New Orleans. Arrive. The river higher than the banks." But it was probably some time before she made out the lengthy table of contents that appears near the center of her second notebook. The great success of Basil Hall's *Travels in North America,* which since publication in 1829 had run through three English editions, worried her but also helped to clear her ideas regarding her own work. Hall had "put the Union in a blaze from one end to the other," she wrote Miss Mitford in July. The hubbub had made her eager to read his book, but she had not obtained a copy until her visit to Philadelphia, from which she had recently returned to Stonington. By that time her first volume, she felt, was in form "and most of the notes for the second collected. I thus escaped influence of any kind from the perusal."

She underestimated the amount of work she had still to do; and she probably undervalued, too, the effect that reading notices of Hall's *Travels* and extracts from it in newspapers and periodicals had had upon her long before she looked between the covers of his volumes. Her notebooks show that she was very conscious of Hall's work while she wrote much of her own. "Describe the Shakers," she jotted down in the midst of a passage on Philadelphia, "because omitted by Capt. Hall." And at another time she wrote:

> I pretend not to understand the philosophy of government. There is nothing so thoroughly out of the way of a woman. She may be brought to turn the whole force of her faculties to the subject, and they *might* prove sufficient to enable her to comprehend something about it — but it must be *à contre coeur*, if she be a true woman. Not causes but effects form the field in which female observation will out-look all the masculine eyes upon earth, but she rarely pauses to ask, "Why are these things so?"

Hall's book made her take stock of her weaknesses; it also helped her to realize her own possible strength. "If the foregoing remarks appear ill-natured," she comments in her second notebook, "I am very sorry for it, but in pages like mine, proposing and possessing no possible claim to notice, but fidelity of the pictures they offer, it would be utter folly not to describe everything simply as I found it." "I cannot speculate," she says another time, "and I cannot reason; but I can see and hear." In a tentative preface contained in her rough draft but later discarded, she frankly summed up her own idea of her book and the reasoning that had guided her choice of materials:

> I greatly doubt if my book contains much valuable instruction; nay, I should not be much surprised if it were called trifling; for to tell the honest truth I suspect that it is *tant soit peu*, gossiping. . . .
> I really do not believe that I have any particular talent to qualify me for the undertaking, but nobody seems to choose to visit America who

has. As to Capt. Hall, he is altogether too wise for the sort of business I have undertaken, and to say the truth, does not appear to have been in the very best temper in the world when he made his North American tour. How is a man whose thoughts are fixed on the philosophy of government to find time for such tiny observations as my notes are filled with? And yet the world is made up of atoms, and though I may dole them out one by one, they are still part and parcel of the great machine we are all so fond of examining.

It was a wise choice. Few readers have quarreled with her for leaving the philosophical discussion of causes to masculine wisdom and cramming her own pages instead with "gossip," with pictures of day-to-day living in America as she had observed it and taken part in it and recorded it in her notes.

X

Mrs. Trollope boarded at Stonington for nearly five months. Except for her fortnight's visit to Philadelphia, where she studied the manners of the citizens and Hervieu lost money by once more exhibiting the *Landing of Lafayette*, she spent the time working at her notebooks and her manuscript. Late in September she was struck by her second autumnal fever in America. It was less severe than the one that had brought her close to death in Cincinnati, but it was a very serious matter. She did not recover until some weeks after she had been moved to Alexandria, Virginia, fifteen miles from Stonington, for a change of air and the attendance of a physician of more than local reputation. Though she gradually gained strength, she continued far from well, and it was decided that she should stay the winter at Alexandria. She occupied her time revising her notes and adding pages to her book.

By spring she was able to lay plans for a final trip in America and set the approximate date for her return to England. Earlier, at Stonington, she had feared that Hervieu's failure to realize funds from the *Landing of Lafayette* had cut off

all chances of a journey to Niagara Falls; without this additional sightseeing she felt that her book would be "very imperfect." Hervieu must have done better during the winter
of 1830–1 than he or she had expected, for with the aid of
what money her hard-pressed husband could send from
England she and her two daughters and Hervieu left Alexandria late in April bound for New York and Niagara. At
New York City she spent five weeks making observations
and taking notes. An American journalist who became acquainted with her during her stay there later spoke of the
"eager avidity" with which she ferreted out her information
and the "rapid flying visits" that she made about the city.
Her desperate hurry to see and know things, he says, occasioned not a little mirth. But she could not afford a more
leisurely view. Her travels in Eastern America were strictly
limited in time and range by her poverty. On May 30 she set
off for Niagara Falls, making the journey by steamboat,
canal packetboat, and stagecoach. After four days at the
Falls she headed once more for New York City, retracing as
little of her former route as was feasible and covering all the
distance as far as Albany by stage. Within a fortnight the
party managed to secure passage and set sail for England.

On August 5, 1831, three years and nine months after she
had taken ship for America, Mrs. Trollope landed at Wool-
wich. She proceeded from there directly to Harrow. The contrast between her hopeful leave-taking and her homecoming
was inevitably clear and painful. She returned to a meanly
furnished tumbledown farmhouse three miles from town that
Mr. Trollope had moved into as a part of his desperate measures to reduce expenses. It may have occurred to her that this
house, with its leaking roof and rotting timbers, was only too
accurate a symbol of the family's circumstances. Her husband, despondent over his mounting debts and persistent,
racking headaches, had lapsed into invalidism. Her own
health had been shaken by the autumnal fevers of America.

The family's last block of capital had been sunk in the disastrous experiment at Cincinnati. The question now was how
long creditors would hold their bills.

Under these conditions Frances Trollope sat down to finish her book. By the end of August she was done. Armed with
a letter of introduction from Miss Mitford, she called on the
publisher Whittaker, who received her civilly and asked her
to leave her manuscript, telling her that he would report on
it in two weeks. When the two anxious weeks had expired,
Mrs. Trollope sent Tom to inquire the fate of her book. Tom
brought back disquieting news. Whittaker had given the
manuscript to Captain Basil Hall, who had not yet returned
it. Mrs. Trollope feared that Hall, having gone over the same
ground but a short time earlier, would be unduly critical.

As a matter of fact, Whittaker could scarcely have chosen
a reader more likely to report favorably on the manuscript.
The author of *Travels in North America* might pretend to
ignore the English liberal press and the American journals
when they accused him of dealing in malicious falsehoods,
but it is a rare man who enjoys being called a liar. Hall could
hardly fail to welcome a book based upon three years' observations in the United States which corroborated his own
statements at almost every point. Soon after Tom's call on
Whittaker, Mrs. Trollope received "a very flattering letter"
from Captain Hall stating that he had strongly advised the
publisher to lose no time in printing her book. Whittaker announced that he was willing to undertake *Domestic Manners,*
dividing the profits with her. "I suppose," Mrs. Trollope confided to Miss Mitford, ". . . that this is as favorable an offer
as a person so utterly unknown can expect. *But,* as we have
been losing money on both sides of the Atlantic, a little
money *in esse* would have been more agreeable than the
hopes he gives *in posse.*"

There followed a nervous period of waiting for publication. Frances Trollope set to writing *The Refugee in America,*

a novel with many of its scenes set in the United States, but
she also managed to find time to put the dingy farmhouse
into better order. When Tom came down from Oxford, the
place "did not seem the same," now that his mother had had
time to brighten it. Anthony lost a part of the wretchedness
that had settled over him. Ever since the return of his father
from America early in 1829, Anthony had shared the gloom
of Harrow Weald with him. Mr. Trollope, when he was not
prostrated by his headaches or attempting to find some way
of making the farm meet expenses, spent his time shut up in
the parlor working on a vast and impracticable project, an
Encyclopedia Ecclesiastica in which he intended to describe
"all ecclesiastical terms, including the denominations of every
fraternity of monks and every convent of nuns, with all their
orders and subdivisions." He felt no need for amusement himself and did not consider that any was necessary for his son;
nor could he sympathize with or alleviate the miseries that
the boy suffered at school. Anthony, who later recalled his
school-days from start to finish as a dreary succession of de-
feats and indignities, singled out the last eighteen months
before his mother's return as "perhaps . . . the worst period
of my life." Mr. Trollope had entered him at Harrow as a
day boarder. A tutor, probably aware of the family's financial
straits, had accepted the boy without the customary fee of
ten guineas but had inflicted exquisite torture upon him by
declaring this act of charity before all the other students in
the pupil-room. Anthony felt that every hand was turned
against him. "What right had a wretched farmer's boy, reeking from a dunghill, to sit next to the sons of peers . . . ?"
He was a pariah. "I know that I skulked, and was odious to
the eyes of those that I admired and envied."

XI

Suddenly, with the publication of *Domestic Manners* in
March, Mrs. Trollope found herself a celebrity; she was

thrown into a whirl of engagements, the lion of the hour.
She wrote Tom that even to him she dared not repeat all the
kind things that people said to her.

> The Countess of Morley told me she was certain that if I drove
> through London proclaiming who I was, I should have the horses taken
> off and be drawn in triumph from one end of town to the other! The
> Honorable Mr. Somebody declared that my thunder storm was the
> finest thing in prose or verse. Lady Charlotte Lindsay *implored* me to
> go on writing — never was anything so delightful. Lady Louisa Stewart
> told me that I had quite put English out of fashion, and that every one
> was talking Yankee talk. In short I was *overpowered*!

The next Wednesday she was to be entertained at Lady
Alderson's — "a splendid party I am told." Celebrity did not
turn her head far, however; she was not so completely overpowered as to take her laurels for granted or to forget the
main object of her writing: "But all this must help the sale
of the next book whatever may happen after." Her worry was
that such lionizing kept her from putting as much time as she
wished into her novel.

At the end of April Mrs. Trollope wrote Miss Mitford that
Whittaker had paid her £250 for the first edition of *Domestic
Manners* and was to give her an additional £200 the next
week for the second edition. In an age of low prices these
were considerable sums. Mrs. Trollope was able to quiet the
most impatient of her husband's creditors and to remove her
family from tumbledown Harrow Weald to the comparative
luxury of Julians Hill. She bought new clothes for herself and
her family, new and splendid furnishings for her home; she
hired servants; she gave gay parties for distinguished guests.
By the end of the year she had realized close to £1,000 from
Domestic Manners and *The Refugee in America.* Her expenditures kept pace with her income. The family's debts
might hover in the background, a shadowy unbidden guest at
her bright assemblies; but after long years of famine Mrs.
Trollope meant to enjoy a period of plenty.

Any second book "by Mrs. Trollope, the author of *Domestic Manners of the Americans*," was assured of an audience. *The Refugee in America* was praised and condemned and held in the public notice by partisan reviewers who judged it by what they had thought of *Domestic Manners*. In large part *The Refugee* is simply run-of-the-mine fiction of its time. Mrs. Trollope was satisfied with no one less than a young earl for her hero, and the Countess of Darcy, his mother, figures prominently in the action. Subscribers to the rental libraries had their expected ration of aristocracy. The plot is made up of deep intrigue, disguise, and pursuit, culminating in a trial at Westminster Hall. There Lord Darcy is cleared of a charge of murder by the last-minute appearance of the girl he loves, with incontrovertible proof of his innocence. The girl is an American, an unspoiled, adaptable maiden who easily sees the merits of imitating English speech and English manners. It is in the American scenes that the novel comes to life, and these contain much clever writing. There is hardly a detail of American life, to be sure, that is not twice-told material for the reader of *Domestic Manners;* but to the average devotee of the three-volume novel *The Refugee's* American settings must have been new and satisfying. Perhaps the most notable fact about this first novel is that in it Mrs. Trollope adopted the practice that she was to follow with rare exceptions throughout her career, one that provided her a reliable market for a quarter-century: she gauged her audience and gave them what they wanted. Critics might abuse her novel as they had abused *Domestic Manners;* so long as her books sold, she did not care greatly. She had no high opinion of herself as a producer of literature; she wrote not for posterity but for money to supply the needs of her family.

Even before *The Refugee* was completed, Mrs. Trollope was planning further projects for supporting her family by her pen. "What does one do to get business with the mags and annuals?" she inquired of Miss Mitford. "Does one say, as at playing écarté, 'I propose,' or must one wait to be asked?' Remember, dear, that I have five children." Within the next year she was to complete *The Abbess*, a highly colored tale of fifteenth-century Italy, and *The Mother's Manual*, a curious satirical essay in rhymed couplets on ways of marrying off young daughters. On June 1, 1833 she set off for Belgium and the Rhine to gather materials for her second travel book. With her she took Henry and Auguste Hervieu, now confirmed in his position as a family retainer.

By the time of Mrs. Trollope's return to Harrow in the fall, she had once more run through her funds. Aided by her brother, Henry Milton, she began a systematic summing up of her family's assets and liabilities. The result was frightening. It was clear that though she might support her husband and children by her writing, there was no hope of her meeting the heavy claims due to Mr. Trollope's creditors. A good part of her marriage settlement could be salvaged and turned into an annuity that could not be seized, but there was little else that might be rescued. The Trollopes' finances had long ago been undermined beyond repair; now the total collapse was not far off. During the winter Mrs. Trollope worked at the manuscript of *Belgium and Western Germany in 1833*. In April came the long impending crash. The family must have had a few hours' warning. Anthony drove his father to the London docks and put him on the Ostend boat. When he came home, the sheriff's officers were already hauling furnishings from the house. Mrs. Trollope may well have viewed the proceedings with a measure of philosophy. She had known for months that they would take place; moreover, she was fortified by her memories. She had gone through the scene once before — four years earlier, at Cincinnati.

XII

Once more Frances Trollope set about establishing her household in a foreign land. In Belgium (at Bruges) finances, though a constant problem, worried her less than in America, for she had now found a way to earn money for herself and her family. But a still graver anxiety before long descended upon the Trollopes. Within a short time Henry and Emily were seriously ailing, and Mrs. Trollope learned past doubt that their illness was consumption in a dangerous form. She began a desperate battle for the lives of her children. When there was no longer any hope that Henry would survive, she worked to make his last months as comfortable as possible, humoring his whims, leaving his bedside only to snatch a few hours' sleep or to care for Emily or to attend to the many other demands of her family. Tom was still at Oxford. Anthony and Cecilia, while they remained, must have helped as best they could; but there were few tasks that could be delegated to them. There was a third invalid to care for. Mr. Trollope's health was steadily declining. But though the duties of her home were more than enough to tax her strength, Mrs. Trollope must keep on with her writing, or sick and well would starve together. "The doctor's vials and the ink-bottle held equal places in my mother's rooms," Anthony recalled years later.

I have written many novels under many circumstances; but I doubt much whether I could write one when my whole heart was by the bedside of a dying son. Her power of dividing herself into two parts, and keeping her intellect by itself clear from the troubles of the world, and fit for the duty it had to do, I never saw equalled.

Mrs. Trollope had a writing-table moved into Henry's room and set herself a rigorous program. She worked at her manuscript for three hours every other night, keeping awake with stiff brews of green tea; on alternate nights she slept heavily by dosing herself with laudanum.

In the fall she found means of sending Cecilia and Anthony beyond the danger of contagion. Cecilia was dispatched to the home of her uncle Henry Milton at Fulham. Anthony, now nineteen, was first sent to an English school at Brussels

kept by the Drurys, old friends of the family, where he served
inefficiently as an usher for room, board, and infrequent
French lessons. In October other friends of the family secured him an opening as a clerk in the London Post Office
at a salary of ninety pounds a year.

When death came to Henry on December 23, 1834, Frances
Trollope allowed herself little time to indulge her grief. Her
second travel book had not realized enough to keep her family from imminent need for further funds. Her novel *Tremordyn Cliff* would bring an additional sum, but she must
set to work on new projects. In February she crossed to London and made arrangements with the publisher Bentley for
a book on Paris and its people. April found her in the French
capital. A few months later she was back at Bruges, with
Paris and the Parisians completed and her second novel of
American life already taking form.

For *The Life and Adventures of Jonathan Jefferson Whitlaw, or Scenes on the Mississippi,* Mrs. Trollope put aside the
lighter tone that she had used to satirize the United States
and its inhabitants in *Domestic Manners* and *The Refugee in
America.* Her present plan was to make a deadly serious attack upon Negro slavery, and she chose as her vehicle a tale
heavy with melodrama and dominated by an appalling villain. Son of a river squatter, Jonathan Jefferson Whitlaw rises
to wealth and power by cunning and total lack of scruples.
He is opposed in his designs by Juno, an aged Negress who
exerts power over whites and blacks alike by preying upon
their superstitious natures. Ultimately Juno proves the nem-
esis of Whitlaw; he dies under the daggers of four slaves
whom she has set upon him and is buried beneath the floor
of her hut. But before his evil career is ended, Whitlaw has
driven Juno's half-white granddaughter, reared as an English
heiress, to escape his threats by suicide; he has also contrived the death of the hero. This enlightened young Kentuckian, who has blocked Whitlaw's plans by championing

the Negroes, dies at the hands of a lynching party. Altogether *Jonathan Jefferson Whitlaw* is a grim tale, full of persecution and violence. It suffers from improbabilities of plotting, but it possesses memorable scenes and characters and is easily one of Mrs. Trollope's strongest performances. Hervieu's fifteen plates are also somber but effective.

Mrs. Trollope wrote much of *Jonathan Jefferson Whitlaw* in scattered snatches of work beside the sickbed of her husband. Late in October 1835, at the age of sixty-one, Thomas Anthony Trollope gave over a life that for some years past had been made up of disappointment, sickness, and futile but heroic labor. Until a few weeks before his death he had worked on at his Encyclopedia Ecclesiastica, the vast quixotic project that was destined never to be finished. He was buried beside Henry in the Protestant cemetery at Bruges. Again Frances Trollope could allow herself little time for mourning. There was no further need to remain out of England, and she established herself and Emily in a house at Hadley, Hertfordshire, twelve miles from London, where she could keep in touch with her publishers. She had lived here only a few weeks when Emily, so long failing of consumption, grew critically ill. In February Mrs. Trollope lost the third member of her family within fourteen months. After a brief space she threw herself into work on a new book. *The Vicar of Wrexhill,* a devastating satire upon the Evangelical clergy, was to become her best-known novel.

XIII

No longer shackled to the sickroom, Mrs. Trollope was entering a new period of her life in which Frances Trollope the mother at last resigned precedence over Frances Trollope the novelist and traveler. In July, with Tom, Cecilia, and Hervieu in tow, she set off for the Continent to gather notes for another travel book. The months in which Mrs. Trollope collected experiences for *Vienna and the Austrians* were probably among the pleasantest of her life. An inveterate lover of novelty, she now enjoyed days of travel by carriage through romantic scenery, visits to old castles and strange cities, a trip by barge down the Danube. Her delight in gay and distinguished company was more than gratified at Vienna. Mélanie, Princess Metternich, made much over her, and Frances Trollope was treated to a succession of dinners, balls, receptions, and parties so dazzling that even those of London seemed poor things by comparison. Seven years earlier Mrs. Trollope's great concern had been whether the fashionables of Cincinnati would grace her entertainments at the Bazaar. She and Hervieu, who sketched Metternich and painted a portrait of the Princess, must have felt that times had changed.

For the next decade Frances Trollope wrote and traveled. Her books provided an income sufficient for her needs and many of her whims. She was seldom in any one place for more than a few months. Cecilia made a good marriage. Anthony continued in the postal service and showed signs of prospering in it, especially after his appointment to a surveyor's clerkship in Ireland. Tom, after a try at teaching, decided upon writing as his profession and accepted his mother's offer to live with her and squire her on her travels. Mrs. Trollope seldom went for long without reminders that, though she had written of many things since 1832, *Domestic Manners* remained her best-known work. In 1839 she allowed Bentley to publish a new edition; she prepared many additional notes as a means of bringing her comments upon the United States up to date. At least one American went to some pains to secure an introduction to her. He professed himself a great admirer and assured Mrs. Trollope that she had done his country a great deal of good. When she was presented at the French court in 1840, Louis Philippe asked her, "with a look of something like fun," if she should like to go back to the United States. She reflected that the King, like herself, had been a refugee in America and "longed to return the question to him!"

While she was in Florence the following year gathering materials for a book on Italy, Mrs. Trollope was invited to visit the studios of some of the most distinguished artists in the city. Among the first names mentioned to her was that of Hiram Powers. She had heard nothing of him since leaving Cincinnati, but she "felt not the slightest doubt" that the artist mentioned would prove to be her old acquaintance. She was not disappointed. "There indeed I found the highly-gifted Hiram Powers, fully emerged from the boyish chrysalis' state, in which I had last seen him, into a full-fledged and acknowledged man of genius. . . ." Powers showed her the portrait busts on which he had been working; but after admiring these she insisted on knowing whether he had never tried his hand on any purely imaginative work. Powers sighed and told her that he had to think of his wife and children; he received a steady stream of orders from people who wanted their likenesses carved in marble, and he "must not risk the loss of this lucrative business" to indulge in flights of the imagination. Nevertheless he at last showed her an ideal figure of Eve that he had shaped in clay. He dared not risk the expense of carving it in marble unless he received an order for the work. In *A Visit to Italy* Mrs. Trollope reproduced her conversation with Powers at length and described his ideal statue in glowing words. After their meeting in Florence, she took to praising Powers on all possible occasions. Her open letter to Edward Everett lauding the "truth-inspired sculptor of Ohio" was printed in the Washington *National Intelligencer*. It paid such high tributes to Powers that a Cincinnati paper not only quoted it in full but spoke of the author of *Domestic Manners* in terms amounting to partial forgiveness. It was Mrs. Trollope who inveigled a wealthy Englishman into Powers's Florence studio and brought him away the first possessor of *The Greek Slave*.

In 1843, a year after the appearance of Charles Dickens's *American Notes,* Frances Trollope published *The Barnabys in America,* her third novel dealing with life in the United States. The simple, somewhat foolish Widow Barnaby was a favorite character whom Mrs. Trollope had already carried through two novels.[4] *The Barnabys in America* is a broad-humored, leisurely, and practically plotless satire upon American customs and American prejudices. In the course of the Barnabys' travels about America the widow's Irish husband changes parts as often as a low comedian on a rural circuit and thus allows his creator to poke fun at a number of American types, including the swaggering, bragging tobacco-chewer and the hypocritical revivalist minister. The widow herself decides to write a book about America, but unlike the author of *Domestic Manners* she shows great adaptability and few scruples; she fits readily into the environment of the moment. She is lionized in the South because she praises slavery and in the North because she condemns it. She is eager for advice about her book and receives large amounts of that commodity. Her advisers differ sharply in their ideas upon the proper handling of particular subjects, but as to the general point of view she should adopt all are agreed. "All I want," one American woman informs her, "is that you should portrait us out to the world for just what we really are, and that is the finest nation upon the surface of God's whole earth, and as far ahead in civilization of Europe in general, and England in particular, as the summer is before winter in heat."

Perhaps Mrs. Trollope meant originally to turn a part of the laughter toward herself; the Widow Barnaby takes notes and asks questions even as she herself had done a dozen years earlier. But the widow is far more often Mrs. Trollope's foil than her likeness. The single sheet of "Justice Done at Last" which the widow reads to an admiring American audience is

---

[4] *The Widow Barnaby* (1839) and *The Widow Wedded* (1840).

a wildly fulsome eulogy on "the free-born, the free-bred, the immortal, and ten hundred thousand times more glorious country," to which all others put together cannot in any respect hold a candle. One member of the audience exclaims: "Admirable!" An American dignitary who is of the party objects to the word. "Admirable? It is *first-rate*, ma'am." There was no doubt in the minds of readers which way the satire pointed, but it was too broad in tone and too familiar in theme to hurt or surprise anyone.

Six years later Mrs. Trollope published her fourth and last novel of American life. She was now within one year of threescore and ten, and she may have felt that it was time to make her peace with the Americans. At least, *The Old World and the New* deals more kindly with the United States than any of her earlier books. The Stormonts come to the New World because they cannot see their way to remaining solvent in England. After inspecting a wild forest tract in New York, they move on to Ohio, where they purchase fifteen hundred acres of land, most of which is already cleared. Their farm is only ten miles from Cincinnati. The Stormonts are much better pleased with this city than Mrs. Trollope had been; they admire its "busy prosperity" and its "magnificent position." Fortunately, they have enough capital to establish themselves without hardship. "Nothing is so difficult as to get along in the United States without ready money," Mrs. Trollope observes. "Nothing is so easy with it."

The Stormonts prosper in the New World even from the start. Before long they decide to build a more spacious residence. The plans for their new house suggest that the creator of Cincinnati's Bazaar had not lost her love for novel architecture. On a bluff overlooking the Ohio River the Stormonts erect a square edifice of three stories, sixty feet to a side, with "a colonnade of perfectly well-proportioned Doric pillars . . . round the entire building." The portico formed by the pillars was twenty feet deep. Within the building, vast halls or galleries met in a spacious cross, "which was lighted — not by a dome, the construction of which would have been difficult and costly, but by ample and well-arranged sky-lights." The fashionable families of Cincinnati are duly impressed; the maneuverings among them to obtain presentations to the Stormonts, Mrs. Trollope tells us, had all the vehemence of a general election. Within six weeks after the English family had moved into their new house, they had become acquainted with "all the most distinguished families among the aristocracy of Cincinnati."

English families in Mrs. Trollope's earlier novels had been glad to shake the dust of the United States from their shoes, but the Stormonts, even when they could return to the Old World in comfort, prefer to stay in Ohio and see their children grow into full-fledged Americans. After all, Mrs. Trollope reflects, twenty years and the advent of the transatlantic steamship have greatly lessened differences between England and America:

It is an obvious and a very agreeable fact, that the social intercourse between the old country and the new, has been rapidly increased, and is still rapidly increasing, in consequence of the great comparative facility with which an excursion across the Atlantic may now be made; and the natural and inevitable effect of this has been the formation of many warm and cordial friendships between individuals who were born of the same race, but with this formidable barrier dividing them.

Now that easy communication between the two countries has been effected, Americans are steadily improving through the benefits of travel. In time they may even learn how to speak English.

XIV

Except for brief excursions, Frances Trollope herself was now content to keep to one place; her years of restless gadding about the face of Europe were past. She and Tom and, after his marriage in 1848, Tom's wife, Theodosia, were set-

tled in Florence, where they were honored members of the
foreign colony. In 1856 Mrs. Trollope published her thirty-
fourth novel and was content, at seventy-six, to relinquish
her post among the writing Trollopes. Though Tom had not
yet produced the historical works for which he is best remembered, he was already a regular contributor to the *Athenæum*
and other periodicals. His wife's slight, melodious verses
were celebrated far beyond their merits. As for Anthony, he
had been writing in his spare time for the last ten years and
had managed the year previous to produce a novel that made
a profit for the publishers and gave its author a slender return for his labors. This novel was *The Warden*, first of the
Barsetshire series. *Barchester Towers* was to appear in 1857.

It is doubtful whether Mrs. Trollope had any but the faintest notion of her younger son's real stature. Since the dark
days at Bruges when the nineteen-year-old Anthony had been
shipped off to a clerkship in the London Post Office, she had
seen him only at infrequent intervals and never for any extended period of time. When, in 1845, he had brought her his
first novel, written in off hours from his duties in the Irish
postal service, she had shown small enthusiasm. Mother and
son had agreed, Anthony tells us in his *Autobiography*, "that
it would be as well that she should not look at it before she
gave it to a publisher. I knew that she did not give me credit
for the sort of cleverness necessary for such work." Though
she found him his first publisher, Frances Trollope seems to
have given her son no great amount of advice or encouragement during the decade in which he groped his way through
two heavy novels on the Anglo-Irish question, a historical romance, a play that came back marked "failure preordained,"
and a guide-book to Ireland that never saw printer's daylight.
Yet when Anthony at last found his true style and subject,
they proclaimed his kinship to his novel-writing mother. His
famed Barsetshire tales of life in an English cathedral town
are interestingly foreshadowed in both setting and character

by *Petticoat Government* (1850), one of his mother's yearly three-volume novels.

Though Mrs. Trollope probably did not foresee the future honors of her line, she had reasons at the end of her career to congratulate herself. Her two surviving children (Cecilia had died in 1849) were free from financial worries such as had harassed the family through so much of her earlier life. Anthony, long married and the father of two sons, held a good position in the Post Office; Tom was making money from his writing, and his wife was an heiress. The Villino Trollope, which Frances Trollope shared with Tom and Theodosia, their six-year-old daughter, and Theo's father, must have satisfied her love for splendid furnishings and imposing architecture. A great marble staircase, vast halls and corridors, a library of five thousand volumes, many of them rare and precious editions, art treasures by the score, a terrace with tessellated marble floor and lofty pillars overlooking grounds dotted with fountains, statues, and cypresses — it was all a far cry from the boarding-houses of America or the dingy poverty of Harrow Weald. Hiram Powers, now at the height of his fame, came to chat with her as he had done years ago in Cincinnati; Elizabeth and Robert Browning were frequent callers. The Villino Trollope was an accepted gathering-place of the many celebrities of society and the arts who passed through Florence; there was no lack of the gay company in which Mrs. Trollope had always delighted.

Frances Trollope lived for another seven years, dying easily and without pain on October 6, 1863, at the age of eighty-three, after an illness of only two days.

XV

A quarter of a century later, when Tom came to characterize his mother's life in his memoirs, he set it down as on the whole "singularly happy." If Tom was right — and he had been in an excellent position to know — few people of her time could lay stronger claims to having built their own happiness through an unusual resourcefulness and resiliency of spirit. Certainly she had drawn more than an average allotment of trouble; the hardships of her American years alone would have been enough to sink many another person. She could write of her years in the United States with lively humor. The fact speaks eloquently for her dauntless character. If the humor of her volumes is often edged with satire, who can blame her? Considering her experiences, as one New World critic was kind enough to remark, she might have written "a worse book" about America!

PREFACE

===

IN offering to the public these volumes* on America, their author would rather be considered as endeavouring to excite fresh attention on a very important subject, than as pretending to furnish complete information upon it.

Although much has already been written on the great experiment, as it has been called, now making in government, on the other side of the Atlantic, there appears to be still room for many interesting details on the influence which the political system of the country has produced on the principles, tastes, and manners, of its domestic life.

The author of the following pages has endeavoured, in some degree, to supply this deficiency, by carefully recording the observations she had an opportunity of making during a residence of three years and six months in different parts of the United States.

She leaves to abler pens the more ambitious task of commenting on the democratic form of the American government; while, by describing, faithfully, the daily aspect of ordinary life, she has endeavoured to shew how greatly the advantage is on the side of those who are governed by the few, instead of the many. The chief object she has had in view is to encourage her countrymen to hold fast by a consti-

---

* The first edition was in two volumes, breaking after Chapter XX.

tution that ensures all the blessings which flow from established habits and solid principles. If they forego these, they will incur the fearful risk of breaking up their repose by introducing the jarring tumult and universal degradation which invariably follow the wild scheme of placing all the power of the state in the hands of the populace.

The United States of America contain a considerable variety of interesting objects in most branches of natural science, besides much that is new, a good deal that is beautiful, and some things that are wonderful. Nevertheless, as it is the moral and religious condition of the people which, beyond every thing else, demands the attention of the philosophical enquirer, the author would consider her work as completely successful, could she but awaken a more general interest on this subject.

HARROW,
March, 1832.

CONTENTS

ILLUSTRATIONS

DOMESTIC MANNERS
OF THE AMERICANS

"On me dit que pourvu que je ne parle ni de l'autorité, ni du culte, ni de la politique, ni de la morale, ni des gens en place, ni de l'opéra, ni des autres spectacles, ni de personne qui tienne à quelque chose, je puis tout imprimer librement."

MARIAGE DE FIGARO

A Key

TO THE NOTES OF THIS EDITION

[T1] *Footnotes by Mrs. Trollope in the first edition of* Domestic Manners of the Americans.

[T5, note] *Footnotes by Mrs. Trollope in the fifth English edition. (For a fuller description of this edition, see* Appendix C.)

[TN] *Excerpts from the notebooks that Mrs. Trollope wrote while composing* Domestic Manners of the Americans. (*See* Appendix B *for a fuller description of them.*)

[TRD] *Excerpts from the rough draft of* Domestic Manners of the Americans. (*See* Appendix B *for a fuller description.*)

[DS] *Notes by the present editor.*

DOMESTIC MANNERS
OF THE
AMERICANS

==

CHAPTER I

Entrance of the Mississippi — Balize

ON the 4th of November, 1827, I sailed from London, accompanied by my son and two daughters; and after a favourable, though somewhat tedious voyage, arrived on Christmas-day at the mouth of the Mississippi.

The first indication of our approach to land was the appearance of this mighty river pouring forth its muddy mass of waters, and mingling with the deep blue of the Mexican Gulf. The shores of this river are so utterly flat, that no object upon them is perceptible at sea, and we gazed with pleasure on the muddy ocean that met us, for it told us we were arrived, and seven weeks of sailing had wearied us; yet it was not without a feeling like regret that we passed from the bright blue waves, whose varying aspect had so long furnished our chief amusement, into the murky stream which now received us.

Large flights of pelicans were seen standing upon the long masses of mud which rose above the surface of the waters, and a pilot came to guide us over the bar, long before any other indication of land was visible.

I never beheld a scene so utterly desolate as this entrance of the Mississippi. Had Dante seen it, he might have drawn images of another Bolgia [1] from its horrors. One only object rears itself above the eddying waters; this is the mast of a vessel long since wrecked in attempting to cross the bar, and it still stands, a dismal witness of the destruction that has been, and a boding prophet of that which is to come.

By degrees bulrushes of enormous growth become visible, and a few more miles of mud brought us within sight of a cluster of huts called the Balize, by far the most miserable station that I ever saw made the dwelling of man, [2] but I was told that many families of pilots and fishermen lived there.

For several miles above its mouth, the Mississippi presents no objects more interesting than mud banks, monstrous bulrushes, and now and then a huge crocodile luxuriating in the slime. Another circumstance that gives to this dreary scene an aspect of desolation, is the incessant appearance of vast quantities of drift wood, which is ever finding its way to the different mouths of the Mississippi. Trees of enormous length, sometimes still bearing their branches, and still oftener their uptorn roots entire, the victims of the frequent hurricane, come floating down the stream. Sometimes several of these, entangled together, collect among their boughs a quantity of floating rubbish, that gives the mass the appearance of a moving island, bearing a forest, with its roots mocking the heavens; while the dishonoured branches lash the tide in idle

---

[1] [DS] In canto XVIII of the *Inferno*, Dante describes "a place in Hell called Malebolge." It is divided into ten concentric trenchlike rings, each of which is a chasm, or *bolgia*, filled with a different class of sinners.

[2] [DS] The Balize was the chief station of pilots at the mouth of the Mississippi.

"From this wretched place — planted in the midst of a boundless swamp or morass — no firm land is in sight, or is within fifty or sixty miles of it. There are about twenty buildings in all, six of which are dwelling-houses. The intercourse between them is carried on exclusively along paths made of planks and trunks of trees laid over the slime and water." — Basil Hall: *Travels in North America* (1829).

vengeance: this, as it approaches the vessel, and glides swiftly past, looks like the fragment of a world in ruins.

As we advanced, however, we were cheered, notwithstanding the season, by the bright tints of southern vegetation. The banks continue invariably flat, but a succession of planless villas, sometimes merely a residence, and sometimes surrounded by their sugar grounds and negro huts, varied the scene. At no one point was there an inch of what painters call a second distance; and for the length of one hundred and twenty miles, from the Balize to New Orleans, and one hundred miles above the town, the land is defended from the encroachments of the river by a high embankment which is called the Levée; without which the dwellings would speedily disappear, as the river is evidently higher than the banks would be without it. When we arrived, there had been constant rains, and of long continuance, and this appearance was, therefore, unusually striking, giving to "this great natural feature" the most unnatural appearance imaginable; and making evident, not only that man had been busy there, but that even the mightiest works of nature might be made to bear his impress; it recalled, literally, Swift's mock heroic,

"Nature must give way to art;"

yet, she was looking so mighty, and so unsubdued all the time, that I could not help fancying she would some day take the matter into her own hands again, and if so, farewell to New Orleans.

It is easy to imagine the total want of beauty in such a landscape; but yet the form and hue of the trees and plants, so new to us, added to the long privation we had endured of all sights and sounds of land, made even these swampy shores seem beautiful. We were, however, impatient to touch as well as see the land; but the navigation from the Balize to New Orleans is difficult and tedious, and the two days that it occupied appeared longer than any we had passed on board.

In truth, to those who have pleasure in contemplating the phenomena of nature, a sea voyage may endure many weeks without wearying. Perhaps some may think that the first glance of ocean and of sky shew all they have to offer; nay, even that that first glance may suggest more of dreariness than sublimity; but to me, their variety appeared endless, and their beauty unfailing. The attempt to describe scenery, even where the objects are prominent and tangible, is very rarely successful; but where the effect is so subtile and so varying, it must be vain. The impression, nevertheless, is perhaps deeper than any other; I think it possible I may forget the sensations with which I watched the long course of the gigantic Mississippi; the Ohio and the Potomac may mingle and be confounded with other streams in my memory, I may even recall with difficulty the blue outline of the Alleghany mountains, but never, while I remember any thing, can I forget the first and last hour of light on the Atlantic.

The ocean, however, and all its indescribable charm, no longer surrounded us; we began to feel that our walk on the quarter-deck was very like the exercise of an ass in a mill; that our books had lost half their pages, and that the other half were known by rote; that our beef was very salt, and our biscuits very hard; in short, that having studied the good ship, Edward, from stem to stern till we knew the name of every sail, and the use of every pulley, we had had enough of her, and as we laid down, head to head, in our tiny beds for the last time, I exclaimed with no small pleasure,

"To-morrow to fresh fields and pastures new."

CHAPTER II

New Orleans — Society — Creoles and Quadroons — Voyage
up the Mississippi

ON first touching the soil of a new land, of a new continent, of a new world, it is impossible not to feel considerable excitement and deep interest in almost every object that meets us. New Orleans presents very little that can gratify the eye of taste, but nevertheless there is much of novelty and interest for a newly arrived European. The large proportion of blacks seen in the streets, all labour being performed by them; the grace and beauty of the elegant Quadroons, the occasional groups of wild and savage looking Indians, the unwonted aspect of the vegetation, the huge and turbid river, with its low and slimy shore, all help to afford that species of amusement which proceeds from looking at what we never saw before.

The town has much the appearance of a French Ville de Province, and is, in fact, an old French colony taken from Spain by France. The names of the streets are French, and the language about equally French and English. The market is handsome and well supplied, all produce being conveyed by the river. We were much pleased by the chant with which the Negro boatmen regulate and beguile their labour on the river; it consists but of very few notes, but they are sweetly harmonious, and the Negro voice is almost always rich and powerful.

By far the most agreeable hours I passed at New Orleans were those in which I explored with my children the forest near the town. It was our first walk in "the eternal forests of the western world," and we felt rather sublime and poetical. The trees, generally speaking, are much too close to be either large or well grown; and, moreover, their growth is often stunted by a parasitical plant, for which I could learn no other name than "Spanish moss;" it hangs gracefully from the boughs, converting the outline of all the trees it hangs upon into that of weeping willows. The chief beauty of the forest in this region is from the luxuriant under-growth of palmetos, which is decidedly the loveliest coloured and most graceful plant I know. The pawpaw, too, is a splendid shrub, and in great abundance. We here, for the first time, saw the wild vine, which we afterwards found growing so profusely in every part of America, as naturally to suggest the idea that the natives ought to add wine to the numerous productions of their plenty-teeming soil.[1] The strong pendant festoons made safe and commodious swings, which some of our party enjoyed, despite the sublime temperament above-mentioned.

Notwithstanding it was mid-winter when we were at New Orleans, the heat was much more than agreeable, and the attacks of the mosquitos incessant, and most tormenting; yet I suspect that, for a short time, we would rather have endured it, than not have seen oranges, green peas, and red pepper, growing in the open air at Christmas. In one of our rambles we ventured to enter a garden, whose bright orange hedge attracted our attention; here we saw green peas fit for the table, and a fine crop of red pepper ripening in the sun. A young Negress was employed on the steps of the house; that she was a slave made her an object of interest to us. She was the first slave we had ever spoken to, and I believe we all

---

[1] [T5, note] The fact, however, is otherwise, and in a very remarkable degree. During my residence in America, I repeatedly tasted native wine from vineyards carefully cultivated, and on the fabrication of which a considerable degree of imported science had been bestowed; but the very best of it was miserable stuff. It should seem that Nature herself requires some centuries of schooling before she becomes perfectly accomplished in ministering to the luxuries of man, and, perhaps as there is no lack of sunshine, the champagne and Bordeaux of the Union may appear simultaneously with a Shakspeare, a Raphael, and a Mozart.

I ANCIENT AND MODERN REPUBLICS

II PHILOSOPHICAL MILLINERY STORE

felt that we could hardly address her with sufficient gentleness. She little dreamed, poor girl, what deep sympathy she
excited; she answered us civilly and gaily, and seemed
amused at our fancying there was something unusual in red
pepper pods; she gave us several of them, and I felt fearful
lest a hard mistress might blame her for it. How very childish
does ignorance make us! and how very ignorant we are upon
almost every subject, where hear-say evidence is all we can
get!

I left England with feelings so strongly opposed to slavery,
that it was not without pain I witnessed its effects around
me. At the sight of every Negro man, woman, and child that
passed, my fancy wove some little romance of misery, as belonging to each of them; since I have known more on the
subject, and become better acquainted with their real situation in America, I have often smiled at recalling what I then
felt.

The first symptom of American equality that I perceived,
was my being introduced in form to a milliner; it was not at
a boarding-house, under the indistinct outline of "Miss
C*****," nor in the street through the veil of a fashionable
toilette, but in the very penetralia of her temple, standing
behind her counter, giving laws to ribbon and to wire, and
ushering caps and bonnets into existence. She was an English
woman, and I was told that she possessed great intellectual
endowments, and much information; I really believe this was
true. Her manner was easy and graceful, with a good deal of
French tournure; and the gentleness with which her fine eyes
and sweet voice directed the movements of a young female
slave, was really touching: the way, too, in which she blended
her French talk of modes with her customers, and her English
talk of metaphysics with her friends, had a pretty air of indifference in it, that gave her a superiority with both.

I found with her the daughter of a judge, eminent, it was
said, both for legal and literary ability, and I heard from

many quarters, after I had left New Orleans, that the society of this lady was highly valued by all persons of talent.[2] Yet were I, traveller-like, to stop here, and set it down as a national peculiarity, or republican custom, that milliners took the lead in the best society, I should greatly falsify facts. I do not remember the same thing happening to me again, and this is one instance among a thousand, of the impression every circumstance makes on entering a new country, and of the propensity, so irresistible, to class all things, however accidental, as national and peculiar. On the other hand, however, it is certain that if similar anomalies are unfrequent in America, they are nearly impossible elsewhere.

In the shop of Miss C°°°°° I was introduced to Mr. M'Clure, a venerable personage, of gentlemanlike appearance, who in the course of five minutes propounded as many axioms ,as "Ignorance is the only devil:" "Man makes his own existence;" and the like. He was of the New Harmony school, or rather the New Harmony school was of him. He was a man of good fortune, (a Scotchman, I believe), who after living a tolerably gay life, had "conceived high thoughts, such as Lycurgus loved, who bade flog the little Spartans," and determined to benefit the species, and immortalize himself, by founding a philosophical school at New Harmony. There was something in the hollow square legislations of Mr. Owen,[3] that struck him as admirable, and he seems, as far as I can understand, to have intended aiding his views, by a sort of

[2] [DS] Miss Mary Carroll was a most unusual milliner, as Mrs. Trollope implies. She was a friend and correspondent of Frances Wright and made use of the little informal gatherings at her millinery shop to defend and promulgate Miss Wright's daring doctrines. Miss Carroll later gave up millinery and opened a bookstore in New Orleans for the sale of liberal books and pamphlets. Her wealthy friends deserted her, and she lost her money and her health. She died, probably of cholera, in 1832.

[3] [DS] Mrs. Trollope's gibe at "hollow square legislations" alludes to the original grand plan that Robert Owen presented to Congress for laying out the buildings of his New Harmony Community in a hollow square one thousand feet to a side. He had constructed a splendid model to illustrate his design, and a print of it was prepared and circulated.

incipient hollow square drilling; teaching the young ideas of all he could catch, to shoot into parallelogramic form and order. This venerable philosopher, like all of his school that I ever heard of, loved better to originate lofty imaginings of faultless systems, than to watch their application to practice. With much liberality he purchased and conveyed to the wilderness a very noble collection of books and scientific instruments; but not finding among men one whose views were liberal and enlarged as his own, he selected a woman to put into action the machine he had organized. As his acquaintance with this lady had been of long standing, and, as it was said, very intimate, he felt sure that no violation of his rules would have place under her sway; they would act together as one being: he was to perform the functions of the soul, and will every thing; she, those of the body, and perform every thing.

The principal feature of the scheme was, that (the first liberal outfit of the institution having been furnished by Mr. M'Clure,) the expense of keeping it up should be defrayed by the profits arising from the labours of the pupils, male and female, which was to be performed at stated intervals of each day, in regular rotation with learned study and scientific research. But unfortunately the soul of the system found the climate of Indiana uncongenial to its peculiar formation, and, therefore, took its flight to Mexico, leaving the body to perform the operations of both, in whatever manner it liked best; and the body, being a French body, found no difficulty in setting actively to work without troubling the soul about it; and soon becoming conscious that the more simple was a machine, the more perfect were its operations, she threw out all that related to the intellectual part of the business, (which to do poor soul justice, it had laid great stress upon), and stirred herself as effectually as ever body did, to draw wealth from the thews and sinews of the youths they had collected. When last I heard of this philosophical establishment, she, and a nephew-son were said to be reaping a golden harvest, as many of the lads had been sent from a distance by indigent parents, for gratuitous education, and possessed no means of leaving it.[4]

---

[4] [DS] Mrs. Trollope's account of Maclure and Madame Fretageot is colored by misinformation and personal feeling. As stated in section IV of the Introduction, Mrs. Trollope had been well enough impressed by Maclure to send her son Henry to his school. Henry's frail health had made New Harmony a disastrous experiment for him, and his mother had had to borrow money from Auguste Hervieu to bring Henry to Cincinnati at a time when she could ill afford to support him there.

William Maclure, born in Scotland in 1763, had made a fortune in business by the time he was forty and thereafter devoted himself to science and the advancement of education. He was deeply interested in the teaching methods of the Swiss educator Pestalozzi and was convinced that a proper education combined mental and physical labor, thus doubling the powers of production and at the same time alleviating the fatigue of labor by a "more agreeable occupation of the mind." Maclure founded the first Pestalozzian school in America at Philadelphia in 1809.

By 1825 Maclure had come to an understanding with Robert Owen and had decided to make Owen's New Harmony Community the center of education in America. Maclure brought his famous "Boatload of Knowledge" to New Harmony, a group containing some of the most distinguished European scientists and educators of the day (many of them did float down the Ohio River to Indiana in a keelboat fitted out and launched at Pittsburgh). All together, Maclure invested $150,000 in his experiment at New Harmony.

Even after the breakup of Owen's socialistic community in 1827, Maclure's school struggled along for a few years. Because of failing health, Maclure began to spend much of his time in Mexico, leaving the management of his New Harmony enterprise to Madame Marie Fretageot, who had for a long time helped him with keeping his finances in order. She had come to America under his auspices to manage the girls' department of his Pestalozzian school at Philadelphia. For some time she had not lived with her husband, a colonel in Napoleon's armies and later commandant of a hospice for invalid soldiers in Paris, and scandal had it that her son was not the child of her marriage.

Maclure's plan was that the upkeep of his school at New Harmony should be paid for from the labors of the students. The scheme was very difficult to keep in motion, and Henry Trollope, like the other pupils, probably had to work hard for his board and tuition. One of Maclure's prospectuses for his school affords an idea of the sort of discipline to which Henry was subjected:

"Young men and young women are received without any expense to them either for teaching or food, lodging or clothing. Hours from five in the morning until eight in the evening, divided as follows: The scholars rise at five; at half past five each goes to his occupation; at seven the bell rings for breakfast; at eight they return to work; at eleven their lessons begin, con-

Our stay in New Orleans was not long enough to permit our entering into society, but I was told that it contained two distinct sets of people, both celebrated, in their way, for their social meetings and elegant entertainments. The first of these is composed of Creole families, who are chiefly planters and merchants, with their wives and daughters; these meet together, eat together, and are very grand and aristocratic; each of their balls is a little Almack's,[5] and every portly dame of the set is as exclusive in her principles as a lady patroness. The other set consists of the excluded but amiable Quadroons, and such of the gentlemen of the former class as can by any means escape from the high places, where pure Creole blood swells the veins at the bare mention of any being tainted in the remotest degree with the Negro stain.

Of all the prejudices I have ever witnessed, this appears to me the most violent, and the most inveterate. Quadroon girls, the acknowledged daughters of wealthy American or Creole fathers, educated with all of style and accomplishments which money can procure at New Orleans, and with all the decorum that care and affection can give; exquisitely beautiful, graceful, gentle, and amiable, these are not admitted, nay, are not on any terms admissible, into the society of the Creole families of Louisiana. They cannot marry; that is to say, no ceremony can render an union with them legal or binding; yet such is the powerful effect of their very peculiar grace, beauty, and sweetness of manner, that unfortunately

---

tinuing until half past two, including half an hour for luncheon; then they return to their occupations until five, when a bell calls them to dinner. Afterwards until half past six they exercise themselves in various ways; then the evening lessons begin and last until eight."

There is no reason to believe that Madame Fretageot lined her own purse from what the pupils managed to produce, and the files of her correspondence, now in the Library of the Workingmen's Institute at New Harmony, indicate that she worked conscientiously for the success of the school.

[5] [DS] Almack's Assembly Rooms in King Street, St. James's, were famous in Mrs. Trollope's time and earlier as the scene of fashionable social functions. Annual balls were given there, with ladies of high rank serving as managers.

they perpetually become the objects of choice and affection. If the Creole ladies have privilege to exercise the awful power of repulsion, the gentle Quadroon has the sweet but dangerous vengeance of possessing that of attraction. The unions formed with this unfortunate race are said to be often lasting and happy, as far as any unions can be so, to which a certain degree of disgrace is attached.

There is a French and an English theatre in the town; but we were too fresh from Europe to care much for either; or, indeed, for any other of the town delights of this city, and we soon became eager to commence our voyage up the Mississippi.

Miss Wright, then less known (though the author of more than one clever volume) than she has since become, was the companion of our voyage from Europe; [6] and it was my purpose to have passed some months with her and her sister at the estate she had purchased in Tennessee. This lady, since become so celebrated as the advocate of opinions that make millions shudder, and some half-score admire, was, at the time of my leaving England with her, dedicated to a pursuit widely different from her subsequent occupations. Instead of becoming a public orator in every town throughout America, she was about, as she said, to seclude herself for life in the deepest forests of the western world, that her fortune, her time, and her talents might be exclusively devoted to aid the cause of the suffering Africans. Her first object was to shew that nature had made no difference between blacks and whites, excepting in complexion; and this she expected to prove by giving an education perfectly equal to a class of black and white children. Could this fact be once fully established, she conceived that the Negro cause would stand on firmer ground than it had yet done, and the degraded rank

---

[6] [DS] For an account of Frances Wright's earlier life, her friendship with Mrs. Trollope, and the circumstances under which she induced Mrs. Trollope to come to the United States, see section II of the Introduction.

which they have ever held amongst civilized nations would be proved to be a gross injustice.

This question of the mental equality, or inequality between us, and the Negro race, is one of great interest, and has certainly never yet been fairly tried; and I expected for my children and myself both pleasure and information from visiting her establishment, and watching the success of her experiment.

The innumerable steam boats, which are the stage coaches and fly waggons of this land of lakes and rivers, are totally unlike any I had seen in Europe, and greatly superior to them. The fabrics which I think they most resemble in appearance, are the floating baths (les bains Vigier) at Paris. The annexed drawing ° will give a correct idea of their form. The room to which the double line of windows belongs, is a very handsome apartment; before each window a neat little cot is arranged in such a manner as to give its drapery the air of a window curtain. This room is called the gentlemen's cabin, and their exclusive right to it is somewhat uncourteously insisted upon. The breakfast, dinner, and supper are laid in this apartment, and the lady passengers are permitted to take their meals there.

On the first of January, 1828, we embarked on board the Belvidere, a large and handsome boat; though not the largest or handsomest of the many which displayed themselves along the wharfs; but she was going to stop at Memphis, the point of the river nearest to Miss Wright's residence, and she was the first that departed after we had got through the custom-house, and finished our sight-seeing. We found the room destined for the use of the ladies dismal enough, as its only windows were below the stern gallery; but both this and the gentlemen's cabin were handsomely fitted up, and the former well carpeted; but oh! that carpet! I will not, I may not describe its condition; indeed it requires the pen of a Swift to

---

° Plate III of the present edition.

do it justice. Let no one who wishes to receive agreeable impressions of American manners, commence their travels in a Mississippi steam boat; for myself, it is with all sincerity I declare, that I would infinitely prefer sharing the apartment of a party of well conditioned pigs to the being confined to its cabin.

I hardly know any annoyance so deeply repugnant to English feelings, as the incessant, remorseless spitting of Americans. I feel that I owe my readers an apology for the repeated use of this, and several other odious words; but I cannot avoid them, without suffering the fidelity of description to escape me. It is possible that in this phrase, "Americans," I may be too general. The United States form a continent of almost distinct nations, and I must now, and always, be understood to speak only of that portion of them which I have seen. In conversing with Americans I have constantly found that if I alluded to any thing which they thought I considered as uncouth, they would assure me it was local, and not national; the accidental peculiarity of a very small part, and by no means a specimen of the whole. "That is because you know so little of America," is a phrase I have listened to a thousand times, and in nearly as many different places. *It may be so* — and having made this concession, I protest against the charge of injustice in relating what I have seen.

III   NEW ORLEANS STEAM BOAT

IV WOOD CUTTER'S CABIN ON THE MISSISSIPPI

CHAPTER III

Company on board the Steam Boat — Scenery of the Mississippi
— Crocodiles — Arrival at Memphis — Nashoba

THE weather was warm and bright, and we found
the guard of the boat, as they call the gallery that runs round
the cabins, a very agreeable station; here we all sat as long
as light lasted, and sometimes wrapped in our shawls, we enjoyed the clear bright beauty of American moonlight long
after every passenger but ourselves had retired. We had a
full complement of passengers on board. The deck, as is usual,
was occupied by the Kentucky flat-boat men, returning from
New Orleans, after having disposed of the boat and cargo
which they had conveyed thither, with no other labour than
that of steering her, the current bringing her down at the rate
of four miles an hour. We had about two hundred of these
men on board, but the part of the vessel occupied by them is
so distinct from the cabins, that we never saw them, except
when we stopped to take in wood; and then they ran, or
rather sprung and vaulted over each other's heads to the
shore, whence they all assisted in carrying wood to supply the
steam engine; the performance of this duty being a stipu-
lated part of the payment of their passage.

From the account given by a man servant we had on board,
who shared their quarters, they are a most disorderly set of
persons, constantly gambling and wrangling, very seldom
sober, and never suffering a night to pass without giving practical proof of the respect in which they hold the doctrines of
equality, and community of property. The clerk of the vessel
was kind enough to take our man under his protection, and
assigned him a berth in his own little nook; but as this was

not inaccessible, he told him by no means to detach his watch or money from his person during the night. Whatever their moral characteristics may be, these Kentuckians are a very noble-looking race of men; their average height considerably exceeds that of Europeans, and their countenances, excepting when disfigured by red hair, which is not unfrequent, extremely handsome.

The gentlemen in the cabin (we had no ladies) would certainly neither, from their language, manners, nor appearance, have received that designation in Europe; but we soon found their claim to it rested on more substantial ground, for we heard them nearly all addressed by the titles of general, colonel, and major. On mentioning these military dignities to an English friend some time afterwards, he told me that he too had made the voyage with the same description of company, but remarking that there was not a single captain among them; he made the observation to a fellow-passenger, and asked how he accounted for it. "Oh, sir, the captains are all on deck," was the reply.

Our honours, however, were not all military, for we had a judge among us. I know it is equally easy and invidious to ridicule the peculiarities of appearance and manner in people of a different nation from ourselves; we may, too, at the same moment, be undergoing the same ordeal in their estimation; and, moreover, I am by no means disposed to consider whatever is new to me as therefore objectionable; but, nevertheless, it was impossible not to feel repugnance to many of the novelties that now surrounded me.

The total want of all the usual courtesies of the table, the voracious rapidity with which the viands were seized and devoured, the strange uncouth phrases and pronunciation; the loathsome spitting, from the contamination of which it was absolutely impossible to protect our dresses; the frightful manner of feeding with their knives, till the whole blade seemed to enter into the mouth; and the still more frightful manner of cleaning the teeth afterwards with a pocket knife, soon forced us to feel that we were not surrounded by the generals, colonels, and majors of the old world; and that the dinner hour was to be any thing rather than an hour of enjoyment.

The little conversation that went forward while we remained in the room, was entirely political, and the respective claims of Adams and Jackson to the presidency were argued with more oaths and more vehemence than it had ever been my lot to hear. Once a colonel appeared on the verge of assaulting a major, when a huge seven-foot Kentuckian gentleman horse-dealer, asked of the heavens to confound them both, and bade them sit still and be d—d. We too thought we should share this sentence; at least sitting still in the cabin seemed very nearly to include the rest of it, and we never tarried there a moment longer than was absolutely necessary to eat.

The unbroken flatness of the banks of the Mississippi continued unvaried for many miles above New Orleans; but the graceful and luxuriant palmetto, the dark and noble ilex, and the bright orange, were every where to be seen, and it was many days before we were weary of looking at them. We occasionally used the opportunity of the boat's stopping to take in wood for a ten minutes' visit to the shore; we in this manner explored a field of sugar canes, and loaded ourselves with as much of the sweet spoil as we could carry. Many of the passengers seemed fond of the luscious juice that is easily expressed from the canes, but it was too sweet for my palate. We also visited, in the same rapid manner, a cotton plantation. A handsome spacious building was pointed out to us as a convent, where a considerable number of young ladies were educated by the nuns.

At one or two points the wearisome level line of forest is relieved by *bluffs,* as they call the short intervals of high ground. The town of Natches is beautifully situated on one of these high spots; the climate here, in the warm season, is as fatal as that of New Orleans; were it not for this, Natches would have great attractions to new settlers. The beautiful contrast that its bright green hill forms with the dismal line of black forest that stretches on every side, the abundant growth of pawpaw, palmetto and orange, the copious variety of sweet-scented flowers that flourish there, all make it appear like an oasis in the desert. Natches is the furthest point to the north at which oranges ripen in the open air, or endure the winter without shelter. With the exception of this sweet spot, I thought all the little towns and villages we passed, wretched looking, in the extreme. As the distance from New Orleans increased, the air of wealth and comfort exhibited in its immediate neighbourhood disappeared, and but for one or two clusters of wooden houses, calling themselves towns, and borrowing some pompous name, generally from Greece or Rome, we might have thought ourselves the first of the human race who had ever penetrated into this territory of bears and alligators. But still from time to time appeared the hut of the wood-cutter, who supplies the steam-boats with fuel, at the risk, or rather with the assurance of early death, in exchange for dollars and whiskey. These sad dwellings are nearly all of them inundated during the winter, and the best of them are constructed on piles, which permit the water to reach its highest level without drowning the wretched inhabitants. These unhappy beings are invariably the victims of ague, which they meet recklessly, sustained by the incessant use of ardent spirits. The squalid look of the miserable wives and children of these men was dreadful, and often as the spectacle was renewed I could never look at it with indifference. Their complexion is of a blueish white, that suggests the idea of dropsy; this is invariable, and the poor little ones wear exactly the same ghastly hue. A miserable cow and a few pigs standing knee-deep in water, distinguish the more prosperous of these dwellings, and on the whole I should say that

I never witnessed human nature reduced so low, as it appeared in the wood-cutters' huts on the unwholesome banks of the Mississippi.

It is said that at some points of this dismal river, crocodiles are so abundant as to add the terror of their attacks to the other sufferings of a dwelling there. We were told a story of a squatter, who having "located" himself close to the river's edge, proceeded to build his cabin. This operation is soon performed, for social feeling and the love of whiskey bring all the scanty neighbourhood round a new comer, to aid him in cutting down trees, and in rolling up the logs, till the mansion is complete. This was done; the wife and five young children were put in possession of their new home, and slept soundly after a long march. Towards day-break the husband and father was awakened by a faint cry, and looking up, beheld relics of three of his children scattered over the floor, and an enormous crocodile, with several young ones around her, occupied in devouring the remnants of their horrid meal. He looked round for a weapon, but finding none, and aware that unarmed he could do nothing, he raised himself gently on his bed, and contrived to crawl from thence through a window, hoping that his wife, whom he left sleeping, might with the remaining children rest undiscovered till his return. He flew to his nearest neighbour and besought his aid; in less than half an hour two men returned with him, all three well armed; but alas! they were too late! the wife and her two babes lay mangled on their bloody bed. The gorged reptiles fell an easy prey to their assailants, who, upon examining the place, found the hut had been constructed close to the mouth of a large hole, almost a cavern, where the monster had hatched her hateful brood.[1]

---

[1] [DS] Mark Twain's comment in *Life on the Mississippi* concerning Mrs. Trollope's crocodile story and the American spinners of tall tales who gave it to her:

"Unfortunate tourists! People humbugged them with stupid and silly lies, and then laughed at them for believing and printing the same. They told

Among other sights of desolation which mark this region, condemned of nature, the lurid glare of a burning forest was almost constantly visible after sun-set, and when the wind so willed, the smoke arising from it floated in heavy vapour over our heads. Not all the novelty of the scene, not all its vastness, could prevent its heavy horror wearying the spirits. Perhaps the dinners and suppers I have described may help to account for this; but certain it is, that when we had wondered for a week at the ceaseless continuity of forest; had first admired, and then wearied of the festooned drapery of Spanish moss; when we had learned to distinguish the different masses of timber that passed us, or that we passed, as a "snag," a "log," or a "sawyer;" [2] when we had finally made up our minds that the gentlemen of the Kentucky and Ohio military establishments, were not of the same genus as those of the Tuilleries and St. James's, we began to wish that we could sleep more

Mrs. Trollope that the alligators — or crocodiles, as she calls them — were terrible creatures; and backed up the statement with a blood-curdling account of how one of these slandered reptiles crept into a squatter cabin one night, and ate up a woman and five children. The woman, by herself, would have satisfied any ordinarily impossible alligator; but no, these liars must make him gorge the five children besides. One would not imagine that jokers of this robust breed would be sensitive — but they were."

For the story of an Indian and a bear who sailed into New Orleans in his canoe, see Appendix A. Mrs. Trollope must have taken it down during her trip up the Mississippi, possibly from the same informant. She included it in the rough draft of her book, but did not finally print it.

[2] [DS] "Those trees which stand perpendicularly in the river, are called 'planters;' those which take hold by the roots, but lie obliquely with the current, yielding to its pressure, appearing and disappearing alternately, are termed 'sawyers;' and those which lie immovably fixed, in the same position as the 'sawyers,' are denominated 'snags.' Many boats have been stove in by 'snags' and 'sawyers,' and sunk with all passengers. At present there is a snag steam-boat stationed on the Mississippi, which has almost entirely cleared it of these obstructions. This boat consists of two hulks, with solid beams of timber uniting the bows. It has a most powerful engine; and when the crew discover a snag, which always lies with the stream, and is known by the ripple on the water, they run down below it for some distance in order to gather head-way — the boat is then run at it full tilt, and seldom fails of breaking off the projecting branch close to the trunk." — Simon Ansley O'Ferrall: *A Ramble of Six Thousand Miles through the United States of America* (1832).

hours away. As we advanced to the northward we were no longer cheered by the beautiful border of palmettos; and even the amusement of occasionally spying out a sleeping crocodile was over.

Just in this state, when we would have fain believed that every mile we went, carried us two towards Memphis, a sudden and violent shock startled us frightfully.

"It is a sawyer!" said one.

"It is a snag!" cried another.

"We are aground!" exclaimed the captain.

"Aground? Good heavens! and how long shall we stay here?"

"The Lord in his providence can only tell, but long enough to tire my patience, I expect."

And the poor English ladies, how fared they the while?

Two breakfasts, two dinners, and a supper did they eat, with the Ohio and Kentucky gentlemen, before they moved an inch. Several steam-boats passed while we were thus enthralled; but some were not strong enough to attempt drawing us off, and some attempted it, but were not strong enough to succeed; at length a vast and mighty "thing of life" approached, threw out grappling irons; and in three minutes the business was done; again we saw the trees and mud slide swiftly past us; and a hearty shout from every passenger on deck declared their joy.

At length we had the pleasure of being told that we had arrived at Memphis; but this pleasure was considerably abated by the hour of our arrival, which was mid-night, and by the rain, which was falling in torrents.

Memphis stands on a high bluff, and at the time of our arrival was nearly inaccessible. The heavy rain which had been falling for many hours would have made any steep ascent difficult, but unfortunately a new road had been recently marked out, which beguiled us into its almost bottomless mud, from the firmer footing of the unbroken cliff. Shoes and

gloves were lost in the mire, for we were glad to avail ourselves of all our limbs, and we reached the grand hotel in a
most deplorable state.

Miss Wright was well known there, and as soon as her arrival was announced, every one seemed on the alert to receive
her, and we soon found ourselves in possession of the best
rooms in the hotel. The house was new, and in what appeared
to me a very comfortless condition, but I was then new to
Western America, and unaccustomed to their mode of "getting along," as they term it. This phrase is eternally in use
among them, and seems to mean existing with as few of the
comforts of life as possible.

We slept soundly however, and rose in the hope of soon
changing our mortar-smelling quarters for Miss Wright's
Nashoba.

But we presently found that the rain which had fallen during the night would make it hazardous to venture through the
forests of Tennessee in any sort of carriage; we therefore had
to pass the day at our queer comfortless hotel. The steam-boat
had wearied me of social meals, and I should have been
thankful to have eaten our dinner of hard venison and peach-
sauce in a private room; but this, Miss Wright said was impossible; the lady of the house would consider the proposal as
a personal affront, and, moreover, it would be assuredly refused. This latter argument carried weight with it, and when
the great bell was sounded from an upper window of the
house, we proceeded to the dining-room. The table was laid
for fifty persons, and was already nearly full. Our party had
the honour of sitting near "the lady," but to check the proud
feelings to which such distinction might give birth, my servant, William, sat very nearly opposite to me. The company
consisted of all the shop-keepers (store-keepers as they are
called throughout the United States) of the little town. The
mayor also, who was a friend of Miss Wright's, was of the
party; he is a pleasing gentlemanlike man, and seems

strangely misplaced in a little town on the Mississippi. We were told that since the erection of this hotel, it has been the custom for all the male inhabitants of the town to dine and breakfast there. They ate in perfect silence, and with such astonishing rapidity that their dinner was over literally before our's was began; the instant they ceased to eat, they darted from the table in the same moody silence which they had preserved since they entered the room, and a second set took their places, who performed their silent parts in the same manner. The only sounds heard were those produced by the knives and forks, with the unceasing chorus of coughing, &c. No women were present except ourselves and the hostess; the good women of Memphis being well content to let their lords partake of Mrs. Anderson's turkeys and venison, (without their having the trouble of cooking for them), whilst they regale themselves on mush and milk at home.[3]

The remainder of the day passed pleasantly enough in rambling round the little town, which is situated at the most beautiful point of the Mississippi; the river is here so wide as to give it the appearance of a noble lake; an island, covered with lofty forest trees divides it, and relieves by its broad mass of shadow the uniformity of its waters. The town stretches in a rambling irregular manner along the cliff, from the Wolf River, one of the innumerable tributaries to the Mississippi, to about a mile below it. Half a mile more of the cliff beyond the town is cleared of trees, and produces good pasture for horses, cows, and pigs; sheep they had none. At either end of this space the forest again rears its dark wall, and seems to say to man, "so far shalt thou come, and no farther!" Courage and industry, however, have braved the warning. Behind this long street the town straggles back into the forest, and the rude path that leads to the more distant log dwellings becomes wilder at every step. The ground is bro-

---

[3] [T5, note] *Mush* is a preparation of Indian corn, bruised to powder, and which when boiled with milk makes excellent porridge.

ken by frequent water-courses, and the bridges that lead across them are formed by trunks of trees thrown over the stream, which support others of smaller growth, that are laid across them. These bridges are not very pleasant to pass, for they totter under the tread of a man, and tremble most frightfully beneath a horse or a waggon; they are, however, very picturesque. The great height of the trees, the quantity of pendant vine branches that hang amongst them; and the variety of gay plumaged birds, particularly the small green parrot, made us feel we were in a new world; and a repetition of our walk the next morning would have pleased us well, but Miss Wright was anxious to get home, and we were scarcely less so to see her Nashoba. A clumsy sort of caravan drawn by two horses was prepared for us; and we set off in high spirits for an expedition of fifteen miles through the forest. To avoid passing one of the bridges above described, which was thought insecure, our negro driver took us through a piece of water, which he assured us was not deep "to matter," however we soon lost sight of our pole, and as we were evidently descending, we gently remonstrated with him on the danger of proceeding, but he only grinned, and flogged in reply; we soon saw the front wheels disappear, and the horses began to plunge and kick most alarmingly, but still without his looking at all disturbed. At length the splinter-bar gave way, upon which the black philosopher said very composedly, "I expect you'll best be riding out upon the horses, as we've got into an unhandsome fix here." Miss Wright, who sat composedly smiling at the scene, said, "Yes, Jacob, that is what we must do;" and with some difficulty we, in this manner, reached the shore, and soon found ourselves again assembled round Mrs. Anderson's fire.

It was soon settled that we must delay our departure till the waters had subsided, but Miss Wright was too anxious to reach home to endure this delay, and she set off again on horseback, accompanied by our man servant, who told me afterwards that they rode through places that might have daunted the boldest hunter, but that "Miss Wright took it quite easy."

The next day we started again, and the clear air, the bright sun, the novel wildness of the dark forest, and our keenly awakened curiosity, made the excursion delightful, and enabled us to bear without shrinking the bumps and bruises we encountered. We soon lost all trace of a road, at least so it appeared to us, for the stumps of the trees, which had been cut away to open a passage, were left standing three feet high. Over these, the high-hung Deerborn, as our carriage was called, passed safely; but it required some miles of experience to convince us that every stump would not be our last; it was amusing to watch the cool and easy skill with which the driver wound his horses and wheels among these stumps. I thought he might have been imported to Bond-street with great advantage. The forest became thicker and more dreary-looking every mile we advanced, but our ever-grinning negro declared it was a right good road, and that we should be sure to get to Nashoba.

And so we did . . . . and one glance sufficed to convince me that every idea I had formed of the place was as far as possible from the truth. Desolation was the only feeling — the only word that presented itself; but it was not spoken. I think, however, that Miss Wright was aware of the painful impression the sight of her forest home produced on me, and I doubt not that the conviction reached us both at the same moment, that we had erred in thinking that a few months passed together at this spot could be productive of pleasure to either.[4] But to do her justice, I believe

<hr>

4 [TRD] The Frances Wright of Nashoba, in dress, looks, and manner, bore no more resemblance to the Miss Wright I had known and admired in London and Paris than did her log cabin to the Tuileries or Buckingham Palace. But, to do her justice, I believe her imagination was so exclusively occupied on the scheme she then had in view that all her other faculties were in a manner suspended, for she appeared perfectly unconscious that

her mind was so exclusively occupied by the object she had
then in view, that all things else were worthless, or indifferent
to her. I never heard or read of any enthusiasm approaching
her's, except in some few instances, in ages past, of religious
fanaticism.

It must have been some feeling equally powerful which enabled Miss Wright, accustomed to all the comfort and refinement of Europe, to imagine not only that she herself could
exist in this wilderness, but that her European friends could
enter there, and not feel dismayed at the savage aspect of the
scene. The annexed plate * gives a faithful view of the
cleared space and buildings which form the settlement. Each
building consisted of two large rooms furnished in the most
simple manner; nor had they as yet collected round them any
of those minor comforts which ordinary minds class among
the necessaries of life. But in this our philosophical friend
seemed to see no evil; nor was there any mixture of affecta-

---

her existence was deprived of all that makes life desirable. I never saw, I
never heard or read, of any enthusiasm approaching hers, except in some few
instances, in ages past, of religious fanaticism. When we arrived at Nashoba,
they were without milk, without beverage of any kind except rain water;
the river Wolf being too distant to send to constantly. Wheat bread they
used but sparingly, and to us the Indian corn bread was uneatable. They
had no vegetables but rice, and some potatoes we brought with us, no meat
but pork, no cheese, no butter; and yet I verily believe that Miss Wright
was unaffectedly surprised at perceiving that I did not find this manner of
life everything that reasonable beings could wish for. She herself made her
meals on a bit of Indian corn bread, and a cup of very indifferent cold water, and while doing so, smiled with the sort of complacency that we may
conceive Peter the Hermit felt when eating his acorns in the wilderness.

I shared her bedroom; it had no ceiling, and the floor consisted of planks
laid loosely upon piles, that raised it some feet from the earth. The rain had
access through the wooden roof, and the chimney, which was of logs, slightly
plaistered with mud, caught fire, at least a dozen times in a day; but Frances Wright stood in the midst of all this desolation, with the air of a conqueror; she would say, perhaps, that she was so, since she had triumphed
over all human weakness.

[For a description of Mrs. Trollope's notebooks and rough draft, see section IX of the Introduction and Appendix A.]

* Plate V of the present edition.

tion in this indifference; it was a circumstance really and truly beneath her notice. Her whole heart and soul were occupied by the hope of raising the African to the level of European intellect; and even now, that I have seen this favourite fabric of her imagination fall to pieces beneath her feet, I cannot recall the self-devotion with which she gave herself to it, without admiration.

The only white persons we found at Nashoba were my amiable friend, Mrs. W°°°°, the sister of Miss Wright, and her husband.[5] I think they had between thirty and forty slaves, including children, but when I was there no school had been established. Books and other materials for the great experiment had been collected, and one or two professors engaged, but nothing was yet organized. I found my friend Mrs. W°°°° in very bad health, which she confessed she attributed to the climate. This naturally so much alarmed me for my children, that I decided upon leaving the place with as little delay as possible, and did so at the end of ten days.

I do not exactly know what was the immediate cause which induced Miss Wright to abandon a scheme which had taken such possession of her imagination, and on which she had expended so much money;[6] but many months had not

---

[5] [DS] Fanny Wright's sister Camilla, her junior and faithful follower, had married Richeson Whitby, the manager of the Nashoba plantation, a year earlier. Though in principle Nashoba advocated free love, Camilla justified her marriage, holding that open violation of the country's civil institutions would prejudice the public against the community.

Mrs. Trollope understandably gained the impression that there were more slaves surrounding her at Nashoba than the records account for. There were not over fifteen at most.

[6] [DS] Fanny Wright's reason for abandoning Nashoba seems to have been simply that it gave no promise of becoming self-supporting. Her own funds were not sufficient to run the plantation at a loss for an indefinite period; her original plan had been to limit her investment in the colony to twelve thousand dollars, but she probably spent much more than that before she had wound up the affairs of Nashoba.

Fanny Wright's life continued unorthodox and eventful. Her lectures at

elapsed before I learnt, with much pleasure, that she and her sister had also left it. I think it probable that she became aware upon returning to Nashoba, that the climate was too hostile to their health. All I know farther of Nashoba is, that Miss Wright having found (from some cause or other) that it was impossible to pursue her object, herself accompanied her slaves to Hayti, and left them there, free, and under the protection of the President.

I found no beauty in the scenery round Nashoba, nor can I conceive that it would possess any even in summer. The trees were so close to each other as not to permit the growth of underwood, the great ornament of the forest at New Orleans, and still less of our seeing any openings, where the varying effects of light and shade might atone for the absence of other objects. The clearing round the settlement appeared to me inconsiderable and imperfect; but I was told that they had grown good crops of cotton and Indian corn. The weather was dry and agreeable, and the aspect of the heavens by night surprisingly beautiful. I never saw moonlight so clear, so pure, so powerful.

We returned to Memphis on the 26th of January, 1828, and found ourselves obliged to pass five days there, awaiting a steam-boat for Cincinnati, to which metropolis of the west, I was now determined to proceed with my family to await the arrival of Mr. Trollope. We were told by every one we spoke to at Memphis, that it was in all respects the finest situation west

Cincinnati and Philadelphia are described farther along in *Domestic Manners*. In New York in 1829, with the help of Robert Dale Owen, Miss Wright started the *Free Enquirer,* a journal that stirred up much excitement and no little wrath. She also bought a church in this city and turned it into her Hall of Science, where she preached freethinking and free love. In 1830 she departed for Europe on the eve of France's July Revolution. In France, despite her teachings of free love, she decided upon marriage to Phiquepal D'Arusmont, formerly a teacher in Maclure's New Harmony school, when it became evident that at the age of thirty-five she was to bear him a child. She returned in 1835 to the United States, where she resumed her crusades, writing and lecturing until near the time of her death, on December 13, 1852, at Cincinnati.

of the Alleghanies. We found many lovely walks among the
broken forest glades around Memphis, which, together with
a morning and evening enjoyment of the effects of a glowing
horizon on the river, enabled us to wait patiently for the boat
that was to bear us away.

CHAPTER IV

Departure from Memphis — Ohio River — Louisville — Cincinnati

ON the 1st of February, 1828, we embarked on board the Criterion, and once more began to float on the "father of waters," as the poor banished Indians were wont to call the Mississippi. The company on board was wonderfully like what we had met in coming from New Orleans; I think they must have all been first cousins; and what was singular, they too had all arrived at high rank in the army. For many a wearisome mile above the Wolf River the only scenery was still forest — forest — forest; the only variety was produced by the receding of the river at some points, and its encroaching on the opposite shore. These changes are continually going on, but from what cause none could satisfactorily explain to me. Where the river is encroaching, the trees are seen growing in water many feet deep; after some time, the water undermines their roots, and they become the easy victims of the first hurricane that blows. This is one source of the immense quantities of drift wood that float into the gulf of Mexico. Where the river has receded, a young growth of cane-brake is soon seen starting up with the rapid vegetation of the climate; these two circumstances in some degree relieve the sameness of the thousand miles of vegetable wall. But we were now approaching the river which is emphatically called "the beautiful," La Belle Riviere of the New Orleans French; and a few days took us, I trust for ever, out of that murky stream which is as emphatically called "the deadly;" and well does it seem to merit the title; the air of its shores is mephitic, and it is said that nothing that ever sunk beneath its muddy surface was known to rise again. As truly does "La Belle Riviere" deserve

its name; the Ohio is bright and clear; its banks are continually varied, as it flows through what is called a rolling
country, which seems to mean a district that cannot shew a
dozen paces of level ground at a time. The primæval forest
still occupies a considerable portion of the ground, and hangs
in solemn grandeur from the cliffs; but it is broken by frequent settlements, where we were cheered by the sight of
herds and flocks. I imagine that this river presents almost
every variety of river scenery; sometimes its clear wave
waters a meadow of level turf; sometimes it is bounded by
perpendicular rocks; pretty dwellings, with their gay porticos are seen, alternately with wild intervals of forest, where
the tangled bear-brake plainly enough indicates what inhabitants are native there. Often a mountain torrent comes pouring its silver tribute to the stream, and were there occasionally a ruined abbey, or feudal castle, to mix the romance
of real life with that of nature, the Ohio would be perfect.

So powerful was the effect of this sweet scenery, that we
ceased to grumble at our dinners and suppers; nay, we almost
learnt to rival our neighbours at table in their voracious rapidity of swallowing, so eager were we to place ourselves again
on the guard, lest we might lose sight of the beauty that was
passing away from us.

Yet these fair shores are still unhealthy. More than once we
landed, and conversed with the families of the wood-cutters,
and scarcely was there one in which we did not hear of some
member who had "lately died of the fever." — They are all
subject to ague,[1] and though their dwellings are infinitely

---

[1] [DS] Ague was so common in Western America that many people
looked upon it as no disease, but a regular part of frontier living. Work
schedules, court dockets, and ministers' calls were adjusted to allow for the
sufferer's recurring attacks. One kind came back daily, another on alternate
days, and still another every third day.

"The symptoms were unmistakable: yawnings and stretching, a feeling
of lassitude, blueness of the fingernails, then little cold sensations which increased until the victim's teeth chattered in his jaws and he 'felt like a harp
with a thousand strings.' As the chills increased, the victim shivered and

better than those on the Mississippi, the inhabitants still look like a race that are selling their lives for gold.

Louisville is a considerable town, prettily situated on the Kentucky, or south side of the Ohio; we spent some hours in seeing all it had to shew; and had I not been told that a bad fever often rages there during the warm season, I should have liked to pass some months there for the purpose of exploring the beautiful country in its vicinity. Frankfort and Lexington are both towns worth visiting though from their being *out of the way* places, I never got to either. The first is the seat of the state government of Kentucky, and the last is, I was told, the residence of several independent families, who, with more leisure than is usually enjoyed in America, have its natural accompaniment, more refinement.

The falls of the Ohio are about a mile below Louisville,[2] and produce a rapid, too sudden for the boats to pass, ex-

shook 'like a miniature earthquake.' After an hour or so warmth returned, then gradually merged into raging heat with racking pains and aching back. The spell ended with copious sweating and a return to normal." — Madge E. Pickard and R. Carlyle Buley: *The Midwest Pioneer: His Ills, Cures, & Doctors* (Crawfordsville, Indiana: R. E. Banta; 1945).

[2] [DS] According to Samuel Cumings's *The Western Pilot* (1829), Louisville's Main Street was already "nearly a mile long, and . . . very compactly built. The town contains probably about 7000 inhabitants. In a commercial point of view, it is far the most important town in the State of Kentucky. The large steam boats, that run between this town and New Orleans, are never able to ascend the falls except in high stages of water. Their cargoes are obliged to be discharged at Shippingport at the foot of the falls, and transported by land to Louisville; from whence they are distributed to their points of destination. The merchants of Louisville are, therefore, from necessity the factors for the important business, which concentrates here. The mouth of Beargrass [Creek] affords an excellent harbour for the steam boats and river craft. . . .

"A canal, which is now in successful progress, and which it is expected will be soon finished, will connect Louisville with Shippingport and remove the barrier to navigation, created by the falls. The canal is a work of stupendous labour. It is two miles in length, in some places 40 feet deep, and of sufficient width to pass the largest class of steam boats. It will afford an immense water power for the mill seats below its locks. — It belongs to an incorporated company, who have already paid in nearly or quite the full amount of the shares taken."

cept in the rainy season. The passengers are obliged to get out below them, and travel by land to Louisville, where they find other vessels ready to receive them for the remainder of the voyage. We were spared this inconvenience by the water being too high for the rapid to be much felt, and it will soon be altogether removed by the Louisville canal coming into operation, which will permit the steam-boats to continue their progress from below the falls to the town.

The scenery on the Kentucky side is much finer than on that of Indiana or Ohio.[3] The State of Kentucky was the darling spot of many tribes of Indians, and was reserved among them as a common hunting ground; it is said that they cannot yet name it without emotion, and that they have a sad and wild lament that they still chaunt to its memory. But their exclusion thence is of no recent date; Kentucky has been longer settled than Illinois, Indiana, or Ohio, and it appears not only more highly cultivated, but more fertile and more picturesque than either. I have rarely seen richer pastures than those of Kentucky. The forest trees, where not too crowded, are of magnificent growth, and the crops are gloriously abundant where the thriftless husbandry has not worn out the soil by unvarying succession of exhausting crops. We were shewn ground which had borne abundant crops of wheat for twenty successive years; but a much shorter period suffices to exhaust the ground, if it were made to produce tobacco without the intermission of some other crop.

We reached Cincinnati on the 10th of February. It is finely situated on the south side of a hill that rises gently from the water's edge; yet it is by no means a city of striking appear-

---

[3] [TRD] . . . excepting at one point, where for a mile or two a fine wall of grey rock, with intervening groups of dark cedars, affords a very agreeable variety. Except at this point the forest on this side continued unvaried by any natural feature. Since we had left New Orleans, I used to think when hearing of the "eternal" forests of A[merica] that people spoke as looking backward to the eternity of time they had endured, but I now began to suspect that it was in looking forward to the eternity of space they covered.

ance; it wants domes, towers, and steeples; but its landing-place is noble, extending for more than a quarter of a mile; it is well paved, and surrounded by neat, though not handsome buildings. I have seen fifteen steam-boats lying there at once, and still half the wharf was unoccupied.

On arriving we repaired to the Washington Hotel, and thought ourselves fortunate when we were told that we were just in time for dinner at the table d'hôte; but when the dining-room door was opened, we retreated with a feeling of dismay at seeing between sixty and seventy men already at table. We took our dinner with the females of the family, and then went forth to seek a house for our permanent accommodation.

We went to the office of an advertising agent, who professed to keep a register of all such information, and described the dwelling we wanted. He made no difficulty, but told us his boy should be our guide through the city, and shew us what we sought; we accordingly set out with him, and he led us up one street, and down another, but evidently without any determinate object; I therefore stopped, and asked him whereabout the houses were which we were going to see.

"I am looking for bills," was his reply.

I thought we could have looked for bills as well without him, and I told him so; upon which he assumed an air of great activity, and began knocking regularly at every door we passed, enquiring if the house was to be let. It was impossible to endure this long, and our guide was dismissed, though I was afterwards obliged to pay him a dollar for his services.

We had the good fortune, however, to find a dwelling before long, and we returned to our hotel, having determined upon taking possession of it as soon as it could be got ready. Not wishing to take our evening meal either with the three score and ten gentlemen of the dining-room, nor yet with the half dozen ladies of the bar-room, I ordered tea in my own chamber. A good-humoured Irish woman came forward with a sort of patronising manner, took my hand, and said, "Och, my honey, ye'll be from the old country. I'll see you will have your tay all to yourselves, honey." With this assurance we retired to my room, which was a handsome one as to its size and bed furniture, but it had no carpet, and was darkened by blinds of paper, such as rooms are hung with, which required to be rolled up, and then fastened with strings very awkwardly attached to the window-frames, whenever light or air were wished for. I afterwards met with these same uncomfortable blinds in every part of America.

Our Irish friend soon reappeared, and brought us tea, together with the never-failing accompaniments of American tea-drinking, hung beef, "chipped up" raw, and sundry sweetmeats of brown sugar hue and flavour. We took our tea, and were enjoying our family talk, relative to our future arrangements, when a loud sharp knocking was heard at our door. My "come in," was answered by the appearance of a portly personage, who proclaimed himself our landlord.

"Are any of you ill?" he began.

"No thank you, sir; we are all quite well," was my reply.

"Then, madam, I must tell you, that I cannot accommodate you on these terms; we have no family tea-drinkings here, and you must live either with me or my wife, or not at all in my house." [4]

new customs

---

[4] [DS] Mrs. Trollope had chosen the hotel of Joseph H. Cromwell, notorious for his arbitrary treatment of his guests.

"Old Cromwell was a sort of hero to us, because he once dismissed old Mrs. Trollope from a hotel on Front street, which he had formerly kept. This and her quarter-deck air, made us quite respectful to him." — A newspaper clipping dated 1848 in the files of the Historical and Philosophical Society of Ohio. Cromwell's house was the Cincinnati Hotel, not the Washington, as Mrs. Trollope calls it. (The *Cincinnati Directory for the Year 1829* lists no Washington Hotel.)

Joe Cowell in his *Thirty Years Passed among the Players* tells of running afoul of Cromwell a year after Mrs. Trollope's experience:

"We put up at the hotel near the landing, kept by Captain Cromwell,

This was said with an air of authority that almost precluded reply, but I ventured a sort of apologistic hint, that we were strangers and unaccustomed to the manners of the country.

"Our manners are very good manners, and we don't wish any changes from England."

I thought of mine host of the Washington afterwards, when reading Scott's "Anne of Geierstein;" he, in truth, strongly resembled the inn-keeper therein immortalized, who made his guests eat, drink, and sleep, just where, when, and how he pleased. I made no farther remonstrance, but determined to hasten my removal. This we achieved the next day to our great satisfaction.

We were soon settled in our new dwelling, which looked neat and comfortable enough, but we speedily found that it was devoid of nearly all the accommodation that Europeans conceive necessary to decency and comfort. No pump, no cistern, no drain of any kind, no dustman's cart, or any other visible means of getting rid of the rubbish, which vanishes with such celerity in London, that one has no time to think of its existence; but which accumulated so rapidly at Cincinnati, that I sent for my landlord to know in what manner refuse of all kinds was to be disposed of.

"Your Help will just have to fix them all into the middle of the street, but you must mind, old woman, that it is the middle. I expect you don't know as we have got a law what forbids throwing such things at the sides of the streets; they

---

and in his little way quite as despotic as his namesake, the poor apology for a king; for after dinner — an operation which was performed by his boarders in three minutes at farthest — myself and two acquaintances I had formed on the road drew towards the fire, and commenced smoking our cigars.

" 'You can't smoke here,' said Captain Cromwell. And we instantly pleaded ignorance of his rules, though they might be thought a little fastidious after our scramble for dinner, and threw our cigars in the fire.

" 'And you can't sit here,' said Captain Cromwell. 'If you want to sit, you must sit in the bar; and if you want to smoke, you can smoke in the bar.'

"Slapping his hand on the table, after the manner of his ancestor dismissing the Long Parliament; and into the bar we went. . . ."

must just all be cast right into the middle, and the pigs soon takes them off."

In truth the pigs are constantly seen doing Herculean service in this way through every quarter of the city; and though it is not very agreeable to live surrounded by herds of these unsavoury animals, it is well they are so numerous, and so active in their capacity of scavengers, for without them the streets would soon be choked up with all sorts of substances in every stage of decomposition.

We had heard so much of Cincinnati, its beauty, wealth, and unequalled prosperity, that when we left Memphis to go thither, we almost felt the delight of Rousseau's novice, "un voyage à faire, et Paris au bout!" — As soon, therefore, as our little domestic arrangements were completed, we set forth to view this "wonder of the west," this "prophet's gourd of magic growth," — this "infant Hercules;" and surely no travellers ever paraded a city under circumstances more favourable to their finding it fair to the sight. Three dreary months had elapsed since we had left the glories of London behind us; for nearly the whole of that time we had beheld no other architecture than what our ship and steam-boats had furnished, and excepting at New Orleans, had seen hardly a trace of human habitations. The sight of bricks and mortar was really refreshing, and a house of three stories looked splendid. Of this splendour we saw repeated specimens, and moreover a brick church, which, from its two little peaked spires, is called the two-horned church. But, alas! the flatness of reality after the imagination has been busy! I hardly know what I expected to find in this city, fresh risen from the bosom of the wilderness, but certainly it was not a little town, about the size of Salisbury, without even an attempt at beauty in any of its edifices, and with only just enough of the air of a city to make it noisy and bustling. The population is greater than the appearance of the town would lead one to expect. This is partly owing to the number of free Negroes who herd together in an obscure part of the city, called little Africa; and partly to the density of the population round the paper-mills and other manufactories. I believe the number of inhabitants exceeds twenty thousand.

We arrived in Cincinnati in February, 1828, and I speak of the town as it was then; several small churches have been built since, whose towers agreeably relieve its uninteresting mass of buildings. At that time I think Main-street, which is the principal avenue, (and runs through the whole town, answering to the High-street of our old cities), was the only one entirely paved. The *troittoir* is of brick, tolerably well laid, but it is inundated by every shower, as Cincinnati has no drains whatever. What makes this omission the more remarkable is, that the situation of the place is calculated both to facilitate their construction and to render them necessary. Cincinnati is built on the side of a hill that begins to rise at the river's edge, and were it furnished with drains of the simplest arrangement, the heavy showers of the climate would keep them constantly clean; as it is, these showers wash the higher streets, only to deposit their filth in the first level spot; and this happens to be in the street second in importance to Main-street, running at right angles to it, and containing most of the large warehouses of the town. This deposit is a dreadful nuisance, and must be productive of miasma during the hot weather.

The town is built, as I believe most American towns are, in squares, as they call them; but these squares are the reverse of our's, being solid instead of hollow. Each consists, or is intended to consist, when the plan of the city is completed, of a block of buildings fronting north, east, west, and south; each house communicating with an alley, furnishing a back entrance. This plan would not be a bad one were the town properly drained, but as it is, these alleys are horrible abominations, and must, I conceive, become worse with every passing year.

To the north, Cincinnati is bounded by a range of forest-

V SETTLEMENT OF NASHOBA

VI RETURNING FROM MARKET

covered hills, sufficiently steep and rugged to prevent their being built upon, or easily cultivated, but not sufficiently high to command from their summits a view of any considerable extent. Deep and narrow water-courses, dry in summer, but bringing down heavy streams in winter, divide these hills into many separate heights, and this furnishes the only variety the landscape offers for many miles round the town. The lovely Ohio is a beautiful feature wherever it is visible, but the only part of the city that has the advantage of its beauty is the street nearest to its bank. The hills of Kentucky, which rise at about the same distance from the river, on the opposite side, form the southern boundary to the basin in which Cincinnati is built.

On first arriving, I thought the many tree-covered hills around, very beautiful, but long before my departure, I felt so weary of the confined view, that Salisbury Plain would have been an agreeable variety. I doubt if any inhabitant of Cincinnati ever mounted these hills so often as myself and my children; but it was rather for the enjoyment of a freer air than for any beauty of prospect, that we took our daily climb. These hills afford neither shrubs nor flowers, but furnish the finest specimens of millepore in the world; and the water-courses are full of fossil productions.

The forest trees are neither large nor well grown, and so close as to be nearly knotted together at top; even the wild vine here loses its beauty, for its graceful festoons bear leaves only when they reach the higher branches of the tree that supports them, both air and light being too scantily found below to admit of their doing more than climbing with a bare stem till they reach a better atmosphere. The herb we call pennyroyal was the only one I found in abundance, and that only on the brows, where the ground had been partially cleared; vegetation is impossible elsewhere, and it is this circumstance which makes the "eternal forests" of America so detestable. Near New Orleans the undergrowth of palmetto and pawpaw is highly beautiful, but in Tennessee, Indiana, and Ohio, I never found the slightest beauty in the forest scenery. Fallen trees in every possible stage of decay, and congeries of leaves that have been rotting since the flood, cover the ground and infect the air. The beautiful variety of foliage afforded by evergreens never occurs, and in Tennessee, and that part of Ohio that surrounds Cincinnati, even the sterile beauty of rocks is wanting. On crossing the water to Kentucky the scene is greatly improved; beech and chesnut, of magnificent growth, border the beautiful river; the ground has been well cleared, and the herbage is excellent; the pawpaw grows abundantly, and is a splendid shrub, though it bears neither fruit nor flowers so far north. The noble tulip tree flourishes here, and blooms profusely.

The river Licking flows into the Ohio nearly opposite Cincinnati; it is a pretty winding stream, and two or three miles from its mouth has a brisk rapid, dancing among white stones, which, in the absence of better rocks, we found very picturesque.

CHAPTER V

Cincinnati — Forest Farm — Mr. Bullock

THOUGH I do not quite sympathise with those who consider Cincinnati as one of the wonders of the earth, I certainly think it a city of extraordinary size and importance, when it is remembered that thirty years ago the aboriginal forest occupied the ground where it stands; and every month appears to extend its limits and its wealth.

Some of the native political economists assert that this rapid conversion of a bear-brake into a prosperous city, is the result of free political institutions; not being very deep in such matters, a more obvious cause suggested itself to me, in the unceasing goad which necessity applies to industry in this country, and in the absence of all resource for the idle. During nearly two years that I resided in Cincinnati, or its neighbourhood, I neither saw a beggar, nor a man of sufficient fortune to permit his ceasing his efforts to increase it; thus every bee in the hive is actively employed in search of that honey of Hybla, vulgarly called money; neither art, science, learning, nor pleasure can seduce them from its pursuit. This unity of purpose, backed by the spirit of enterprise, and joined with an acuteness and *total* absence of probity, where interest is concerned, which might set canny Yorkshire at defiance, may well go far towards obtaining its purpose.

The low rate of taxation, too, unquestionably permits a more rapid accumulation of individual wealth than with us; but till I had travelled through America, I had no idea how much of the money collected in taxes returns among the people, not only in the purchase of what their industry furnishes, but in the actual enjoyment of what is furnished. Were

I an English legislator, instead of sending sedition to the Tower, I would send her to make a tour of the United States. I had a little leaning towards sedition myself when I set out, but before I had half completed my tour I was quite cured.

I have read much of the "few and simple wants of rational man," and I used to give a sort of dreamy acquiescence to the reasoning that went to prove each added want an added woe. Those who reason in a comfortable London drawing-room know little about the matter. Were the aliments which sustain life all that we wanted, the faculties of the hog might suffice us; but if we analyze an hour of enjoyment, we shall find that it is made up of agreeable sensations occasioned by a thousand delicate impressions on almost as many nerves; where these nerves are sluggish from never having been awakened, external objects are less important, for they are less perceived; but where the whole machine of the human frame is in full activity, where every sense brings home to consciousness its touch of pleasure or of pain, then every object that meets the senses is important as a vehicle of happiness or misery. But let no frames so tempered visit the United States, or if they do, let it be with no longer pausing than will store the memory with images, which, by the force of contrast, shall sweeten the future.

> "Guarda e passa (e poi) ragioniam di lor." [1]

The "simple" manner of living in Western America was more distasteful to me from its levelling effects on the manners of the people, than from the personal privations that it rendered necessary; and yet, till I was without them, I was in no degree aware of the many pleasurable sensations derived from the little elegancies and refinements enjoyed by the middle classes in Europe. There were many circum-

---

[1] [DS] *"Guarda e passa,"* etc.: "Look and pass (and afterward) let us speak of them." Mrs. Trollope has adapted Dante's line (*Inferno*, III, 51), which reads: *"non ragioniam di lor, ma guarda e passa"* — "let us not speak of them, but look and pass."

stances, too trifling even for my gossiping pages, which
pressed themselves daily and hourly upon us, and which
forced us to remember painfully that we were not at home.
It requires an abler pen than mine to trace the connection
which I am persuaded exists between these deficiencies and
the minds and manners of the people. All animal wants are
supplied profusely at Cincinnati, and at a very easy rate; but,
alas! these go but a little way in the history of a day's enjoyment. The total and universal want of manners, both in males
and females, is so remarkable, that I was constantly endeavouring to account for it. It certainly does not proceed from
want of intellect. I have listened to much dull and heavy conversation in America, but rarely to any that I could strictly
call silly, (if I except the every where privileged class of very
young ladies). They appear to me to have clear heads and
active intellects; are more ignorant on subjects that are only
of conventional value, than on such as are of intrinsic importance; but there is no charm, no grace in their conversation. I very seldom during my whole stay in the country heard
a sentence elegantly turned, and correctly pronounced from
the lips of an American. There is always something either
in the expression or the accent that jars the feelings and shocks
the taste.[2]

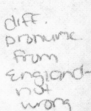

diff.
pronunc
from
England—
not
wrong

---

[2] [T5, note] In most instances, though perhaps not quite in all, many of
these observations are inapplicable to the higher classes of society in the Atlantic cities. There are mansions, for instance, in all of them, wherein little
or nothing which can be required by the most refined habits of the educated
middle classes, is so conspicuously wanting as to deserve the remarks made
in the text; nay, in many of them, as the reader will find distinctly stated in
the description of the best houses at New York, the richness of the decorations exceed[s] what it is usual to find among persons of similar rank in
Europe. Nevertheless, the text may stand unchallenged as referring to that
portion of the Union which it was intended to describe. As to what follows,
relating to the ordinary tone of conversation, it must in truth be allowed to
have had in the year 1831 a much more extended application. The intercourse with England, which, happily it is to be hoped for both countries,
has increased, and is daily so rapidly increasing between us, must speedily
render the remark as obsolete as that of Madame de Staël, who describes
English ladies of the highest rank as sitting for hours superintending the

I will not pretend to decide whether man is better or worse off for requiring refinement in the manners and customs of the society that surrounds him, and for being incapable of enjoyment without them; but in America that polish which removes the coarser and rougher parts of our nature is unknown and undreamed of. There is much substantial comfort, and some display in the larger cities; in many of the more obvious features they are as Paris or as London, being all large assemblies of active and intelligent human beings — but yet they are wonderfully unlike in nearly all their moral features. Now God forbid that any reasonable American, (of whom there are so many millions), should ever come to ask me what I mean; I should find it very difficult, nay, perhaps, utterly impossible, to explain myself; but, on the other hand, no European who has visited the Union, will find the least difficulty in understanding me. I am in no way competent to judge of the political institutions of America; and if I should occasionally make an observation on their effects, as they meet my superficial glance, they will be made in the spirit, and with the feeling of a woman, who is apt to tell what her first impressions may be, but unapt to reason back from effects to their causes. Such observations, if they be unworthy of much attention, are also obnoxious to little reproof: but there are points of national peculiarity of which women may judge as ably as men, — all that constitutes the external of society may be fairly trusted to us.[3]

faulty reasoning & judgment

---

boiling of the tea-kettle, while awaiting the termination of the bacchanalian orgies of their husbands. But such lingering tea-drinkings have been in England, and such heavy and ungraceful conversation has been heard to drawl through the drawing-rooms of the republic. On our part we scruple not to acknowledge our obligation to the neighbours who have taught us, during the intimate intercourse of the last twenty years, to amend the above-mentioned abomination indifferently well; nor will our trans-atlantic brothers and sisters, now become our neighbours too, long refuse to confess, that nothing but a personal familiarity with their avowed models could suffice to obliterate all national dissimilarity of manners.

[3] [TN] The study of manners, though greatly important, is not too profound for their capacity, and the minutiæ of which it is composed, suits bet-

Captain Hall, when asked what appeared to him to constitute the greatest difference between England and America,
replied, like a gallant sailor, "the want of loyalty." Were the
same question put to me, I should answer, "the want of refinement."

Were Americans, indeed, disposed to assume the plain unpretending deportment of the Switzer in the days of his picturesque simplicity, (when, however, he never chewed tobacco), it would be in bad taste to censure him; but this is
not the case. Jonathan will be a fine gentleman, but it must
be in his own way. Is he not a free-born American? Jonathan,
however, must remember, that if he will challenge competition with the old world, the old world will now and then look
out to see how he supports his pretensions.

With their hours of business, whether judicial or mercantile, civil or military, I have nothing to do; I doubt not they
are all spent wisely and profitably; but what are their hours
of recreation? Those hours that with us are passed in the enjoyment of all that art can win from nature; when, if the
elaborate repast be more deeply relished than sages might
approve, it is redeemed from sensuality by the presence of
elegance and beauty. What is the American pendant to this?
I will not draw any comparisons between a good dinner party
in the two countries; I have heard American gentlemen say,
that they could perceive no difference between them; but in
speaking of general manners, I may observe, that it is rarely
they dine in society, except in taverns and boarding-houses.
Then they eat with the greatest possible rapidity, and in total
silence; I have heard it said by American ladies, that the
hours of greatest enjoyment to the gentlemen were those in
which a glass of gin cock-tail, or egg-nog, receives its highest

(handwritten margin note: no time for play?)

ter the minute and lynx-like optics of the female, than with the enlarged
and elevated views of things taken by the male traveler.

[A discussion of Mrs. Trollope's view concerning her relation to the
"male traveler" and Captain Hall in particular is given in section IX of the
Introduction.]

relish from the absence of all restraint whatever; and when there were no ladies to trouble them.

Notwithstanding all this, the country is a very fine country, well worth visiting for a thousand reasons; nine hundred and ninety-nine of these are reasons founded on admiration and respect; the thousandth is, that we shall feel the more contented with our own. The more unlike a country through which we travel is to all we have left, the more we are likely to be amused; every thing in Cincinnati had this newness, and I should have thought it a place delightful to visit, but to tarry there was not to feel at home.

My home, however, for a time it was to be. We heard on every side, that of all the known places on "the globe called earth," Cincinnati was the most favourable for a young man to settle in; and I only awaited the arrival of Mr. T. to fix our son there, intending to continue with him till he should feel himself sufficiently established. We accordingly determined upon making ourselves as comfortable as possible. I took a larger house which, however, I did not obtain without considerable difficulty, as, notwithstanding fourteen hundred new dwellings had been erected the preceding year, the demand for houses greatly exceeded the supply. We became acquainted with several amiable people, and we beguiled the anxious interval that preceded Mr. T.'s joining us by frequent excursions in the neighbourhood, which not only afforded us amusement, but gave us an opportunity of observing the mode of life of the country people.

We visited one farm, which interested us particularly from its wild and lonely situation, and from the entire dependence of the inhabitants upon their own resources. It was a partial clearing in the very heart of the forest. The house was built on the side of a hill, so steep that a high ladder was necessary to enter the front door, while the back one opened against the hill side; at the foot of this sudden eminence ran a clear stream, whose bed had been deepened into a little

reservoir, just opposite the house. A noble field of Indian-
corn stretched away into the forest on one side, and a few
half-cleared acres, with a shed or two upon them, occupied
the other, giving accommodation to cows, horses, pigs, and
chickens innumerable. Immediately before the house was a
small potatoe garden, with a few peach and apple trees. The
house was built of logs, and consisted of two rooms, besides
a little shanty or lean-to, that was used as a kitchen. Both
rooms were comfortably furnished with good beds, drawers,
&c. The farmer's wife, and a young woman who looked like
her sister, were spinning, and three little children were playing about. The woman told me that they spun and wove all
the cotton and woollen garments of the family, and knit all
the stockings; her husband, though not a shoe-maker by
trade, made all the shoes. She manufactured all the soap and
candles they used, and prepared her sugar from the sugar-
trees on their farm. All she wanted with money, she said, was
to buy coffee, tea, and whiskey, and she could "get enough
any day by sending a batch of butter and chicken to market."
They used no wheat, nor sold any of their corn, which,
though it appeared a very large quantity, was not more than
they required to make their bread and cakes of various kinds,
and to feed all their live stock during the winter. She did not
look in health, and said they had all had ague in "the fall;"
but she seemed contented, and proud of her independence;
though it was in somewhat a mournful accent that she said,
" 'Tis strange to us to see company: I expect the sun may rise
and set a hundred times before I shall see another *human*
that does not belong to the family."

I have been minute in the description of this forest farm,
as I think it the best specimen I saw of the back-wood's independence, of which so much is said in America. These
people were indeed independent, Robinson Crusoe was
hardly more so, and they eat and drink abundantly; but yet
it seemed to me that there was something awful and almost

they are wrong b/c not like rw

unnatural in their loneliness. No village bell ever summoned them to prayer, where they might meet the friendly greeting of their fellow-men. When they die, no spot sacred by ancient reverence will receive their bones — Religion will not breathe her sweet and solemn farewell upon their grave; the husband or the father will dig the pit that is to hold them, beneath the nearest tree; he will himself deposit them within it, and the wind that whispers through the boughs will be their only requiem. But then they pay neither taxes nor tythes, are never expected to pull off a hat or to make a curtsy, and will live and die without hearing or uttering the dreadful words, "God save the king."

*   *   *   *   *   *

About two miles below Cincinnati, on the Kentucky side of the river, Mr. Bullock, the well known proprietor of the Egyptian Hall,[4] has bought a large estate, with a noble house upon it. He and his amiable wife were devoting themselves to the embellishment of the house and grounds; and certainly

[4] [DS] William Bullock's *Sketch of a Journey through the Western States* (1827) may have helped the Trollopes to choose Cincinnati for their business venture (see note to section II of my Introduction). According to Charles Anderson, the Bullocks gave a dinner party for Mrs. Trollope a few months after she had come to Cincinnati, with the notables of Cincinnati gathered for the occasion.

William Bullock started his career as a jeweler and goldsmith in Liverpool in 1808. He collected curiosities in his spare time and four years later opened his museum. It was so successful that he took his collections to London, where he became famous for his exhibits in Egyptian Hall, Piccadilly. In 1822 he went to Mexico for fresh materials and on his return opened a popular exhibit called "Modern Mexico." He also published a widely read book on his travels. In 1827 he visited the United States on his way back from a second visit to Mexico. Stopping at Cincinnati, he was so much impressed with this city and its environs that he bought a large estate on the Kentucky bank of the Ohio directly opposite Cincinnati with the purpose of establishing a "rural town to be called Hygeia," and laid out an elaborate plan calling for a museum, a town hall, a library, two parks, a market, a brewery, a theater, a bath, a fountain, schools, churches, and inns. Bullock returned to Cincinnati with his family in the spring of 1828 to begin this project. It did not prosper, and he sold his estate shortly after Mrs. Trollope left Cincinnati. Nothing seems to be known of his later life.

there is more taste and art lavished on one of their beautiful saloons, than all Western America can shew elsewhere. It is impossible to help feeling that Mr. Bullock is rather out of his element in this remote spot, and the gems of art he has brought with him, shew as strangely there, as would a bower of roses in Siberia, or a Cincinnati fashionable at Almack's. The exquisite beauty of the spot, commanding one of the finest reaches of the Ohio, the extensive gardens, and the large and handsome mansion, have tempted Mr. Bullock to spend a large sum in the purchase of this place, and if any one who has passed his life in London could endure such a change, the active mind and sanguine spirit of Mr. Bullock might enable him to do it; but his frank, and truly English hospitality, and his enlightened and enquiring mind, seemed sadly wasted there. I have since heard with pleasure that Mr. Bullock has parted with this beautiful, but secluded mansion.

CHAPTER VI

Servants — Society — Evening Parties

THE greatest difficulty in organising a family establishment in Ohio, is getting servants, or, as it is there called,
"getting help," for it is more than petty treason to the Republic, to call a free citizen a *servant*. The whole class of young
women, whose bread depends upon their labour, are taught
to believe that the most abject poverty is preferable to
to domestic service. Hundreds of half-naked girls work in the
paper-mills, or in any other manufactory, for less than half
the wages they would receive in service; but they think their
equality is compromised by the latter, and nothing but the
wish to obtain some particular article of finery will ever induce them to submit to it. A kind friend, however, exerted
herself so effectually for me, that a tall stately lass soon presented herself, saying, "I be come to help you." The intelligence was very agreeable, and I welcomed her in the most
gracious manner possible, and asked what I should give her
by the year.

"Oh Gimini!" exclaimed the damsel, with a loud laugh,
"you be a downright Englisher, sure enough. I should like
to see a young lady engage by the year in America! I hope I
shall get a husband before many months, or I expect I shall
be an outright old maid, for I be most seventeen already; besides, mayhap I may want to go to school. You must just give
me a dollar and half a week, and mother's slave, Phillis, must
come over once a week, I expect, from t'other side the water,
to help me clean."

I agreed to the bargain, of course, with all dutiful submission; and seeing she was preparing to set to work in a yellow
dress parsemé with red roses, I gently hinted, that I thought

it was a pity to spoil so fine a gown, and that she had better change it.

" 'Tis just my best and my worst," she answered, "for I've got no other."

And in truth I found that this young lady had left the paternal mansion with no more clothes of any kind than what she had on. I immediately gave her money to purchase what was necessary for cleanliness and decency, and set to work with my daughters to make her a gown. She grinned applause when our labour was completed, but never uttered the slightest expression of gratitude for that, or for any thing else we could do for her. She was constantly asking us to lend her different articles of dress, and when we declined it, she said, "Well, I never seed such grumpy folks as you be; there is several young ladies of my acquaintance what goes to live out now and then with the old women about the town, and they and their gurls always lends them what they asks for; I guess you Inglish thinks we should poison your things, just as bad as if we was Negurs." And here I beg to assure the reader, that whenever I give conversations they were not made à loisir, but were written down immediately after they occurred, with all the verbal fidelity my memory permitted.

This young lady left me at the end of two months, because I refused to lend her money enough to buy a silk dress to go to a ball, saying, "Then 'tis not worth my while to stay any longer."

I cannot imagine it possible that such a state of things can be desirable, or beneficial to any of the parties concerned. I might occupy a hundred pages on the subject, and yet fail to give an adequate idea of the sore, angry, ever wakeful pride that seemed to torment these poor wretches.[1] In many

---

[1] [DS] A passage in Harriet Martineau's Society in America (1837) is quite possibly aimed at Mrs. Trollope (whom she did not like):

"The study of the economy of domestic service was a continual amusement to me. What I saw would fill a volume. Many families are, and have for years been, as well off for domestics as any family in England; and I

of them it was so excessive, that all feeling of displeasure, or even of ridicule, was lost in pity. One of these was a pretty girl, whose natural disposition must have been gentle and kind; but her good feelings were soured, and her gentleness turned to morbid sensitiveness, by having heard a thousand and a thousand times that she was as good as any other lady, that all men were equal, and women too, and that it was a sin and a shame for a free-born American to be treated like a servant.[2]

When she found she was to dine in the kitchen, she turned up her pretty lip, and said, "I guess that's 'cause you don't think I'm good enough to eat with you. You'll find that won't do here." I found afterwards that she rarely ate any dinner at

---

must say that among the loudest complainers there were many who, from fault of either judgment or temper, deserved whatever difficulty they met with. This is remarkably the case with English ladies settled in America. They carry with them habits of command, and expectations of obedience; and when these are found utterly to fail, they grow afraid of their servants. Even when they have learned the theory that domestic service is a matter of contract, an exchange of service for recompense, the authority of the employer extending no further than to require the performance of the service promised, — when the ladies have learned to assent in words to this, they are still apt to be annoyed at things which in no way concern them. If one domestic chooses to wait at table with no cap over her scanty chevelure, and in spectacles, — if another goes to church on Sunday morning, dressed exactly like her mistress, the lady is in no way answerable for the bad taste of her domestics. But English residents often cannot learn to acquiesce in these things; nor in the servants doing their work in their own way; nor in their dividing their time as they please between their mistress's work and their own. The consequence is, that they soon find it impossible to get American help at all. . . ."

[2] [DS] "Well, life *am* strange! I am again cookless. I imprudently turned old Smith off and took a young girl, who left me in four days. Why? Her lover would not allow her to stay in a family where she did not eat at table with the lady. I had read of such things in Mrs. Trollope, and thought them quite impossible. In the place from which I took her, she had done all the cooking, washing and chamber work of the house — was, in fine the only servant, for the compensation of six dollars a month. But then, she sat at table!!! oh ho!" — Julia Ward Howe (author of "The Battle Hymn of the Republic"), writing to her sister from South Boston, Massachusetts, in 1844 or 1845.

all, and generally passed the time in tears. I did every thing in my power to conciliate and make her happy, but I am sure she hated me. I gave her very high wages, and she staid till she had obtained several expensive articles of dress, and then, *un beau matin*, she came to me full dressed, and said, "I must go." "When shall you return, Charlotte?" "I expect you'll see no more of me." And so we parted. Her sister was also living with me, but her wardrobe was not yet completed, and she remained some weeks longer, till it was.

I fear it may be called bad taste to say so much concerning my domestics, but, nevertheless, the circumstances are so characteristic of America that I must recount another history relating to them. A few days after the departure of my ambitious belle, my cries for "Help" had been so effectual that another young lady presented herself, with the usual preface "I'm come to help you." I had been cautioned never to ask for a reference for character, as it would not only rob me of that help, but entirely prevent my ever getting another; so, five minutes after she entered she was installed, bundle and all, as a member of the family. She was by no means handsome, but there was an air of simple frankness in her manner that won us all. For my own part, I thought I had got a second Jeanie Deans; for she recounted to me histories of her early youth, wherein her plain good sense and strong mind had enabled her to win her way through a host of cruel stepmothers, faithless lovers, and cheating brothers. Among other things, she told me, with the appearance of much emotion, that she had found, since she came to town, a cure for all her sorrows, "Thanks and praise for it, I have got religion!" and then she asked if I would spare her to go to Meeting every Tuesday and Thursday evening; "You shall not have to want me, Mrs. Trollope, for our minister knows that we have all our duties to perform to man, as well as to God, and he makes the Meeting late in the evening that they may not cross one another." Who could refuse? Not I, and Nancy had leave to go to Meeting two evenings in the week, besides Sundays.

One night, that the mosquitoes had found their way under my net, and prevented my sleeping, I heard some one enter the house very late; I got up, went to the top of the stairs, and, by the help of a bright moon, recognised Nancy's best bonnet. I called to her; "You are very late," said I, "what is the reason of it?" "Oh, Mrs. Trollope," she replied, "I am late, indeed! We have this night had seventeen souls added to our flock. May they live to bless this night! But it has been a long sitting, and very warm; I'll just take a drink of water, and get to bed; you shan't find me later in the morning for it." Nor did I. She was an excellent servant, and performed more than was expected from her; moreover, she always found time to read the Bible several times in the day, and I seldom saw her occupied about any thing without observing that she had placed it near her.

At last she fell sick with the cholera,[3] and her life was despaired of. I nursed her with great care, and sat up the greatest part of two nights with her. She was often delirious, and all her wandering thoughts seemed to ramble to heaven. "I have been a sinner," she said, "but I am safe in the Lord Jesus." When she recovered, she asked me to let her go into the country for a few days, to change the air, and begged me to lend her three dollars.

While she was absent a lady called on me, and enquired, with some agitation, if my servant, Nancy Fletcher, were at home. I replied that she was gone into the country. "Thank God," she exclaimed, "never let her enter your doors again, she is the most abandoned woman in the town: a gentleman who knows you, has been told that she lives with you, and

---

[3] [T5, note] Not the Asiatic cholera, which at that time had not visited America. [The Asiatic cholera swept America in 1832; in Cincinnati the death toll rose as high as 351 persons in three weeks.]

that she boasts of having the power of entering your house at any hour of the night." She told many other circumstances, unnecessary to repeat, but all tending to prove that she was a very dangerous inmate.

I expected her home the next evening, and I believe I passed the interval in meditating how to get rid of her without an *eclaircissement*. At length she arrived, and all my study having failed to supply me with any other reason than the real one for dismissing her, I stated it at once. Not the slightest change passed over her countenance, but she looked steadily at me, and said, in a very civil tone, "I should like to know who told you." I replied that it could be of no advantage to her to know, and that I wished her to go immediately. "I am ready to go," she said, in the same quiet tone, "but what will you do for your three dollars?" "I must do without them, Nancy; good morning to you." "I must just put up my things," she said, and left the room. About half an hour afterwards, when we were all assembled at dinner, she entered with her usual civil composed air, "Well, I am come to wish you all good bye," and with a friendly good-humoured smile she left us.

This adventure frightened me so heartily, that, notwithstanding I had the dread of cooking my own dinner before my eyes, I would not take any more young ladies into my family without receiving some slight sketch of their former history. At length I met with a very worthy French woman, and soon after with a tidy English girl to assist her; and I had the good fortune to keep them till a short time before my departure: so, happily, I have no more misfortunes of this nature to relate.

Such being the difficulties respecting domestic arrangements, it is obvious, that the ladies who are brought up amongst them cannot have leisure for any great developement of the mind: it is, in fact, out of the question; and, remembering this, it is more surprising that some among them should be very pleasing, than that none should be highly instructed.

Had I passed as many evenings in company in any other town that I ever visited as I did in Cincinnati, I should have been able to give some little account of the conversations I had listened to; but, upon reading over my notes, and then taxing my memory to the utmost to supply the deficiency, I can scarcely find a trace of any thing that deserves the name. Such as I have, shall be given in their place. But, whatever may be the talents of the persons who meet together in society, the very shape, form, and arrangement of the meeting is sufficient to paralyze conversation. The women invariably herd together at one part of the room, and the men at the other; but, in justice to Cincinnati, I must acknowledge that this arrangement is by no means peculiar to that city, or to the western side of the Alleghanies. Sometimes a small attempt at music produces a partial reunion; a few of the most daring youths, animated by the consciousness of curled hair and smart waistcoats, approach the piano-forte, and begin to mutter a little to the half-grown pretty things, who are comparing with one another "how many quarters' music they have had." Where the mansion is of sufficient dignity to have two drawing-rooms, the piano, the little ladies, and the slender gentlemen are left to themselves, and on such occasions the sound of laughter is often heard to issue from among them. But the fate of the more dignified personages, who are left in the other room, is extremely dismal. The gentlemen spit, talk of elections and the price of produce, and spit again.[4] The ladies look at each other's dresses till they know

---

[4] [DS] Mrs. Trollope's observations on tobacco-chewing here and elsewhere in *Domestic Manners* may well have had something to do with the following letter to the editor of the Cincinnati *Mirror* (March 2, 1833):

"Mr. Editor: — Are you a *tobacco-chewer?* — I know you are not, for I took the trouble to ascertain before I seated myself at my desk. Is it not a most abominable practice? . . . .

"This has been called the 'age of improvements,' the 'age of novels,' the

every pin by heart; talk of Parson Somebody's last sermon on the day of judgment, on Dr. T'otherbody's new pills for dyspepsia, till the "tea" is announced, when they all console themselves together for whatever they may have suffered in keeping awake, by taking more tea, coffee, hot cake and custard, hoe cake, johny cake, waffle cake, and dodger cake, pickled peaches, and preserved cucumbers, ham, turkey, hung beef, apple sauce, and pickled oysters than ever were prepared in any other country of the known world. After this massive meal is over, they return to the drawing-room, and it always appeared to me that they remained together as long as they could bear it, and then they rise *en masse,* cloak, bonnet, shawl, and exit.

'age of lectures,' &c. For my part, I think it is more especially the *age of tobacco-chewers,* than of any thing else. If a lady meet a cousin in the street, and have a question to ask him, before he can answer, out must come a black mass of the noxious weed, large enough to scent the air for a rod around. Again, if one take a gentleman's arm for a short evening stroll, and there happens to be a slight breeze, ten to one if she don't the next day find the skirt of her dress as completely bespattered and besprinkled, as if she had been caught in a shower of tobacco juice. And if a lady be seated in the theatre by the side of one of these inveterate *chewers,* every time he addresses a word to her, her olfactories meet with such a salutation as will set her to dreaming of any thing but the aromatic flowers of Paradise. A few months since, a gentleman whom from his external appearance you would suppose to have never looked upon a tobacco-stem without shuddering, drew his chair close up to mine, and while he was asking my company at any approaching Ball at the Bazaar, he was also actually cutting a mouthful of the vile stuff from a 'plug' which he had just taken from his pocket. You may be sure, Mr. Editor, that I had a 'previous engagement elsewhere,' for that evening. . . .

"The particular object of this epistle, is to recommend to the ladies of this city, the formation among themselves of a *Society for the suppression of Tobacco-chewing.* . . ."

CHAPTER VII

Market — Museum — Picture Gallery — Academy of Fine Arts —
Drawing School — Phrenological Society — Miss Wright's Lecture

PERHAPS the most advantageous feature in Cincinnati is its market, which, for excellence, abundance, and cheapness, can hardly, I should think, be surpassed in any part of the world, if I except the luxury of fruits, which are very inferior to any I have seen in Europe. There are no butchers, fishmongers, or indeed any shops for eatables, except *bakeries,* as they are called, in the town; every thing must be purchased at market; and to accomplish this, the busy housewife must be stirring betimes, or, 'spite of the abundant supply, she will find her hopes of breakfast, dinner, and supper for the day defeated, the market being pretty well over by eight o'clock.

The beef is excellent, and the highest price when we were there, four cents (about two-pence) the pound.[1] The mutton was inferior, and so was veal to the eye, but it ate well, though not very fat; the price was about the same. The poultry was excellent; fowls or full-sized chickens, ready for table, twelve cents, but much less if bought alive, and not quite fat; turkeys about fifty cents, and geese the same. The Ohio fur-

---

[1] [TN] The prices of many articles rose considerably during our stay, yet were they still such when we left the place two years after as probably to be still [blank space] and I am decidedly of opinion that to whomever abundance of cheap beef steaks can be a means of enjoyment, Cincinnati must be the happiest spot on earth.

[TRD, a little later in the same paragraph] [They had] all kinds of vegetables that we have in Covent Garden, except sea-cale, artichokes, califlowers and brocoli, cheap and abundant, but these had not made their appearance in the Cincinnati Market when I was there; their absence, however, was more than atoned for, in my opinion, by the profuse abundance of tomatoes. . . .

nishes several sorts of fish, some of them very good, and always to be found cheap and abundant in the market. Eggs, butter, nearly all kinds of vegetables, excellent, and at moderate prices. From June till December tomatoes (the great luxury of the American table in the opinion of most Europeans) may be found in the highest perfection in the market for about sixpence the peck. They have a great variety of beans unknown in England, particularly the lima-bean, the seed of which is dressed like the French harrico; it furnishes a very abundant crop, and is a most delicious vegetable: could it be naturalised with us it would be a valuable acquisition. The Windsor, or broad-bean, will not do well there; Mr. Bullock had them in his garden, where they were cultivated with much care; they grew about a foot high and blossomed, but the pod never ripened. All the fruit I saw exposed for sale in Cincinnati was most miserable. I passed two summers there, but never tasted a peach worth eating. Of apricots and nectarines I saw none; strawberries very small, raspberries much worse; gooseberries very few, and quite uneatable; currants about half the size of ours, and about double the price; grapes too sour for tarts; apples abundant, but very indifferent, none that would be thought good enough for an English table; pears, cherries, and plums most miserably bad. The flowers of these regions were at least equally inferior: whether this proceeds from want of cultivation or from peculiarity of soil I know not, but after leaving Cincinnati, I was told by a gentleman who appeared to understand the subject, that the state of Ohio had no indigenous flowers or fruits. The water-melons, which in that warm climate furnish a delightful refreshment, were abundant and cheap; but all other melons very inferior to those of France, or even of England, when ripened in a common hot-bed.

From the almost total want of pasturage near the city, it is difficult for a stranger to divine how milk is furnished for its supply, but we soon learnt that there are more ways than one

of keeping a cow. A large proportion of the families in the
town, particularly of the poorer class, have one, though apparently without any accommodation whatever for it. These
animals are fed morning and evening at the door of the house,
with a good mess of Indian corn, boiled with water; while
they eat, they are milked, and when the operation is completed the milk-pail and the meal-tub retreat into the dwelling, leaving the republican cow to walk away, to take her
pleasure on the hills, or in the gutters, as may suit her fancy
best. They generally return very regularly to give and take
the morning and evening meal; though it more than once
happened to us, before we were supplied by a regular milk
cart, to have our jug sent home empty, with the sad news that
"the cow was not come home, and it was too late to look for
her to breakfast now." Once, I remember, the good woman
told us that she had overslept herself, and that the cow had
come and gone again, "not liking, I expect, to hanker about
by herself for nothing, poor thing."

Cincinnati has not many lions to boast, but among them
are two museums of natural history; both of these contain
many respectable specimens, particularly that of Mr. Dorfeuille, who has, moreover, some highly interesting Indian
antiquities. He is a man of taste and science, but a collection
formed strictly according to their dictates, would by no
means satisfy the western metropolis. The people have a most
extravagant passion for wax figures, and the two museums vie
with each other in displaying specimens of this barbarous
branch of art. As Mr. Dorfeuille cannot trust to his science for
attracting the citizens, he has put his ingenuity into requisition, and this has proved to him the surer aid of the two. He
has constructed a pandæmonium in an upper story of his
museum, in which he has congregated all the images of horror that his fertile fancy could devise; dwarfs that by machinery grow into giants before the eyes of the spectator;
imps of ebony with eyes of flame; monstrous reptiles devour-

ing youth and beauty; lakes of fire, and mountains of ice; in short, wax, paint and springs have done wonders. "To give the scheme some more effect," he makes it visible only through a grate of massive iron bars, among which are arranged wires connected with an electrical machine in a neighbouring chamber; should any daring hand or foot obtrude itself within the bars, it receives a smart shock, that often passes through many of the crowd, and the cause being unknown, the effect is exceedingly comic; terror, astonishment, curiosity, are all set in action, and all contribute to make "Dorfeuille's Hell" one of the most amusing exhibitions imaginable.[2]

---

[2] [DS] The showing of the *Infernal Regions,* or "Dorfeuille's Hell," was Mrs. Trollope's own idea. Her activities at the Western Museum are narrated at length in section V of the Introduction, but the description of Cincinnati's "Hell" written by Linus S. Everett, a Bostonian who visited it not many months after it was set up on July 4, 1828, may be of some interest here:

"It is located — for the reader must understand that it has 'a local habitation and a name' — in the attic story of the lower Museum in Cincinnati. The whole length of this infernal place is about twenty feet — its breadth ten or twelve. In the centre is seated his Infernal Highness 'as large as life.' This diabolical personage sits on a throne of darkness of sufficient elevation to give him a commanding view of the abyss on either side. His body is clad in a sable robe, which, however, discloses that all-essential appendage — a 'cloven foot.' In his left hand he holds a pitch-fork, like a weaver's beam; while his right is pointed towards an inscription directly in front, 'Whoever enters here leaves hope behind!' His head is adorned with a huge crown, and his face, (which by the way is not the most pleasant) is wo[e]fully ornamented with a hoary beard, made of horses' tails! To give importance to this King of Hell, his neck is so constructed as to admit of his giving a nod of recognition to the spectator; and his glaring eye-balls are made to roll most horribly by means of some machinery in the room below. This is a brief, but correct description of this man-made devil, and will enable the reader to form an idea of the interest thrown upon the scene by his presence.

"On the right hand of the devil above described, and on the left of the spectator, is seen one department of this hell, which is denominated the *hell* of ice; a most heretical place, where the damned, instead of being burned in fire and brimstone, are *frozen* in eternal death! This department is filled with wax figures representing persons of all ages and conditions — and among others, I observed a beautiful child, represented as in the greatest agony, frozen fast to the foot of the infernal throne. But what added much to the *effect,* was the condition of a poor old negro just entering upon a

There is also a picture gallery at Cincinnati, and this was a circumstance of much interest to us, as our friend Mr. H., who had accompanied Miss Wright to America, in the expectation of finding a good opening in the line of historical painting, intended commencing his experiment at Cincinnati. It would be invidious to describe the picture gallery; [3] I have

state of perpetual freezing; a sad predicament, truly, for one so constitutionally fond of a warm climate! In the corners of *this* part of hell, were to be seen several *imps* waiting the orders of his Majesty, 'grinning ghastly a horrible smile' at the miseries of their unfortunate subjects.

"On the left of the devil, which is to the right of the beholder, is the *hell of fire*. In this department, are seen the skeletons of persons, thrown into various positions, the sockets of their eyes, their nostrils &c. &c. filled with some bright substance resembling fire; presenting to the eye one of the most loathesome and disgusting scenes that imagination can portray! While the heart is pained with beholding these *representatives* of misery, the ear is saluted with a subterranean noise, produced by some instruments of discord in the apartment below, resembling the imaginary groans of the damned! Taken all together, it presents a scene well calculated to alarm weak minds. . . ."

[3] [DS] "Mr. H.," the young French artist Auguste Jean Jacques Hervieu, who accompanied Mrs. Trollope throughout her American adventures, figures prominently in the Introduction.

Some idea of Cincinnati's picture gallery can be obtained from an advertisement of it in the Cincinnati *National Republican* for June 20, 1828:

"GALLERY OF HISTORICAL PAINTINGS.

"The citizens of Cincinnati and its vicinity are respectfully informed, that an exhibition of SPLENDID PAINTINGS is now ready for their reception, at the *Corner of Main and Upper Market streets,* where may be seen the following interesting representations:

"TRUMBULL's grand Historical Painting of the DECLARATION OF INDEPENDENCE; Painted on a canvass of 252 square feet; — on which is represented the correct LIKENESS of each of the immortal Signers of the Declaration of the Independence of our country, for the support of which they pledged 'their lives, fortunes and sacred honor,' which led to such glorious results, and has been the means of establishing the greatest Republic in the universe.

"An Original Painting, on a canvass of 336 square feet, representing *"Napoleon and his Army, crossing the Alps.*

"The View comprehends the CONVENT OF CHARTREUX, situated near the summit of the mountain St. Bernard, and the VILLAGE OF ST. PIERRE in the distance.

no doubt, that some years hence it will present a very different appearance. Mr. H. was very kindly received by many of the gentlemen of the city, and though the state of the fine arts there gave him but little hope that he should meet with much success, he immediately occupied himself in painting a noble historical picture of the landing of General Lafayette at Cincinnati.

Perhaps the clearest proof of the little feeling for art that existed at that time in Cincinnati, may be drawn from the result of an experiment originated by a German, who taught drawing there. He conceived the project of forming a chartered academy of fine arts; and he succeeded in the beginning to his utmost wish, or rather, "they fooled him to the top of his bent." Three thousand dollars were subscribed, that is to say, names were written against different sums to that amount, a house was chosen, and finally, application was made to the government, and the charter obtained, rehearsing formally the names of the subscribing members, the pro-

---

"On a canvass of 180 square feet, the renowned
BATTLE OF ABOUKIR,
The last battle of Bonaparte in the Egyptian campaign against the Turks.
"Panorama View of the
CITY OF LYONS,
The Capital of Southern France; painted on 400 square feet of canvass.
"City of Jerusalem and its Environs.
"GEN. BOLIVAR HUNTING BISONS.
"View of the *Upper Market Space & Main St. of Cincinnati.*
"Cosmoramic View of GREENWICH HOSPITAL.
"The curious Metamorphoses of WASHINGTON, LAFAYETTE and BOLIVAR, who change from one to the other, as you change your point of sight.
"View of the PALACE OF WHITEHALL.
"THE SPLENDID CRYSTALLOMANCY, which represents the lively business and bustle in the Streets and Market of CINCINNATI, all in motion and action: never, for a moment, is to be seen the same scene. This is highly interesting to the scientific; and must be a treat to the optician.
"The Gallery is open every day and evening, Sundays excepted. Admittance 25 cents.
"Smoking within the Gallery prohibited."

fessors, and the officers. So far did the steam of their zeal impel them, but at this point it was let off; the affair stood still, and I never heard the academy of fine arts mentioned afterwards.[4]

---

[4] [DS] Frederick Eckstein and his Academy of Fine Arts received much publicity in Cincinnati newspapers, especially the *Chronicle*, during the spring, summer, and fall of 1828. In March the Academy was launched with a charter from the city, a board of eighteen directors, and rooms in the "college edifice." Thereafter articles in the city's newspapers praised the project from time to time with more rhetoric than detail. By August, Eckstein was apparently in financial difficulties. He tried to raise funds through an exhibition of "such Paintings as belong to the Academy and such as can be procured by loan." The fate of the Academy's exhibition is described in a letter to the editor of the *Chronicle* (December 20, 1828):

"It is well known that some enterprising but deluded persons have been for the last year, laboring to establish in this city an Academy of Fine Arts, and that the first exhibition has just ended. Now although there were near two hundred specimens of the fine arts, all handsomely arranged, — many of them pieces of interest, and indeed, of extraordinary merit, and more than all, the efforts of our talented native artists, yet such is the commendable taste of our worthy citizens, that the Academy has been closed for the want of sufficient patronage to pay the door keeper, and furnish tallow candles to light it up in the evenings. After having been open six weeks, it is computed that not more than one hundred and fifty of the 20,000 inhabitants of Cincinnati, have visited it, and perhaps one half of that number were induced to do so, because they were, in one way and another, admitted without the payment of their twenty-five cents. On the other hand, hundreds and hundreds of persons, night after night, for months past, have visited the Circus to witness the feats of a clown riding at full speed with his head on the saddle and his heels in the air."

By the end of another month Eckstein had given up all attempt to keep the Academy in operation. With the help of his wife, he had opened a private school offering "an elementary, literary and scientific English education" to young ladies. Later he moved this school to Kentucky.

The same letter that relates the failure of Eckstein's exhibition gives the history of another project for the enlightenment of the community that was hailed with much fanfare:

"Again, certain busy members of society have lately been making an effort to get up a Mechanic's Institute in this city, the avowed object of which, is the promotion of the *arts:* After several weeks of puffing and other outdoor arrangements, a public meeting was called at Talbot's school room to organize the society, and behold, *fifteen* persons attended. A few nights afterwards, the American Dog Appollo advertised that he would *see company.* Some two or three hundred persons were present, and such was the case for several succeeding nights." In fairness it should be said that the Mechanic's Institute later did well in Cincinnati.

This same German gentleman, on seeing Mr. H.'s sketches, was so well pleased with them, that he immediately proposed his joining him in his drawing school, with an agreement, I believe, that his payment from it should be five hundred dollars a year. Mr. H. accepted the proposal, but the union did not last long, and the cause of its dissolution was too American to be omitted. Mr. H. prepared his models, and attended the class, which was numerous, consisting both of boys and girls. He soon found that the "sage called Decipline" was not one of the assistants, and he remonstrated against the constant talking, and running from one part of the room to another, but in vain; finding, however, that he could do nothing till this was discontinued, he wrote some rules, enforcing order, for the purpose of placing them at the door of the academy. When he shewed them to his colleague, he shook his head, and said, "Very goot, very goot in Europe, but America boys and gals vill not bear it, dey will do just vat dey please; Suur, dey vould all go avay next day." "And you will not enforce these regulations *si nécessaires*, Monsieur?" "O lar! not for de vorld." "*Eh bien*, Monsieur, I must leave the young republicans to your management."

I heard another anecdote that will help to show the state of art at this time in the west. Mr. Bullock was shewing to some gentlemen of the first standing, the very *élite* of Cincinnati, his beautiful collection of engravings, when one among them exclaimed, "Have you really done all these since you came here? How hard you must have worked!"

I was also told of a gentleman of High Cincinnati *ton* and critical in his taste for the fine arts, who, having a drawing put into his hands, representing Hebe and the bird, umquhile sacred to Jupiter, demanded in a satirical tone, "What is this?" "Hebe," replied the alarmed collector. "Hebe," sneered the man of taste, "What the devil has Hebe to do with the American eagle?"

We had not been long at Cincinnati when Dr. Caldwell,

the Spurzheim of America, arrived there for the purpose of delivering lectures on phrenology.[5] I attended his lectures, and was introduced to him. He has studied Spurzheim and Combe diligently, and seems to understand the science to which he has devoted himself; but neither his lectures nor his conversation had that delightful truth of genuine enthusiasm, which makes listening to Dr. Spurzheim so great a treat. His lectures, however, produced considerable effect. Between twenty and thirty of the most erudite citizens decided upon forming a phrenological society. A meeting was called, and fully attended; a respectable number of subscribers' names was registered, the payment of subscriptions being arranged for a future day. President, vice-president, treasurer, and secretary, were chosen; and the first meeting dissolved with every appearance of energetic perseverance in scientific research.

The second meeting brought together one-half of this learned body, and they enacted rules and laws, and passed resolutions, sufficient, it was said, to have filled three folios.

A third day of meeting arrived, which was an important one, as on this occasion the subscriptions were to be paid. The treasurer came punctually, but found himself alone. With patient hope, he waited two hours for the wise men of the

---

[5] [DS] Dr. Charles Caldwell had gone to Europe in 1821 to buy books for the Medical Department of Transylvania College at Lexington, Kentucky, in which he taught. In Europe he took up phrenology, and on his return to the West he began to give public lectures on the subject. At one of these he is reported to have said: "There are only three great heads in the United States, one is that of Daniel Webster, another that of Henry Clay, and the last," indicating his own, "modesty prevents me from mentioning."

On April 5, 1828 the *Cincinnati Chronicle* carried this announcement:

"PHRENOLOGY

"Professor Caldwell of Transylvania University, is delivering a course of Phrenological Lectures in the Western Museum of this city. Those persons who are desirous of becoming acquainted with this new and fashionable science, will do well to avail themselves of the present opportunity of hearing the lectures of its distinguished propagandist in the west."

The *Chronicle* ran a series of seven articles upon phrenology, beginning with the issue of April 12.

west, but he waited in vain: and so expired the Phrenological Society of Cincinnati.

I had often occasion to remark that the spirit of enterprise or improvement seldom glowed with sufficient ardour to resist the smothering effect of a demand for dollars. The Americans love talking. All great works, however, that promise a profitable result, are sure to meet support from men who have enterprise and capital sufficient to await the return; but where there is nothing but glory, or the gratification of taste to be expected, it is, I believe, very rarely that they give any thing beyond "their most sweet voices."

Perhaps they are right. In Europe we see fortunes crippled by a passion for statues, or for pictures, or for books, or for gems; for all and every of the artificial wants that give grace to life, and tend to make man forget that he is a thing of clay.[6] They are wiser in their generation on the other side of the Atlantic; I rarely saw any thing that led to such oblivion there.

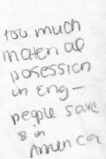

too much material posession in Eng — people save $ in America

Soon after Dr. Caldwell's departure, another lecturer appeared upon the scene, whose purpose of publicly addressing the people was no sooner made known, than the most violent sensation was excited.

That a lady of fortune, family, and education, whose youth had been passed in the most refined circles of private life, should present herself to the people as a public lecturer, would naturally excite surprise any where, and the *nil admirari* of the old world itself, would hardly be sustained before such a spectacle; but in America, where women are guarded by a seven-fold shield of habitual insignificance, it caused an effect that can hardly be described. "Miss Wright, of Nashoba, is going to lecture at the court-house," sounded

---

[6] [TN] . . . all contributing to the grace and refinement of life — but here such things are never heard of as articles of personal expense, or even of national ambition. They are known to exist, that is matter of history, but for the feelings they inspire among the sons and daughters of Europe, I believe they are no more comprehended here than the pleasure of scalping an enemy is by us.

from street to street, and from house to house. I shared the
surprise, but not the wonder; I knew her extraordinary gift
of eloquence, her almost unequalled command of words, and
the wonderful power of her rich and thrilling voice; and I
doubted not that if it was her will to do it, she had the power
of commanding the attention, and enchanting the ear of any
audience before whom it was her pleasure to appear.[7] I was

[7] [TRD] This was, I believe, the first lecture Miss Wright delivered publicly; but there was no appearance of agitation, or faltering of any kind. [It
was, as a matter of fact, Fanny Wright's second public appearance. She had
delivered the Fourth of July address at New Harmony only a few weeks
earlier.]

[DS] Mrs. Trollope is not the only witness to Miss Wright's powers of
oratory. "Oliver Oldschool" wrote in a letter to the *Chronicle* (August 30,
1828):

"Sir, I was attracted last Sunday by curiosity to the Court-house to hear
a lecture from the celebrated Miss Wright on the subject of *free enquiry*. If
chaste diction, and logical deduction from assumed data, delivered with an
air of determined purpose, breathing an indomitable fortitude, that seemed
to court persecution and martyrdom, heightened by persuasive smiles and
earnest gestures be eloquence, she possesses it. But her's is not the eloquence of truth, nor the advice of wisdom, but the siren song that lures and
deceives the more it charms. . . ."

A letter quoted in note 4 of this chapter in regard to Eckstein's Academy
also has a word to say of Miss Wright's success: "Witness the immense
crowds who, lecture after lecture, have thronged the Court-house, and hung
with delight upon the eloquent accents of Miss Frances Wright, when pouring forth her glowing anathemas upon the artificial institution of marriage,
while *he* who ministers in holy things, was preaching to empty pews, upon
the inestimable importance of connubial constancy."

Fanny Wright stated that her purpose was to "take up the cause of in-
sulted reason and outraged humanity" against the hysterical preachings of
revivalists, who had of late been especially active and successful in Cincinnati. She intended to counteract the works of these "ghostly expounders of
damnation" by exalting "true knowledge" as opposed to beliefs and opinions that cannot be verified by the senses. She delivered her lectures at the
Courthouse on three successive Sundays. The first two discourses were fairly
general in character, a compound of theories garnered from Jeremy Ben-
tham and Robert Owen; but the last of the three was a direct attack upon
Christian churches and religious institutions, which brought down upon her
head the wrath of the united clergy, including the Catholic bishop. Nevertheless, the lectures were so popular that she repeated them by special request of Cincinnati's theater.

Mrs. Trollope's friend Mrs. P°°°°, who accompanied her to hear Miss
Wright, was probably Mrs. William Price. Mrs. Trollope's friendship with
the Prices is discussed in section VI of the Introduction.

most anxious to hear her, but was almost deterred from attempting it, by the reports that reached me of the immense crowd that was expected. After many consultations, and hearing that many other ladies intended going, my friend Mrs. P****, and myself, decided upon making the attempt, accompanied by a party of gentlemen, and found the difficulty less than we anticipated, though the building was crowded in every part. We congratulated ourselves that we had had the courage to be among the number, for all my expectations fell far short of the splendour, the brilliance, the overwhelming eloquence of this extraordinary orator.

Her lecture was upon the nature of true knowledge, and it contained little that could be objected to, by any sect or party; it was intended as an introduction to the strange and startling theories contained in her subsequent lectures, and could alarm only by the hints it contained that the fabric of human wisdom could rest securely on no other base than that of human knowledge.

There was, however, one passage from which commonsense revolted; it was one wherein she quoted that phrase of mischievous sophistry, "all men are born free and equal."

This false and futile axiom, which has done, is doing, and will do so much harm to this fine country, came from Jefferson; and truly his life was a glorious commentary upon it. I pretend not to criticise his written works, but common-sense enables me to pronounce this, his favourite maxim, false.

Few names are held in higher estimation in America, than that of Jefferson; it is the touchstone of the democratic party, and all seem to agree that he was one of the greatest of men; yet I have heard his name coupled with deeds which would make the sons of Europe shudder. The facts I allude to are spoken openly by all, not whispered privately by a few; and in a country where religion is the tea-table talk, and its strict observance a fashionable distinction, these facts are recorded, and listened to, without horror, nay, without emotion.

Mr. Jefferson is said to have been the father of children by almost all his numerous gang of female slaves. These wretched offspring were also the lawful slaves of their father, and worked in his house and plantations as such; in particular, it is recorded that it was his especial pleasure to be waited upon by them at table, and the hospitable orgies for which his Montecielo was so celebrated, were incomplete, unless the goblet he quaffed were tendered by the trembling hand of his own slavish offspring.[8]

I once heard it stated by a democratical adorer of this great man, that when, as it sometimes happened, his children by Quadroon slaves were white enough to escape suspicion of their origin, he did not pursue them if they attempted to escape, saying laughingly, "Let the rogues get off, if they can; I will not hinder them." This was stated in a large party, as a

[8] [T5, note] Some years after my return from America, I met at Paris an American gentleman holding a diplomatic situation in that city, who assured me, that the real political principles of Mr. Jefferson were exactly the reverse of what he publicly expressed, and that it was impossible any man could be less a democrat than he was.

[DS] The scandalous story that fathered Jefferson with broods of slave children was probably invented by James Thomson Callender, a British refugee who had fled to America to escape prosecution for libel in England. Callender met his death by drowning in the James River after a drunken spree; one historian has commented that he thus found his grave "in congenial mud." By 1802 the story of Jefferson's numerous slave progeny was widely circulated, and a song went the rounds to be sung to the tune of "Yankee Doodle":

> Of all the damsels on the green,
> On mountain, or in valley,
> A lass so luscious ne'er was seen
> As Monticellian Sally.
> Yankee doodle, who's the noodle?
> What wife was half so handy?
> To breed a flock of slaves for stock,
> A blackamoor's the dandy.

Jefferson refused to contradict the "thousands of calumnies so industriously propagated" against him, maintaining that though the press is a noble institution when it stays "within the pale of truth," it is "impotent when it abandons itself to falsehood."

proof of his kind and noble nature, and was received by all with approving smiles.

If I know any thing of right or wrong, if virtue and vice be indeed something more than words, then was this great American an unprincipled tyrant, and most heartless libertine.

But to return to Miss Wright, — it is impossible to imagine any thing more striking than her appearance. Her tall and majestic figure, the deep and almost solemn expression of her eyes, the simple contour of her finely formed head, unadorned, excepting by its own natural ringlets; her garment of plain white muslin, which hung around her in folds that recalled the drapery of a Grecian statue, all contributed to produce an effect, unlike any thing I had ever seen before, or ever expect to see again.

CHAPTER VIII

Absence of public and private Amusement — Churches and
Chapels — Influence of the Clergy — A Revival

I NEVER saw any people who appeared to live so
much without amusement as the Cincinnatians. Billiards are
forbidden by law, so are cards. To sell a pack of cards in Ohio
subjects the seller to a penalty of fifty dollars. They have no
public balls, excepting, I think, six, during the Christmas
holidays. They have no concerts. They have no dinner parties.

They have a theatre, which is, in fact, the only public amusement of this triste little town; but they seem to care little
about it, and either from economy or distaste, it is very poorly
attended. Ladies are rarely seen there, and by far the larger
proportion of females deem it an offence against religion to
witness the representation of a play. It is in the churches and
chapels of the town that the ladies are to be seen in full costume; and I am tempted to believe that a stranger from the
continent of Europe would be inclined, on first reconnoitering
the city, to suppose that the places of worship were the theatres and cafés of the place. No evening in the week but
brings throngs of the young and beautiful to the chapels and
meeting-houses, all dressed with care, and sometimes with
great pretension; it is there that all display is made, and all
fashionable distinction sought. The proportion of gentlemen
attending these evening meetings is very small, but often, as
might be expected, a sprinkling of smart young clerks make
this sedulous display of ribbons and ringlets intelligible and
natural. Were it not for the churches, indeed, I think there
might be a general bonfire of best bonnets, for I never could
discover any other use for them.

work @ the home

The ladies are too actively employed in the interior of their houses to permit much parading in full dress for morning visits. There are no public gardens or lounging shops of fashionable resort, and were it not for public worship, and private tea-drinkings, all the ladies in Cincinnati would be in danger of becoming perfect recluses.

The influence which the ministers of all the innumerable religious sects throughout America, have on the females of their respective congregations, approaches very nearly to what we read of in Spain, or in other strictly Roman Catholic countries. There are many causes for this peculiar influence. Where equality of rank is affectedly acknowledged by the rich, and clamorously claimed by the poor, distinction and pre-eminence are allowed to the clergy only. This gives them high importance in the eyes of the ladies. I think, also, that it is from the clergy only that the women of America receive that sort of attention which is so dearly valued by every female heart throughout the world. With the priests of America, the women hold that degree of influential importance which, in the countries of Europe, is allowed them throughout all orders and ranks of society, except, perhaps, the very lowest; and in return for this they seem to give their hearts and souls into their keeping. I never saw, or read, of any country where religion had so strong a hold upon the women, or a slighter hold upon the men.

I mean not to assert that I met with no men of sincerely religious feelings, or with no women of no religious feelings at all; but I feel perfectly secure of being correct as to the great majority in the statement I have made.

We had not been many months in Cincinnati when our curiosity was excited by hearing the "revival" talked of by every one we met throughout the town. "The revival will be very full" — "We shall be constantly engaged during the revival" — were the phrases we constantly heard repeated, and for a long time, without in the least comprehending what was meant; but at length I learnt that the un-national church of America required to be roused, at regular intervals, to greater energy and exertion. At these seasons the most enthusiastic of the clergy travel the country, and enter the cities and towns by scores, or by hundreds, as the accommodation of the place may admit, and for a week or fortnight, or, if the population be large, for a month; they preach and pray all day, and often for a considerable portion of the night, in the various churches and chapels of the place. This is called a Revival.

I took considerable pains to obtain information on this subject; but in detailing what I learnt I fear that it is probable I shall be accused of exaggeration; all I can do is cautiously to avoid deserving it. The subject is highly interesting, and it would be a fault of no trifling nature to treat it with levity.

These itinerant clergymen are of all persuasions, I believe, except the Episcopalian, Catholic, Unitarian, and Quaker.[1] I heard of Presbyterians of all varieties; of Baptists of I know not how many divisions; and of Methodists of more denominations than I can remember; whose innumerable shades of varying belief, it would require much time to explain, and

---

[1] [T5, note] The critics who have from time to time reproached me with undue severity in my strictures on the domestic manners of the Americans, have said that a candid examination of matters at home would have shown me that what I reprobated might be found in England, as well as in the United States. In most cases I have felt that this might be rebutted, not by altogether denying the charge, but by showing that what I complained of in the Union as indicative of imperfect civilisation, if existing at all with us, could only be met with among persons in a much lower station of life than any I have quoted as specimens of society in America.

But on the subject treated in the present chapter, justice compels me to avow that no such pleading can avail me.

That such fearful profanation of the holy name of religion has rapidly increased among us since the year 1827, in which I quitted England for America, is most sadly certain, and may account for its exhibition being as new to me, as it was painful. The want of a national church, and of that guardian protection which its episcopal authority seems to promise against its desecration by the ever-varying innovations of sectarian licence, appeared to account for all the profanations I witnessed. But this explanation fails me now.

more to comprehend. They enter all the cities, towns, and villages of the Union, in succession; I could not learn with sufficient certainty to repeat, what the interval generally is between their visits. These itinerants are, for the most part, lodged in the houses of their respective followers, and every evening that is not spent in the churches and meeting-houses, is devoted to what would be called parties by others, but which they designate as prayer meetings. Here they eat, drink, pray, sing, hear confessions, and make converts. To these meetings I never got invited, and therefore I have nothing but hear-say evidence to offer, but my information comes from an eye-witness, and one on whom I believe I may depend. If one half of what I heard may be believed, these social prayer meetings are by no means the most [least] curious, or the least important part of the business.

It is impossible not to smile at the close resemblance to be traced between the feelings of a first-rate Presbyterian or Methodist lady, fortunate enough to have secured a favourite Itinerant for her meeting, and those of a first-rate London Blue, equally blest in the presence of a fashionable poet. There is a strong family likeness among us all the world over.

The best rooms, the best dresses, the choicest refreshments solemnize the meeting. While the party is assembling, the load-star of the hour is occupied in whispering conversations with the guests as they arrive. They are called brothers and sisters, and the greetings are very affectionate. When the room is full, the company, of whom a vast majority are always women, are invited, intreated, and coaxed to confess before their brothers and sisters, all their thoughts, faults, and follies.

These confessions are strange scenes; the more they confess, the more invariably are they encouraged and caressed. When this is over, they all kneel, and the Itinerant prays extempore. They then eat and drink; and then they sing hymns, pray, exhort, sing, and pray again, till the excitement reaches a very high pitch indeed. These scenes are going on at some house or other every evening during the revival, nay, at many at the same time, for the churches and meeting-houses cannot give occupation to half the Itinerants, though they are all open throughout the day, and till a late hour in the night, and the officiating ministers succeed each other in the occupation of them.

It was at the principal of the Presbyterian churches that I was twice witness to scenes that made me shudder; in describing one, I describe both, and every one; the same thing is constantly repeated.

It was in the middle of summer, but the service we were recommended to attend did not begin till it was dark. The church was well lighted, and crowded almost to suffocation. On entering, we found three priests standing side by side, in a sort of tribune, placed where the altar usually is, handsomely fitted up with crimson curtains, and elevated about as high as our pulpits. We took our places in a pew close to the rail which surrounded it.

The priest who stood in the middle was praying; the prayer was extravagantly vehement, and offensively familiar in expression; when this ended, a hymn was sung, and then another priest took the centre place, and preached. The sermon had considerable eloquence, but of a frightful kind. The preacher described, with ghastly minuteness, the last feeble fainting moments of human life, and then the gradual progress of decay after death, which he followed through every process up to the last loathsome stage of decomposition. Suddenly changing his tone, which had been that of sober accurate description, into the shrill voice of horror, he bent forward his head, as if to gaze on some object beneath the pulpit. And as Rebecca made known to Ivanhoe what she saw through the window, so the preacher made known to us what he saw in the pit that seemed to open before him. The device was certainly a happy one for giving effect to his description of hell. No image that fire, flame, brimstone, molten lead, or red-hot pincers could supply; with flesh, nerves, and sinews quivering under them, was omitted. The perspiration ran in streams from the face of the preacher; his eyes rolled, his lips were covered with foam, and every feature had the deep expression of horror it would have borne, had he, in truth, been gazing at the scene he described. The acting was excellent. At length he gave a languishing look to his supporters on each side, as if to express his feeble state, and then sat down, and wiped the drops of agony from his brow.

The other two priests arose, and began to sing a hymn. It was some seconds before the congregation could join as usual; every up-turned face looked pale and horror struck. When the singing ended, another took the centre place, and began in a sort of coaxing affectionate tone, to ask the congregation if what their dear brother had spoken had reached their hearts? Whether they would avoid the hell he had made them see? "Come, then!" he continued, stretching out his arms towards them, "come to us, and tell us so, and we will make you see Jesus, the dear gentle Jesus, who shall save you from it. But you must come to him! You must not be ashamed to come to him! This night you shall tell him that you are not ashamed of him; we will make way for you; we will clear the bench for anxious sinners to sit upon. Come, then! come to the anxious bench, and we will shew you Jesus! Come! Come! Come!"

Again a hymn was sung, and while it continued, one of the three was employed in clearing one or two long benches that went across the rail, sending the people back to the lower part of the church. The singing ceased, and again the people were invited, and exhorted not to be ashamed of Jesus, but to put themselves upon "the anxious benches," and lay their heads on his bosom. "Once more we will sing," he concluded, "that we may give you time." And again they sung a hymn.

And now in every part of the church a movement was perceptible, slight at first, but by degrees becoming more decided.

Young girls arose, and sat down, and rose again; and then the pews opened, and several came tottering out, their hands clasped, their heads hanging on their bosoms, and every limb trembling, and still the hymn went on; but as the poor creatures approached the rail their sobs and groans became audible. They seated themselves on the "anxious benches;" the hymn ceased, and two of the three priests walked down from the tribune, and going, one to the right, and the other to the left, began whispering to the poor tremblers seated there. These whispers were inaudible to us, but the sobs and groans increased to a frightful excess. Young creatures, with features pale and distorted, fell on their knees on the pavement, and soon sunk forward on their faces; the most violent cries and shrieks followed, while from time to time a voice was heard in convulsive accents, exclaiming, "Oh Lord!" "Oh Lord Jesus!" "Help me, Jesus!" and the like.

Meanwhile the two priests continued to walk among them; they repeatedly mounted on the benches, and trumpet-mouthed proclaimed to the whole congregation, "the tidings of salvation," and then from every corner of the building arose in reply, short sharp cries of "Amen!" "Glory!" "Amen!" while the prostrate penitents continued to receive whispered comfortings, and from time to time a mystic caress. More than once I saw a young neck encircled by a reverend arm. Violent hysterics and convulsions seized many of them, and when the tumult was at the highest, the priest who remained above, again gave out a hymn as if to drown it.

It was a frightful sight to behold innocent young creatures, in the gay morning of existence, thus seized upon, horror struck, and rendered feeble and enervated for ever. One young girl, apparently not more than fourteen, was supported in the arms of another, some years older; her face was pale as death; her eyes wide open, and perfectly devoid of meaning; her chin and bosom wet with slaver; she had every appearance of idiotism. I saw a priest approach her, he took her delicate hand, "Jesus is with her! Bless the Lord!" he said, and passed on.

Did the men of America value their women as men ought to value their wives and daughters, would such scenes be permitted among them?

It is hardly necessary to say that all who obeyed the call to place themselves on the "anxious benches" were women, and by far the greater number, very young women. The congregation was, in general, extremely well dressed, and the smartest and most fashionable ladies of the town were there; during the whole revival the churches and meeting-houses were every day crowded with well dressed people.

It is thus the ladies of Cincinnati amuse themselves; to attend the theatre is forbidden; to play cards is unlawful; but they work hard in their families, and must have some relaxation. For myself, I confess that I think the coarsest comedy ever written would be a less detestable exhibition for the eyes of youth and innocence than such a scene.

CHAPTER IX

Schools — Climate — Water Melons — Fourth of July — Storms —
Pigs — Moving Houses — Mr. Flint — Literature

CINCINNATI contains many schools, but of their rank or merit I had very little opportunity of judging; the only one which I visited was kept by Dr. Lock, a gentleman who appears to have liberal and enlarged opinions on the subject of female education.[1] Should his system produce practical results proportionably excellent, the ladies of Cincinnati will probably some years hence be much improved in their powers of companionship. I attended the annual public exhibition at this school, and perceived, with some surprise, that the higher branches of science were among the studies of the pretty creatures I saw assembled there. One lovely girl of sixteen *took her degree* in mathematics, and another was examined in moral philosophy. They blushed so sweetly, and looked so beautifully puzzled and confounded, that it might have been difficult for an abler judge than I was to decide how far they merited the diploma they received.

This method of letting young ladies graduate, and granting them diplomas on quitting the establishment, was quite new to me; at least, I do not remember to have heard of any thing similar elsewhere. I should fear that the time allowed to the fair

---

[1] [DS] Dr. John Locke (1792–1856) was a New Englander by birth and a graduate of Yale College. He had failed in the practice of medicine before he took a position as a teacher in a school for young women at Windsor, Vermont. In 1822 he came to Cincinnati and established Locke's Female Academy, which had a high reputation in the West for many years. Probably Mrs. Trollope's two daughters, Emily and Cecilia, attended this school while they remained at Cincinnati. Locke was a pioneer in the teaching of science; he also carried on scientific investigations of his own, especially in regard to the nature of magnetism, and made several trips to Europe to keep abreast of new developments.

graduates of Cincinnati for the acquirement of these various branches of education would seldom be sufficient to permit their reaching the eminence in each which their enlightened instructor anticipates. "A quarter's" mathematics, or "two quarters'" political economy, moral philosophy, algebra, and quadratic equations, would seldom, I should think, enable the teacher and the scholar, by their joint efforts, to lay in such a stock of these sciences as would stand the wear and tear of half a score of children, and one help.

*   *   *   *   *   *

Towards the end of May we began to feel that we were in a climate warmer than any we had been accustomed to, and my son suffered severely from the effects of it. A bilious complaint, attended by a frightful degree of fever, seized him, and for some days we feared for his life. The treatment he received was, I have no doubt, judicious, but the quantity of calomel prescribed was enormous. I asked one day how many grains I should prepare, and was told to give half a teaspoonful. The difference of climate must, I imagine, make a difference in the effect of this drug, or the practice of the old and new world could hardly differ so widely as it does in the use of it. Anstey, speaking of the Bath physicians, says,

> "No one e'er viewed
> Any one of the medical gentlemen stewed." [2]

---

[2] [DS] Christopher Anstey in *The New Bath Guide . . . a Series of Poetical Epistles* (1766) remarks upon the failure of doctors to take the curative waters that they prescribe for their patients:

> *Though some think the lawyer may choose to* demur,
> *And the priest till another occasion* defer;
> *And both, to be better prepared for herea'ter,*
> *Take a smack of the brimstone contained in the water,*
> *But, what is surprising, no mortal e'er view'd*
> *Any one of the physical gentlemen stewed;*
> *Since the day that King Blodud first found out these bogs,*
> *And thought them so good for himself and his hogs,*
> *Not one of the faculty ever has tried*
> *These excellent waters to cure his own hide. . . .*

But I can vouch, upon my own experience, that no similar imputation lies against the gentlemen who prescribe large quantities of calomel in America. To give one instance in proof of this, when I was afterwards in Montgomery county, near Washington, a physician attended one of our neighbours, and complained that he was himself unwell. "You must take care of yourself, Doctor," said the patient; "I do so," he replied, "I took forty grains of calomel yesterday, and I feel better than I did." Repeated and violent bleeding was also had recourse to in the case of my son, and in a few days he was able to leave his room, but he was dreadfully emaciated, and it was many weeks before he recovered his strength.

As the heat of the weather increased we heard of much sickness around us. The city is full of physicians, and they were all to be seen driving about in their cabs at a very alarming rate. One of these gentlemen told us, that when a medical man intended settling in a new situation, he always, if he knew his business, walked through the streets at night, before he decided. If he saw the dismal twinkle of the watchlight from many windows he might be sure that disease was busy, and that the "location" might suit him well. Judging, by this criterion, Cincinnati was far from healthy, I began to fear for our health, and determined to leave the city; but, for a considerable time I found it impossible to procure a dwelling out of it. There were many boarding-houses in the vicinity, but they were all overflowing with guests. We were advised to avoid, as much as possible, walking out in the heat of the day;

The doctors of Western America depended a great deal upon calomel and blood-letting as cures for the fever. Some doctors prescribed as much as one hundred grains of calomel for a single dose, and there is a record of one doctor who gave a cholera patient a pound in one day without fatal effect. Frequent and heavy dosage sometimes caused the patient's gums to soften and his teeth to fall out. A ballad of eleven stanzas recites the "dier effects" of the drug; it ends:

> And when I must Resign my breath
> Pray let me die a natural death
> And bid you all a long farewell
> Without one dose of Calomel.

but the mornings and evenings were delightful, particularly
the former, if taken sufficiently early. For several weeks I was
never in bed after four o'clock, and at this hour I almost daily
accompanied my "help" to market, where the busy novelty of
the scene afforded me much amusement.

Many waggon-loads of enormous water-melons were
brought to market every day, and I was sure to see groups
of men, women, and children seated on the pavement round
the spot where they were sold, sucking in prodigious quantities of this watery fruit. Their manner of devouring them is
extremely unpleasant; the huge fruit is cut into half a dozen
sections, of about a foot long, and then, dripping as it is with
water, applied to the mouth, from either side of which pour
copious streams of the fluid, while, ever and anon, a mouthful
of the hard black seeds are shot out in all directions, to the
great annoyance of all within reach. When I first tasted this
fruit I thought it very vile stuff indeed, but before the end of
the season we all learned to like it. When taken with claret
and sugar it makes delicious wine and water.

It is the custom for the gentlemen to go to market at Cincinnati; the smartest men in the place, and those of the
"highest standing" do not scruple to leave their beds with the
sun, six days in the week, and, prepared with a mighty basket, to sally forth in search of meat, butter, eggs, and vegetables. I have continually seen them returning, with their
weighty basket on one arm and an enormous ham depending
from the other.[3]

[3] [TRD] Meantime the lady wife at home, has either to wash her numerous progeny, or present them at the breakfast table unwashed — then to
make the coffee, fry ham and beef steaks plus onions, make and bake hot
rolls, besides preparing a few *et cæteras* of corn dodgers, johnny cakes, and
waffles. All this, and often more, the silk and lace, the feather and flower
wearer of the evening before, is expected to perform; for "her help," if indeed she be so blest as to have one, is just washing the linen, or just scrubbing the "keeping room" or just scouring the pots and kettles; or she may
be employed, just as the annexed drawing represents her, eating a piece of
water melon, that she has successfully scrambled for, with the children.
[The drawing was never printed.]

And now arrived the 4th of July, that greatest of all American festivals. On the 4th of July, 1776, the declaration of their independence was signed, at the State-house in Philadelphia.

To me, the dreary coldness and want of enthusiasm in American manners is one of their greatest defects, and I therefore hailed the demonstrations of general feeling which this day elicits with real pleasure. On the 4th of July the hearts of the people seem to awaken from a three hundred and sixty-four days' sleep; they appear high-spirited, gay, animated, social, generous, or at least liberal in expense; and would they but refrain from spitting on that hallowed day, I should say, that on the 4th of July, at least, they appeared to be an amiable people. It is true that the women have but little to do with the pageantry, the splendour, or the gaiety of the day; but, setting this defect aside, it was indeed a glorious sight to behold a jubilee so heartfelt as this; [4] and had they

---

[4] [DS] An early Cincinnati Fourth of July is described in the *Chronicle* for July 7, 1827:

"The fifty-first anniversary of American Independence was celebrated in this city on Wednesday last, with the usual ceremonies. The procession, composed of the volunteer military corps, some of the mechanical societies, and citizens, was formed at the foot of Broadway, and about 12 o'clock passed down Front and up Main street to the First Presbyterian church. — After a prayer by the Rev. J. Lyon, a revolutionary soldier, which was followed by an appropriate Oration, very handsomely delivered by Robert T. Lytle Esq. The audience was large and respectable. Major General Brown, and several other officers of the army were present. In the evening the public Gardens, the Theatre and the Museums were visited by a large concourse of citizens. Nothing occurred to mar the general order and harmony of the day."

But spitting was not the only vice that sometimes marred such occasions if we judge from an editorial in the *Chronicle* just before the Fourth of July two years later:

"We recommend to our citizens generally, the suppression, on that day, of all party feelings and animosity; the observance of order, decorum, and *temperance*. In regard to this last matter, we can assure those who are not already apprized of the fact, that public sentiment does not, at the present day, require that a man should get intoxicated to show his patriotism, on the *fourth of July*. Such has been the change of opinion, on this subject, that we feel warranted in saying that a man's *love of country* will not be seriously

not the bad taste and bad feeling to utter an annual oration, with unvarying abuse of the mother country, to say nothing of the warlike manifesto called the Declaration of Independence, our gracious king himself might look upon the scene and say that it was good; nay, even rejoice, that twelve millions of bustling bodies, at four thousand miles distance from his throne and his altars, should make their own laws, and drink their own tea, after the fashion that pleased them best.

*   *   *   *   *   *

One source of deep interest to us, in this new clime, was the frequent recurrence of thunder-storms. Those who have only listened to thunder in England have but a faint idea of the language which the gods speak when they are angry. Thomson's description, however, will do: it is hardly possible that words can better paint the spectacle, or more truly echo to the sound, than his do.[5] The only point he does not reach is

---

questioned, though he should fail on Saturday next, to become *uproarious,* or omit his accustomed performance of serpentine evolutions in our streets."

[5] [DS] From "Summer" in James Thomson's *The Seasons* (1726–30):

> And following slower, in explosion vast,
> The thunder raises his tremendous voice.
> At first, heard solemn o'er the verge of heaven,
> The tempest growls; but as it nearer comes,
> And rolls its awful burden on the wind,
> The lightnings flash a larger curve, and more
> The noise astounds — till over head a sheet
> Of livid flame discloses wide, then shuts
> And opens wider, shuts and opens still
> Expansive, wrapping ether in a blaze.
> Follows the loosen'd aggravated roar,
> Enlarging, deepening, mingling, peal on peal
> Crush'd horrible, convulsing heaven and earth.
> . . . Amid Caernarvon's mountains rages loud
> The repercussive roar; with mighty crush,
> Into the flashing deep, from the rude rocks
> Of Penmaen Mawr heap'd hideous to the sky,
> Tumble the smitten cliffs; and Snowdon's peak,
> Dissolving, instant yields his wintry load.
> Far-seen, the heights of heathy Cheviot blaze,
> And Thulè bellows through her utmost isles.

the vast blaze of rose-coloured light that ever and anon sets the landscape on fire.

In reading this celebrated description in America, and observing how admirably true it was to nature there, I seemed to get a glimpse at a poet's machinery, and to perceive, that in order to produce effect he must give his images more vast than he finds them in nature; but the proportions must be just, and the colouring true. Every thing seems colossal on this great continent; if it rains, if it blows, if it thunders, it is all done *fortissimo;* but I often felt terror yield to wonder and delight, so grand, so glorious were the scenes a storm exhibited. Accidents are certainly more frequent than with us, but not so much so as reasonably to bring terror home to one's bosom every time a mass of lurid clouds is seen rolling up against the wind.

*   *   *   *   *   *

It seems hardly fair to quarrel with a place because its staple commodity is not pretty, but I am sure I should have liked Cincinnati much better if the people had not dealt so very largely in hogs. The immense quantity of business done in this line would hardly be believed by those who had not witnessed it. I never saw a newspaper without remarking such advertisements as the following:

"Wanted, immediately, 4,000 fat hogs."

"For sale, 2,000 barrels of prime pork."

But the annoyance came nearer than this; if I determined upon a walk up Main-street, the chances were five hundred to one against my reaching the shady side without brushing by a snout fresh dripping from the kennel; [6] when we had

---

6 [DS] From the journal of Cyrus P. Bradley, a young Dartmouth College student who visited Cincinnati in 1835:

"There is a good deal, far too much, of mud and dirt and stagnant water about the streets; if the cholera approaches, it will set them a scrubbing. Swine are here in abundance — to be expected in this vast pork market. Remembered Mrs. Trollope's amusing descriptions of her adventures with the

screwed our courage to the enterprise of mounting a certain noble-looking sugar-loaf hill, that promised pure air and a fine view, we found the brook we had to cross, at its foot, red with the stream from a pig slaughter-house; while our noses, instead of meeting "the thyme that loves the green hill's breast," were greeted by odours that I will not describe, and which I heartily hope my readers cannot imagine; our feet, that on leaving the city had expected to press the flowery sod, literally got entangled in pigs' tails and jawbones: and thus the prettiest walk in the neighbourhood was interdicted for ever.

*　　*　　*　　*　　*　　*

One of the sights to stare at in America is that of houses moving from place to place. We were often amused by watching this exhibition of mechanical skill in the streets. They make no difficulty of moving dwellings from one part of the town to another. Those I saw travelling were all of them frame-

---

hogs in the streets of Cincinnati. Perhaps they are not much exaggerated — for the beasts *are* impudent. They know enough to give way to a carriage, but as to a foot passenger he must always turn out; they won't budge an inch for a whole regiment, and no one wishes to come in contact with their filthiness. . . .

"But apropos of swine, it is giving them a grain too much liberty to allow of their running at large in the streets. In a morning paper I saw a notice of one of these ravenous beasts seizing a young child by the arm, tearing him from his mother's doorstep into the gutter, where, had it not been for the child's screams and the interference of a gentleman, he would inevitably have devoured it."

One more quotation, and from a different source:

". . . Take care of the pigs. Two portly sows are trotting up behind this carriage, and a select party of half-a-dozen gentlemen hogs have just now turned the corner. Here is a solitary swine lounging homeward by himself. . . . He is a free-and-easy, careless, indifferent kind of pig . . . turning up the news and small-talk of the city in the shape of cabbage-stalks and offal. . . . He is in every respect a republican pig, going wherever he pleases, and mingling with the best society, on an equal, if not superior footing, for every one makes way when he appears, and the haughtiest give him the wall, if he prefer it. . . . They are the city scavengers, these pigs." — Charles Dickens's description of Broadway, New York, in *American Notes* (1842).

houses, that is, built wholly of wood, except the chimneys; but it is said that brick buildings are sometimes treated in the same manner. The largest dwelling that I saw in motion was one containing two stories of four rooms each; forty oxen were yoked to it. The first few yards brought down the two stacks of chimneys, but it afterwards went on well. The great difficulties were the first getting it in motion and the stopping exactly in the right place. This locomotive power was extremely convenient at Cincinnati, as the constant improvements going on there made it often desirable to change a wooden dwelling for one of brick; and whenever this happened, we were sure to see the ex No. 100 of Main-street or the ex No. 55 of Second-street creeping quietly out of town, to take possession of a humble suburban station on the common above it.

*   *   *   *   *   *

The most agreeable acquaintance I made in Cincinnati, and indeed one of the most talented men I ever met, was Mr. Flint, the author of several extremely clever volumes, and the editor of the Western Monthly Review.[7] His conversational powers are of the highest order: he is the only person I remember to have known with first-rate powers of satire, and even of sarcasm, whose kindness of nature and of manner remained perfectly uninjured. In some of his critical notices there is a strength and keenness second to nothing of the kind I have ever read. He is a warm patriot, and so true-hearted an American, that we could not always be of the same opinion on all the subjects we discussed; but whether it were the force and brilliancy of his language, his genuine and manly sincerity of feeling, or his bland and gentleman-like manner that beguiled me, I know not, but certainly he is the only Ameri-

---

[7] [DS] An account of Timothy Flint, his acquaintance with Mrs. Trollope, and his somewhat acid description of her and her activities in Cincinnati is given in section VI of the Introduction.

can I ever listened to whose unqualified praise of his country did not appear to me somewhat overstrained and ridiculous.

On one occasion, but not at the house of Mr. Flint, I passed an evening in company with a gentleman said to be a scholar and a man of reading; he was also what is called a *serious* gentleman, and he appeared to have pleasure in feeling that his claim to distinction was acknowledged in both capacities. There was a very amiable *serious* lady in the company, to whom he seemed to trust for the development of his celestial pretensions, and to me he did the honour of addressing most of his terrestrial superiority. The difference between us was, that when he spoke to her, he spoke as to a being who, if not his equal, was at least deserving high distinction; and he gave her smiles, such as Michael might have vouchsafed to Eve. To me he spoke as Paul to the offending Jews; he did not, indeed, shake his raiment at me, but he used his pocket-handkerchief so as to answer the purpose; and if every sentence did not end with "I am clean," pronounced by his lips, his tone, his look, his action, fully supplied the deficiency.

Our poor Lord Byron, as may be supposed, was the bull's-eye against which every dart in his black little quiver was aimed. I had never heard any serious gentleman talk of Lord Byron at full length before, and I listened attentively. It was evident that the noble passages which are graven on the hearts of the genuine lovers of poetry had altogether escaped the serious gentleman's attention; and it was equally evident that he knew by rote all those that they wish the mighty master had never written. I told him so, and I shall not soon forget the look he gave me.

Of other authors his knowledge was very imperfect, but his criticisms very amusing. Of Pope, he said, "He is so entirely gone by, that in *our* country it is considered quite fustian to speak of him."

But I persevered, and named "the Rape of the Lock" as evincing some little talent, and being in a tone that might still hope for admittance in the drawing-room; but, on the mention of this poem, the serious gentleman became almost as strongly agitated as when he talked of Don Juan; and I was unfeignedly at a loss to comprehend the nature of his feelings, till he muttered, with an indignant shake of the handkerchief, "The very title!"

At the name of Dryden he smiled, and the smile spoke as plainly as a smile could speak, "How the old woman twaddles!"

"We only know Dryden by quotations, Madam, and these, indeed, are found only in books that have long since had their day."

"And Shakspeare, sir?"

"Shakspeare, Madam, is obscene, and, thank God, WE are sufficiently advanced to have found it out! If we must have the abomination of stage plays, let them at least be marked by the refinement of the age in which we live."

This was certainly being *au courant du jour*.

Of Massenger he knew nothing. Of Ford he had never heard. Gray had had his day. Prior he had never read, but understood he was a very childish writer. Chaucer and Spenser he tied in a couple, and dismissed by saying, that he thought it was neither more nor less than affectation to talk of authors who wrote in a tongue no longer intelligible.

This was the most literary conversation I was ever present at in Cincinnati.[8]

In truth, there are many reasons which render a very general diffusion of literature impossible in America. I can scarcely class the universal reading of newspapers as an exception to this remark; if I could, my statement would be exactly the reverse, and I should say that America beat the world in letters. The fact is, that throughout all ranks of so-

---

[8] [T1] The pleasant, easy, unpretending talk on all subjects, which I enjoyed in Mr. Flint's family, was an exception to every thing else I met at Cincinnati.

ciety, from the successful merchant, which is the highest, to
the domestic serving man, which is the lowest, they are all
too actively employed to read, except at such broken moments as may suffice for a peep at a newspaper. It is for this
reason, I presume, that every *American newspaper* is more
or less a magazine, wherein the merchant may scan while he
holds out his hand for an invoice, "Stanzas by Mrs. Hemans,"
or a garbled extract from Moore's Life of Byron; the lawyer
may study his brief faithfully, and yet contrive to pick up the
valuable dictum of some American critic, that "Bulwer's
novels are decidedly superior to Sir Walter Scott's;" nay, even
the auctioneer may find time, as he bustles to his tub, or his
tribune, to support his pretensions to polite learning, by
glancing his quick eye over the columns, and reading that
"Miss Mitford's descriptions are indescribable." If you buy a
yard of ribbon, the shop-keeper lays down his newspaper,
perhaps two or three, to measure it. I have seen a brewer's
dray-man perched on the shaft of his dray and reading one
newspaper, while another was tucked under his arm; and I
once went into the cottage of a country shoe-maker, of the
name of Harris, where I saw a newspaper half full of "original" poetry, directed to Madison F. Harris. To be sure of the
fact, I asked the man if his name were Madison. "Yes, Madam,
Madison Franklin Harris is my name." The last and the lyre
divided his time, I fear too equally, for he looked pale and
poor.

This, I presume, is what is meant by the general diffusion
of knowledge, so boasted of in the United States; such as it is,
the diffusion of it is general enough, certainly; but I greatly
doubt its being advantageous to the population.

The only reading men I met with were those who made
letters their profession; and of these, there were some who
would hold a higher rank in the great Republic (not of America, but of letters), did they write for persons less given to
the study of magazines and newspapers; and they might hold

a higher rank still, did they write for the few and not for the many. I was always drawing a parallel, perhaps a childish one, between the external and internal deficiency of polish and of elegance in the native volumes of the country.[9] Their compositions have not that condensation of thought, or that elaborate finish, which the consciousness of writing for the scholar and the man of taste is calculated to give; nor have their dirty blue paper and slovenly types [10] the polished elegance that fits a volume for the hand or the eye of the fastidious epicure in literary enjoyment. The first book I bought in America was the "Chronicles of the Cannongate." On asking the price, I was agreeably surprised to hear a dollar and a half named, being about one sixth of what I used to pay for its fellows in England; but on opening the grim pages, it was long before I could again call them cheap. To be sure the pleasure of a bright well-printed page ought to be quite lost sight of in the glowing, galloping, bewitching course that the imagination sets out upon with a new Waverley novel; and so it was with me till I felt the want of it; and then I am almost ashamed to confess how often, in turning the thin dusky pages, my poor earth-born spirit paused in its pleasure, to sigh for hot-pressed wire-wove.

---

[9] [T5, note] That the compositions of Dr. Chan[n]ing are a brilliant exception to this remark need hardly be stated; except by the occasional (and rare) use of a few words not familiar to us in the sense in which he employs them, his writings may stand a comparison with almost any in the English language.

[10] [T1] I must make an exception in favour of the American Quarterly Review. To the eye of the body it is in all respects exactly the same thing as the English Quarterly Review.

CHAPTER X

Removal to the country — Walk in the forest — Equality

AT length my wish of obtaining a house in the country was gratified. A very pretty cottage, the residence of a gentleman who was removing into town, for the convenience of his business as a lawyer,[1] was to let, and I immediately secured it. It was situated in a little village about a mile and a half from the town, close to the foot of the hills formerly mentioned as the northern boundary of it. We found ourselves much more comfortable here than in the city. The house was pretty and commodious, our sitting-rooms were cool and airy; we had got rid of the detestable mosquitoes, and we had an ice-house that never failed. Besides all this, we had the pleasure of gathering our tomatoes from our own garden, and receiving our milk from our own cow. Our manner of life was infinitely more to my taste than before; it gave us all the privileges of rusticity, which are fully as incompatible with a residence in a little town of Western America as with a residence in London. We lived on terms of primæval intimacy with our cow, for if we lay down on our lawn she did not scruple to take a sniff at the book we were reading, but then she gave us her own sweet breath in re-

---

[1] [DS] Major Daniel Gano, Mrs. Trollope's landlord, must have presented a striking appearance even for 1828:

"He was distinguished for wearing a large perfectly white, cambric ruffle, down the open bosom of his shirt adorned with a beautiful breastpin, and the *old fashioned Revolutionary* plaited cue of his hair, tied with black ribbon in a bow, and hanging down his back between his shoulders; and even for modern times, he never gave it up, and retained, in his toilet this mark of the old Revolutionary forefathers of this country, to the day of his shroud and coffin." — Judge Carter: *The Old Court House: Reminiscences and Anecdotes* (Cincinnati, 1880).

turn.[2] The verge of the cool-looking forest that rose opposite
our windows was so near, that we often used it as an extra
drawing-room, and there was no one to wonder if we went
out with no other preparation than our parasols, carrying
books and work enough to while away a long summer day in
the shade; the meadow that divided us from it was covered
with a fine short grass, that continued for a little way under
the trees, making a beautiful carpet, while sundry logs and
stumps furnished our sofas and tables. But even this was not
enough to satisfy us when we first escaped from the city, and
we determined upon having a day's enjoyment of the wildest
forest scenery we could find. So we packed up books, albums,
pencils, and sandwiches, and, despite a burning sun, dragged
up a hill so steep that we sometimes fancied we could rest
ourselves against it by only leaning forward a little. In panting and in groaning we reached the top, hoping to be refreshed by the purest breath of heaven; but to have tasted the
breath of heaven we must have climbed yet farther, even to
the tops of the trees themselves, for we soon found that the
air beneath them stirred not, nor ever had stirred, as it
seemed to us, since first it settled there, so heavily did it
weigh upon our lungs.

---

[2] [DS] At least some American readers of *Domestic Manners* thought
this sentence especially noteworthy, for the following letter to the editor appears in the *Cincinnati Mirror* for November 2, 1833:

"TROLLOPE'S FOLLY

"Although the good people of Cincinnati appear disposed to bear the
strictures and calumnies of Mrs. Trollope with all commendable patience and
submission, yet, Messrs. Editors, I am happy to hear, that a volume is in
progress with the above title, which will contain a brief review of Mrs. Trollope's domestic manners, and will be embellished or rather illustrated with
a north and south view of the Bazaar, otherwise called Trollope's Folly; together with some enlarged sketches from Johnston's scrap-book, and an original drawing, illustrative of a passage in page 90 of her book, where she observes, 'We lived on terms of primeval intimacy with our cow; for if we lay
down on our lawn, she did not scruple to take a sniff at the book we were
reading.' "

Apparently the book was never published; I have found no other allusion to it.

Still we were determined to enjoy ourselves, and forward we went, crunching knee deep through aboriginal leaves, hoping to reach some spot less perfectly air-tight than our landing-place. Wearied with the fruitless search, we decided on reposing awhile on the trunk of a fallen tree; being all considerably exhausted, the idea of sitting down on this tempting log was conceived and executed simultaneously by the whole party, and the whole party sunk together through its treacherous surface into a mass of rotten rubbish that had formed part of the pith and marrow of the eternal forest a hundred years before.

We were by no means the only sufferers by the accident; frogs, lizards, locusts, katiedids, beetles, and hornets, had the whole of their various tenements disturbed, and testified their displeasure very naturally by annoying us as much as possible in return; we were bit, we were stung, we were scratched; and when, at last, we succeeded in raising ourselves from the venerable ruin, we presented as woeful a spectacle as can well be imagined. We shook our (not ambrosial) garments, and panting with heat, stings, and vexation, moved a few paces from the scene of our misfortune, and again sat down; but this time it was upon the solid earth.

We had no sooner began to "chew the cud" of the bitter fancy that had beguiled us to these mountain solitudes than a new annoyance assailed us. A cloud of mosquitoes gathered round, and while each sharp proboscis sucked our blood, they teased us with their humming chorus, till we lost all patience, and started again on our feet, pretty firmly resolved never to try the *al fresco* joys of an American forest again. The sun was now in its meridian splendour, but our homeward path was short, and down hill, so again packing up our preparations for felicity, we started homeward, or, more properly speaking, we started, for in looking for an agreeable spot in this dungeon forest we had advanced so far from the verge of the hill that we had lost all trace of the precise spot where we had entered it. Nothing was to be seen but multitudes of tall, slender, melancholy stems, as like as peas, and standing within a foot of each other. The ground, as far as the eye could reach (which certainly was not far), was covered with an unvaried bed of dried leaves; no trace, no track, no trail, as Mr. Cooper would call it, gave us a hint which way to turn; and having paused for a moment to meditate, we remembered that chance must decide for us at last, so we set forward, in no very good mood, to encounter new misfortunes. We walked about a quarter of a mile, and coming to a steep descent, we thought ourselves extremely fortunate, and began to scramble down, nothing doubting that it was the same we had scrambled up. In truth, nothing could be more like, but, alas! things that are like are not the same; when we had slipped and stumbled down to the edge of the wood, and were able to look beyond it, we saw no pretty cottage with the shadow of its beautiful acacias coming forward to meet us: all was different; and, what was worse, all was distant from the spot where we had hoped to be. We had come down the opposite side of the ridge, and had now to win our weary way a distance of three miles round its base. I believe we shall none of us ever forget that walk. The bright, glowing, furnace-like heat of the atmosphere seems to scorch as I recal it. It was painful to tread, it was painful to breathe, it was painful to look round; every object glowed with the reflection of the fierce tyrant that glared upon us from above.

We got home alive, which agreeably surprised us; and when our parched tongues again found power of utterance, we promised each other faithfully never to propose any more parties of pleasure in the grim stove-like forests of Ohio.

We were now in daily expectation of the arrival of Mr. T.; but day after day, and week after week passed by, till we began to fear some untoward circumstance might delay his coming till the Spring; at last, when we had almost ceased to look out for him, on the road which led from the town, he arrived, late at night, by that which leads across the country from Pitzburgh. The pleasure we felt at seeing him was greatly increased by his bringing with him our eldest son, which was a happiness we had not hoped for. Our walks and our drives now became doubly interesting. The young men, fresh from a public school, found America so totally unlike all the nations with which their reading had made them acquainted, that it was indeed a new world to them. Had they visited Greece or Rome they would have encountered objects with whose images their minds had been long acquainted; or had they travelled to France or Italy they would have seen only what daily conversation had already rendered familiar; but at our public schools America (except perhaps as to her geographical position) is hardly better known than Fairy Land; and the American character has not been much more deeply studied than that of the Anthropophagi: all, therefore, was new, and every thing amusing.

The extraordinary familiarity of our poor neighbours startled us at first, and we hardly knew how to receive their uncouth advances, or what was expected of us in return; however, it sometimes produced very laughable scenes. Upon one occasion two of my children set off upon an exploring walk up the hills; they were absent rather longer than we expected, and the rest of our party determined upon going out to meet them; we knew the direction they had taken, but thought it would be as well to enquire at a little public-house at the bottom of the hill, if such a pair had been seen to pass. A woman, whose appearance more resembled a Covent Garden market-woman than any thing else I can remember, came out and answered my question with the most jovial good humour in the affirmative, and prepared to join us in our search. Her look, her voice, her manner, were so exceedingly coarse and vehement, that she almost frightened me; she passed her arm within mine, and to the inexpressible amusement of my young people, she dragged me on, talking and questioning me without ceasing. She lived but a short distance from us, and I am sure intended to be a very good neighbour; but her violent intimacy made me dread to pass her door; my children, including my sons, she always addressed by their Christian names, excepting when she substituted the word "honey;" this familiarity of address, however, I afterwards found was universal throughout all ranks in the United States.

My general appellation amongst my neighbours was "the English old woman," but in mentioning each other they constantly employed the term "lady;" and they evidently had a pleasure in using it, for I repeatedly observed, that in speaking of a neighbour, instead of saying Mrs. Such-a-one, they described her as "the lady over the way what takes in washing," or as "that there lady, out by the Gulley, what is making dip-candles." Mr. Trollope was as constantly called "the old man," while draymen, butchers' boys, and the labourers on the canal were invariably denominated "them gentlemen;" nay, we once saw one of the most gentlemanlike men in Cincinnati introduce a fellow in dirty shirt sleeves, and all sorts of detestable et cetera, to one of his friends, with this formula, "D***** let me introduce this gentleman to you."

Our respective titles certainly were not very important; but the eternal shaking hands with these ladies and gentlemen was really an annoyance, and the more so, as the near approach of the gentlemen was always redolent of whiskey and tobacco.

But the point where this republican equality was the most distressing was in the long and frequent visitations that it produced. No one dreams of fastening a door in Western America; I was told that it would be considered as an affront by the whole neighbourhood. I was thus exposed to perpetual, and most vexatious interruptions from people whom I had often never seen, and whose names still oftener were unknown to me.

Those who are native there, and to the manner born, seem to pass over these annoyances with more skill than I could ever acquire. More than once I have seen some of my acquaintance beset in the same way, without appearing at all distressed by it; they continued their employment or conversation with me, much as if no such interruption had taken place; when the visitor entered, they would say, "How do you do?" and shake hands.

"Tolerable, I thank ye, how be you?" was the reply.

If it was a female, she took off her hat; if a male, he kept it on, and then taking possession of the first chair in their way, they would retain it for an hour together, without uttering another word; at length, rising abruptly, they would again shake hands, with, "Well, now I must be going, I guess," and so take themselves off, apparently well contented with their reception.

I could never attain this philosophical composure; I could neither write nor read, and I always fancied I must talk to them. I will give the minutes of a conversation which I once set down after one of their visits, as a specimen of their tone and manner of speaking and thinking. My visitor was a milkman.

"Well now, so you be from the old country? Ay — you'll see sights here, I guess."

"I hope I shall see many."

"That's a fact. I expect your little place of an island don't grow such dreadful fine corn as you sees here?"

"It grows no corn at all, sir." [3]

" Possible! no wonder, then, that we reads such awful stories in the papers of your poor people being starved to death."

"We have wheat, however."

"Ay, for your rich folks, but I calculate the poor seldom gets a belly full."

---

[3] [T1] *Corn* always means Indian corn, or maize.

"You have certainly much greater abundance here."

"I expect so. Why they do say, that if a poor body contrives to be smart enough to scrape together a few dollars, that your King George always comes down upon 'em, and takes it all away. Don't he?"

"I do not remember hearing of such a transaction."

"I guess they be pretty close about it. Your papers ben't like ourn, I reckon? Now we says and prints just what we likes."

"You spend a good deal of time in reading the newspapers." [4]

"And I'd like you to tell me how we can spend it better. How should freemen spend their time, but looking after their government, and watching that them fellers as we gives offices to, doos their duty, and gives themselves no airs?"

"But I sometimes think, sir, that your fences might be in more thorough repair, and your roads in better order, if less time was spent in politics."

"The Lord! to see how little you knows of a free country! Why, what's the smoothness of a road, put against the freedom of a free-born American? And what does a broken zigzag signify, comparable to knowing that the men what we have been pleased to send up to Congress, speaks handsome and straight, as we chooses they should?" [5]

---

[4] [T5, note] Here, again, I fear I must allow that the ten years which have passed over us have been sufficient to destroy the characteristic and national poignancy of this description. If the reading-rooms of the rich throughout the Union have during this period increased their collections of European literature, the beer houses of England have in a tenfold ratio multiplied their half-penny newspapers — nor can the presses of the republic any longer consider themselves as distinguished by the licence boasted of by my friend the milkman, of "printing just what they likes." Indeed, if recent reports be true, this doubtful blessing has crossed the Atlantic, and abides now solely and wholly in Great Britain.

[5] [T5, note] This too, is now, at least, as much English as American. Having imported so largely before the introduction of steam, what may we not expect after it? Some projectors go so far as to predict that in the course of time, or perhaps, when the hoped-for establishment of balloons is fully organised, we shall have a President sent over by way of an experiment.

"It is from a sense of duty, then, that you all go to the liquor store to read the papers?"

"To be sure it is, and he'd be no true born American as didn't. I don't say that the father of a family should always be after liquor, but I do say that I'd rather have my son drunk three times in a week, than not look after the affairs of his country."

*   *   *   *   *   *

Our autumn walks were delightful; the sun ceased to scorch; the want of flowers was no longer peculiar to Ohio; and the trees took a colouring, which in richness, brilliance, and variety, exceeded all description. I think it is the maple, or sugar-tree, that first sprinkles the forest with rich crimson; the beech follows, with all its harmony of golden tints, from pale yellow up to brightest orange. The dog-wood gives almost the purple colour of the mulberry; the chesnut softens all with its frequent mass of delicate brown, and the sturdy oak carries its deep green into the very lap of winter. These tints are too bright for the landscape painter; the attempt to follow nature in an American autumn scene must be abortive. The colours are in reality extremely brilliant, but the medium through which they are seen increases the effect surprisingly. Of all the points in which America has the advantage of England, the one I felt most sensibly was the clearness and brightness of the atmosphere. By day and by night this exquisite purity of air gives tenfold beauty to every object. I could hardly believe the stars were the same; the Great Bear looked like a constellation of suns; and Jupiter justified all the fine things said of him in those beautiful lines, from I know not what spirited pen, beginning,

> "I looked on thee, Jove! till my gaze
> Shrunk, smote by the pow'r of thy blaze." [6]

[6] [T5, note] As I have never been able to discover the author of these lines, nor to meet with them any where, except in the Bristol newspaper (the

I always remarked that the first silver line of the moon's crescent attracted the eye on the first day, in America, as strongly as it does here on the third. I observed another phenomenon in the crescent moon of that region, the cause of which I less understood. That appearance which Shakspeare describes as "the new moon, with the old moon in her lap," [7] and which I have heard ingeniously explained as the effect of *earth light*, was less visible there than here.

Cuyp's clearest landscapes have an atmosphere that approaches nearer to that of America than any I remember on canvas; but even Cuyp's *air* cannot reach the lungs, and, therefore, can only give an idea of half the enjoyment; for it makes itself felt as well as seen, and is indeed a constant source of pleasure.

Our walks were, however, curtailed in several directions

Mercury), from whence I copied them, I think I shall do my readers a benefit if I transcribe them here.

TO THE PLANET JUPITER
"I look'd on thee, Jove! till my gaze
Shrunk, smote by the power of thy blaze,
For in heaven, from the sunset's red throne
To the zenith, thy rival was none.
From thy orb rush'd a torrent of light,
That made the stars dim in thy sight;
And the half-risen moon seem'd to die,
And leave thee the realm of the sky.
I look'd on the ocean's broad breast,
The purple was pale in the west;
But down shot thy long silver spire,
And the waves were like arrows of fire.
I turn'd from the infinite main,
Thy light was the light of the plain;
'T was the beacon that blazed on the hill,
Thou wert proud, pure, magnificent, still.
A cloud spread its wing over heaven,
By the light of thy splendor 't was riven;
And I saw thy bright front through it shine
Like a god from the depth of his shrine!"

[7] [DS] The concordances list no such line in Shakespeare. Apparently Mrs. Trollope is thinking of the ballad "Sir Patrick Spens":
Late, late yestreen I saw the new moone,
Wi the auld moone in hir arme,
And I feir, I feir, my deir master,
That we will cum to harme.

by my old Cincinnati enemies, the pigs; immense droves of them were continually arriving from the country by the road that led to most of our favourite walks; they were often fed and lodged in the prettiest valleys, and worse still, were slaughtered beside the prettiest streams. Another evil threatened us from the same quarter, that was yet heavier. Our cottage had an ample piazza, (a luxury almost universal in the country houses of America), which, shaded by a group of acacias, made a delightful sitting-room; from this favourite spot we one day perceived symptoms of building in a field close to it; with much anxiety we hastened to the spot, and asked what building was to be erected there.

" 'Tis to be a slaughter-house for hogs," was the dreadful reply. As there were several gentlemen's houses in the neighbourhood, I asked if such an erection might not be indicted as a nuisance.

"A what?"

"A nuisance," I repeated, and explained what I meant.

"No, no," was the reply, "that may do very well for your tyrannical country, where a rich man's nose is more thought of than a poor man's mouth; but hogs be profitable produce here, and we be too free for such a law as that, I guess."

During my residence in America, little circumstances like the foregoing often recalled to my mind a conversation I once held in France with an old gentleman on the subject of their active police, and its omnipresent gens d'armerie; "Croyez moi, Madame, il n'y a que ceux, à qui ils ont à faire, qui les trouvent de trop." [8] And the old gentleman was right, not only in speaking of France, but of the whole human family, as philosophers call us. The well disposed, those whose own feeling of justice would prevent their annoying others, will never complain of the restraints of the law. All the freedom enjoyed in America, beyond what is enjoyed in England, is

---

[8] [DS] *"Croyez moi,"* etc.: "Believe me, madam, only the people they deal with think there are too many of them."

enjoyed solely by the disorderly at the expense of the orderly; and were I a stout knight, either of the sword or of the pen, I would fearlessly throw down my gauntlet, and challenge the whole Republic to prove the contrary; but being, as I am, a feeble looker on, with a needle for my spear, and "I talk" for my device, I must be contented with the power of stating the fact, perfectly certain that I shall be contradicted by one loud shout from Maine to Georgia.

CHAPTER XI

Religion

I HAD often heard it observed before I visited America, that one of the great blessings of its constitution was the absence of a national religion, the country being thus exonerated from all obligation of supporting the clergy; those only contributing to do so whose principles led them to it. My residence in the country has shewn me that a religious tyranny may be exerted very effectually without the aid of the government,[1] in a way much more oppressive than the paying of

_____

[1] [TN] I shall not expect to escape the charge of impossible exaggeration if I describe the species of petty persecution that I have seen exercised on religious subjects in America. The whole people appear to be divided into an almost endless variety of religious factions; I was told in Cincinnati that to be well received in society it was indispensably necessary to declare that you belonged to some one of these factions — it did not much matter which — as far as I could make out, the Methodists were considered as the most pious, the Presbyterians as the most powerful, the Episcopalians and the Catholics as the most genteel, the Universalists as the most liberal, the Swedenborgians as the most musical, the Unitarians as the most enlightened, the Quakers as the most amiable, the dancing Shakers the most amusing, and the Jews as the most interesting. Besides these there are dozens more of fancy religions whose designations I cannot remember, but declaring yourself to belong to any one of them as far as I could learn was sufficient to constitute you a respectable member of society. Having thus declared yourself, your next submission must be that of unqualified obedience to the will and pleasure of your elected pastor, or you will run a great risk of being "passed out of the church." This was a phrase that I perpetually heard, and upon enquiry I found that it did not mean being passed neck and heels out of the building at the discretion of the sexton, but a sort of congregational excommunication which infallibly betides those who venture to [do] any thing that their pastor and master disapproves. I once heard a lady say "I must not wear high bows on my bonnet, or I shall be passed out of our church" and another "I must not go to see the dancing at the theatre or I shall be passed out of our church" and another "I must not confess that I visit Mrs. J. or I shall be passed out of our church, for they say she does not belong to any church in the town." I think I am tolerant not only in religion but of all opinions that differ from my own, but this does not prevent my seeing

tithe, and without obtaining any of the salutary decorum, which I presume no one will deny is the result of an established mode of worship.

As it was impossible to remain many weeks in the country without being struck with the strange anomalies produced by its religious system, my early notes contain many observations on the subject; but as nearly the same scenes recurred in every part of the country, I state them here, not as belonging to the west alone, but to the whole Union, the same cause producing the same effect every where.

The whole people appear to be divided into an almost endless variety of religious factions, and I was told, that to be well received in society, it was necessary to declare yourself as belonging to some one of these. Let your acknowledged belief be what it may, you are said to be *not a Christian*, unless you attach yourself to a particular congregation. Besides the broad and well-known distinctions of Episcopalian, Catholic, Presbyterian, Calvinist, Baptist, Quaker, Swedenborgian, Universalist, Dunker, &c. &c. &c.; there are innumerable others springing out of these, each of which assumes a church government of its own; of this, the most intriguing and factious individual is invariably the head; and in order, as it should seem, to shew a reason for this separation, each congregation invests itself with some queer variety of external observance that has the melancholy effect of exposing *all* religious ceremonies to contempt.

It is impossible, in witnessing all these unseemly vagaries, not to recognise the advantages of an established church as a sort of head-quarters for quiet unpresuming Christians, who are contented to serve faithfully, without insisting upon having each a little separate banner, embroidered with a device of their own imagining.

----

that the end of true and rational religion is better obtained when the government of the church is confided to the hands of those who act in conformity & obedience to it.

The Catholics alone appear exempt from the fury of division and sub-division that has seized every other persuasion. Having the Pope for their common head, regulates, I presume, their movements, and prevents the outrageous display of individual whim which every other sect is permitted.

I had the pleasure of being introduced to the Catholic bishop of Cincinnati, and have never known in any country a priest of a character and bearing more truly apostolic.[2] He was an American, but I should never have discovered it from his pronunciation or manner. He received his education partly in England, and partly in France. His manners were highly polished; his piety active and sincere, and infinitely more mild and tolerant than that of the factious Sectarians who form the great majority of the American priesthood.

I believe I am sufficiently tolerant; but this does not prevent my seeing that the object of all religious observances is better obtained, when the government of the church is confided to the wisdom and experience of the most venerated among the people, than when it is placed in the hands of every tinker and tailor who chooses to claim a share in it. Nor is this the only evil attending the want of a national religion, supported by the State. As there is no legal and fixed provision for the clergy, it is hardly surprising that their services are confined to those who can pay them. The vehement

---

[2] [DS] The Right Reverend Edward Dominic Fenwick was born in Maryland in 1768. He studied in Belgium at the Dominican College of Bornheim and after his ordination remained there as a professor and administrator until the French Revolutionists invaded Belgium. He was thrown into prison, but was released and allowed to go on to England when he produced proofs that he was an American citizen. In England he entered a monastery of his order, but in 1805 he came to the United States with three other priests to introduce the Dominican Order in America. For some years he spent most of his waking hours on horseback traveling throughout the states of Ohio and Kentucky in his labors to establish the Roman Catholic Church in the West. He had already founded eight churches before he built Cincinnati's first Catholic church in 1819. During his later years he carried on much missionary work among the Indians, and it was on one of these visitations that he died of cholera in 1832.

expressions of insane or hypocritical zeal, such as were exhibited during "the Revival," can but ill atone for the want of village worship, any more than the eternal talk of the admirable and unequalled government, can atone for the continual contempt of social order. Church and State hobble along, side by side, notwithstanding their boasted independence. Almost every man you meet will tell you, that he is occupied in labours most abundant for the good of his country; and almost every woman will tell you, that besides those things that are within (her house) she has coming upon her daily the care of all the churches. Yet spite of this universal attention to the government, its laws are half asleep; and spite of the old women and their Dorcas societies, atheism is awake and thriving.

In the smaller cities and towns prayer-meetings take the place of almost all other amusements; but as the thinly scattered population of most villages can give no parties, and pay no priests, they contrive to marry, christen, and bury without them. A stranger taking up his residence in any city in America must think the natives the most religious people upon earth; but if chance lead him among her western villages, he will rarely find either churches or chapels, prayer or preacher; except, indeed, at that most terrific saturnalia, "a camp-meeting." I was much struck with the answer of a poor woman, whom I saw ironing on a Sunday. "Do you make no difference in your occupations on a Sunday?" I said. "I beant a Christian, Ma'am; we have got no opportunity," was the reply. It occurred to me, that in a country where "all men are equal," the government would be guilty of no great crime, did it so far interfere as to give them all *an opportunity* of becoming Christians if they wished it. But should the federal government dare to propose building a church, and endowing it, in some village that has never heard "the bringing home of bell and burial," it is perfectly certain that not only the sovereign state where such an abomination was proposed, would rush into the Congress to resent the odious interference, but that all the other states would join the clamour, and such an intermeddling administration would run great risk of impeachment and degradation.

Where there is a church-government so constituted as to deserve human respect, I believe it will always be found to receive it, even from those who may not assent to the dogma of its creed; and where such respect exists, it produces a decorum in manners and language often found wanting where it does not. Sectarians will not venture to rhapsodise, nor infidels to scoff, in the common intercourse of society. Both are injurious to the cause of rational religion, and to check both must be advantageous.

It is certainly possible that some of the fanciful variations upon the ancient creeds of the Christian Church, with which transatlantic religionists amuse themselves, might inspire morbid imaginations in Europe as well as in America; but before they can disturb the solemn harmony *here*, they must prelude by a defiance, not only to common sense, but what is infinitely more appalling, to common usage. They must at once rank themselves with the low and the illiterate, for only such prefer the eloquence of the tub to that of the pulpit. The aristocracy must ever, as a body,[3] belong to the established Church, and it is but a small proportion of the influential classes who would be willing to allow that they do not belong to the aristocracy. That such feelings influence the professions of men it were ignorance or hypocrisy to deny; and that nation is wise who knows how to turn even such feelings into a wholesome stream of popular influence.

As a specimen of the tone in which religion is mixed in the ordinary intercourse of society, I will transcribe the notes I took of a conversation, at which I was present, at Cincinnati; I wrote them immediately after the conversation took place.

---

[3] [T5, note] Vide recantation and apology in the note to chapter eight.

Dr. A.

"I wish, Mrs. M., that you would explain to me what a revival is. I hear it talked of all over the city, and I know it means something about Jesus Christ and religion; but that is all I know, will you instruct me farther?"

Mrs. M.

"I expect, Dr. A., that you want to laugh at me. But that makes no difference. I am firm in my principles, and I fear no one's laughter." [4]

[4] [DS] In Mrs. Trollope's rough draft the colloquy is longer by two passages, and additional characters speak. At this point Mr. B. breaks into the conversation:

"*Mr. B.:* Assuredly you are right, my dear madam. There can be nothing to fear in the laughter of those who differ from us in opinion. Perhaps you will laugh at me when I confess I do not believe in the devil?

"*Mrs. M.:* Indeed, Mr. B., I do not feel at all inclined to laugh."

Later, just after Mrs. A. declares that she has been brought up to consider the Bible nothing better than an old newspaper, there is a second and longer passage that Mrs. Trollope decided to leave out of her final manuscript:

"*Mrs. M.:* And I have been brought up to look upon it as the only light of life through Our Lord and Saviour Jesus Christ.

"*Mr. W.:* It is amusing enough, to be sure, to mark the variety of opinions we meet with. Why, there is my good little wife now, she thinks that being dipped in the river has washed away all her sins, and that to be a perfect saint it is only necessary to believe every syllable from the first of Genesis to the book of Revelations.

"*Mrs. V.:* Why, that is undertaking for a great work certainly. My father was a Presbyterian clergyman, but he never taught me to believe all the Bible. I no more believe that Jesus Christ is God, than I believe I am.

"*Mr. W.:* There are but few who do, I fancy, at present.

"*Mrs. M.:* I beg your pardon — every body does that has the grace of Our Lord Jesus Christ, and the help of the Holy Spirit.

"*Mr. J.:* Well, my good friends, I really feel some right to speak of things spiritual, for I began by being an Episcopal clergyman; I then took to the Calvinistic line; another year's reading and writing brought me to Universalism — and now I am where my reason has placed me, and the result of all my experience is to feel convinced that the Bible is good for nothing.

"*Mrs. M.:* And yet, Mr. J., it is certainly written by God himself.

"*Mr. J.:* I can only say, Mrs. M., that if you deem it proper to worship the author of that book, it is very lucky you are not my wife — for I most assuredly should not approve it."

Dr. A.

"Well, but what is a revival?"

Mrs. M.

"It is difficult, very difficult, to make those see who have no light; to make those understand whose souls are darkened. A revival means just an elegant kindling of the spirit; it is brought about to the Lord's people by the hands of his saints, and it means salvation in the highest."

Dr. A.

"But what is it the people mean by talking of feeling the revival? and waiting in spirit for the revival? and the extacy of the revival?"

Mrs. M.

"Oh Doctor! I am afraid that you are too far gone astray to understand all that. It is a glorious assurance, a whispering of the everlasting covenant, it is the bleating of the lamb, it is the welcome of the shepherd, it is the essence of love, it is the fulness of glory, it is being in Jesus, it is Jesus being in us, it is taking the Holy Ghost into our bosoms, it is sitting ourselves down by God, it is being called to the high places, it is eating, and drinking, and sleeping in the Lord, it is becoming a lion in the faith, it is being lowly and meek, and kissing the hand that smites, it is being mighty and powerful, and scorning reproof, it is — "

(The next three speeches in the book — those of Mrs. O., Mrs. A., and Dr. A. — do not appear in the rough draft. There are minor differences in wording throughout the colloquy.)

Mrs. Trollope probably heard a good deal of such talk at the home of Dr. and Mrs. William Price in Cincinnati. Thomas Adolphus Trollope tells us in his autobiography that the Doctor professed complete atheism and Mrs. Price was given to saying that he thought no more of the Bible than of an old newspaper. (See section VI of the Introduction to this edition.)

Dr. A.

"Thank you, Mrs. M., I feel quite satisfied; and I think I understand a revival now almost as well as you do yourself."

Mrs. A.

"My! Where can you have learnt all that stuff, Mrs. M.?"

Mrs. M.

"How benighted you are! From the holy book, from the Word of the Lord, from the Holy Ghost, and Jesus Christ themselves."

Mrs. A.

"It does seem so droll to me, to hear you talk of 'the Word of the Lord.' Why, I have been brought up to look upon the Bible as nothing better than an old newspaper."

Mrs. O.

"Surely you only say this for the sake of hearing what Mrs. M. will say in return — you do not mean it?"

Mrs. A.

"La, yes! to be sure I do."

Dr. A.

"I profess that I by no means wish my wife to read all she might find there. — What says the Colonel, Mrs. M.?"

Mrs. M.

"As to that, I never stop to ask him. I tell him every day that I believe in Father, Son, and Holy Ghost, and that it is his duty to believe in them too, and then my conscience is clear, and I don't care what he believes. Really, I have no notion of one's husband interfering in such matters."

Dr. A.

"You are quite right. I am sure I give my wife leave to believe just what she likes; but she is a good woman, and does not abuse the liberty; for she believes nothing."

It was not once, nor twice, nor thrice, but many many times, during my residence in America, that I was present when subjects which custom as well as principle had taught me to consider as fitter for the closet than the tea-table, were thus lightly discussed. I hardly know whether I was more startled at first hearing, in little dainty namby pamby tones, a profession of Atheism over a teacup, or at having my attention called from a Johnny cake, to a rhapsody on election and the second birth.

But, notwithstanding this revolting license, persecution exists to a degree unknown, I believe, in our well-ordered land since the days of Cromwell. I had the following anecdote from a gentleman perfectly well acquainted with the circumstances. A tailor sold a suit of clothes to a sailor a few moments before he sailed, which was on a Sunday morning. The corporation of New York prosecuted the tailor, and he was convicted, and sentenced to a fine greatly beyond his means to pay. Mr. F., a lawyer of New York, defended him with much eloquence, but in vain. His powerful speech, however, was not without effect, for it raised him such a host of Presbyterian enemies as sufficed to destroy his practice. Nor was this all: his nephew was at the time preparing for the bar, and soon after the above circumstance occurred his certificates were presented, and refused, with this declaration, "that no man of the name and family of F. should be admitted." I have met this young man in society; he is a person of very considerable talent, and being thus cruelly robbed of his profession, has become the editor of a newspaper.

CHAPTER XII

Peasantry, compared to that of England — Early marriages — Charity — Independence and equality — Cottage prayer-meeting

MOHAWK, as our little village was called, gave us an excellent opportunity of comparing the peasants of the United States with those of England, and of judging the average degree of comfort enjoyed by each. I believe Ohio gives as fair a specimen as any part of the Union; if they have the roughness and inconveniences of a new state to contend with, they have higher wages and cheaper provisions; if I err in supposing it a mean state in point of comfort, it certainly is not in taking too low a standard.

Mechanics, if good workmen, are certain of employment, and good wages, rather higher than with us; the average wages of a labourer throughout the Union is ten dollars a month, with lodging, boarding, washing, and mending; if he lives at his own expense he has a dollar a day. It appears to me that the necessaries of life, that is to say, meat, bread, butter, tea, and coffee, (not to mention whiskey), are within the reach of every sober, industrious, and healthy man who chooses to have them; and yet I think that an English peasant, with the same qualifications, would, in coming to the United States, change for the worse. He would find wages somewhat higher, and provisions in Western America considerably lower; but this statement, true as it is, can lead to nothing but delusion if taken apart from other facts, fully as certain, and not less important, but which require more detail in describing, and which perhaps cannot be fully comprehended, except by an eye-witness. The American poor are accustomed to eat meat three times a day; I never enquired into the habits of any cottagers in Western America, where this was not the case. I found afterwards in Maryland, Pennsylvania, and other parts of the country, where the price of meat was higher, that it was used with more economy; yet still a much larger portion of the weekly income is thus expended than with us. Ardent spirits, though lamentably cheap,[1] still cost something, and the use of them among the men, with more or less of discretion, according to the character, is universal. Tobacco also grows at their doors, and is not taxed; yet this too costs something, and the air of heaven is not in more general use among the men at America, than chewing tobacco. I am not now pointing out the evils of dram-drinking, but it is evident, that where this practice prevails universally, and often to the most frightful excess, the consequence must be, that the money spent to obtain the dram is less than the money lost by the time consumed in drinking it. Long, disabling, and expensive fits of sickness are incontestably more frequent in every part of America, than in England, and the sufferers have no aid to look to, but what they have saved, or what they may be enabled to sell. I have never seen misery exceed what I have witnessed in an American cottage where disease has entered.

But if the condition of the labourer be not superior to that of the English peasant, that of his wife and daughters is incomparably worse. It is they who are indeed the slaves of the soil. One has but to look at the wife of an American cottager, and ask her age, to be convinced that the life she leads is one of hardship, privation, and labour. It is rare to see a woman in this station who has reached the age of thirty, without losing every trace of youth and beauty. You continually see women with infants on their knee, that you feel sure are their grand-children, till some convincing proof of

---

[1] [T1] About a shilling a gallon is the retail price of good whiskey. If bought wholesale, or of inferior quality, it is much cheaper.

the contrary is displayed. Even the young girls, though
often with lovely features, look pale, thin, and haggard. I do
not remember to have seen in any single instance among the
poor, a specimen of the plump, rosy, laughing physiognomy
so common among our cottage girls. The horror of domestic
service, which the reality of slavery, and the fable of equality,
have generated, excludes the young women from that sure
and most comfortable resource of decent English girls; and
the consequence is, that with a most irreverend freedom of
manner to the parents, the daughters are, to the full extent of
the word, domestic slaves. This condition, which no periodical
merry-making, no village *fête*, ever occurs to cheer, is only
changed for the still sadder burdens of a teeming wife. They
marry very young; in fact, in no rank of life do you meet with
young women in that delightful period of existence between
childhood and marriage, wherein, if only tolerably well spent,
so much useful information is gained, and the character takes
a sufficient degree of firmness to support with dignity the
more important parts of wife and mother. The slender, childish thing, without vigour of mind or body, is made to stem a
sea of troubles that dims her young eye and makes her cheek
grow pale, even before nature has given it the last beautiful
finish of the full-grown woman.

"We shall get along," is the answer in full, for all that can
be said in way of advice to a boy and girl who take it into
their heads to go before a magistrate and "get married." And
they do get along, till sickness overtakes them, by means perhaps of borrowing a kettle from one and a tea-pot from another; but intemperance, idleness, or sickness will, in one
week, plunge those who are even getting along well, into utter
destitution; and where this happens, they are completely without resource.

The absence of poor-laws is, without doubt, a blessing to
the country, but they have not that natural and reasonable
dependence on the richer classes which, in countries dif-

ferently constituted, may so well supply their place. I suppose there is less alms-giving in America than in any other Christian country on the face of the globe. It is not in the temper of the people either to give or to receive.

I extract the following pompous passage from a Washington paper of Feb. 1829, (a season of uncommon severity and distress,) which, I think, justifies my observation.

"Among the liberal evidences of sympathy for the suffering poor of this city, two have come to our knowledge which deserve to be especially noticed: the one a donation by the President of the United States to the committee of the ward in which he resides of fifty dollars; the other the donation by a few of the officers of the war department to the Howard and Dorcas Societies, of seventy-two dollars." When such mention is made of a gift of about nine pounds sterling from the sovereign magistrate of the United States, and of thirteen pounds sterling as a contribution from one of the state departments, the inference is pretty obvious, that the sufferings of the destitute in America are not liberally relieved by individual charity.

I had not been three days at Mohawk-cottage before a pair of ragged children came to ask for medicine for a sick mother; and when it was given to them, the eldest produced a handful of cents, and desired to know what he was to pay. The superfluous milk of our cow was sought after eagerly, but every new comer always proposed to pay for it. When they found out that "the English old woman" did not sell any thing, I am persuaded they by no means liked her the better for it; but they seemed to think, that if she were a fool it was no reason they should be so too, and accordingly the borrowing, as they called it, became very constant, but always in a form that shewed their dignity and freedom. One woman sent to borrow a pound of cheese; another half a pound of coffee; and more than once an intimation accompanied the milk-jug, that the milk must be fresh, and unskimmed: on one occasion the messenger refused milk, and said, "Mother only wanted a little cream for her coffee."

I could never teach them to believe, during above a year that I lived at this house, that I would not sell the old clothes of the family; and so pertinacious were they in bargain-making, that often, when I had given them the articles which they wanted to purchase, they would say, "Well, I expect I shall have to do a turn of work for this; you may send for me when you want me." But as I never did ask for the turn of work, and as this formula was constantly repeated, I began to suspect that it was spoken solely to avoid uttering that most un-American phrase "I thank you."

rude?

There was one man whose progress in wealth I watched with much interest and pleasure. When I first became his neighbour, himself, his wife, and four children, were living in one room, with plenty of beef-steaks and onions for breakfast, dinner, and supper, but with very few other comforts. He was one of the finest men I ever saw, full of natural intelligence and activity of mind and body, but he could neither read nor write. He drank but little whiskey, and but rarely chewed tobacco, and was therefore more free from that plague spot of spitting which rendered male colloquy so difficult to endure. He worked for us frequently, and often used to walk into the drawing-room and seat himself on the sofa, and tell me all his plans. He made an engagement with the proprietor of the wooded hill before mentioned, by which half the wood he could fell was to be his own. His unwearied industry made this a profitable bargain, and from the proceeds he purchased the materials for building a comfortable frame (or wooden) house; he did the work almost entirely himself. He then got a job for cutting rails, and, as he could cut twice as many in a day as any other man in the neighbourhood, he made a good thing of it. He then let half his pretty house, which was admirably constructed, with an ample portico, that kept it always cool. His next step was contracting for the building a wooden bridge, and when I left Mohawk he had fitted up his half of the building as an hotel and grocery store; and I have no doubt that every sun that sets sees him a richer man than when it rose. He hopes to make his son a lawyer, and I have little doubt that he will live to see him sit in congress; when this time arrives, the woodcutter's son will rank with any other member of congress, not of courtesy, but of right, and the idea that his origin is a disadvantage, will never occur to the imagination of the most exalted of his fellow-citizens.

This is the only feature in American society that I recognise as indicative of the equality they profess. Any man's son may become the equal of any other man's son, and the consciousness of this is certainly a spur to exertion; on the other hand, it is also a spur to that coarse familiarity, untempered by any shadow of respect, which is assumed by the grossest and the lowest in their intercourse with the highest and most refined. This is a positive evil, and, I think, more than balances its advantages.

And here again it may be observed, that the theory of equality may be very daintily discussed by English gentlemen in a London dining-room, when the servant, having placed a fresh bottle of cool wine on the table, respectfully shuts the door, and leaves them to their walnuts and their wisdom; but it will be found less palatable when it presents itself in the shape of a hard, greasy paw, and is claimed in accents that breathe less of freedom than of onions and whiskey. Strong, indeed, must be the love of equality in an English breast if it can survive a tour through the Union.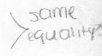

There was one house in the village which was remarkable from its wretchedness. It had an air of *in*decent poverty about it, which long prevented my attempting an entrance; but at length, upon being told that I could get chicken and eggs there whenever I wanted them, I determined upon venturing. The door being opened to my knock, I very nearly abandoned my almost blunted purpose; I never beheld such a den of filth and misery: a woman, the very image of dirt and disease, held a squalid imp of a baby on her hip bone while she kneaded her dough with her right fist only. A great lanky girl, of twelve years old, was sitting on a barrel, gnawing a corn cob; when I made known my business, the woman answered, "No, not I; I got no chickens to sell, nor eggs neither; but my son will, plenty I expect. Here, Nick," (bawling at the bottom of a ladder), "here's an old woman what wants chickens." Half a moment brought Nick to the bottom of the ladder, and I found my merchant was one of a ragged crew, whom I had been used to observe in my daily walk, playing marbles in the dust, and swearing lustily; he looked about ten years old.

"Have you chicken to sell, my boy?"

"Yes, and eggs too, more nor what you'll buy."

Having enquired price, condition, and so on, I recollected that I had been used to give the same price at market, the feathers plucked, and the chicken prepared for the table, and I told him that he ought not to charge the same.

"Oh for that, I expect I can fix 'em as well as ever them was, what you got in market."

"You fix them?"

"Yes to be sure, why not?"

"I thought you were too fond of marbles."

He gave me a keen glance, and said, "You don't know I. — When will you be wanting the chickens?"

He brought them at the time directed, extremely well "fixed," and I often dealt with him afterwards. When I paid him, he always thrust his hand into his breeches pocket, which I presume, as being *the keep,* was fortified more strongly than the dilapidated outworks, and drew from thence rather more dollars, half-dollars, levies, and fips, than his dirty little hand could well hold. My curiosity was excited,

and though I felt an involuntary disgust towards the young
Jew, I repeatedly conversed with him.

"You are very rich, Nick," I said to him one day, on his
making an ostentatious display of change, as he called it; he
sneered with a most unchildish expression of countenance,
and replied, "I guess 'twould be a bad job for I, if that was all
I'd got to shew."

I asked him how he managed his business. He told me that
he bought eggs by the hundred, and lean chicken by the
score, from the waggons that passed their door on the way to
market; that he fatted the latter in coops he had made himself, and could easily double their price, and that his eggs
answered well too, when he sold them out by the dozen.

"And do you give the money to your mother?"

"I expect not," was the answer, with another sharp glance
of his ugly blue eyes.

"What do you do with it, Nick?"

His look said plainly, what is that to you? but he only answered, quaintly enough, "I takes care of it."

How Nick got his first dollar is very doubtful; I was told
that when he entered the village store, the person serving
always called in another pair of eyes; but having obtained it,
the spirit, activity, and industry, with which he caused it to
increase and multiply, would have been delightful in one of
Miss Edgeworth's dear little clean bright-looking boys, who
would have carried all he got to his mother; but in Nick it
was detestable. No human feeling seemed to warm his young
heart, not even the love of self-indulgence, for he was not
only ragged and dirty, but looked considerably more than
half starved, and I doubt not his dinners and suppers half fed
his fat chickens.

I by no means give this history of Nick, the chicken merchant, as an anecdote characteristic in all respects of America; the only part of the story which is so, is the independence
of the little man, and is one instance out of a thousand, of the

hard, dry, calculating character that is the result of it. Probably Nick will be very rich; perhaps he will be President. I once got so heartily scolded for saying, that I did not think all American citizens were equally eligible to that office, that I shall never again venture to doubt it.

Another of our cottage acquaintance was a market-gardener, from whom we frequently bought vegetables; from the wife of this man we one day received a very civil invitation to "please to come and pass the evening with them in prayer." The novelty of the circumstance, and its great dissimilarity to the way and manners of our own country, induced me to accept the invitation, and also to record the visit here.

We were received with great attention, and a place was assigned us on one of the benches that surrounded the little parlour. Several persons, looking like mechanics and their wives, were present; every one sat in profound silence, and with that quiet subdued air, that serious people assume on entering a church. At length, a long, black, grim-looking man entered; his dress, the cut of his hair, and his whole appearance, strongly recalled the idea of one of Cromwell's fanatics. He stepped solemnly into the middle of the room, and took a chair that stood there, but not to sit upon it; he turned the back towards him, on which he placed his hands, and stoutly uttering a sound between a hem and a cough, he deposited freely on either side of him a considerable portion of masticated tobacco. He then began to preach. His text was "Live in hope," and he continued to expound it for two hours in a drawling, nasal tone, with no other respite than what he allowed himself for expectoration. If I say that he repeated the words of his text a hundred times, I think I shall not exceed the truth, for that allows more than a minute for each repetition, and in fact the whole discourse was made up of it. The various tones in which he uttered it might have served as a lesson on emphasis; as a question — in accents of triumph

— in accents of despair — of pity — of threatening — of authority — of doubt — of hope — of faith. Having exhausted every imaginable variety of tone, he abruptly said, "Let us pray," and twisting his chair round, knelt before it. Every one knelt before the seat they had occupied, and listened for another half hour to a rant of miserable, low, familiar jargon, that he presumed to *improvisé* to his Maker as a prayer. In this, however, the cottage apostle only followed the example set by every preacher throughout the Union, excepting those of the Episcopalian and Catholic congregations; *they* only do not deem themselves privileged to address the Deity in strains of crude and unweighed importunity. These ranters may sometimes be very much in earnest, but surely the least we can say of it is, that they

"Praise their God amiss."

I enquired afterwards of a friend, well acquainted with such matters, how the grim preacher of "Hope" got paid for his labours, and he told me that the trade was an excellent one, for that many a gude wife bestowed more than a tithe of what her gude man trusted to her keeping, in rewarding the zeal of these self-chosen apostles. These sable ministers walk from house to house, or if the distance be considerable, ride on a comfortable ambling nag. They are not only as empty as wind, but resemble it in other particulars; for they blow where they list, and no man knoweth whence they come, nor whither they go. When they see a house that promises comfortable lodging and entertainment, they enter there, and say to the good woman of the house, "Sister, shall I pray with you?" If the answer be favourable, and it is seldom otherwise, he instals himself and his horse till after breakfast the next morning. The best meat, drink, and lodging are his, while he stays, and he seldom departs without some little contribution in money for the support of the crucified and suffering church. Is it not strange that "the most intelligent people in the world" should prefer such a religion as this, to a form established by the wisdom and piety of the ablest and best among the erring sons of men, solemnly sanctioned by the nation's law, and rendered sacred by the use of their fathers?

It would be well for all reasoners on the social system to observe steadily, and with an eye obscured by no beam of prejudice, the result of the experiment that is making on the other side of the Atlantic. If I mistake not, they might learn there, better than by any abstract speculation, what are the points on which the magistrates of a great people should dictate to them, and on what points they should be left freely to their own guidance. I sincerely believe, that if a fire-worshipper, or an Indian Brahmin, were to come to the United States, prepared to preach and pray in English, he would not be long without a "very respectable congregation."

The influence of a religion, sanctioned by the government, could in no country, in the nineteenth century, interfere with the speculations of a philosopher in his closet, but it might, and must, steady the weak and wavering opinions of the multitude. There is something really pitiable in the effect produced by the want of this rudder oar. I knew a family where one was a Methodist, one a Presbyterian, and a third a Baptist; and another, where one was a Quaker, one a declared Atheist, and another an Universalist. These are all females, and all moving in the best society that America affords; but one and all of them as incapable of reasoning on things past, present, and to come, as the infants they nourish, yet one and all of them perfectly fit to move steadily and usefully in a path marked out for them. But I shall be called an itinerant preacher myself if I pursue this theme.[2]

---

[2] [T5, note] Since this chapter was written, I have sometimes been led to doubt whether the national and *authorised* indifference in matters of religious belief, which I deprecated in the United States, may not be productive of less moral evil than the *unauthorised* individual secessions from the national worship which I have witnessed in England.

The Methodist, Presbyterian, Baptist, Quaker, Atheist, and Universalist

As I have not the magic power of my admirable friend, Miss Mitford, to give grace and interest to the humblest rustic details,[3] I must not venture to linger among the cottages that surrounded us; but before I quit them I must record the pleasing recollection of one or two neighbours of more companionable rank, from whom I received so much friendly attention, and such unfailing kindness, in all my little do-

---

ladies mentioned in the text, acted, one and all of them, upon a universally recognised and received national principle — that each had a right to choose a creed and mode of worship for herself. There was no rebellion in it against paternal, or any other authority: no domestic disunion followed; and the disapprobation with which so loose, unstable, and unscriptural a system may be contemplated, can only be directed against the short-sighted legislation, which originated this rope of sand.

No violation of filial respect and duty, no social schism, no renegade turning from the venerable church, which for ages had regulated and cherished the piety of their forefathers, attends this republican indulgence for fancy religions. But widely different is the spectacle presented here, when similar licence is assumed. When every young lady claims a right to be her own bishop, and every parent, who ventures to doubt the lawfulness of her calling, is liable to hear himself doomed to eternal perdition by the voice of his child, the matter assumes a different aspect, — as different, indeed, as the act of wantonly pulling down York Minster, and using for the deed the rails of its own altar, from that of thoughtlessly chipping the stones in a quarry, from whence, if skill and will were not wanting, another Minster might be reared.

[3] [DS] Mary Russell Mitford, novelist and dramatist, author of the still delightful *Our Village*, was a special confidante of Mrs. Trollope, whom she once characterized as "a lively, brilliant woman of the world, with a warm, blunt, cordial manner." It was Miss Mitford who introduced Mrs. Trollope to Whittaker, the publisher of *Domestic Manners*. Mrs. Trollope had written asking her for her help shortly before taking ship back to England:

"You know, I believe, that I have looked and listened since I have been here with a view to publication, and you know also, dear friend — for how can you help it? — that I am as utterly unknown in the world of letters as your dog May was before you immortalized him. What I would ask is such a letter of introduction to your publisher as would enable me to present myself before him without feeling as if I had dropped upon him from the moon.

"My book is gossiping, and without pretension most faithfully true to the evidence of my senses, and written without a shadow of (previous) feeling for or against the things described. I have about thirty outline sketches by Hervieu, not of scenery, but of manners, which I think will help the book greatly. I am well aware that it is difficult to bring a first effort to the light, but I think your powerful name will help me much."

mestic embarrassments, that I shall never recall the memory of Mohawk, without paying an affectionate tribute to these far distant friends. I wish it were within the range of hope, that I might see them again, in my own country, and repay, in part, the obligations I owe them.

CHAPTER XIII

Theatre — Fine Arts — Delicacy — Shaking Quakers — Big-Bone
Lick — Visit of the President

THE theatre at Cincinnati is small, and not very brilliant in decoration, but in the absence of every other amusement our young men frequently attended it, and in the bright clear nights of autumn and winter, the mile and a half of distance was not enough to prevent the less enterprising members of the family from sometimes accompanying them. The great inducement to this was the excellent acting of Mr. and Mrs. Alexander Drake,[1] the managers. Nothing could be more distinct than their line of acting, but the great versatility of their powers enabled them often to appear together. Her cast was the highest walk of tragedy, and his the broadest comedy; but yet, as Goldsmith says of his sister heroines, I have known them change characters for a whole evening together, and have wept with him and laughed with her, as it was their will and pleasure to ordain. I think in his comedy he was superior to any actor I ever saw in the same parts, except Emery. Alexander Drake's comedy was like that of the French, who never appear to be acting at all; he was himself the comic being the author aimed at depicting. Let him speak whose words he would, from Shakspeare to Colman, it was impossible not to feel that half the fun was his own; he had, too, in a very high degree, the power that Fawcett possessed, of drawing tears by a sudden touch of natural feeling. His comic songs might have set the gravity of the judges and bishops together at defiance. Liston is great, but Alexander Drake was greater.

---

[1] [T] Mr. Drake was an Englishman.

Mrs. Drake, formerly Miss Denny, greatly resembles Miss O'Neil; a proof of this is, that Mr. Kean, who had heard of the resemblance, arrived at New York late in the evening, and having repaired to the theatre, saw her for the first time across the stage, and immediately exclaimed, "that's Miss Denny." Her voice, too, has the same rich and touching tones, and is superior in power. Her talent is decidedly first-rate. Deep and genuine feeling, correct judgment, and the most perfect good taste, distinguish her play in every character. Her last act of Belvidera is superior in tragic effect to any thing I ever saw on the stage, the one great exception to all comparison, Mrs. Siddons, being set aside.[2]

---

[2] [DS] The Drakes were great friends of Mrs. Trollope's during her stay in Cincinnati, and helped her when she attempted to realize funds by staging musical and dramatic entertainments at the Bazaar (see section VII of the Introduction). Not everyone saw them quite so favorably as did Mrs. Trollope. Joe Cowell describes the Drakes as they appeared to him in the fall of 1829:

"I was making some inquiries of the barkeeper about the theatre, when a man about my own age and size, very shabby, very dirty, and very deaf, introduced himself as Alexander Drake, the manager, curled his right hand round his ear, and, in a courteous whisper, invited me to 'take something.' He was a kind, familiar, lighthearted creature, [and] told me, with apparent glee, that he was over head and ears in debt to the company and everybody else; that that night he had given the use of the theatre, and the performers had tendered their services, to an old actor who expected a 'meeting of his creditors;' but that he had been obliged to close the theatre for the simple reason that it wasn't fashionable! . . . Mrs. Drake has been very successful as a star since the time I speak of; she is one out of six or seven ladies who have by turns been called 'the Mrs. Siddons of America;' but what for, for the life of me I never could find out; but as the baptizers, in all probability, never saw THE Mrs. Siddons, they should stand excused for taking her name in vain.

"Old Drake [Alexander's father] had been a strolling manager in the West of England, and some years before had brought to this country a large family of children, all educated to sing, dance, fight combats, paint scenes, play the fiddle, and everything else; and by wandering through the then wilderness, and giving entertainments at the numerous small towns which were daily ejecting the forest, he had made money by their combined exertions in that primitive dramatic way. But this portion of the Union had in a very few years outgrown even his boys and girls, and the march of improvement had marched rather beyond the point of his experience. . . . Alexander Drake had been intrusted by his father with this [the

It was painful to see these excellent performers playing to a miserable house, not a third full, and the audience probably not including half a dozen persons who would prefer their playing to that of the vilest strollers. In proof of this, I saw

Cincinnati] branch of the concern, and had got in debt and ·got on the *limits,* and could not move out of the state till relieved by the insolvent law; and Old Drake was at Frankfort, Kentucky, waiting for this company, to open the theatre there, and they could not move for want of funds. . . .

"[Alexander Drake] gave me an invitation to witness the performance; and after a pleasant chat — for he was a delightful companion — and 'taking something' till the time for commencing, excused himself for being obliged to leave, in consequence of having to 'study Charles Surface, who went on in the third act.' If he had never played the part before, he had an extraordinary 'swallow;' for he was perfect, and performed it much better than I have often seen it done by those who consider such characters their line of business; and he was a *low comedian* and an *excellent one,* which may probably account for the unfitness of his dress: he wore white trousers of that peculiar cut you sometimes see frisk round the stage in what is called a sailor's hornpipe, and, being very short, exposed a pair of boots on which Day and Martin [blacking] had never deigned to shine; no gloves, a round hat, and the same blue coat and brass buttons I had already been introduced to, buttoned up to the top. His wife was the Lady Teazle; a very fine looking woman, and plenty of her. I was not then accustomed to the peculiar *twang* in the pronunciation of the west end of the United States, which, in consequence, sounded uncouth and unlady-Teazle-like to me; for though Sir Peter particularly boasts that he has chosen a wife 'bred altogether in the country,' he didn't mean, I suppose, the Western country; but, at any rate, she got great applause; everybody seemed very much pleased with her, and she seemed very much pleased with herself. . . . I don't know if it was considered a *fashionable* house. There were about a hundred persons present. . . .

"I shall neither mention names nor particularly describe the party I saw the first morning I went to rehearsal huddled round the fire, in what was called the green-room. In one corner, on the floor, was a pallet-bed and some stage properties, evidently used to make shift to cook with, such as tin cups and dishes, a brass breastplate, and an iron helmet half full of boiled potatoes, which I was informed, was the domestic paraphernalia of the housekeeper and ladies'-dresser. She was . . . very busily employed in roasting coffee on a sheet of thunder, and stirring it round with one of Macbeth's daggers, for 'on the blade and dudgeon, gouts' of rose-pink still remained.

"I soon got acquainted with the ladies and gentlemen. . . . I perched myself on a throne-chair, by the side of Mrs. Drake, who was seated next the fire, on a bass drum. I found her a most joyous, affable creature, full of conundrums and good nature; she made some capital jokes about her peculiar position; martial music — sounds by distance made more sweet; and an excellent rhyme to drum, which I am very sorry I have forgotten."

them, as managers, give place to paltry third-rate actors from London, who would immediately draw crowded houses, and be overwhelmed with applause.

Poor Drake died just before we left Ohio, and his wife, who, besides her merit as an actress, is a most estimable and amiable woman, is left with a large family. I have little, or rather no doubt, of her being able to obtain an excellent engagement in London, but her having property in several of the Western theatres will, I fear, detain her in a neighbourhood, where she is neither understood nor appreciated.[3] She told me many very excellent professional anecdotes collected during her residence in the West; one of these particularly amused me as a specimen of Western idiom. A lady who professed a great admiration for Mrs. Drake had obtained her permission to be present upon one occasion at her theatrical toilet. She was dressing for some character in which she was to stab herself, and her dagger was lying on the table. The visitor took it up, and examining it with much emotion, exclaimed, "What! do you really jab this into yourself sevagarous?"

We also saw the great American star, Mr. Forrest.[4] What he may become I will not pretend to prophesy; but when I saw him play Hamlet at Cincinnati, not even Mrs. Drake's sweet Ophelia could keep me beyond the third act. It is true that I have seen Kemble, Macready, Kean, Young, C. Kemble, Cook, and Talma play Hamlet, and I might not, perhaps, be

3 [DS] After Alexander Drake's death Mrs. Drake kept on with her career and in 1832 was a star performer at the Park Theater in New York. She married Captain Cutter, a poet who was once well known for his "Song of Steam." Cutter courted the bottle more assiduously than the muse, and the marriage was an unhappy one. She was still living in 1852.

4 [DS] Edwin Forrest was still in his early twenties when Mrs. Trollope saw him at the Cincinnati theater, but he was already idolized in the United States. He had made his first great success playing Othello in New York in 1826. It was nearly two decades later that he began his famous hostilities with the English tragedian William Charles Macready, which led to the Astor Place Riot in New York City, in which thirty-six persons were wounded and twenty-two killed.

a very fair judge of this young actor's merits; but I was greatly
amused when a gentleman, who asked my opinion of him,
told me upon hearing it, that he would not advise me to state
it freely in America, "for they would not bear it."

The theatre was really not a bad one, though the very poor
receipts rendered it impossible to keep it in high order; but
an annoyance infinitely greater than decorations indifferently
clean, was the style and manner of the audience.[5] Men came
into the lower tier of boxes without their coats; and I have
seen shirt sleeves tucked up to the shoulder; the spitting was
incessant, and the mixed smell of onions and whiskey was
enough to make one feel even the Drakes' acting dearly
bought by the obligation of enduring its accompaniments.[6]

culture

[5] [DS] According to the *Cincinnati Directory*, 1829, the theater covered
a lot 50 by 100 feet in size. It had a large stage, a pit, two tiers of boxes,
and a "spacious gallery, with commodious lobbies, punch room, &c.," and
seated 800 persons.

A poster dated May 1, 1830 suggests that Mrs. Trollope was not without some basis for her remarks upon the manners of Cincinnati audiences.
It reads in part:

"I. Gentlemen will be particular in not disturbing the audience by loud
talking in the Bar-Room, nor by personal altercations in any part of the
house.

"II. Gentlemen in the boxes and in the pit are expected not to wear
their hats nor to stand nor sit on the railing, during the performance; as
they will thereby prevent the company behind, and in the lobby, from seeing the stage. Those in the side boxes will endeavor to avoid leaning forward as, from the construction of the house, the projection of one person's
head must interrupt the view of several others on the same line of seats.

"III. The practice of cracking nuts, now abandoned in all well regulated Theatres, should be entirely avoided during the time the curtain is up;
as it must necessarily interfere with the pleasure of those who feel disposed
to attend to the performance.

"IV. Persons in the upper Boxes and Gallery will be careful to avoid the
uncourteous habit of throwing nutshells, apples, etc., into the Pit; and those
in the Pit are cautioned against clambering over the balustrade into the
Boxes, either during or at the end of the Performance.

"V. Persons in the Gallery are requested not to disturb the harmony of
the House by boisterous conduct, either in language or by striking with
sticks on the seats or bannisters, etc. . . ."

[6] [T5, note] I have had the pleasure of being told by a variety of American travellers, whom I have met in England, France, and Germany, that
since the publication of this statement, this annoyance at the theatres, not

The bearing and attitudes of the men are perfectly indescribable; the heels thrown higher than the head, the entire rear of the person presented to the audience, the whole length supported on the benches, are among the varieties that these exquisite posture-masters exhibit. The noises, too, were perpetual, and of the most unpleasant kind; the applause is expressed by cries and thumping with the feet, instead of clapping; and when a patriotic fit seized them, and "Yankee Doodle" was called for, every man seemed to think his reputation as a citizen depended on the noise he made.

Two very indifferent figurantes, probably from the Ambigu Comique, or la Gaieté, made their appearance at Cincinnati while we were there; and had Mercury stepped down, and danced a *pas seul* upon earth, his godship could not have produced a more violent sensation. But wonder and admiration were by no means the only feelings excited; horror and dismay were produced in at least an equal degree. No one,

---

only at Cincinnati, but throughout all the cities of the Union, has been greatly lessened.

[DS] Shortly after the appearance of *Domestic Manners*, as a matter of fact, "a Trollope!" or "Trollope!" became a familiar cry in America. The *New-York Mirror* for January 12, 1833 states that Mrs. Trollope's name was already a "by-word in taverns and in the pit of the theatres, which, we doubt not, pleases her vastly. She has, nevertheless, although in a most ungracious way, 'done the state some service.' Spitters and chewers, look to it; and ye indolent beings, who lounge on two chairs with your feet on the mantel-piece, remember Mr. Herview's [*sic*] sketches, and be no more guilty of a *Trollope!*"

Patrick Shirreff in *A Tour through North America* (1835) reports concerning his visit to the Park Theater at New York to see Fanny Kemble in *The Wonder*:

"At the end of the second act, I observed a gentleman in the second tier of boxes in an indelicate posture in front of the box. Three were similarly situated, at the end of the third act, when several voices in the pit called out, 'A Trollope, a Trollope,' and a general hissing and hooting from the same quarter had the effect of inducing the offenders speedily to withdraw."

Henry T. Tuckerman in *America and Her Commentators* (1864) says: "Until recently the sight of a human foot protruding over the gallery of a western theater was hailed with the instant and vociferous challenge, apparently undisputed as authoritative, of 'Trollope,' whereupon the obnoxious member was withdrawn from sight."

I believe, doubted their being admirable dancers, but every one agreed that the morals of the Western world would never recover the shock. When I was asked if I had ever seen any thing so dreadful before, I was embarrassed how to answer; for the young women had been exceedingly careful, both in their dress and in their dancing, to meet the taste of the people; but had it been Virginie in her most transparent attire, or Taglioni in her most remarkable pirouette, they could not have been more reprobated. The ladies altogether forsook the theatre; the gentlemen muttered under their breath, and turned their heads aside when the subject was mentioned; the clergy denounced them from the pulpit; and if they were named at the meetings of the saints, it was to show how deep the horror such a theme could produce. I could not but ask myself if virtue were a plant, thriving under one form in one country, and flourishing under a different one in another? If these Western Americans are right, then how dreadfully wrong are we! It is really a very puzzling subject.[7]

---

[7] [DS] From the *North American Review* (January 1833), published not among the Western Americans but at Boston:

"What then is this puzzle? What is 'the transparent attire of *Virginie*,' and the 'remarkable *pirouette* of Taglioni?' The attire of an opera dancer in Europe, which Mrs. Trollope judiciously designates as 'transparent,' appears to consist of flesh-coloured pantaloons, fitted as tight to the limbs as the skin they are designed to imitate; and over these, one single covering of gauze or some other transparent material, stopping several inches *above* the knee. This is *the entire dress,* in which the opera dancers at London appear in public before mixed multitudes, — before crowds of men and women assembled in the theatre. This is the dress, in which the matrons and maidens of Great Britain behold, unblushing and delighted, the public appearance of persons of their own sex. So much for the dress. As for the dancing, particularly that part of it for which even Mrs. Trollope's lively and graphic pen could find no epithet more discriminative than 'remarkable,' it is remarkable indeed, and for two reasons; — first, that females, not lost to shame, should be found to perform it, on the stage; and second, that they should find men and women of character to countenance the exhibition in the boxes. The *pirouette,* in a word, is a movement, in which a woman, dressed as we have described, poising herself on one limb, extends the other to its full length, at right angles, and in this *graceful* attitude spins round, some eight or ten times, leaving her drapery, 'transparent' and short as it is at the best, to be carried up, by the centrifugal force imparted to it by the revolu-

But this was not the only point on which I found my notions of right and wrong utterly confounded; hardly a day
passed in which I did not discover that something or other
that I had been taught to consider lawful as eating, was held
in abhorrence by those around me; many words to which I
had never heard an objectionable meaning attached, were
totally interdicted, and the strangest paraphrastic sentences
substituted. I confess it struck me, that notwithstanding a
general stiffness of manner, which I think must exceed that
of the Scribes and Pharisees, the Americans have imaginations that kindle with alarming facility. I could give
many anecdotes to prove this, but will content myself with
a few.

A young German gentleman of perfectly good manners,
once came to me greatly chagrined at having offended one of
the principal families in the neighbourhood, by having pronounced the word *corset* before the ladies of it. An old female
friend had kindly overcome her own feelings so far as to
mention to him the cause of the coolness he had remarked,
and strongly advised his making an apology. He told me that
he was perfectly well disposed to do so, but felt himself
greatly at a loss how to word it.

An English lady who had long kept a fashionable boarding-
school in one of the Atlantic cities, told me that one of her
earliest cares with every new comer, was the endeavour to
substitute real delicacy for this affected precision of manner;
among many anecdotes, she told me one of a young lady
about fourteen, who on entering the receiving room, where
she only expected to see a lady who had enquired for her,
and finding a young man with her, put her hands before her

tion of the dancer, as far as it will go. This we believe is an unexaggerated
description of that scene, which Mrs. Trollope sneers at the ladies of Cincinnati for regarding with horror. Is there a father or a mother, a husband or
wife, a brother or sister in Christendom,
        '*If damned Custom had not brazed them so,*'
who would view it with any thing but horror?"

VII THE SOLEMNITY OF JUSTICE

VIII DEBATE BETWEEN OWEN AND CAMPBELL

eyes, and ran out of the room again, screaming "A man! a man! a man!"

On another occasion, one of the young ladies in going up stairs to the drawing-room, unfortunately met a boy of fourteen coming down, and her feelings were so violently agitated, that she stopped panting and sobbing, nor would pass on till the boy had swung himself up on the upper banisters, to leave the passage free.

At Cincinnati there is a garden where the people go to eat ices, and to look at roses. For the preservation of the flowers, there is placed at the end of one of the walks a sign-post sort of daub, representing a Swiss peasant girl, holding in her hand a scroll, requesting that the roses might not be gathered. Unhappily for the artist, or for the proprietor, or for both, the petticoat of this figure was so short as to shew her ancles. The ladies saw, and shuddered; and it was formally intimated to the proprietor, that if he wished for the patronage of the ladies of Cincinnati, he must have the petticoat of this figure lengthened. The affrighted purveyor of ices sent off an express for the artist and his paint pot. He came, but unluckily not provided with any colour that would match the petticoat; the necessity, however, was too urgent for delay, and a flounce of blue was added to the petticoat of red, giving bright and shining evidence before all men of the immaculate delicacy of the Cincinnati ladies.

I confess I was sometimes tempted to suspect that this ultra refinement was not very deep seated. It often appeared to me like the consciousness of grossness, that wanted a veil; but the veil was never gracefully adjusted. Occasionally, indeed, the very same persons who appeared ready to faint at the idea of a statue, would utter some unaccountable sally that was quite startling, and which made me feel that the indelicacy of which we were accused had its limits. The following anecdote is hardly fit to tell, but it explains what I mean too well to be omitted.

A young married lady, of *high standing* and most fastidious delicacy, who had been brought up at one of the Atlantic seminaries of highest reputation, told me that her house, at the distance of half a mile from a populous city, was unfortunately opposite a mansion of worse than doubtful reputation. "It is abominable," she said, "to see the people that go there; they ought to be exposed. I and another lady, an intimate friend of mine, did make one of them look foolish enough last summer: she was passing the day with me, and, while we were sitting at the window, we saw a young man we both knew ride up there, we went into the garden and watched at the gate for him to come back, and when he did, we both stepped out, and I said to him, 'Are you not ashamed, Mr. William D., to ride by my house and back again in that manner?' I never saw a man look so foolish!"

In conversing with ladies on the customs and manners of Europe, I remarked a strong propensity to consider every thing as wrong to which they were not accustomed.[8]

I once mentioned to a young lady that I thought a pic-nic party would be very agreeable, and that I would propose it to some of our friends. She agreed that it would be delightful, but she added, "I fear you will not succeed; we are not used to such sort of things here, and I know it is considered very indelicate for ladies and gentlemen to sit down together on the grass."

I could multiply anecdotes of this nature; but I think these sufficient to give an accurate idea of the tone of manners in this particular, and I trust to justify the observations I have made.

One of the spectacles which produced the greatest astonishment on us all was the Republican simplicity of the courts of justice. We had heard that the judges indulged themselves

---

[8] [T5, note] Can this be fairly stated as peculiar to the ladies of America? Most assuredly not, and the observation therefore, as applied peculiarly to them, is either invidious or unmeaning. — PECCAVI!

on the bench in those extraordinary attitudes which, doubt-less, some peculiarity of the American formation leads them to find the most comfortable. Of this we were determined to judge for ourselves, and accordingly entered the court when it was in full business, with three judges on the bench. The annexed sketch ° will better describe what we saw than any thing I can write.

Our winter passed rapidly away, and pleasantly enough, by the help of frosty walks, a little skaiting, a visit to Big-Bone Lick, and a visit to the shaking Quakers, a good deal of chess, and a good deal of reading, notwithstanding we were almost in the back woods of Western America.

The excursion to Big-Bone Lick, in Kentucky, and that to the Quaker village, were too fatiguing for females at such a season, but our gentlemen brought us home mammoth bones and shaking Quaker stories in abundance.[9]

These singular people, the shaking Quakers of America, give undeniable proof that communities may exist and pros-per, for they have continued for many years to adhere strictly to this manner of life, and have been constantly increasing in wealth. They have formed two or three different societies in distant parts of the Union, all governed by the same gen-eral laws, and all uniformly prosperous and flourishing.[10]

° Plate VII of the present edition.

[9] [T5, note] In one of Miss Sedgwick's excellent novels — "Clarence," if I mistake not, the authoress introduces a description of one of these com-munities, embracing many particulars on the justice of which our travellers had no means of forming an opinion. If this description be as correct as those of Miss Sedgwick generally are, *absurdity* is certainly the least of the objec-tions to be urged against them."

[DS] Catharine Maria Sedgwick describes the Shakers in *Redwood* (1824). In her preface Miss Sedgwick states that her "sketch . . . was drawn from personal observation." There is nothing very shocking about it. Indeed, the author felt sure that she had put down nothing that "would wound the feelings even of a single individual of that obscure sect."

[10] [DS] The Shaker community that Mr. Trollope and his two sons Henry and Thomas Adolphus visited was at Mount Lebanon, about twenty-five miles from Cincinnati. The autobiography of Thomas Adolphus Trol-lope adds detail:

There must be some sound and wholesome principle at work in these establishments to cause their success in every undertaking, and this principle must be a powerful one, for it has to combat much that is absurd and much that is mischievous.

The societies are generally composed of about an equal proportion of males and females, many of them being men and their wives; but they are all bound by their laws not to cohabit together. Their religious observances are wholly confined to singing and dancing of the most grotesque kind, and this repeated so constantly as to occupy much time; yet these people become rich and powerful wherever they settle themselves. Whatever they manufacture, whatever their farms produce, is always in the highest repute, and brings the highest price in the market. They receive all strangers with great courtesy, and if they bring an introduction they are lodged and fed for any length of time they choose to stay;

"We did not eat in company with the members, though faring, as I have said, exactly as they did, but we were present at their religious worship, or at what stood in the place of such. This consisted in a species of dance, if the uncouth jumping or 'shaking' which they practised could be so called. The men and women were assembled and danced in the same room, but not together. They jumped and 'shook' themselves in two divided bodies. Any spectator would be disposed to imagine that the whole object of the performance was bodily exercise. It seemed to be carried on to the utmost extent that breath and bodily fatigue would permit. Many were mopping the perspiration from their faces. No laughing or gladness or exhilaration whatever appeared to accompany or to be caused by the exercise. All was done with an air of perfect solemnity.

"All the men and all the women seemed to be in the enjoyment of excellent health. Most of them seemed to be somewhat more than well nourished — rather tending to obesity. They were florid, round-faced, sleek and heavy in figure. I observed no laughter, and very little conversation among them. The women were almost all in the prime of life, and many young. But there was a singular absence of good looks among them. Some had regular features enough, but they were all heavy, fat, dull-looking, like well-kept animals. I could not spy one pair of bright eyes in the place."

The Shakers established eleven communities between 1787 and 1794 in New York and New England; during the first quarter of the nineteenth century seven more were founded in Ohio, Kentucky, and Indiana. In 1840 the total membership of these communities was about six thousand. According to *Time* (July 28, 1947), there are about fifty members of the cult today.

they are not asked to join in their labours, but are permitted to do so if they wish it.

The Big-Bone Lick was not visited, and even partially examined, without considerable fatigue.[11]

It appeared from the account of our travellers, that the spot which gives the region its elegant name is a deep bed of blue clay, tenacious and unsound, so much so as to render it both difficult and dangerous to traverse. The digging it has been found so laborious that no one has yet hazarded the expense of a complete search into its depths for the gigantic relics so certainly hidden there. The clay has never been moved without finding some of them; and I think it can hardly be doubted that money and perseverance would procure a more perfect specimen of an entire mammoth than we have yet seen.[12]

And now the time arrived that our domestic circle was again to be broken up. Our eldest son was to be entered at Oxford, and it was necessary that his father should accompany him; and, after considerable indecision, it was at length determined that I and my daughters should remain another year, with our second son. It was early in February, and our travellers prepared themselves to encounter some sharp gales upon the mountains, though the great severity of the cold

[11] [DS] Big Bone Lick, in Kentucky, was something over twenty miles from Cincinnati by wagon road. "The waters are strongly impregnated with salts, and send up a vapour of sulphuretted hydrogen gas. It is at this place, where the huge organick remains of the mammoth have been dug up in large quantities; and it was here, where, according to the tradition of the Delaware Indians, as related by Mr. Jefferson, such herds of them came as to destroy the game of the red men. . . . An English traveller, who called his name Thomas Ashe, and who carried off to England several waggon loads of the bones, dug out of this Lick; gives it as his opinion that the animal was of the lion kind, called *megalonyx*, or great lion. He says that 'his shoulder blade was of the size of a breakfast table; that he was 60 feet in length, and 25 feet in height; that his figure was magnificent; — his looks determined; his gait stately, and his voice tremendous!' " — Samuel Cumings: *The Western Pilot* (1829).

[12] [T1] Since the above was written an immense skeleton, nearly perfect, has been extracted.

appeared to be past. We got buffalo robes and double shoes prepared for them, and they were on the eve of departure when we heard that General Jackson, the newly-elected President, was expected to arrive immediately at Cincinnati, from his residence in the West, and to proceed by steam-boat to Pittsburgh, on his way to Washington. This determined them not to fix the day of their departure till they heard of his arrival, and then, if possible, to start in the same boat with him; the decent dignity of a private conveyance not being deemed necessary for the President of the United States.

The day of his arrival was however quite uncertain, and we could only determine to have every thing very perfectly in readiness, let it come when it would. This resolution was hardly acted upon when the news reached us that the General had arrived at Louisville, and was expected at Cincinnati in a few hours. All was bustle and hurry at Mohawk-cottage; we quickly dispatched our packing business, and this being the first opportunity we had had of witnessing such a demonstration of popular feeling, we all determined to be present at the debarkation of the great man. We accordingly walked to Cincinnati, and secured a favourable station at the landing-place, both for the purpose of seeing the first magistrate and of observing his reception by the people. We had waited but a few moments when the heavy panting of the steam-engines and then a discharge of cannon told that we were just in time; another moment brought his vessel in sight.

Nothing could be better of its kind than his approach to the shore: the noble steam-boat which conveyed him was flanked on each side by one of nearly equal size and splendour; the roofs of all three were covered by a crowd of men; cannon saluted them from the shore as they passed by, to the distance of a quarter of a mile above the town; there they turned about, and came down the river with a rapid but stately motion, the three vessels so close together as to appear one mighty mass upon the water.

When they arrived opposite the principal landing they swept gracefully round, and the side vessels, separating themselves from the centre, fell a few feet back, permitting her to approach before them with her honoured freight. All this manœuvring was extremely well executed, and really beautiful.

The crowd on the shore awaited her arrival in perfect stillness. When she touched the bank the people on board gave a faint huzza, but it was answered by no note of welcome from the land: this cold silence was certainly not produced by any want of friendly feeling towards the new President; during the whole of the canvassing he had been decidedly the popular candidate at Cincinnati, and, for months past, we had been accustomed to the cry of "Jackson for ever" from an overwhelming majority; but enthusiasm is not either the virtue or the vice of America.

More than one private carriage was stationed at the water's edge to await the General's orders, but they were dismissed with the information that he would walk to the hotel. Upon receiving this intimation the silent crowd divided itself in a very orderly manner, leaving a space for him to walk through them. He did so, uncovered, though the distance was considerable, and the weather very cold; but he alone (with the exception of a few European gentlemen who were present) was without a hat. He wore his grey hair, carelessly, but not ungracefully arranged, and, spite of his harsh gaunt features, he looks like a gentleman and a soldier. He was in deep mourning, having very recently lost his wife; they were said to have been very happy together, and I was pained by hearing a voice near me exclaim, as he approached the spot where I stood, "There goes Jackson, where is his wife?" Another sharp voice, at a little distance, cried, "Adams for ever!" And these sounds were all I heard to break the silence.[13]

---

[13] [DS] Though the men in the crowd kept their hats on, it was probably courtesy rather than any lack of enthusiasm that made all except two unreconstructed Adams-and-Clay men remain silent while the General,

"They manage these matters better" in the East, I have no doubt, but as yet I was still in the West, and still inclined to think, that however meritorious the American character may be, it is not amiable.

Mr. T. and his sons joined the group of citizens who waited upon him to the hotel, and were presented to the President in form; that is, they shook hands with him. Learning that he intended to remain a few hours there, or more properly, that it would be a few hours before the steam-boat would be

---

dressed in mourning for his wife, who had died scarcely more than a month earlier, left his steamboat and walked through the mass of people to the Cincinnati Hotel. The *National Republican* (Tuesday, January 27, 1829) found no lack of warmth in the reception of the President-elect:

"Gen. Jackson and suite very unexpectedly arrived here about two o'clock on Saturday last, on board the steam boat Pennsylvania. . . . Notwithstanding the shortness of the notice, the decks of the steam boats, and indeed every kind of vessel on the river, presented a mass of heads, and our spacious wharf was thronged with thousands of our fellow citizens, all anxious to behold the defender of his country's liberties, and their choice as Chief Magistrate of the Republic. The crowds of ladies waved their handkerchiefs, and the men greeted the veteran hero with hearty cheers. — The General spent the afternoon at the Cincinnati Hotel, and the evening at the Broadway Hotel; and at both houses he was almost incessantly occupied in taking by the hand the crowds of both sexes, and of all ages, who waited on him. . . .

"About ten o'clock on Saturday night Gen. Jackson went on board the Pennsylvania, attended by a committee of our citizens, who will accompany him to Pittsburgh. A number of our citizens chartered the steam boat Fulton, to escort the General as far as Maysville; on board of which an excellent band of music volunteered their services, and the boats left here closely lashed together. . . . An address was delivered by Mr. L. C. Lavin, one of our teachers, to Gen. Jackson; and the General's reply was so affecting as to leave but few dry eyes among his auditors. On the return voyage, the Rev. William Burke preached a sermon to the passengers, which was listened to with deep and solemn attention."

The man who shouted: "There goes Jackson, where is his wife?" was probably alluding to a bit of muckraking that Adams newspapers had made much use of in the recent campaign. Mrs. Jackson had formerly been married to a man in East Tennessee. He had used her badly, and she had begun divorce proceedings, which dragged on for many years. When Jackson married her, both he and she understood that the decree had been granted. According to the story, the decree was not made final until a few days after the marriage; thus Jackson's marriage, his opponents maintained, was illegal, and at the time of the campaign he was still living in adultery.

ready to proceed, Mr. T. secured berths on board, and returned, to take a hasty dinner with us. At the hour appointed by the captain, Mr. T. and his son accompanied the General on board; and by subsequent letters I learnt that they had conversed a good deal with him, and were pleased by his conversation and manners, but deeply disgusted by the brutal familiarity to which they saw him exposed at every place on their progress at which they stopped; I am tempted to quote one passage, as sufficiently descriptive of the manner, which so painfully grated against their European feelings.

"There was not a hulking boy from a keel-boat who was not introduced to the President, unless, indeed, as was the case with some, they introduced themselves: for instance, I was at his elbow when a greasy fellow accosted him thus: —

" 'General Jackson, I guess?'

"The General bowed assent.

" 'Why they told me you was dead.'

" 'No! Providence has hitherto preserved my life.'

" 'And is your wife alive too?'

"The General, apparently much hurt, signified the contrary, upon which the courtier concluded his harangue, by saying, 'Aye, I thought it was the one or the t'other of ye.' "

CHAPTER XIV

American Spring — Controversy between Messrs. Owen
and Campbell — Public ball — Separation of the sexes —
American freedom — Execution

THE American spring is by no means so agreeable as
the American autumn; both move with faultering step, and
slow; but this lingering pace, which is delicious in autumn, is
most tormenting in the spring. In the one case you are about
to part with a friend, who is becoming more gentle and agreeable at every step, and such steps can hardly be made too
slowly; but in the other you are making your escape from a
dreary cavern, where you have been shut up with black frost
and biting blasts, and where your best consolation was being
smoke-dried.

But, upon second thoughts, I believe it would be more
correct, instead of complaining of the slow pace of the American spring, to declare that they have no spring at all. The
beautiful autumn often lingers on till Christmas, after which
winter can be trifled with no longer, and generally keeps a
stubborn hold through the months which we call spring,
when he suddenly turns his back, and summer takes his place.

The inconceivable uncertainty of the climate is, however,
such, that I will not venture to state about what time this
change takes place, for it is certain, that let me name what
time I would, it would be easy for any weather journaliser to
prove me wrong, by quoting that the thermometer was at 100
at a period which my statement included in the winter; or
50 long after I made the summer commence.

The climate of England is called uncertain, but it can

never, I think, be so described by any who have experienced
that of the United States. A gentleman, on whose accuracy
I could depend, told me he had repeatedly known the thermometer vary above 40 degrees in the space of twelve hours.
This most unpleasant caprice of the temperature is, I conceive, one cause of the unhealthiness of the climate.

At length, however, after shivering and shaking till we
were tired of it, and having been half ruined in fire-wood
(which, by the way, is nearly as dear as at Paris, and dearer
in many parts of the Union), the summer burst upon us full
blown, and the ice-house, the piazza, and the jalousies were
again in full requisition.

It was in the early summer of this year (1829) that Cincinnati offered a spectacle unprecedented, I believe, in any
age or country. Mr. Owen, of Lanark, of New Harmony, of
Texas, well known to the world by all or either of these additions, had challenged the whole religious public of the United
States to discuss with him publicly the truth or falsehood of
all the religions that had ever been propagated on the face of
the earth; stating, further, that he undertook to prove that
they were all equally false, and nearly equally mischievous.
This most appalling challenge was conveyed to the world
through the medium of New Orleans newspapers, and for
some time it remained unanswered; at length the Reverend
Alexander Campbell, from Bethany, (not of Judæa, but of
Kentucky,) proclaimed, through the same medium, that he
was ready to take up the gauntlet. The place fixed for this
extraordinary discussion was Cincinnati; the time, the second
Monday in May, 1829, being about a year from the time the
challenge was accepted; thus giving the disputants time to
prepare themselves.[1]

---

[1] [DS] The *Cincinnati Chronicle* (April 25, 1829) states that the debate
began on Monday, April 13. "There was, each day of the debate, an audience of more than 1200 persons, many of whom were strangers, attracted to
our city by the novelty and importance of the discussion." Like Mrs. Trollope, it praises the "Christian forbearance" of Campbell and the "philo-

Mr. Owen's preparation, however, could only have been such as those who run may read, for, during the interval, he traversed great part of North America, crossed the Atlantic twice, visited England, Scotland, Mexico, Texas, and I know not how many places besides.

Mr. Campbell, I was told, passed this period very differently, being engaged in reading with great research and perseverance all the theological works within his reach. But whatever confidence the learning and piety of Mr. Campbell might have inspired in his friends, or in the Cincinnati Chris-

---

sophic complacency" of Owen. The discussions were later published as a book and widely read.

Alexander Campbell (1788–1866), chief founder of the Disciples of Christ, commonly known as the Christian Church, was born in Ireland, but came to America in 1809. By the time of his debate with Owen, he was well known as a writer and debater upon religious subjects, and his "little country printing office" between 1823 and 1830 issued 46,000 volumes. His center of operations was Bethany, Virginia (not Kentucky, as Mrs. Trollope says), near Wheeling.

Robert Owen (1771–1858), British socialist, social reformer, and pioneer in co-operative movements, was born in Wales, the son of a shopkeeper. By 1794 he had already worked his way up from a draper's apprenticeship through managership of one of Manchester's largest mills to become a substantial manufacturer in his own right. In 1799 he bought the New Lanark Mills in Scotland. At New Lanark he set up a model community and proceeded to show that good wages and living-conditions for the employees were compatible with prosperity for the employer.

In 1824, after much crusading for more and more ambitious social reforms in England, he came to America, where he had purchased the land and buildings of Harmonie, in Indiana, from the Rappites, a communal religious sect. In 1825 he began his co-operative experiment at the spot, now christened New Harmony; about one thousand persons had taken up residence at his invitation. There were many disputes and dissensions; by the spring of 1827 Owen left New Harmony for England. In 1828 he was back in America with a plan for establishing communal colonies in the provinces of Texas and Coahuila in Mexico. It was while he was on his way to Mexico that he issued the challenge mentioned by Mrs. Trollope. He had for a long time preached rationalism and denounced all religions. His negotiations in Mexico came to an end when he found that the Mexican government would not allow the degree of religious toleration that he demanded for his proposed colonies. In the early spring of 1829 he revisited New Harmony, where nearly all traces of his social experiment had disappeared. From there he went on to Cincinnati for his debate with Campbell, which occupied eight successive days, April 13–20.

tians in general, it was not, as it appeared, sufficient to induce Mr. Wilson, the Presbyterian minister of the largest church in the town, to permit the display of them within its walls. This refusal was greatly reprobated, and much regretted, as the curiosity to hear the discussion was very general, and no other edifice offered so much accommodation.

A Methodist meeting-house, large enough to contain a thousand persons, was at last chosen; a small stage was arranged round the pulpit, large enough to accommodate the disputants and their stenographers; the pulpit itself was throughout the whole time occupied by the aged father of Mr. Campbell, whose flowing white hair, and venerable countenance, constantly expressive of the deepest attention, and the most profound interest, made him a very striking figure in the group. Another platform was raised in a conspicuous part of the building, on which were seated seven gentlemen of the city, selected as moderators.

The chapel was equally divided, one half being appropriated to ladies, the other to gentlemen; and the door of entrance reserved for the ladies was carefully guarded by persons appointed to prevent any crowding or difficulty from impeding their approach. I suspect that the ladies were indebted to Mr. Owen for this attention; the arrangements respecting them on this occasion were by no means American.

When Mr. Owen rose, the building was thronged in every part; the audience, or congregation, (I hardly know which to call them) were of the highest rank of citizens, and as large a proportion of best bonnets fluttered there, as the "two-horned church" itself could boast.

It was in the profoundest silence, and apparently with the deepest attention, that Mr. Owen's opening address was received; and surely it was the most singular one that ever Christian men and women sat to listen to.

When I recollect its object, and the uncompromising manner in which the orator stated his mature conviction that the whole history of the Christian mission was a fraud, and its sacred origin a fable, I cannot but wonder that it was so listened to; yet at the time I felt no such wonder. Never did any one practise the *suaviter in modo* with more powerful effect than Mr. Owen. The gentle tone of his voice; his mild, sometimes playful, but never ironical manner; the absence of every vehement or harsh expression; the affectionate interest expressed for "the whole human family;" the air of candour with which he expressed his wish to be convinced he was wrong, if he indeed were so — his kind smile — the mild expression of his eyes — in short, his whole manner, disarmed zeal, and produced a degree of tolerance that those who did not hear him would hardly believe possible.

Half an hour was the time allotted for each haranguer; when this was expired, the moderators were seen to look at their watches. Mr. Owen, too, looked at his (without pausing) smiled, shook his head, and said in a parenthesis "a moment's patience," and continued for nearly another half hour.

Mr. Campbell then arose; his person, voice, and manner all greatly in his favour. In his first attack he used the arms, which in general have been considered as belonging to the other side of the question. He quizzed Mr. Owen most unmercifully; pinched him here for his parallelograms; hit him there for his human perfectibility, and kept the whole audience in a roar of laughter. Mr. Owen joined in it most heartily himself, and listened to him throughout with the air of a man who is delighted at the good things he is hearing, and exactly in the cue to enjoy all the other good things that he is sure will follow. Mr. Campbell's watch was the only one which reminded us that we had listened to him for half an hour; and having continued speaking for a few minutes after he had looked at it, he sat down with, I should think, the universal admiration of his auditory.

Mr. Owen again addressed us; and his first five minutes

were occupied in complimenting Mr. Campbell with all the strength his exceeding hearty laughter had left him. But then he changed his tone, and said the business was too serious to permit the next half hour to pass so lightly and so pleasantly as the last; and then he read us what he called his twelve fundamental laws of human nature. These twelve laws he has taken so much trouble to circulate to all the nations of the earth, that it must be quite unnecessary to repeat them here. To me they appear twelve truisms, that no man in his senses would ever think of contradicting; but how any one can have conceived that the explanation and defence of these laws could furnish forth occupation for his pen and his voice, through whole years of unwearying declamation, or how he can have dreamed that they could be twisted into a refutation of the Christian religion, is a mystery which I never expect to understand.[2]

---

[2] [DS] Owen summarized his Twelve Laws in his rebuttal speech on the first day of the debate:

"1. That man, at his birth, is ignorant of everything relative to his own organization, and that he has not been permitted to create the slightest part of his natural propensities, faculties, or qualities, physical or mental.

"2. That no two infants, at birth, have yet been known to possess precisely the same organization, while the physical, mental, and moral differences, between all infants, are formed without their knowledge or will.

"3. That each individual is placed, at birth, without his knowledge or consent, within circumstances, which, acting upon his peculiar organization, impress the general character of those circumstances upon the infant, child, and man. Yet that the influence of these circumstances is, to a certain degree, modified by the peculiar natural organization of each individual.

"4. That no infant has the power of deciding at what period of time, or in what part of the world, he shall come into existence; of whom he shall be born, in what distinct religion he shall be trained to believe, or by what other circumstances he shall be surrounded from birth to death.

"5. That each individual is so created, that when young, he may be made to receive impressions, to produce either true ideas or false notions, and beneficial or injurious habits, and to retain them with great tenacity.

"6. That each individual is so created, that he must believe according to the strongest impressions that are made on his feelings and other faculties, while his belief in no case depends upon his will.

"7. That each individual is so created, that he must like that which is pleasant to him, or that which produces agreeable sensations on his individual organization, and he must dislike that which creates in him unpleas-

From this time Mr. Owen entrenched himself behind his twelve laws, and Mr. Campbell, with equal gravity, confined himself to bringing forward the most elaborate theological authorities in evidence of the truth of revealed religion.

Neither appeared to me to answer the other; but to confine themselves to the utterance of what they had uppermost in their own minds when the discussion began. I lamented this on the side of Mr. Campbell, as I am persuaded he would

---

ant and disagreeable sensations; while he cannot discover, previous to experience, what those sensations should be.

"8. That each individual is so created, that the sensations made upon his organization, although pleasant and delightful at their commencement, and for some duration, generally become, when continued beyond a certain period, without change, disagreeable and painful. While, on the contrary, when a too rapid change of sensations is made on his organization, it dissipates, weakens, and otherwise injures his physical, intellectual, and moral powers and enjoyments.

"9. That the highest health, the greatest progressive improvements, and the most permanent happiness of each individual depend in a great degree upon the proper cultivation of all his physical, intellectual, and moral faculties and powers, from infancy to maturity, and upon all these parts of his nature being duly called into action, at their proper period, and temperately exercised, according to the strength and capacity of the individual.

"10. That the individual is made to possess and to acquire the *worst* character, when his organization at birth has been compounded of the most inferior propensities, faculties, and qualities of our common nature, and when so organized, has been placed, from birth to death, amidst the most vicious or worst circumstances.

"11. That the individual is made to possess and to acquire a *medium* character when his original organization has been created *superior,* and when the circumstances which surround him, from birth to death, produce continued *vicious* or *unfavourable* impressions. Or, when his organization has been formed of inferior materials, and the circumstances in which he has been placed, from birth to death, are of a character to produce *superior* impressions only. Or, when there has been some mixture of *good* and *bad* qualities, in the original organization, and when it has been also placed, through life, in various circumstances of *good* and *evil.* This last compound has been hitherto the common lot of mankind.

"12. That the individual is made the most *superior* of his species, when his original organization has been compounded of the best proportions of the best ingredients of which human nature is formed, and when the circumstances which surround him, from birth to death, are of a character to produce only *superior* impressions; or, in other words, when the circumstances or laws, institutions and customs, in which he is placed, are in unison with his nature."

have been much more powerful had he trusted more to himself and less to his books. Mr. Owen is an extraordinary man, and certainly possessed of talent, but he appears to me so utterly benighted in the mists of his own theories, that he has quite lost the power of looking through them, so as to get a peep at the world as it really exists around him.

At the conclusion of the debate (which lasted for fifteen sittings) Mr. Campbell desired the whole assembly to sit down. They obeyed. He then requested all who wished well to Christianity to rise, and a very large majority were in an instant on their legs. He again requested them to be seated, and then desired those who believed not in its doctrines to rise, and a few gentlemen and one lady obeyed. Mr. Owen protested against this manœuvre, as he called it, and refused to believe that it afforded any proof of the state of men's minds, or of women's either; declaring, that not only was such a result to be expected, in the present state of things, but that it was the duty of every man who had children to feed, not to hazard the sale of his hogs, or his iron, by a declaration of opinions which might offend the majority of his customers. It was said, that at the end of the fifteen meetings the numerical amount of the Christians and the Infidels of Cincinnati remained exactly what it was when they began.

This was a result that might have been perhaps anticipated; but what was much less to have been expected, neither of the disputants ever appeared to lose their temper. I was told they were much in each other's company, constantly dining together, and on all occasions expressed most cordially their mutual esteem.

All this I think could only have happened in America. I am not quite sure that it was very desirable it should have happened any where.[3]

---

[3] [TRD] [Mrs. Trollope crossed out the following passage in her rough draft. It is heavily scored and much amended between the lines in a cramped and minute hand.]

In noting the various brilliant events which diversified our residence in the western metropolis, I have omitted to mention the Birth-day Ball, as it is called, a festivity which, I believe, has place on the 22nd of February, in every town and city throughout the Union. It is the anniversary of the birth of General Washington, and well deserves to be marked by the Americans as a day of jubilee.

I was really astonished at the *coup d'œil* on entering, for I saw a large room filled with extremely well-dressed company, among whom were many very beautiful girls. The gentlemen also were exceedingly smart, but I had not yet been long enough in Western America not to feel startled at recognising in almost every full-dressed *beau* that passed me, the master or shopman that I had been used to see behind the counter, or lolling at the door of every shop in the city. The fairest and finest *belles* smiled and smirked on them with as much zeal and satisfaction as I ever saw bestowed on an eldest son, and I therefore could feel no doubt of their being considered as of the highest rank. Yet it must not be supposed that there is no distinction of classes: at this same ball I was looking among the many very beautiful girls I saw there for one more beautiful still, with whose lovely face I had been particularly struck at the school examination I have mentioned. I could not find her, and asked a gentleman why the beautiful Miss C. was not there.

This probably could only have happened in America, where a man's abstract opinions, be they right or wrong, can seldom greatly influence his fortune, or his reception in society, and where one mode of faith is almost as profitable as another, & having no faith at all seems to excite no disputes & little surprise. Therefore [they] venture fearlessly to associate together, nor have I yet heard of any instance in which doing so has been invidiously remarked upon. This at least is a state of things most devoutly to be wished for, as it is I conceive the only state in which those who are led can feel quite sure of the sincerity of those who lead. Where no motive of worldly interest recommends one faith to the teacher in preference to another, the taught are at least sure of not being led to labour in the vineyard of the preacher — instead of that of the Lord.

"You do not yet understand our aristocracy," he replied, "the family of Miss C. are mechanics."

"But the young lady has been educated at the same school as these, whom I see here, and I know her brother has a shop in the town, quite as large, and apparently as prosperous, as those belonging to any of these young men. What is the difference?"

"He is a mechanic; he assists in making the articles he sells; the others call themselves merchants."

The dancing was not quite like, yet not very unlike, what we see at an assize or race-ball in a country town. They call their dances cotillions instead of quadrilles, and the figures are called from the orchestra in English, which has a very ludicrous effect on European ears.

The arrangements for the supper were very singular, but eminently characteristic of the country. The gentlemen had a splendid entertainment spread for them in another large room of the hotel, while the poor ladies had each a plate put into their hands, as they pensively promenaded the ballroom during their absence; and shortly afterwards servants appeared, bearing trays of sweetmeats, cakes, and creams.[4] The fair creatures then sat down on a row of chairs placed round the walls, and each making a table of her knees, began eating her sweet, but sad and sulky repast. The effect was extremely comic; their gala dresses and the decorated room forming a contrast the most unaccountable with their uncomfortable and forlorn condition.

This arrangement was owing neither to economy nor want of a room large enough to accommodate the whole party, but purely because the gentlemen liked it better. This was the answer given me, when my curiosity tempted me to ask why

_____

[4] [TN] ". . . and creams in abundance, and I was told that after I left the room pickled *oysters* & ices *followed* the other good things by way of bonne bouche."

the ladies and gentlemen did not sup together; and this was the answer repeated to me afterwards by a variety of people to whom I put the same question.

I am led to mention this feature of American manners very frequently, not only because it constantly recurs, but because I consider it as being in a great degree the cause of that universal deficiency in good manners and graceful demeanour, both in men and women, which is so remarkable.

Where there is no court, which every where else is the glass wherein the higher orders dress themselves, and which again reflected from them to the classes below, goes far towards polishing, in some degree, a great majority of the population, it is not [to] be expected that manner should be made so much a study, or should attain an equal degree of elegance; but the deficiency, and the total difference, is greater than this cause alone could account for. The hours of enjoyment are important to human beings every where, and we every where find them preparing to make the most of them. Those who enjoy themselves only in society, whether intellectual or convivial, prepare themselves for it, and such make but a poor figure when forced to be content with the sweets of solitude; while, on the other hand, those to whom retirement affords the greatest pleasure, seldom give or receive much in society. Wherever the highest enjoyment is found by both sexes in scenes where they meet each other, both will prepare themselves to appear with advantage there. The men will not indulge in the luxury of chewing tobacco, or even of spitting, and the women will contrive to be capable of holding a higher post than that of unwearied tea-makers.

In America, with the exception of dancing, which is almost wholly confined to the unmarried of both sexes, all the enjoyments of the men are found in the absence of the women. They dine, they play cards, they have musical meetings, they have suppers, all in large parties, but all without women. Were it not that such is the custom, it is impossible but that

they would have ingenuity enough to find some expedient for
sparing the wives and daughters of the opulent the sordid offices of household drudgery which they almost all perform in
their families. Even in the slave states, though they may not
clear-starch and iron, mix puddings and cakes one half of
the day, and watch them baking the other half, still the very
highest occupy themselves in their household concerns, in
a manner that precludes the possibility of their becoming
elegant and enlightened companions. In Baltimore, Philadelphia, and New York, I met with some exceptions to
this; but speaking of the country generally, it is unquestionably true.

Had I not become heartily tired of my prolonged residence
in a place I cordially disliked, and which moreover I began to
fear would not be attended with the favourable results we
had anticipated, I should have found an almost inexhaustible
source of amusement in the notions and opinions of the people I conversed with; and as it was, I often did enjoy this in
a considerable degree.

We received, as I have mentioned, much personal kindness;
but this by no means interfered with the national feeling of,
I believe, unconquerable dislike, which evidently lives at the
bottom of every truly American heart against the English.
This shows itself in a thousand little ways, even in the midst
of the most kind and friendly intercourse, but often in a manner more comic than offensive.

Sometimes it was thus. — "Well, now, I think your government must just be fit to hang themselves for that last war they
cooked up; it has been the ruin of you I expect, for it has just
been the making of us."

Then. — "Well, I do begin to understand your broken English better than I did; but no wonder I could not make it out
very well at first, as you come from London; for every body
knows that London slang is the most dreadful in the world.
How queer it is now, that all the people that live in London

should put the *h* where it is not, and never will put it where it is."

I was egotistical enough to ask the lady who said this, if she found that I did so.

"No; you do not," was the reply; but she added, with a complacent smile, "it is easy enough to see the pains you take about it: I expect you have heard how we Americans laugh at you all for it, and so you are trying to learn our way of pronouncing."

One lady asked me very gravely, if we had left home in order to get rid of the vermin with which the English of all ranks were afflicted? "I have heard from unquestionable authority," she added, "that it is quite impossible to walk through the streets of London without having the head filled."

I laughed a little, but spoke not a word. She coloured highly, and said, "There is nothing so easy as to laugh, but truth is truth, laughed at or not."

I must preface the following anecdote by observing that in America nearly the whole of the insect tribe are classed under the general name of bug; the unfortunate cosmopolite known by that name amongst us is almost the only one not included in this term. A lady abruptly addressed me with, "Don't you hate chintzes, Mrs. Trollope?"

"No, indeed," I replied, "I think them very pretty."

"There now! if that is not being English! I reckon you call that loving your country; well, thank God! we Americans have something better to love our country for than that comes to; we are not obliged to say that we like nasty filthy chintzes to shew that we are good patriots."

"Chintzes? what are chintzes?"

"Possible! do you pretend you don't know what chintzes are? Why the nasty little stinking blood-suckers that all the beds in London are full of."

I have since been informed that *chinche* is Spanish for bug;

but at the time the word suggested only the material of a curtain.

Among other instances of that species of modesty so often seen in America, and so unknown to us, I frequently witnessed one, which, while it evinced the delicacy of the ladies, gave opportunity for many lively sallies from the gentlemen. I saw the same sort of thing repeated on different occasions at least a dozen times; *e. g.* a young lady is employed in making a shirt, (which it would be a symptom of absolute depravity to name), a gentleman enters, and presently begins the sprightly dialogue with "What are you making, Miss Clarissa?"

"Only a frock for my sister's doll, sir."

"A frock? not possible. Don't I see that it is not a frock? Come, Miss Clarissa, what is it?"

" 'Tis just an apron for one of our Negroes, Mr. Smith."

"How can you, Miss Clarissa! why is not the two sides joined together? I expect you were better tell me what it is."

"My! why then Mr. Smith, it is just a pillow-case."

"Now that passes, Miss Clarissa! 'Tis a pillow-case for a giant then. Shall I guess, Miss?"

"Quit, Mr. Smith; behave yourself, or I'll certainly be affronted."

Before the conversation arrives at this point, both gentleman and lady are in convulsions of laughter. I once saw a young lady so hard driven by a wit, that to prove she was making a bag, and nothing but a bag, she sewed up the ends before his eyes, shewing it triumphantly, and exclaiming, "there now! what can you say to that?"

One of my friends startled me one day by saying in an affectionate, but rather compassionate tone, "How will you bear to go back to England to live, and to bring up your children in a country where you know you are considered as no better than the dirt in the streets?"

I begged she would explain.

"Why, you know I would not affront you for any thing; but the fact is, we Americans know rather more than you think for, and certainly if I was in England I should not think of associating with anything but lords. I have always been among the first here, and if I travelled I should like to do the same. I don't mean, I'm sure, that I would not come to see you, but you know you are not lords, and therefore I know very well how you are treated in your own country."

I very rarely contradicted statements of this kind, as I found it less trouble, and infinitely more amusing, to let them pass; indeed, had I done otherwise, it would have been of little avail, as among the many conversations I held in America respecting my own country, I do not recollect a single instance in which it was not clear that I knew much less about it than those I conversed with.

On the subject of national glory, I presume I got more than my share of buffeting; for being a woman, there was no objection to their speaking out. One lady, indeed, who was a great patriot, evinced much delicacy towards me, for upon some one speaking of New Orleans, she interrupted them, saying, "I wish you would not talk of New Orleans;" and, turning to me, added with great gentleness, "It must be so painful to your feelings to hear that place mentioned!"

The immense superiority of the American to the British navy was a constant theme, and to this I always listened, as nearly as possible, in silence. I repeatedly heard it stated, (so often, indeed, and from such various quarters, that I think there must be some truth in it), that the American sailors fire with a certainty of slaughter, whereas our shots are sent very nearly at random. "This," said a naval officer of high reputation, "is the blessed effect of your game laws; your sailors never fire at a mark; whilst our free tars, from their practice in pursuit of game, can any of them split a hair." But the favourite, the constant, the universal sneer that met me every where, was on our old-fashioned attachments to things ob-

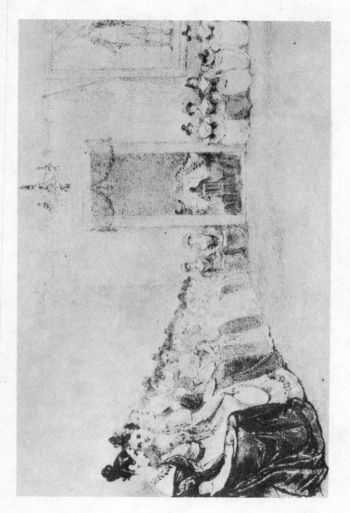

IX CINCINNATI BALL ROOM

X MISS CLARISSA AND MR. SMITH

solete. Had they a little wit among them, I am certain they would have given us the cognomen of "My Grandmother, the British," for that is the tone they take, and it is thus they reconcile themselves to the crude newness of every thing around them.

"I wonder you are not sick of kings, chancellors, and archbishops, and all your fustian of wigs and gowns," said a very clever gentleman to me once, with an affected yawn, "I protest the very sound almost sets me to sleep."

It is amusing to observe how soothing the idea seems, that they are more modern, more advanced than England. Our classic literature, our princely dignities, our noble institutions, are all gone-by relics of the dark ages.

This, and the vastness of their naked territory, make up the flattering unction which is laid upon the soul, as an antidote to the little misgiving which from time to time arises, lest their large country be not of quite so much importance among the nations, as a certain paltry old-fashioned little place that they wot of.

I was once sitting with a party of ladies, among whom were one or two young girls, whose curiosity was greater than their patriotism, and they asked me many questions respecting the splendour and extent of London. I was endeavouring to satisfy them by the best description I could give, when we were interrupted by another lady, who exclaimed, "Do hold your tongues, girls, about London; if you want to know what a beautiful city is, look at Philadelphia; when Mrs. Trollope has been there, I think she will allow that it is better worth talking about than that great overgrown collection of nasty, filthy, dirty streets, that they call London."

Once in Ohio, and once in the district of Columbia, I had an atlas displayed before me, that I might be convinced by the evidence of my own eyes what a very contemptible little country I came from. I shall never forget the gravity with which, on the latter occasion, a gentleman drew out his graduated pencil-case, and shewed me, past contradiction, that the whole of the British dominions did not equal in size one of their least important states; nor the air with which, after the demonstration, he placed his feet upon the chimney-piece, considerably higher than his head, and whistled Yankee Doodle.

Their glorious institutions, their unequalled freedom, were, of course, not left unsung.

I took some pains to ascertain what they meant by their glorious institutions, and it is with no affectation of ignorance that I profess I never could comprehend the meaning of the phrase, which is, however, on the lip of every American, when he talks of his country. I asked if by their institutions they meant their hospitals and penitentiaries. "Oh no! we mean the glorious institutions which are coeval with the revolution." "Is it," I asked, "your institution of marriage, which you have made purely a civil and not a religious rite, to be performed by a justice of peace, instead of a clergyman?"

"Oh no! we speak of our divine political institutions."

Yet still I was in the dark, nor can I guess what they mean, unless they call incessant electioneering, without pause or interval for a single day, for a single hour, of their whole existence, "a glorious institution."

Their unequalled freedom, I think, I understand better. Their code of common law is built upon ours; and the difference between us is this, in England the laws are acted upon, in America they are not.

I do not speak of the police of the Atlantic cities; I believe it is well arranged: in New York it is celebrated for being so; but out of the range of their influence, the contempt of law is greater than I can venture to state, with any hope of being believed. Trespass, assault, robbery, nay, even murder, are often committed without the slightest attempt at legal interference.

During the summer that we passed most delightfully in

Maryland, our rambles were often restrained in various directions by the advice of our kind friends, who knew the manners and morals of the country. When we asked the cause, we
were told, "There is a public-house on that road, and it will
not be safe to pass it."

The line of the Chesapeak and Ohio canal passed within a
few miles of Mrs. S°°°'s residence. It twice happened during
our stay with her, that dead bodies were found partially concealed near it. The circumstance was related as a sort of
half hour's wonder; and when I asked particulars of
those who, on one occasion, brought the tale, the reply
was, "Oh, he was murdered I expect; or may-be he died of
the canal fever; but they say he had marks of being throttled."
No inquest was summoned; and certainly no more sensation
was produced by the occurrence than if a sheep had been
found in the same predicament.

The abundance of food and the scarcity of hanging were
also favourite topics, as proving their superiority to England.
They are both excellent things, but I do not admit the inference. A wide and most fertile territory, as yet but thinly inhabited, may easily be made to yield abundant food for its
population: and where a desperate villain knows, that when
he has made his town or his village "too hot to hold him," he
has nothing to do but to travel a few miles west, and be sure
of finding plenty of beef and whiskey, with no danger that
the law shall follow him, it is not extraordinary that execu-
tions should be rare.

Once during our residence at Cincinnati, a murderer of uncommon atrocity was taken, tried, convicted, and condemned
to death. It had been shewn on his trial, that some years before he had murdered a wife and child at New Orleans, but little notice had been taken of it at the time. The crime which
had now thrown him into the hands of justice was the recent
murder of a second wife, and the chief evidence against him
was his own son.

The day of his execution was fixed, and the sensation produced was so great from the strangeness of the occurrence, (no white man having ever been executed at Cincinnati,) that persons from sixty miles' distance came to be present at it.[5]

---

[5] [DS] The Cincinnati newspapers for late July and August 1829 had a good deal to say of this murder and the events that followed it. J. Birdsell (or Birdsall), after driving his children from the home, had cut off his wife's head with an ax. After sentence of hanging had been passed on him, a group of doctors, lawyers, and ministers — the "aristocrats of the three professions," according to a letter in the *Advertiser* signed "One of the People" — submitted a petition to Governor Trimble, arguing that Birdsell was insane and asking that in accordance with a law passed in 1818 his sentence be commuted to life imprisonment. The Governor granted the petition, but Birdsell refused to give his written consent as required by the law before the sentence could be changed. The sequel is best described in the *Cincinnati Chronicle* (August 1, 1829):

"Under the sentence of the court he was to have been hung on Friday, the 24th ultimo. Without any effort having been made to disseminate a knowledge of this fact, the crowd began to assemble the day previous from the surrounding regions, and before 10 o'clock of the day of execution, our streets were literally thronged with men, women, and children — old age, youth and infancy; these, commingled with our own population, the parade of the military, and the general suspension of business, were well calculated to create an impression that our city was engaged in some grand jubilee, or joyous national festival. Our work shops, stores, offices, and we are deeply pained to say, many of our parlours were deserted. Every body seemed to be in the streets, and all impatient for the arrival of the appointed hour.

"The professors too of *galvanism,* in our city, had united and burnished up their plates of copper and zinc, and having procured the Circus were busily engaged in *selling* tickets of admission to those who felt desirous of continuing the fun by witnessing the horrible contortions to be produced upon the dead body of Birdsell after the penalty of the law had been paid. A species of public exhibition unheard of, we believe, in the history of any community, and totally at variance with all the decencies and refinements of civilized and religious life.

"The only shadow of gloom that seemed to pervade the vast multitude arose from the fear that the prisoner might accept of a commutation of his punishment into confinement for life. . . . The reports, however, from the prison during the forenoon were confirmatory of his determination to die upon the gallows, and the delight of the crowd was just in proportion to their belief on that determination.

"By 12 o'clock the city, except in that quarter which overlooked the place of execution, was almost tenantless. The streets were as silent and desolate as though the plague had swept through them.

"We have heard the number of persons assembled around the gallows es-

Meanwhile some unco' good people began to start doubts as to the righteousness of hanging a man, and made application to the Governor of the State [6] of Ohio, to commute the sentence into imprisonment. The Governor for some time refused to interfere with the sentence of the tribunal before which he had been tried; but at length, frightened at the unusual situation in which he found himself, he yielded to the importunity of the Presbyterian party who had assailed him, and sent off an order to the sheriff accordingly. But this order was not to reprieve him, but to ask him if he pleased to be reprieved, and sent to the penitentiary instead of being hanged.

The sheriff waited upon the criminal, and made his proposal, and was answered, "If any thing could make me agree to it, it would be the hope of living long enough to kill you and my dog of a son: however, I won't agree; you shall have the hanging of me."

The worthy sheriff, to whom the ghastly office of executioner is assigned, said all in his power to persuade him to sign the offered document, but in vain; he obtained nothing but abuse for his efforts.

The day of execution arrived; the place appointed was the side of a hill, the only one cleared of trees near the town; and many hours before the time fixed, we saw it entirely cov-

---

timated at from 15 to 25,000 of whom it is supposed that more than one half were females. When the prisoner, after the rope was placed round his neck, agreed to the commutation, we are told there was a general burst of indignation and disappointment, and that torrents of bitter imprecations were poured out upon the criminal, the Executive, and all of those who had petitioned for a commutation of the punishment. As the crowd returned from the gallows to the city, they reminded one of a funeral procession, except so far as the occasional outbreakings of their deep disappointment indicated the source of their wobegone looks. Now it must not be understood that this feeling of indignation arose from the fact that a murderer was about to escape . . . it was simply because they had been cheated out of the sport of seeing a man hung."

[6] [T1] The Governors of states have the same power over life and death as is vested, with us, in the crown.

ered by an immense multitude of men, women, and children. At length the hour arrived, the dismal cart was seen slowly mounting the hill, the noisy throng was hushed into solemn silence; the wretched criminal mounted the scaffold, when again the sheriff asked him to sign his acceptance of the commutation proposed; but he spurned the paper from him, and cried aloud, "Hang me!"

Mid-day was the moment appointed for cutting the rope; the sheriff stood, his watch in one hand, and a knife in the other; the hand was lifted to strike, when the criminal stoutly exclaimed, "I sign;" and he was conveyed back to prison, amidst the shouts, laughter, and ribaldry of the mob.

I am not fond of hanging, but there was something in all this that did not look like the decent dignity of wholesome justice.[7]

---

[7] [T5, note] It was not till after I had left the United States that the frightful details of Lynch law reached me. These details are now well known throughout Europe, and must surely be received as a confirmation of the statements made in the foregoing chapter, respecting the insufficiency of the laws, or at least of the manner in which they are enforced, for preventing and punishing crime. Yet these statements are among those which brought upon me the most positive accusations of having falsified facts, and grossly misstated what I saw.

[DS] Lynch law and the question of Negro slavery play important parts in Mrs. Trollope's novel *The Life and Adventures of Jonathan Jefferson Whitlaw; or Scenes on the Mississippi*, published, with fifteen illustrations by Hervieu, in London in 1836. For a fuller description of this novel, see section XII of the Introduction.

CHAPTER XV

Camp-Meeting

IT was in the course of this summer that I found the opportunity I had long wished for, of attending a camp-meeting, and I gladly accepted the invitation of an English lady and gentleman to accompany them in their carriage to the spot where it is held; this was in a wild district on the confines of Indiana.

The prospect of passing a night in the back woods of Indiana was by no means agreeable, but I screwed my courage to the proper pitch, and set forth determined to see with my own eyes, and hear with my own ears, what a camp-meeting really was. I had heard it said that being at a camp-meeting was like standing at the gate of heaven, and seeing it opening before you; I had heard it said, that being at a camp-meeting was like finding yourself within the gates of hell; in either case there must be something to gratify curiosity, and compensate one for the fatigue of a long rumbling ride and a sleepless night.

We reached the ground about an hour before midnight, and the approach to it was highly picturesque. The spot chosen was the verge of an unbroken forest, where a space of about twenty acres appeared to have been partially cleared for the purpose. Tents of different sizes were pitched very near together in a circle round the cleared space; behind them were ranged an exterior circle of carriages of every description, and at the back of each were fastened the horses which had drawn them thither. Through this triple circle of defence we distinguished numerous fires burning brightly within it; and still more numerous lights flickering from the trees that were left in the enclosure. The moon was in meridian splendour above our heads.

We left the carriage to the care of a servant, who was to prepare a bed in it for Mrs. B. and me, and entered the inner circle. The first glance reminded me of Vauxhall, from the effect of the lights among the trees, and the moving crowd below them; but the second shewed a scene totally unlike any thing I had ever witnessed. Four high frames, constructed in the form of altars, were placed at the four corners of the enclosure; on these were supported layers of earth and sod, on which burned immense fires of blazing pine-wood. On one side a rude platform was erected to accommodate the preachers, fifteen of whom attended this meeting, and with very short intervals for necessary refreshment and private devotion, preached in rotation, day and night, from Tuesday to Saturday.

When we arrived, the preachers were silent; but we heard issuing from nearly every tent mingled sounds of praying, preaching, singing, and lamentation. The curtains in front of each tent were dropped, and the faint light that gleamed through the white drapery, backed as it was by the dark forest, had a beautiful and mysterious effect, that set the imagination at work; and had the sounds which vibrated around us been less discordant, harsh, and unnatural, I should have enjoyed it; but listening at the corner of a tent, which poured forth more than its proportion of clamour, in a few moments chased every feeling derived from imagination, and furnished realities that could neither be mistaken or forgotten.

Great numbers of persons were walking about the ground, who appeared like ourselves to be present only as spectators; some of these very unceremoniously contrived to raise the drapery of this tent, at one corner, so as to afford us a perfect view of the interior.

The floor was covered with straw, which round the sides

XI CAMP MEETING, INDIANA, 1829

XII "HERE'S TO YOU, COLONEL."
"SAD WEATHER, MAJOR."

was heaped in masses, that might serve as seats, but which at that moment were used to support the heads and the arms of the close-packed circle of men and women who kneeled on the floor.

Out of about thirty persons thus placed, perhaps half a dozen were men. One of these, a handsome looking youth of eighteen or twenty, kneeled just below the opening through which I looked. His arm was encircling the neck of a young girl who knelt beside him, with her hair hanging dishevelled upon her shoulders, and her features working with the most violent agitation; soon after they both fell forward on the straw, as if unable to endure in any other attitude the burning eloquence of a tall grim figure in black, who, standing erect in the centre, was uttering with incredible vehemence an oration that seemed to hover between praying and preaching; his arms hung stiff and immoveable by his side, and he looked like an ill-constructed machine, set in action by a movement so violent, as to threaten its own destruction, so jerkingly, painfully, yet rapidly, did his words tumble out; the kneeling circle ceasing not to call in every variety of tone, on the name of Jesus; accompanied with sobs, groans, and a sort of low howling [1] inexpressibly painful to listen to. But my attention was speedily withdrawn from the preacher, and the circle round him, by a figure which knelt alone at some distance; it was a living image of Scott's Macbriar, as young, as wild, and as terrible. His thin arms tossed above his head, had forced themselves so far out of the sleeves, that they were bare to the elbow; his large eyes glared frightfully, and he continued to scream without an instant's intermission the word "Glory!" with a violence that seemed to swell every vein

---

[1] [TRD] . . . and a sort of low howling so closely resembling that of a distant wolf that they must have caught it from thence — but my attention was speedily . . .

[DS] The section of the rough draft devoted to the camp meeting is headed: "Camp Meeting on the borders of Indiana and Ohio, August 14th 1829."

to bursting. It was too dreadful to look upon long, and we turned away shuddering.

We made the circuit of the tents, pausing where attention was particularly excited by sounds more vehement than ordinary. We contrived to look into many; all were strewed with straw, and the distorted figures that we saw kneeling, sitting, and lying amongst it, joined to the woeful and convulsive cries, gave to each, the air of a cell in Bedlam.

One tent was occupied exclusively by Negroes. They were all full-dressed, and looked exactly as if they were performing a scene on the stage. One woman wore a dress of pink gauze trimmed with silver lace; another was dressed in pale yellow silk; one or two had splendid turbans; and all wore a profusion of ornaments. The men were in snow white pantaloons, with gay coloured linen jackets. One of these, a youth of coal-black comeliness, was preaching with the most violent gesticulations, frequently springing high from the ground, and clapping his hands over his head. Could our missionary societies have heard the trash he uttered, by way of an address to the Deity, they might perhaps have doubted whether his conversion had much enlightened his mind.

At midnight a horn sounded through the camp, which, we were told, was to call the people from private to public worship; and we presently saw them flocking from all sides to the front of the preachers' stand. Mrs. B. and I contrived to place ourselves with our backs supported against the lower part of this structure, and we were thus enabled to witness the scene which followed without personal danger. There were about two thousand persons assembled.

One of the preachers began in a low nasal tone, and, like all other Methodist preachers, assured us of the enormous depravity of man as he comes from the hands of his Maker, and of his perfect sanctification after he had wrestled sufficiently with the Lord to get hold of him, *et cætera*. The admiration of the crowd was evinced by almost constant cries of "Amen! Amen!" "Jesus! Jesus!" "Glory! Glory!" and the like. But this comparative tranquillity did not last long: the preacher told them that "this night was the time fixed upon for anxious sinners to wrestle with the Lord;" that he and his brethren "were at hand to help them," and that such as needed their help were to come forward into "the pen." The phrase forcibly recalled Milton's lines —

> "Blind mouths! that scarce themselves know how to hold
> A sheep-hook, or have learned aught else, the least
> That to the faithful herdsman's art belongs!
> — But when they list their lean and flashy songs,
> Grate on their scrannel pipes of wretched straw; —
> The hungry sheep look up, and are not fed!
> But swoln with wind, and the rank mist they draw,
> Rot inwardly — and foul contagion spread."

"The pen" was the space immediately below the preachers' stand; we were therefore placed on the edge of it, and were enabled to see and hear all that took place in the very centre of this extraordinary exhibition.

The crowd fell back at the mention of the *pen*, and for some minutes there was a vacant space before us. The preachers came down from their stand and placed themselves in the midst of it, beginning to sing a hymn, calling upon the penitents to come forth. As they sung they kept turning themselves round to every part of the crowd, and, by degrees, the voices of the whole multitude joined in chorus. This was the only moment at which I perceived any thing like the solemn and beautiful effect, which I had heard ascribed to this woodland worship. It is certain that the combined voices of such a multitude, heard at dead of night, from the depths of their eternal forests, the many fair young faces turned upward, and looking paler and lovelier as they met the moon-beams, the dark figures of the officials in the middle of the circle, the lurid glare thrown by the altar-fires on the woods beyond, did altogether produce a fine and solemn effect, that I shall not easily forget; but ere I had well enjoyed it, the scene changed, and sublimity gave place to horror and disgust.

The exhortation nearly resembled that which I had heard at "the Revival," but the result was very different; for, instead of the few hysterical women who had distinguished themselves on that occasion, above a hundred persons, nearly all females, came forward, uttering howlings and groans, so terrible that I shall never cease to shudder when I recall them. They appeared to drag each other forward, and on the word being given, "let us pray," they all fell on their knees; but this posture was soon changed for others that permitted greater scope for the convulsive movements of their limbs; and they were soon all lying on the ground in an indescribable confusion of heads and legs. They threw about their limbs with such incessant and violent motion, that I was every instant expecting some serious accident to occur.

But how am I to describe the sounds that proceeded from this strange mass of human beings? I know no words which can convey an idea of it. Hysterical sobbings, convulsive groans, shrieks and screams the most appalling, burst forth on all sides. I felt sick with horror. As if their hoarse and overstrained voices failed to make noise enough, they soon began to clap their hands violently. The scene described by Dante was before me: —

> "Quivi sospiri, pianti, ed alti guai
> Risonavon per l'aere ——
> —— Orribili favelle
> Parole di dolore, accenti d'ira
> Voci alti e fioche, *e suon di man con elle*." [2]

---

[2] [DS] *Inferno*, III, 22–7:
Here sighs, plaints, and loud wailings
Resounded through the air . . .
. . . horrible outcries,
Words of pain, accents of anger,
Voices loud and hoarse, and sounds of hands among them.

Many of these wretched creatures were beautiful young females. The preachers moved about among them, at once exciting and soothing their agonies. I heard the muttered "Sister! dear sister!" I saw the insidious lips approach the cheeks
of the unhappy girls; I heard the murmured confessions of
the poor victims, and I watched their tormentors, breathing
into their ears consolations that tinged the pale cheek with
red. Had I been a man, I am sure I should have been guilty
of some rash act of interference; nor do I believe that such a
scene could have been acted in the presence of Englishmen
without instant punishment being inflicted; not to mention
the salutary discipline of the tread-mill, which, beyond all
question, would, in England, have been applied to check so
turbulent and so vicious a scene.

After the first wild burst that followed their prostration, the
moanings, in many instances, became loudly articulate; and
I then experienced a strange vibration between tragic and
comic feeling.

A very pretty girl, who was kneeling in the attitude of
Canova's Magdalene immediately before us, amongst an immense quantity of jargon, broke out thus: "Woe! woe to the
backsliders! hear it, hear it Jesus! when I was fifteen my
mother died, and I backslided, oh Jesus, I backslided! take
me home to my mother, Jesus! take me home to her, for I am
weary! Oh John Mitchel! John Mitchel!" and after sobbing
piteously behind her raised hands, she lifted her sweet face
again, which was as pale as death, and said, "Shall I sit on the
sunny bank of salvation with my mother? my own dear
mother? oh Jesus, take me home, take me home!"

Who could refuse a tear to this earnest wish for death in
one so young and so lovely? But I saw her, ere I left the
ground, with her hand fast locked, and her head supported by
a man who looked very much as Don Juan might, when sent
back to earth as too bad for the regions below.

One woman near us continued to "call on the Lord," as it is

termed, in the loudest possible tone, and without a moment's interval, for the two hours that we kept our dreadful station. She became frightfully hoarse, and her face so red as to make me expect she would burst a blood-vessel. Among the rest of her rant, she said, "I will hold fast to Jesus, I never will let him go; if they take me to hell, I will still hold him fast, fast, fast!"

The stunning noise was sometimes varied by the preachers beginning to sing; but the convulsive movements of the poor maniacs only became more violent. At length the atrocious wickedness of this horrible scene increased to a degree of grossness, that drove us from our station; we returned to the carriage at about three o'clock in the morning, and passed the remainder of the night in listening to the ever increasing tumult at the pen. To sleep was impossible. At day-break the horn again sounded, to send them to private devotion; and in about an hour afterwards I saw the whole camp as joyously and eagerly employed in preparing and devouring their most substantial breakfasts as if the night had been passed in dancing; and I marked many a fair but pale face, that I recognised as a demoniac of the night, simpering beside a swain, to whom she carefully administered hot coffee and eggs. The preaching saint and the howling sinner seemed alike to relish this mode of recruiting their strength.

After enjoying abundance of strong tea, which proved a delightful restorative after a night so strangely spent, I wandered alone into the forest,[3] and I never remember to have found perfect quiet more delightful.

---

[3] [TRD] . . . I wandered alone into the forest, where I committed to paper a part of what I had witnessed — my memory therefore has not cheated me — and the above statement may be depended upon as strictly true, though by no means so full of circumstances as I would have made it, but common decency forbids my dwelling on much that I saw; and nothing can excuse the mention of it but the burning indignation which makes me feel exposure of such atrocity to be a duty.

We soon after left the ground; but before our departure we learnt that a very *satisfactory* collection had been made by the preachers, for Bibles, Tracts, and *all other religious purposes*.

CHAPTER XVI

Danger of rural excursions — Sickness

IT is by no means easy to enjoy the beauties of American scenery in the west, even when you are in a neighbourhood that affords much to admire; at least, in doing so, you run considerable risk of injuring your health. Nothing is considered more dangerous than exposure to mid-day heat, except exposure to evening damp; and the twilight is so short, that if you set out on an expedition when the fervid heat subsides, you can hardly get half a mile before "sun down," as they call it, warns you that you must run or drive home again, as fast as possible, for fear you should get "a chill."

I believe we braved all this more than any one else in the whole country, and if we had not, we should have left Cincinnati without seeing any thing of the country around it.

Though we kept steadily to our resolution of passing no more sylvan hours in the forests of Ohio, we often spent entire days in Kentucky, tracing the course of a "creek," or climbing the highest points within our reach, in the hope of catching a glimpse of some distant object. A beautiful reach of the Ohio, or the dark windings of the pretty Licking, were indeed always the most remarkable features in the landscape.

There was one spot, however, so beautiful that we visited it again and again; it was by no means free from mosquitoes; and being on the bank of a stream, with many enormous trees lying on the half-cleared ground around, it was just such a place as we had been told a hundred times was particularly "dangerous;" nevertheless, we dared every thing for the sake of dining beside our beautiful rippling stream, and watching the bright sunbeams dancing on the grassy bank, at such a distance from our retreat that they could not heat us. A little below the basin that cooled our wine was a cascade of sufficient dimensions to give us all the music of a waterfall, and all the sparkling brightness of clear water when it is broken again and again by jutting crags.

To sit beside this miniature cascade, and read, or dream away a day, was one of our greatest pleasures.

It was indeed a mortifying fact, that whenever we found out a picturesque nook, where turf, and moss, and deep shade, and a crystal stream, and fallen trees, majestic in their ruin, tempted us to sit down, and be very cool and very happy, we invariably found that that spot lay under the imputation of malaria.

A row upon the Ohio was another of our favourite amusements; but in this, I believe, we were also very singular, for often, when enjoying it, we were shouted at, by the young free-borns on the banks, as if we had been so many monsters.

The only rural amusement in which we ever saw any of the natives engaged was eating strawberries and cream in a pretty garden about three miles from the town; here we actually met three or four carriages; a degree of dissipation that I never witnessed on any other occasion. The strawberries were tolerable strawberries, but the cream was the vilest sky-blue, and the charge half a dollar to each person; which being about the price of half a fat sheep, I thought "pretty considerable much," if I may be permitted to use an expressive phrase of the country.

We had repeatedly been told, by those who knew the land, that the *second summer* was the great trial to the health of Europeans settled in America; but we had now reached the middle of our second August, and with the exception of the fever one of my sons had suffered from, the summer after our arrival, we had all enjoyed perfect health; but I was now doomed to feel the truth of the above prediction, for before the end of August I fell low before the monster that is for ever stalking through that land of lakes and rivers, breathing fever and death around. It was nine weeks before I left my room, and when I did, I looked more fit to walk into the Potter's Field, (as they call the English burying-ground) than any where else.

Long after my general health was pretty well restored, I suffered from the effect of the fever in my limbs, and lay in bed reading several weeks after I had been pronounced convalescent. Several American novels were brought me. Mr. Flint's Francis Berrian is excellent; a little wild and romantic, but containing scenes of first-rate interest and pathos. Hope Leslie, and Redwood, by Miss Sedgewick [Catharine Maria Sedgwick], an American lady, have both great merit; and I now first read the whole of Mr. Cooper's novels. By the time these American studies were completed, I never closed my eyes without seeing myriads of bloody scalps floating round me; long slender figures of Red Indians crept through my dreams with noiseless tread; panthers glared; forests blazed; and whichever way I fled, a light foot, a keen eye, and a long rifle were sure to be on my trail. An additional ounce of calomel hardly sufficed to neutralize the effect of these raw-head and bloody-bones adventures. I was advised to plunge immediately into a course of fashionable novels. It was a great relief to me; but as my head was by no means very clear, I sometimes jumbled strangely together the civilized rogues and assassins of Mr. Bulwer, and the wild men, women, and children slayers of Mr. Cooper; and, truly, between them, I passed my dreams in very bad company.

Still I could not stand, nor even sit upright. What was I to read next? A happy thought struck me. I determined upon beginning with Waverley, and reading through (not for the first time certainly) the whole series. And what a world did I enter upon! The wholesome vigour of every page seemed to communicate itself to my nerves; I ceased to be languid and fretful, and though still a cripple, I certainly enjoyed myself

most completely, as long as my treat lasted; but this was a
shorter time than any one would believe, who has not found
how such volumes melt, before the constant reading of a long
idle day. When it was over, however, I had the pleasure of
finding that I could walk half a dozen yards at a time, and
take short airings in an open carriage; and better still, could
sleep quietly.

It was no very agreeable conviction which greeted my recovery, that our Cincinnati speculation for my son would in
no way answer our expectation; and very soon after, he was
again seized with the bilious fever of the country, which terminated in that most distressing of all maladies, an ague. I
never witnessed its effects before, and therefore made myself
extremely miserable at what those around me considered of
no consequence.

I believe this frightful complaint is not immediately dangerous; but I never can believe that the violent and sudden
prostration of strength, the dreadfully convulsive movements
which distort the limbs, the livid hue that spreads itself over
the complexion, can take place without shaking the seat of
health and life.[1] Repeatedly we thought the malady cured,
and for a few days the poor sufferer believed himself restored
to health and strength; but again and again it returned upon
him, and he began to give himself up as the victim of ill

---

[1] [DS] As one sufferer described the effects:
"You felt as though you had gone through some sort of collision, thrash-
ing-machine or jarring-machine, and came out not killed, but next thing to
it. You felt weak, as though you had run too far after something, and then
didn't catch it. You felt languid, stupid and sore, and was down in the
mouth and heel and partially raveled out. Your back was out of fix, your
head ached and your appetite crazy. Your eyes had too much white in
them, your ears, especially after taking quinine, had too much roar in
them, and your whole body and soul were entirely woebegone, disconsolate,
sad, poor, and good for nothing. . . . You didn't quite make up your mind
to commit suicide, but sometimes wished some accident would happen to
knock either the malady or yourself out of existence." — Quoted in Madge
E. Pickard and R. Carlyle Buley: *The Midwest Pioneer: His Ills, Cures, &
Doctors* (Crawfordsville, Indiana: R. E. Banta; 1945).

health. My own health was still very infirm, and it took but little time to decide that we must leave Cincinnati. The only impediment to this was, the fear that Mr. Trollope, who was to join us in the spring, might have set out, and thus arrive at Cincinnati after we had left it. However, as the time he had talked of leaving England was later in the season, I decided upon running the risk; but the winter had set in with great severity, and the river being frozen, the steam-boats could not run; the frost continued unbroken through the whole of February, and we were almost weary of waiting for its departure, which was to be the signal of ours.

The breaking up of the ice, on the Licking and Ohio, formed a most striking spectacle. At night the river presented a solid surface of ice, but in the morning it shewed a collection of floating ice-bergs, of every imaginable size and form, whirling against each other with frightful violence, and with a noise unlike any sound I remember.

This sight was a very welcome one, as it gave us hopes of immediate departure, but my courage failed, when I heard that one or two steam-boats, weary of waiting, meant to start on the morrow. The idea of running against these floating islands was really alarming, and I was told by many, that my fears were not without foundation, for that repeated accidents had happened from this cause; and then they talked of the little Miami river, whose mouth we were to pass, sending down masses of ice that might stop our progress; in short, we waited patiently and prudently, till the learned in such matters told us that we might start with safety.

CHAPTER XVII

Departure from Cincinnati — Society on board the Steam-boat —
Arrival at Wheeling — Bel Esprit

WE quitted Cincinnati the beginning of March, 1830, and I believe there was not one of our party who did not experience a sensation of pleasure in leaving it.[1] We had seen again and again all the queer varieties of it's little world; had amused ourselves with it's consequence, it's taste, and it's ton, till they had ceased to be amusing. Not a hill was left unclimbed, nor a forest path unexplored; and, with the exception of two or three individuals, who bore heads and hearts peculiar to no clime, but which are found scattered through the world, as if to keep us every where in good humour with it, we left nought to regret at Cincinnati. The only regret was, that we had ever entered it; for we had wasted health, time, and money there.

We got on board the steam-boat which was to convey us to Wheeling at three o'clock. She was a noble boat, by far the finest we had seen.[2] The cabins were above, and the deck

---

[1] [DS] For an account of Mrs. Trollope's circumstances at the time when she left Cincinnati and her plans in starting eastward, see sections VII and VIII of the Introduction.

[2] [DS] The *Lady Franklin* was a steamboat of two hundred tons, with high-pressure boiler, built at Portsmouth, Ohio, in 1829; sunk by collision in 1835.

The *Belvidere*, which carried Mrs. Trollope from New Orleans to Memphis, had a low-pressure boiler and weighed one hundred and sixty tons; it was built at Portsmouth, Ohio, in 1825, and was retired, worn out, in 1831.

The *Criterion*, which brought her from Memphis to Cincinnati, had a high-pressure boiler and weighed two hundred tons; it was built at New Albany, Indiana, in 1828. The date when it was retired or lost is not given in James Hall's *Notes on the Western States* (1838), the source of these statistics.

passengers, as they are called, were accommodated below. In front of the ladies' cabin was an ample balcony, sheltered by an awning; chairs and sofas were placed there, and even at that early season, nearly all the female passengers passed the whole day there. The name of this splendid vessel was the Lady Franklin. By the way, I was often amused by the evident fondness which the Americans shew for titles. The wives of their eminent men constantly receive that of "Lady." We heard of Lady Washington, Lady Jackson, and many other "ladies." The eternal recurrence of their militia titles is particularly ludicrous, met with, as they are, among the tavern-keepers, market-gardeners, &c. But I think the most remarkable instance which we noticed of this sort of aristocratical longing occurred at Cincinnati. Mr. T— in speaking of a gentleman of the neighbourhood, called him Mr. M—. "General M—, sir," observed his companion. "I beg his pardon," rejoined Mr. T—, "but I was not aware of his being in the army." "No, sir, not in the army," was the reply, "but he was surveyor-general of the district." [3]

The weather was delightful; all trace of winter had disappeared, and we again found ourselves moving rapidly up the stream, and enjoying all the beauty of the Ohio.

Of the male part of the passengers we saw nothing, excepting at the short silent periods allotted for breakfast, dinner, and supper, at which we were permitted to enter their cabin, and place ourselves at their table.

In the Lady Franklin we had decidedly the best of it, for we had our beautiful balcony to sit in. In all respects, indeed,

---

[3] [DS] From Godfrey T. Vigne's *Six Months in America* (1832):

"An English gentleman assured me that, being on board a steamer on the Ohio river, he was first introduced by a friend as plain Mr., then as Captain; soon after he was addressed as Major, and before the end of the day he was formally introduced as a General. There is usually a Major, or an Aide, as they call themselves, in every stage-coach company. The captain of a steam-boat, who was presiding at the dinner table, happened to ask rather loudly, 'General, a little fish!' and was immediately answered in the affirmative by twenty-five out of the thirty gentlemen who were present."

our accommodations were very superior to what we had found in the boat which brought us from New Orleans to Memphis, where we were stowed away in a miserable little chamber close aft, under the cabin, and given to understand by the steward, that it was our duty there to remain "till such time as the bell should ring for meals."

The separation of the sexes, so often mentioned, is no where more remarkable than on board the steam-boats. Among the passengers on this occasion we had a gentleman and his wife, who really appeared to suffer from the arrangement. She was an invalid, and he was extremely attentive to her, as far, at least, as the regulations permitted. When the steward opened the door of communication between the cabins, to permit our approaching the table, her husband was always stationed close to it, to hand her to her place; and when he accompanied her again to the door, he always lingered for a moment or two on the forbidden threshold, nor left his station, till the last female had passed through. Once or twice he ventured, when all but his wife were on the balcony, to sit down beside her for a moment in our cabin, but the instant either of us entered, he started like a guilty thing and vanished.

While mentioning the peculiar arrangements which are thought necessary to the delicacy of the American ladies, or to the comfort of the American gentlemen, I am tempted to allude to a story which I saw in the papers respecting the visits which it was stated Captain Basil Hall persisted in making to his wife and child on board a Mississippi steam-boat, after being informed that doing so was contrary to law. Now I happen to know that neither himself or Mrs. Hall ever entered the ladies' cabin during the whole voyage, as they occupied a state-room which Captain Hall had secured for his party. The veracity of newspaper statements is, perhaps, nowhere quite unimpeachable, but if I am not greatly mistaken, there are more direct falsehoods circulated by the

American newspapers than by all the others in the world, and the one great and never-failing source of these voluminous works of imagination is England and the English. How differently would such a voyage be managed on the other side the Alantic, were such a mode of travelling possible there. Such long calm river excursions would be perfectly delightful, and parties would be perpetually formed to enjoy them. Even were all the parties strangers to each other, the knowledge that they were to eat, drink, and steam away together for a week or fortnight, would induce something like a social feeling in any other country.

It is true that the men became sufficiently acquainted to game together, and we were told that the opportunity was considered as so favourable, that no boat left New Orleans without having as cabin passengers one or two gentlemen from that city whose profession it was to drill the fifty-two elements of a pack of cards to profitable duty. This doubtless is an additional reason for the strict exclusion of the ladies from their society. The constant drinking of spirits is another, for though they do not scruple to chew tobacco and to spit incessantly in the presence of women, they generally prefer drinking and gaming in their absence.

I often used to amuse myself with fancying the different scene which such a vessel would display in Europe. The noble length of the gentlemen's cabin would be put into requisition for a dance, while that of the ladies, with their delicious balcony, would be employed for refreshments, instead of sitting down in two long silent melancholy rows, to swallow as much coffee and beef-steak as could be achieved in ten minutes. Then song and music would be heard borne along by the midnight breeze; but on the Ohio, when light failed to shew us the bluffs, and the trees, with their images inverted in the stream, we crept into our little cots, listening to the ceaseless churning of the engine, in hope it would prove a lullaby till morning.

We were three days in reaching Wheeling,[4] where we arrived at last, at two o'clock in the morning, an uncomfortable
hour to disembark with a good deal of luggage, as the steam-
boat was obliged to go on immediately; but we were instantly
supplied with a dray, and in a few moments found ourselves
comfortably seated before a good fire, at an hotel near the
landing-place; our rooms, with fires in them, were immediately ready for us, and refreshments brought, with all that
sedulous attention which in this country distinguishes a slave
state.[5] In making this observation I am very far from intend-

---

[4] [TRD] We were three days in reaching Wheeling; one of these was
Sunday. An American Sunday, passed before the eyes of any of the natives,
is a day of penance indeed. It matters not who are the individuals, or what
their opinions; *fear* does the work of principle; and for one who wished to
pass this day in the listless apathy of perfect idleness, I have met hundreds
who confessed they dared not do otherwise. To write is a scandal; to read,
except the Bible, a crime. To be heard to touch a piano would produce a
much stronger feeling of horror, than to be heard swearing, on any other
day of the week; nor do I believe that there is any crime in the decalogue,
the perpetration of which would produce so strong an expression of public
indignation, as singing a song on a Sunday.

Our Sunday on the Ohio steam boat was dull enough, for there was no
creeping into a corner with a book. The only trace of amusement I can remember was endeavoring to make an old lady define what might be done,
and what might not be done on a Sunday. It was her opinion that we ought
not to cook, or permit cooking on the day set apart for the Lord; but that
we should bring ourselves, humbly, to be content with what could be
cooked on Saturday: "I never," she said, kindling with conscious merit, "I
never suffer a pot to be put upon the fire in my house, on the Sabbath Day."
"Do you take no tea, Madam?" said I. "Oh yes, I always have my tea."
"Then in this case, Madam, the difference between good and evil, is the
same as that between a pot and a kettle." This joke, however, was hardly
witty enough to furnish out amusement for the twelve hours of daylight;
and I heartily wished during their course, that the Jews had hit upon any
other expedient in the world, for keeping every seventh day holy, than sitting with our hands before us.

We passed many towns, of high sounding names but none that appeared
of much importance; we were told, however, that one or two of them had
a bank. Many of their names end in *opilis* and I remember that they were
always pronounced opol*is*, a very strong emphasis resting on the last syllable.

[5] [T5, note] This passage was written during my short stay at Wheeling, and before I had seen any thing of slavery beyond the condition of domestic slaves in one or two well-ordered families. I permitted the passage,
however, to be published as it stood in my MS. because it spoke faithfully

ing to advocate the system of slavery; I conceive it to be essentially wrong; but so far as my observation has extended, I think its influence is far less injurious to the manners and morals of the people than the fallacious ideas of equality, which are so fondly cherished by the working classes of the white population in America. That these ideas are fallacious, is obvious, for in point of fact the man possessed of dollars does command the services of the man possessed of no dollars; but these services are given grudgingly, and of necessity, with no appearance of cheerful good-will on the one side, or of kindly interest on the other. I never failed to mark the difference on entering a slave state. I was immediately comfortable, and at my ease, and felt that the intercourse between me and those who served me, was profitable to both parties and painful to neither.

It was not till I had leisure for more minute observation that I felt aware of the influence of slavery upon the owners of slaves; when I did, I confess I could not but think that the citizens of the United States had contrived, by their political alchymy, to extract all that was most noxious both in

the impression received when it was written. Nay, notwithstanding that the detestation of slavery increased with me, as it must do with all disinterested lookers-on, in proportion to their opportunities of watching its consequences, I still think that when seen as we then saw it its effect will appear less injurious to the country than the false, futile, and preposterous tone assumed by the white population when compelled by necessity to sell their labour in domestic service.

A little reflection, however, will show that this false note itself is in fact generated solely by the existence of slavery. It is this which renders the idea of domestic service shameful; and had the federal government courage and influence to abolish this iniquitous abuse of power, they would, at the same moment that they righteously did justice to the negro, relieve their country from one of the chief causes of its inferiority in all the graces of civilisation; for it is the struggle of proud but powerless poverty with unprivileged but powerful wealth which stagnates the progress of civilisation, as well as of order, in the United States. Were the sinful and unnatural spectacle of a race degraded by legalised tyranny removed, the gradation of ranks INEVITABLE in the progress of all society would take place naturally, and of necessity, leaving tranquillity and leisure for the progress of refinement.

democracy and in slavery, and had poured the strange mixture through every vein of the moral organization of their country.

Wheeling is in the state of Virginia, and appears to be a flourishing town. It is the point at which most travellers from the West leave the Ohio, to take the stages which travel the mountain road to the Atlantic cities.

It has many manufactories, among others, one for blowing and cutting glass, which we visited. We were told by the workmen that the articles finished there were equal to any in the world; but my eyes refused their assent. The cutting was very good, though by no means equal to what we see in daily use in London; but the chief inferiority is in the material, which is never altogether free from colour. I had observed this also in the glass of the Pittsburgh manufactory, the labour bestowed on it always appearing greater than the glass deserved. They told us also, that they were rapidly improving in the art, and I have no doubt that this was true.

Wheeling has little of beauty to distinguish it, except the ever lovely Ohio, to which we here bade adieu, and a fine bold hill, which rises immediately behind the town. This hill, as well as every other in the neighbourhood, is bored for coal. Their mines are all horizontal. The coal burns well, but with a very black and dirty cinder.

We found the coach, by which we meant to proceed to Little Washington, full, and learnt that we must wait two days before it would again leave the town. Posting was never heard of in the country, and the mail travelled all night, which I did not approve of; we therefore found ourselves compelled to pass two days at the Wheeling hotel.

I know not how this weary interval would have worn away, had it not been for the fortunate circumstance of our meeting with a *bel esprit* among the boarders there. We descended to the common sitting room (for private parlours there are none) before breakfast the morning after our arrival; several ordinary individuals entered, till the party amounted to eight or nine. Again the door opened, and in swam a female, who had once certainly been handsome, and who, it was equally evident, still thought herself so. She was tall, and well formed, dressed in black, with many gaudy trinkets about her: a scarlet *fichu* relieved the sombre colour of her dress, and a very smart little cap at the back of her head set off an immense quantity of sable hair, which naturally, or artificially, adorned her forehead. A becoming quantity of rouge gave the finishing touch to her figure, which had a degree of pretension about it that immediately attracted our notice. She talked fluently, and without any American restraint, and I began to be greatly puzzled as to who or what she could be; a lady, in the English sense of the word, I was sure she was not, and she was as little like an American female of what they call good standing. A beautiful girl of seventeen entered soon after, and called her "Ma," and both mother and daughter chattered away, about themselves and their concerns, in a manner that greatly increased my puzzle.

After breakfast, being much in want of amusement, I seated myself by her, and entered into conversation. I found her nothing loth, and in about a minute and a half she put a card into my hand, setting forth, that she taught the art of painting upon velvet in all its branches.

She stated to me, with great volubility, that no one but herself and her daughter knew any thing of this invaluable branch of art; but that for twenty-five dollars they were willing to communicate all they knew.

In five minutes more she informed me that she was the author of some of the most cutting satires in the language; and then she presented me a paper, containing a prospectus, as she called it, of a novel, upon an entirely new construction. I was strangely tempted to ask her if it went by steam, but she left me no time to ask any thing, for, continuing the autobiography she had so obligingly begun, she said, "I used to

write against all the Adams faction. I will go up stairs in a
moment and fetch you down my sat-heres against that side.
But oh! my dear madam! it is really frightful to think how
talent is neglected in this country. Ah! I know what you are
going to say, my dear madam, you will tell me that it is not
so in yours. I know it! but alas! the Atlantic! However, I
really must tell you how I have been treated: not only did I
publish the most biting sat-heres against the Adams faction,
but I wrote songs and odes in honour of Jackson; and my
daughter, Cordelia, sang a splendid song of my writing, before eight hundred people, entirely and altogether written in
his praise; and would you believe it, my dear madam, he has
never taken the slightest notice of me, or made me the least
remuneration. But you can't suppose I mean to bear it quietly? No! I promise him that is not my way. The novel I have
just mentioned to you was began as a sentimental romance
(that, perhaps, after all, is my real forte), but after the provo-
cation I received at Washington, I turned it into a sat-hereical
novel, and I now call it *Yankee Doodle Court.* By the way,
my dear madam, I think if I could make up my mind to cross
that terrible Atlantic, I should be pretty well received, after
writing Yankee Doodle Court!"

I took the opportunity of a slight pause to ask her to what
party she now belonged, since she had forsworn both Adams
and Jackson.

"Oh Clay! Clay for ever! he is a real true-hearted republican; the others are neither more nor less than tyrants." [6]

---

[6] [DS] Anyone looking for evidence that Mrs. Trollope contrived caricatures on occasion without benefit of fact would probably fasten upon this
sketch of an authoress whose "sat-hereical" work is called, of all things,
Yankee Doodle Court. But the book is in the Library of Congress. It contains 146 pages and is entitled *The Reign of Reform, or, Yankee Doodle
Court, by a Lady* (Baltimore: Printed for the Authoress; 1830).

The authoress, Mrs. Margaret Botsford, carries out the purpose that she
avowed to Mrs. Trollope of attacking Jackson and lauding Clay, and her peculiar style of doing so has much the flavor of her conversation as Mrs. Trollope reports it. The "Advertisement" reads:

When next I entered the sitting-room she again addressed me, to deplore the degenerate taste of the age.

"Would you believe it? I have at this moment a comedy ready for representation; I call it 'The Mad Philosopher.' It is really admirable, and its success certain, if I could get it played. I assure you the neglect I meet with amounts perfectly to persecution. But I have found out how to pay them, and to make my own fortune. Sat-here, (as she constantly pronounced satire) sat-here is the only weapon that can re-

---

"That a *female* writer should thus oppose a *majority*, and attack even the *'Wise men of Gotham,'* (alone and unaided as she is,) may excite much astonishment — even among the *minority;* but she *fears naught*, when con-[s]cious of employing her pen in a *just* cause."

The whole book is made up of dialogues between Colonel Hardfare and Major Dauntless. A sample follows:

"Major Dauntless: . . . we are an *enthusiastic* people, and when *genuine* merit is too apparent to be *mistaken*, the shouts of a multitude will bring forth the *Western luminary*, who has withdrawn its effulgence for a *while*, but to dazzle with *tenfold lustre*, when the *proper* time shall arrive; and the clouds which *unjust prejudice* and *base calumny*, gathered to obscure a star of too great *magnitude* to be long concealed, will *disperse*. . . .

"Col. Hardfare: Bravo! Major *Dauntless*! you are a true *Patriot*! Success to the *Star of the West*!

"Maj. Dauntless: Aye, Col., no *mistake* there! rely on it. Now I will give a specimen of Major *Dauntless's* plain, *blunt rhyme*, on the subject — which I have written *extemporaneously*, as you will perceive; but if it is to the *purpose*, that's all we require. It is addressed to

The *wise* Princes of the Reign of *'Reform.'*

If the shoe should fit you — wear *it* —
If it pinch *you* — grin *and* bear *it* —
If the lash should smart — *don't flinch*!
It will not help the case an inch. . . .
And, tho' their barque's 'tough Hickory!'
The cry's for 'Clay! *and* Victory!'
Kentucky's sons have seen their error —
Indignant at this 'Reign of terror!'
They now resolve to stop the sway!
And eager to bring out their Clay,
Which is of finest Porcelain *kind*,
None to compare, will others find!
Then hark! the West cries out 'Huzza!'
We'll beat 'tough Hickory' *with* 'Clay.'"

venge neglect, and I flatter myself I know how to use it. Do me the favour to look at this."

She then presented me with a tiny pamphlet, whose price, she informed me, was twenty-five cents, which I readily paid to become the possessor of this *chef d'œuvre*. The composition was pretty nearly such as I anticipated, excepting that the English language was done to death by her pen still more than by her tongue. The epigraph, which was subscribed "original," was as follows:

> "Your popularity's on the decline:
> You had your triumph! now I'll have mine."

These are rather a favourable specimen of the verses that follow.

In a subsequent conversation she made me acquainted with another talent, informing me that she had played the part of Charlotte, in *Love à la mode,* when General Lafayette honoured the theatre at Cincinnati with his presence.

She now appeared to have run out the catalogue of her accomplishments; and I came to the conclusion that my new acquaintance was a strolling player: but she seemed to guess my thoughts, for she presently added, "It was a Thespian corps that played before the General." [7]

---

[7] [DS] The Cincinnati *Advertiser* (May 25, 1825) reports: "The Thespian Society having got up a play and Entertainments, for the purpose, the General was requested to grace the Theatre with his presence, with which he complied. . . ." The play may have been Charles Macklin's *Love à la Mode: an Afterpiece in Two Acts* (1760).

Mrs. Botsford dates one of her poems "Cincinnati, 1817," and was possibly living in Cincinnati when General Lafayette visited the city. The poem ("To W. V.") is contained in her *Viola, or the Heiress of St. Valverde, an Original Poem in Five Cantos, to which is Annexed, Patriotic Songs, Sonnets, &c., by a Lady of Philadelphia* (Louisville: Printed by S. Penn, Jr.; 1820). She also published *Adelaide: A New and Original Novel, by a Lady of Philadelphia* (Philadelphia: Printed by Dennis Heartt; 1816).

CHAPTER XVIII

Departure for the Mountains in the Stage — Scenery of the
Alleghany — Haggerstown

THE weather was bleak and disagreeable during the two days we were obliged to remain at Wheeling. I had got heartily tired of my gifted friend; we had walked up every side of the rugged hill, and I set off on my journey towards the mountains with more pleasure than is generally felt in quitting a pillow before day-light, for a cold corner in a rumbling stage-coach.

This was the first time we had got into an American stage, though we had traversed above two thousand miles of the country, and we had all the satisfaction in it, which could be derived from the conviction that we were travelling in a foreign land. This vehicle had no step, and we climbed into it by a ladder; when that was removed I remembered, with some dismay, that the females at least were much in the predicament of sailors, who, "in danger have no door to creep out:" but when a misfortune is absolutely inevitable, we are apt to bear it remarkably well; who would utter that constant petition of ladies on rough roads, "let me get out," when compliance would oblige the pleader to make a step of five feet before she could touch the ground?

The coach had three rows of seats, each calculated to hold three persons, and as we were only six, we had, in the phrase of Milton, to "inhabit lax" this exalted abode, and, accordingly, we were for some miles tossed about like a few potatoes in a wheel-barrow. Our knees, elbows, and heads required too much care for their protection to allow us leisure to look out of the windows; but at length the road became smoother, and we became more skilful in the art of balancing ourselves, so as to meet the concussion with less danger of dislocation.

We then found that we were travelling through a very beautiful country, essentially different in its features from what we had been accustomed to round Cincinnati: it is true we had left *"la belle rivière"* behind us, but the many limpid and rapid little streams that danced through the landscape to join it, more than atoned for its loss.

The country already wore an air of more careful husbandry, and the very circumstance of a wide and costly road (though not a very smooth one), which in theory might be supposed to injure picturesque effect, was beautiful to us, who, since we had entered the muddy mouth of the Mississippi, had never seen any thing except a steam-boat and the *levée* professing to have so noble an object as public accommodation. Through the whole of the vast region we had passed, excepting at New Orleans itself, every trace of the art of man appeared to be confined to the individual effort of "getting along," which, in western phrase, means contriving to live with as small a portion of the incumbrances of civilized society as possible.

This road was made at the expense of the government as far as Cumberland, a town situated among the Alleghany mountains, and, from the nature of the ground, must have been a work of great cost.[1] I regretted not having counted the number of bridges between Wheeling and Little Washington, a distance of thirty-four miles; over one stream only

[1] [DS] Mrs. Trollope traveled the famous National Road, or Cumberland Road, the great artery of traffic westward in the first half of the nineteenth century. It was begun at Cumberland, Maryland, in 1808 and carried across the Alleghenies to Wheeling, Virginia (a distance of 130 miles), in the next nine years. By 1833 it was brought to Columbus, Ohio, and two decades later carried as far as Vandalia, Illinois. According to original estimate, the section from Cumberland to Wheeling was to take $1,750,000, but it actually cost a good deal more. The National Road today forms part of transcontinental U. S. Highway Number 40.

there are twenty-five, all passed by the road. They frequently occurred within a hundred yards of each other, so serpentine is its course; they are built of stone, and sometimes very neatly finished.

Little Washington is in Pennsylvania, across a corner of which the road runs. This is a free state, but we were still waited upon by Negroes, hired from the neighbouring state of Virginia. We arrived at night, and set off again at four in the morning; all, therefore, that we saw of Little Washington was its hotel, which was clean and comfortable. The first part of the next day's journey was through a country much less interesting: its character was unvaried for nearly thirty miles, consisting of an uninterrupted succession of forest-covered hills. As soon as we had wearily dragged to the top of one of these, we began to rumble down the other side as rapidly as our four horses could trot; and no sooner arrived at the bottom than we began to crawl up again; the trees constantly so thick and so high as to preclude the possibility of seeing fifty yards in any direction.

The latter part of the day, however, amply repaid us. At four o'clock we began to ascend the Alleghany mountains: the first ridge on the western side is called Laurel Hill, and takes its name from the profuse quantity of evergreens with which it is covered; not any among them, however, being the shrub to which we give the name of laurel.

The whole of this mountain region, through ninety miles of which the road passes, is a garden. The almost incredible variety of plants, and the lavish profusion of their growth, produce an effect perfectly enchanting. I really can hardly conceive a higher enjoyment than a botanical tour among the Alleghany mountains, to any one who had science enough to profit by it.

The magnificent rhododendron first caught our eyes; it fringes every cliff, nestles beneath every rock, and blooms around every tree. The azalia, the shumac, and every variety of that beautiful mischief, the kalmia, are in equal profusion. Cedars of every size and form were above, around, and underneath us; firs more beautiful and more various than I had ever seen, were in equal abundance, but I know not whether they were really such as I had never seen in Europe, or only in infinitely greater splendour and perfection of growth; the species called the hemlock is, I think, second to the cedar only, in magnificence. Oak and beech, with innumerable roses and wild vines, hanging in beautiful confusion among their branches, were in many places scattered among the evergreens. The earth was carpeted with various mosses and creeping plants, and though still in the month of March, not a trace of the nakedness of winter could be seen. Such was the scenery that shewed us we were indeed among the far-famed Alleghany mountains.

As our noble terrace-road, the Semplon [2] of America, rose higher and higher, all that is noblest in nature was joined to all that is sweetest. The blue tops of the higher ridges formed the outline; huge masses of rock rose above us on the left, half hid at intervals by the bright green shrubs, while to the right we looked down upon the tops of the pines and cedars which clothed the bottom.

I had no idea of the endless variety of mountain scenery. My notions had been of rocks and precipices, of torrents and of forest trees, but I little expected that the first spot which should recal the garden scenery of our beautiful England would be found among the mountains: yet so it was. From the time I entered America I had never seen the slightest approach to what we call pleasure-grounds; a few very worthless and scentless flowers were all the specimens of gardening I had seen in Ohio; no attempt at garden scenery was ever dreamed of, and it was with the sort of delight with which one meets an old friend, that we looked on the lovely mixture

[2] [DS] An allusion to the famous road built by Napoleon over the Simplon Pass in the Swiss Alps.

of trees, shrubs, and flowers, that now continually met our eyes. Often, on descending into the narrow vallies, we found a little spot of cultivation, a garden or a field, hedged round with shumacs, rhododendrons, and azalias, and a cottage covered with roses. These vallies are spots of great beauty; a clear stream is always found running through them, which is generally converted to the use of the miller, at some point not far from the road; and here, as on the heights, great beauty of coloring is given to the landscape, by the bright hue of the vegetation, and the sober grey of the rocks.

The first night we passed among the mountains recalled us painfully from the enjoyment of nature to all the petty miseries of personal discomfort. Arrived at our inn, a forlorn parlour, filled with the blended fumes of tobacco and whiskey, received us; and chilled, as we began to feel ourselves with the mountain air, we preferred going to our cold bed-rooms rather than sup in such an atmosphere. We found linen on the beds which they assured us had only been used *a few nights;* every kind of refreshment we asked for we were answered, "We do not happen to have that article."

We were still in Pennsylvania, and no longer waited upon by slaves; it was, therefore, with great difficulty that we procured a fire in our bed-rooms from the surly-looking *young lady* who condescended to officiate as chamber-maid, and with much more, that we extorted clean linen for our beds; that done, we patiently crept into them supperless, while she made her exit muttering about the difficulty of "fixing English folks."

The next morning cheered our spirits again; we now enjoyed a new kind of alpine witchery; the clouds were floating around, and below us, and the distant peaks were indistinctly visible as through a white gauze veil, which was gradually lifted up, till the sun arose, and again let in upon us the full glory of these interminable heights.

We were told before we began the ascent, that we should

find snow four inches deep on the road; but as yet we had seen none, and indeed it was with difficulty we persuaded ourselves that we were not travelling in the midst of summer. As we proceeded, however, we found the northern declivities still covered with it, and at length, towards the summit, the road itself had the promised four inches. The extreme mildness of the air, and the brilliant hue of the evergreens, contrasted strangely with this appearance of winter; it was difficult to understand how the snow could help melting in such an atmosphere.

Again and again we enjoyed all the exhilarating sensations that such scenes must necessarily inspire, but in attempting a continued description of our progress over these beautiful mountains, I could only tell again of rocks, cedars, laurels, and running streams, of blue heights, and green vallies, yet the continually varying combinations of these objects afforded us unceasing pleasure. From one point, pre-eminently above any neighbouring ridge, we looked back upon the enormous valley of the West. It is a stupendous view; but having gazed upon it for some moments, we turned to pursue our course, and the certainty that we should see it no more, raised no sigh of regret.

We dined, on the second day, at a beautiful spot, which we were told was the highest point on the road, being 2,846 feet above the level of the sea. We were regaled luxuriously on wild turkey and mountain venison; which latter is infinitely superior to any furnished by the forests of the Mississippi, or the Ohio. The vegetables also were extremely fine, and we were told by a pretty girl, who superintended the slaves that waited on us, (for we were again in Virginia), that the vegetables of the Alleghany were reckoned the finest in America. She told us also, that wild strawberries were profusely abundant, and very fine; that their cows found for themselves, during the summer, plenty of flowery food, which produced a copious supply of milk; that their spring gave them the purest water, of icy coldness in the warmest seasons; and that the climate was the most delicious in the world, for though the thermometer sometimes stood at ninety, their cool breeze never failed them. What a spot to turn hermit in for a summer! My eloquent mountaineer gave me some specimens of ground plants, far unlike any thing I had ever seen. One particularly, which she called the ground pine, is peculiar, as she told me, to the Alleghany, and in some places runs over whole acres of ground; it is extremely beautiful. The rooms were very prettily decorated with this elegant plant, hung round it in festoons.

In many places the clearing has been considerable; the road passes through several fine farms, situated in the sheltered hollows; we were told that the wolves continue to annoy them severely, but that panthers, the terror of the West, are never seen, and bears very rarely. Of snakes, they confessed they had abundance, but very few that were considered dangerous.

In the afternoon we came in sight of the Monongehala [Monongahela] river; and its banks gave us for several miles a beautiful succession of wild and domestic scenery. In some points, the black rock rises perpendicularly from its margin, like those at Chepstow; at others, a mill, with its owner's cottage, its corn-plat, and its poultry, present a delightful image of industry and comfort.

Brownsville is a busy looking little town built upon the banks of this river; it would be pretty, were it not stained by the hue of coal. I do not remember in England to have seen any spot, however near a coal mine, so dyed in black as Wheeling and Brownsville. At this place we crossed the Monongehala, in a flat ferry-boat, which very commodiously received our huge coach and four horses.

On leaving the black little town, we were again cheered by abundance of evergreens, reflected in the stream, with fantastic piles of rock, half visible through the pines and cedars above, giving often the idea of a vast gothic castle. It was a folly, I confess, but I often lamented they were not such; the travelling for thousands of miles, without meeting any nobler trace of the ages that are passed, than a mass of rotten leaves, or a fragment of fallen rock, produces a heavy, earthly, matter-of-fact effect upon the imagination, which can hardly be described, and for which the greatest beauty of scenery can furnish only an occasional and transitory remedy.[3]

Our second night in the mountains was past at a solitary house of rather forlorn appearance; but we fared much better than the night before, for they gave us clean sheets, a good fire, and no scolding. We again started at four o'clock in the morning, and eagerly watched for the first gleam of light that should show the same lovely spectacle we had seen the day before; nor were we disappointed, though the show was somewhat different. The vapours caught the morning ray, as it first darted over the mountain top, and passing it to the scene below, we seemed enveloped in a rainbow.

We had now but one ridge left to pass over, and as we reached the top, and looked down on the new world before us, I hardly knew whether most to rejoice that

"All the toil of the long-pass'd way"

was over, or to regret that our mountain journey was drawing to a close.

The novelty of my enjoyment had doubtless added much to its keenness. I have never been familiar with mountain scenery. Wales has shewn me all I ever saw, and the region of the Alleghany Alps in no way resembles it. It is a world of

---

[3] [T5, note] I have been severely ridiculed by some American friends for my superstitious clinging to the memory of the little mouldering works of man amid the boundless and eternal majesty of nature. For a moment the observation seems too pompously powerful to permit an answer. But is it true to our human nature? If we be pigmies — as in truth we are — it is vain to struggle against the fact; and the past doings of our father pigmies will (to such as know any thing about their fathers) have an interest, for the total absence of which neither rocks nor rivers can long atone.

mountains rising around you in every direction, and in every
form; savage, vast, and wild; yet almost at every step, some
lovely spot meets your eye, green, bright, and blooming, as
the most cherished nook belonging to some noble Flora in
our own beautiful land. It is a ride of ninety miles through
kalmias, rhododendrons, azalias, vines and roses; sheltered
from every blast that blows by vast masses of various coloured
rocks, on which

> "Tall pines and cedars wave their dark green crests."

While in every direction you have a back-ground of blue
mountain tops, that play at bo-peep with you in the clouds.[4]

After descending the last ridge we reached Haggerstown
[Hagerstown], a small neat place, between a town and a village; and here by the piety of the Presbyterian coach-masters,
we were doomed to pass an entire day, and two nights, "as
the accommodation line must not run on the sabbath."

I must, however, mention, that this day of enforced rest
was *not* Sunday. Saturday evening we had taken in at Cumberland a portly passenger, whom we soon discovered to be
one of the proprietors of the coach. He asked us, with great
politeness, if we should wish to travel on the sabbath, or to
delay our journey. We answered that we would rather proceed; "The coach, then, shall go on to-morrow," replied the
liberal coach-master, with the greatest courtesy; and accordingly we travelled all Sunday, and arrived at Haggerstown
on Sunday night. At the door of the inn our civil proprietor
left us; but when we enquired of the waiter at what hour

---

4 [TRD] Nor is there any danger that sameness should weary, for every
three or four miles present a pretty little cottage, whose rustic colonnade
generally contains a mingled group of black and white children to gaze at
the daily show of the huge coach and four. Sometimes a beautiful dancing
stream calls together a little town, by the convenience it offers to the miller;
and wherever this happens the mixture of flowering shrubs, with the cultivation of the little gardens, suggests ideas of luxury and pleasure; though assuredly it was the hand of nature, and not taste, that planted them there.

XIII METHODIST PREACHER
Baltimore

XIV MEMBER OF CONGRESS

we were to start on the morrow, he told us that we should be obliged to pass the whole of Monday there, as the coach which was to convey us forward would not arrive from the east, till Tuesday morning.

Thus we discovered that the waiving the sabbath-keeping by the proprietor, was for his own convenience, and not for ours, and that we were to be tied by the leg for four-and-twenty hours notwithstanding. This was quite a Yankee trick.

Luckily for us, the inn at Haggerstown was one of the most comfortable I ever entered. It was there that we became fully aware that we had left Western America behind us. Instead of being scolded, as we literally were at Cincinnati, for asking for a private sitting-room, we here had two, without asking at all. A waiter, quite *comme il faut,* summoned us to breakfast, dinner, and tea, which we found prepared with abundance, and even elegance. The master of the house met us at the door of the eating-room, and, after asking if we wished for any thing not on the table, retired. The charges were in no respect higher than at Cincinnati.

A considerable creek, called Conococheque Creek, runs near the town, and the valley through which it passes is said to be the most fertile in America.

On leaving Haggerstown we found, to our mortification, that we were not to be the sole occupants of the bulky accommodation, two ladies and two gentlemen appearing at the door ready to share it with us. We again started, at four o'clock, by the light of a bright moon, and rumbled and nodded through roads considerably worse than those over the mountains.

As the light began to dawn we discovered our ladies to be an old woman and her pretty daughter.

Soon after day-light we found that our pace became much slower than usual, and that from time to time our driver addressed to his companion on the box many and vehement exclamations.[5] The gentlemen put their heads out, to ask what was the matter, but could get no intelligence, till the mail overtook us, when both vehicles stopped, and an animated colloquy of imprecations took place between the coachmen. At length we learnt that one of our wheels was broken in such a manner as to render it impossible for us to proceed. Upon this the old lady immediately became a principal actor in the scene. She sprung to the window, and addressing the set of gentlemen who completely filled the mail, exclaimed "Gentlemen! can't you make room for two? Only me and my daughter?" The *naïve* simplicity of this request set both the coaches into an uproar of laughter. It was impossible to doubt that she acted upon the same principle as the pious Catholic, who addressing heaven with a prayer for himself alone, added *"pour ne pas fatiguer ta miséricorde."* [6] Our laugh, however, never daunted the old woman, or caused her for a moment to cease the reiteration of her request, "only for two of us, gentlemen! can't you find room for two?"

Our situation was really very embarrassing, but not to laugh was impossible. After it was ascertained that our own vehicle could not convey us, and that the mail had not even room for two, we decided upon walking to the next village, a distance, fortunately, of only two miles, and awaiting there the repair of the wheel. We immediately set off, at the brisk pace that six o'clock and a frosty morning in March were likely to inspire, leaving our old lady and her pretty daughter considerably in the rear; our hearts having been rather hardened by the exclusive nature of her prayer for aid.

---

[5] [TRD] . . . with sundry observations, all containing that most unfailing expletive "God D-mn." The gentlemen put their heads out, to ask what was the matter, but could get no intelligence till the mail overtook us, when both vehicles stopped, and an animated colloquy of G-d d-mns between the drivers, accompanied by the pointing of the mail coachman's whip to our wheels, convinced us that something was wrong. We insisted upon knowing what, and at length learnt that one of the wheels was broken to pieces.

[6] [DS] *"pour ne pas fatiguer,"* etc.: "in order not to tire out Thy mercy."

When we had again started upon our new wheel, the driver, to recover the time he had lost, drove rapidly over a very rough road, in consequence of which, our self-seeking old lady fell into a perfect agony of terror, and her cries of "we shall be over! oh, Lord! we shall be over! we must be over! we shall be over!" lasted to the end of the stage, which with laughing, walking, and shaking, was a most fatiguing one.

CHAPTER XIX

Baltimore — Catholic Cathedral — St. Mary's College — Sermons
— Infant School

AS we advanced towards Baltimore the look of cultivation increased, the fences wore an air of greater neatness, the houses began to look like the abodes of competence and comfort, and we were consoled for the loss of the beautiful mountains by knowing that we were approaching the Atlantic.

From the time of quitting the Ohio river, though, unquestionably, it merits its title of "the beautiful," especially when compared with the dreary Mississippi, I strongly felt the truth of an observation I remembered to have heard in England, that little rivers were more beautiful than great ones. As features in a landscape, this is assuredly the case. Where the stream is so wide that the objects on the opposite shore are indistinct, all the beauty must be derived from the water itself; whereas, when the stream is narrow, it becomes only a part of the composition. The Monongahela, which is in size between the Wye and the Thames, is infinitely more picturesque than the Ohio.

To enjoy the beauty of the vast rivers of this vast country you must be upon the water; and then the power of changing the scenery by now approaching one shore, and now the other, is very pleasing; but travelling as we now did, by land, the wild, rocky, narrow, rapid little rivers we encountered, were a thousand times more beautiful. The Potapsco, near which the road runs, as you approach Baltimore, is at many points very picturesque. The large blocks of grey rock, now close upon its edge, and now retiring to give room for a few acres of bright green herbage, give great interest and variety to its course.

Baltimore is, I think, one of the handsomest cities to approach in the Union. The noble column erected to the memory of Washington, and the Catholic Cathedral, with its beautiful dome, being built on a commanding eminence, are seen at a great distance. As you draw nearer, many other domes and towers become visible, and as you enter Baltimore-street, you feel that you are arrived in a handsome and populous city.

We took up our quarters at an excellent hotel, where the coach stopped, and the next day were fortunate enough to find accommodation in the house of a lady, well known to many of my European friends. With her and her amiable daughter, we spent a fortnight very agreeably, and felt quite aware that if we had not arrived in London or Paris, we had, at least, left far behind the "half-horse, half-alligator" tribes of the West, as the Kentuckians call themselves.

Baltimore is in many respects a beautiful city; it has several handsome buildings, and even the private dwelling-houses have a look of magnificence, from the abundance of white marble with which many of them are adorned. The ample flights of steps, and the lofty door frames, are in most of the best houses formed of this beautiful material.

This has been called the city of monuments, from its having the stately column erected to the memory of General Washington, and which bears a colossal statue of him at the top; and another pillar of less dimensions, recording some victory; I forget which.[1] Both these are of brilliant white marble. There are also several pretty marble fountains in different parts of the city, which greatly add to its beauty. These are

---

[1] [TRD] . . . and another [column] of less dimensions recording the decisive battle of Bunker Hill[!].

not, it is true, quite so splendid as that of the Innocents, or many others at Paris, but they are fountains of clear water, and they are built of white marble. There is one which is sheltered from the sun by a roof supported by light columns; it looks like a temple dedicated to the genius of the spring. The water flows into a marble cistern, to which you descend by a flight of steps of delicate whiteness, and return by another. These steps are never without groups of negro girls, some carrying the water on their heads, with that graceful steadiness of step, which requires no aid from the hand; some tripping gaily with their yet unfilled pitchers; many of them singing in the soft rich voice, peculiar to their race; and all dressed with that strict attention to taste and smartness, which seems the distinguishing characteristic of the Baltimore females of all ranks.

The Catholic Cathedral is considered by all Americans as a magnificent church, but it can hardly be so classed by any one who has seen the churches of Europe; its interior, however, has an air of neatness that amounts to elegance. The form is a Greek cross, having a dome in the centre; but the proportions are ill-preserved; the dome is too low, and the arches which support it are flattened, and too wide for their height. On each side of the high altar are chapels to the Saviour and the Virgin. The altars in these, as well as the high altar, are of native marble of different colours, and some of the specimens are very beautiful. The decorations of the altar are elegant and costly. The prelate is a cardinal, and bears, moreover, the title of "Archbishop of Baltimore."

There are several paintings in different parts of the church, which we heard were considered as very fine. There are two presented by Louis XVIII.; one of these is the Descent from the Cross, by Paulin Guirin; the other a copy from Rubens, (as they told us) of a legend of St. Louis in the Holy Land; but the composition of the picture is so abominably bad, that I conceive the legend of its being after Rubens, must be as fabulous as its subject.[2] The admiration in which these pictures are held, is an incontestable indication of the state of art in the country.

We attended mass in this church the Sunday after our arrival, and I was perfectly astonished at the beauty and splendid appearance of the ladies who filled it. Excepting on a very brilliant Sunday at the Tuilleries, I never saw so shewy a display of morning costume, and I think I never saw any where so many beautiful women at one glance. They all appeared to be in full dress, and were really all beautiful.

The sermon (I am very attentive to sermons) was a most extraordinary one. The priest began by telling us, that he was about to preach upon a vice that he would not "mention or name" from the beginning of his sermon to the end.

Having thus excited the curiosity of his hearers, by proposing a riddle to them, he began.

Adam, he said, was most assuredly the first who had committed this sin, and Cain the next; then, following the advice given by the listener, in the Plaideurs, "Passons au déluge, je vous prie;"[3] he went on to mention the particular propriety of Noah's family on this point; and then continued, "Now observe, what did God shew the greatest dislike to? What was it that Jesus was never even accused of? What was it Joseph hated the most? Who was the disciple that Jesus chose for his friend?" and thus he went on for nearly an hour, in a strain that was often perfectly unintelligible to me, but which, as far as I could comprehend it, appeared to be a sort of *exposé* and commentary upon private anecdotes which he had found, or fancied he had found in the Bible. I never saw the attention of a congregation more strongly excited, and I

---

[2] [DS] Probably Mrs. Trollope failed to hear her informant correctly and mistook *Steuben* for *Rubens*. The picture of St. Louis burying a dead soldier in sight of the fortifications of Tunis, which still hangs in the Baltimore Cathedral, was painted by Baron Charles de Steuben.

[3] [DS] *"Passons au déluge,"* etc.: "Pray, let's pass on to the Flood." — Racine's *Les Plaideurs*.

really wished, in Christian charity, that something better had rewarded it.

There are a vast number of churches and chapels in the city, in proportion to its extent, and several that are large and well-built; the Unitarian church is the handsomest I have ever seen dedicated to that mode of worship. But the prettiest among them is a little *bijou* of a thing belonging to the Catholic college. The institution is dedicated to St. Mary, but this little chapel looks, though in the midst of a city, as if it should have been sacred to St. John of the wilderness. There is a sequestered little garden behind it, hardly large enough to plant cabbages in, which yet contains a Mount Calvary, bearing a lofty cross. The tiny path which leads up to this sacred spot, is not much wider than a sheep-track, and its cedars are but shrubs, but all is in proportion; and notwithstanding its fairy dimensions, there is something of holiness, and quiet beauty about it, that excites the imagination strangely. The little chapel itself has the same touching and impressive character. A solitary lamp, whose glare is tempered by delicately painted glass, hangs before the altar. The light of day enters dimly, yet richly, through crimson curtains, and the silence with which the well-lined doors opened from time to time, admitting a youth of the establishment, who, with noiseless tread, approached the altar, and kneeling, offered a whispered prayer, and retired, had something in it more calculated, perhaps, to generate holy thoughts, than even the swelling anthem heard beneath the resounding dome of St. Peter's.

Baltimore has a handsome museum, superintended by one of the Peale family, well known for their devotion to natural science, and to works of art. It is not their fault if the specimens which they are enabled to display in the latter department are very inferior to their splendid exhibitions in the former.

The theatre was closed when we were in Baltimore, but we

were told that it was very far from being a popular or fashionable amusement. We were, indeed, told this every where
throughout the country, and the information was generally
accompanied by the observation, that the opposition of the
clergy was the cause of it. But I suspect that this is not the
principal cause, especially among the men, who, if they were
so implicit in their obedience to the clergy, would certainly
be more constant in their attendance at the churches; nor
would they, moreover, deem the theatre more righteous because an English actor, or a French dancer, performed there;
yet on such occasions the theatres overflow. The cause, I
think, is in the character of the people. I never saw a population so totally divested of gaiety; there is no trace of this feeling from one end of the Union to the other. They have no
fêtes, no fairs, no merry-makings, no music in the streets, no
Punch, no puppet-shows. If they see a comedy or a farce,
they may laugh at it; but they can do very well without it;
and the consciousness of the number of cents that must be
paid to enter a theatre, I am very sure turns more steps from
its door than any religious feeling. A distinguished publisher
of Philadelphia told me that no comic publication had ever
yet been found to answer in America.[4]

---

[4] [T5, note] This is an observation which, though probably quite true at
the time it was made, must never be repeated. Major Downing's *Letters*
prove, much beyond the power of contradiction, that humour, rich and original, does exist in the United States; and the popularity of the work shows
with equal certainty, that when such a treat is given to them, the people
know how to enjoy it. Whether a work treating of a subject less vitally near
and dear to every bosom than the BANK would have produced an equal sensation, may perhaps be doubted — but this matters little. If an artist can be
found skilful enough to dress such a subject in all the whimsical harle-
quinade of the most exquisite humour, without for a moment losing sight of
his commercial object, the glory of the achievement must assuredly be increased by its difficulty: and if American citizens are gay-spirited enough to
chuckle at, and enjoy wit, that expends itself on a grave subject, which is
both the most familiar and the most important to them, it is easy to predict,
that, in the progress of time, when other topics shall come to divide the public mind with dollars, they will chuckle at, and enjoy wit, otherwise
employed.

We arrived at Baltimore at the season of the "Conference."
I must be excused from giving any very distinct explanation
of this term, as I did not receive any. From what I could
learn, it much resembles a Revival. We entered many
churches, and heard much preaching, and not one of the reverend orators could utter the reproach,

"Peut-on si bien prêcher qu'elle ne dorme au sermon?" [5]

for I never even dosed at any. There was one preacher whose
manner and matter were so peculiar, that I took the liberty
of immediately writing down a part of his discourse as a
specimen. I confess I began writing in the middle of a sentence, for I waited in vain for a beginning. It was as follows: —

"Nevertheless, we must not lose sight of the one important,
great, and only object; for the Lord is mighty, his works are
great, likewise wonderful, likewise wise, likewise merciful;
and, moreover, we must ever keep in mind, and close to our
hearts, all his precious blessings, and unspeakable mercies,
and overflowing; and, moreover we must never lose sight
of, no, never lose sight of, nor ever cease to remember, nor
ever let our souls forget, nor ever cease to dwell upon, and
to reverence, and to welcome, and to bless, and to give thanks,

_____

This, indeed, is already proved by the cordial reception given to the in-
imitable Slick, which, whether by a native hand or not, is as heartily enjoyed on the other side of the Atlantic as it is by all genuine lovers of true
humour on this.

[DS] Seba Smith's creation Major Downing, a down-East Yankee who
commented upon current affairs with shrewdness disguised as simplicity, became highly popular in the United States in the 1830's and for many years
thereafter. Through Major Downing, Smith became the inaugurator of the
long line of American homespun humorists that includes such figures as
Hosea Biglow (created by James Russell Lowell), Josh Billings (H. W.
Shaw), and Will Rogers.

Sam Slick, the shrewd but boastful itinerant Yankee clockmaker and
peddler, was fathered by the Canadian humorist Thomas Chandler Halibur-
ton. _The Clockmaker_ (1837–40), first of the Sam Slick series, tells of this
hero's adventures selling clocks to the farmers of Nova Scotia.

[5] [DS] _"Peut-on si bien,"_ etc.: "Can one preach so well that she'll not
sleep through the sermon?"

and to sing hosanna, and give praise," —— and here my fragment of paper failed, but this strain continued, without a
shadow of meaning that I could trace, and in a voice inconceivably loud, for more than an hour.[6] After he had finished
his sermon, a scene exactly resembling that at the Cincinnati
Revival, took place. Two other priests assisted in calling forward the people, and in whispering comfort to them. One of
these men roared out in the coarsest accents, "Do you want
to go to hell to-night?" The church was almost entirely filled
with women, who vied with each other in howlings and contortions of the body; many of them tore their clothes nearly
off. I was much amused, spite of the indignation and disgust
the scene inspired, by the vehemence of the negro part of the
congregation; they seemed determined to bellow louder than
all the rest, to shew at once their piety and their equality.

At this same chapel, a few nights before, a woman had
fallen in a fit of ecstasy from the gallery, into the arms of the
people below, a height of twelve feet. A young slave who

[6] [TN] On Monday evening 15 March [1830] we went with Miss Johnson to a Methodist meeting. . . .

This strain . . . was continued . . . for above an hour. It would have
been impossible for the preacher to have sustained this tone, had he not occasionally relieved himself by suddenly changing his voice into a note as unlike it as possible — in this falsetto he continued for a few minutes and then
roared forth again in his former key. After the sermon a psalm was sung by
the congregation — and then they prayed; upon which a most disgusting
scene ensued, similar to what I have already described at the Revival at
Cincinnati. The most frightful groans, the most appalling cries, issued from
every part of the church. Upon this the priests began another hymn as if to
drown it [sic] and then besought all anxious Christians to come forth and
speak their words, enforcing the invitation by saying "do you want to go to
hell tonight, or will you rest with Jesus" etc. etc. Flocks of wretched women
pressed forward and began to vie with each other in the most violent howlings and contortions of the body. They tore their hair, they tore their clothes
while cries of "take us home, Jesus," and "Amen, amen," pronounced in a
sharp short tone like the bark of a dog rose without intermission from all
parts of the church. One poor wretch went into violent convulsions, and ever
and anon, as the screams grew louder, the priests began singing, evidently to
drown the dreadful sounds. I was much amused, spite of the indignation and
disgust the scene inspired, with the vehemence of the Negro part of the
congregation. . . .

waited upon us at table, when this was mentioned, said, that similar accidents had frequently happened, and that once she had seen it herself. Another slave in the house told us, that she "liked religion right well, but that she never took fits in it, 'cause she was always fixed in her best, when she went to chapel, and she did not like to have all her best clothes broke up."

We visited the infant school, instituted in this city by Mr. Ibbertson, an amiable and intelligent Englishman. It was the first infant school, properly so called, which I had ever seen, and I was greatly pleased with all the arrangements, and the apparent success of them. The children, of whom we saw about a hundred, boys and girls, were between eighteen months and six years. The apartment was filled with all sorts of instructive and amusing objects; a set of Dutch toys, arranged as a cabinet of natural history, was excellent; a numerous collection of large wooden bricks filled one corner of the room; the walls were hung with gay papers of different patterns, each representing some pretty group of figures; large and excellent coloured engravings of birds and beasts were exhibited in succession as the theme of a little lesson; and the sweet flute of Mr. Ibbertson gave tune and time to the prettiest little concert of chirping birds that I ever listened to.

A geographical model, large enough to give clear ideas of continent, island, cape, isthmus, et cetera, all set in water, is placed before the children, and the pretty creatures point their little rosy fingers with a look of intense interest, as they are called upon to shew where each of them is to be found. The dress, both of boys and girls, was elegantly neat, and their manner, when called upon to speak individually, was well-bred, intelligent, and totally free from the rude indifference, which is so remarkably prevalent in the manners of American children. Mr. Ibbertson will be a benefactor to the Union, if he becomes the means of spreading the admirable method by which he has polished the manner, and awakened the intellect of these beautiful little Republicans. I have conversed with many American ladies on the total want of discipline and subjection which I observed universally among children of all ages, and I never found any who did not both acknowledge and deplore the truth of the remark. In the state of Ohio they have a law (I know not if it exist elsewhere), that if a father strike his son, he shall pay a fine of ten dollars for every such offence. I was told by a gentleman of Cincinnati, that he had seen this fine inflicted there, at the requisition of a boy of twelve years of age, whose father, he proved, had struck him for lying. Such a law, they say, generates a spirit of freedom. What else may it generate?

Mr. Ibbertson, who seems perfectly devoted, heart and head to the subject, told me that he was employed in organizing successive schools that should receive the pupils as they advanced in age. If he prove himself as capable of completing education, as he appears to be of beginning it, his institution will be a very valuable one.[7] It would, indeed, be valuable any where; but in America, where discipline is not, where, from the shell, they are beings "that cannot rule, nor ever will be ruled," it is invaluable.

About two miles from Baltimore is a fort, nobly situated on the Patapsco, and commanding the approach from the Chesapeak-bay. As our visit was on a Sunday we were not permitted to enter it. The walk to this fort is along a fine terrace of beautiful verdure, which commands a magnificent view of the city, with its columns, towers, domes, and shipping; and also of the Patapsco river, which is here so wide as to present almost a sea view. This terrace is ornamented with abundance of evergreens, and wild roses innumerable, but, the whole region has the reputation of being unhealthy, and the fort itself most lamentably so. Before leaving the city of

---

[7] [DS] Apparently Mr. Ibbertson's work did not prosper; Mrs. Trollope seems to be the only chronicler of this Baltimore school.

monuments, I must not omit naming one reared to the growing wealth of the country; Mr. Barham's hotel is said to be the most splendid in the Union, and it is certainly splendid enough for a people more luxurious than the citizens of the republic appear yet to be.[8] I heard different, and, indeed, perfectly contradictory accounts of the success of the experiment; but at least every one seemed to agree that the liberal projector was fully entitled to exclaim,

> " 'Tis not in mortals to command success;
> I have done more, Jonathan, I've deserved it."

After enjoying a very pleasant fortnight, the greater part of which was passed in rambling about this pretty city and its environs, we left it, not without regret, and all indulging the hope that we should be able to pay it another visit.

---

[8] [DS] Mrs. Trollope probably means the hotel of David Barnum (not Barham): *"Barnum's,* or *The City Hotel,* is the most distinguished. It is situate at the south-west corner of Calvert and Fayette Streets, and is of the following dimensions: 120 feet front, 6 stories high, and 213 feet in depth. No expense has been spared either for the materials used, or the quality of the furniture, it being the intention of the proprietor, *David Barnum,* to merit the patronage of the public, by having everything suited to their ease and comfort." — Charles Varle: *A Complete View of Baltimore* (1833).

"Barnum's City Hotel" was built in 1825–6 and survived until April 4, 1889. It enjoyed nation-wide fame in the 1830's and 1840's.

CHAPTER XX

Voyage to Washington — Capitol — City of Washington —
Congress — Indians — Funeral of a Member of Congress

BY far the shortest route to Washington, both as to distance and time, is by land; but I much wished to see the celebrated Chesapeak bay, and it was therefore decided that we should take our passage in the steam-boat. It is indeed a beautiful little voyage, and well worth the time it costs; but as to the beauty of the bay, it must, I think, be felt only by sailors. It is, I doubt not, a fine shelter for ships, from the storms of the Atlantic, but its very vastness prevents its striking the eye as beautiful: it is, in fact, only a fine sea view. But the entrance from it into the Potomac river is very noble, and is one of the points at which one feels conscious of the gigantic proportions of the country, without having recourse to a graduated pencil-case.

The passage up this river to Washington is interesting, from many objects that it passes, but beyond all else, by the view it affords of Mount Vernon, the seat of General Washington. It is there that this truly great man passed the last years of his virtuous life, and it is there that he lies buried: it was easy to distinguish, as we passed, the cypress that waves over his grave.

The latter part of the voyage shews some fine river scenery; but I did not discover this till some months afterwards, for we now arrived late at night.

Our first object the next morning was to get a sight of the capitol, and our impatience sent us forth before breakfast. The mists of morning still hung around this magnificent building when first it broke upon our view, and I am not sure that the effect produced was not the greater for this circumstance. At all events, we were struck with admiration and surprise. None of us, I believe, expected to see so imposing a structure on that side the Atlantic. I am ill at describing buildings, but the beauty and majesty of the American capitol might defy an abler pen than mine to do it justice. It stands so finely too, high, and alone.

The magnificent western façade is approached from the city by terraces and steps of bolder proportions than I ever before saw. The elegant eastern front, to which many persons give the preference, is on a level with a newly-planted but exceedingly handsome inclosure, which, in a few years, will offer the shade of all the most splendid trees which flourish in the Union, to cool the brows and refresh the spirits of the members. The view from the capitol commands the city and many miles around, and it is itself an object of imposing beauty to the whole country adjoining.

We were again fortunate enough to find a very agreeable family to board with; and soon after breakfast left our comfortless hotel near the water, for very pleasant apartments in F. street.[1]

I was delighted with the whole aspect of Washington; light, cheerful, and airy, it reminded me of our fashionable watering-places. It has been laughed at by foreigners, and even by natives, because the original plan of the city was upon an enormous scale, and but a very small part of it has been as yet executed.[2] But I confess I see nothing in the least degree ridiculous about it; the original design, which was as beautiful as it was extensive, has been in no way departed from, and all that has been done has been done well. From the base of the hill on which the capitol stands extends a street of most magnificent width, planted on each side with

---

[1] [T1] The streets that intersect the great avenues in Washington are distinguished by the letters of the alphabet.

[2] [DS] The population of Washington in 1830 was 18,827.

trees, and ornamented by many splendid shops. This street, which is called Pennsylvania Avenue, is above a mile in length, and at the end of it is the handsome mansion of the President; conveniently near to his residence are the various public offices, all handsome, simple, and commodious; ample areas are left round each, where grass and shrubs refresh the eye. In another of the principal streets is the general post-office, and not far from it a very noble town-hall. Towards the quarter of the President's house are several handsome dwellings, which are chiefly occupied by the foreign ministers. The houses in the other parts of the city are scattered, but without ever losing sight of the regularity of the original plan; and to a person who has been travelling much through the country, and marked the immense quantity of new manufactories, new canals, new rail-roads, new towns, and new cities, which are springing, as it were, from the earth in every part of it, the appearance of the metropolis rising gradually into life and splendour, is a spectacle of high historic interest.

Commerce had already produced large and handsome cities in America before she had attained to an individual political existence, and Washington may be scorned as a metropolis, where such cities as Philadelphia and New York exist; but I considered it as the growing metropolis of the growing population of the Union, and it already possesses features noble enough to sustain its dignity as such.

The residence of the foreign legations and their families gives a tone to the society of this city which distinguishes it greatly from all others. It is also, for a great part of the year, the residence of the senators and representatives, who must be presumed to be the *élite* of the entire body of citizens, both in respect to talent and education. This cannot fail to make Washington a more agreeable abode than any other city in the Union.

The total absence of all sights, sounds, or smells of commerce, adds greatly to the charm. Instead of drays you see handsome carriages; and instead of the busy bustling hustle of men, shuffling on to a sale of "dry goods" or "prime broad stuffs," you see very well-dressed personages lounging leisurely up and down Pennsylvania Avenue.

Mr. Pishey Thompson, the English bookseller, with his pretty collection of all sorts of pretty literature, fresh from London, and Mr. Somebody, the jeweller, with his brilliant shop full of trinkets, are the principal points of attraction and business.[3] What a contrast to all other American cities! The members, who pass several months every year in this lounging easy way, with no labour but a little talking, and with the *douceur* of eight dollars a day to pay them for it, must feel the change sadly when their term of public service is over.

There is another circumstance which renders the evening parties at Washington extremely unlike those of other places in the Union; this is the great majority of gentlemen. The expense, the trouble, or the necessity of a ruling eye at home, one or all of these reasons, prevents the members' ladies from accompanying them to Washington; at least, I heard of very few who had their wives with them. The female society is chiefly to be found among the families of the foreign ministers, those of the officers of state, and of the few members, the wealthiest and most aristocratic of the land, who bring their families with them. Some few independent persons reside in or near the city, but this is a class so thinly scattered that they can hardly be accounted a part of the population.

But, strange to say, even here a theatre cannot be supported for more than a few weeks at a time. I was told that gambling is the favourite recreation of the gentlemen, and that it is carried to a very considerable extent; but here, as elsewhere within the country, it is kept extremely well out

---

[3] [DS] "Mr. Somebody, the jeweller," was probably James Galt, establisher of Galt & Bro., Inc., which still flourishes.

of sight. I do not think I was present with a pack of cards a dozen times during more than three years that I remained in the country. Billiards are much played, though in most places the amusement is illegal. It often appeared to me that the old women of a state made the laws, and the young men broke them.

Notwithstanding the diminutive size of the city, we found much to see, and to amuse us.

The patent office is a curious record of the fertility of the mind of man when left to its own resources; but it gives ample proof also that it is not under such circumstances it is most usefully employed. This patent office contains models of all the mechanical inventions that have been produced in the Union, and the number is enormous. I asked the man who shewed these, what proportion of them had been brought into use, he said about one in a thousand; he told me also, that they chiefly proceeded from mechanics and agriculturists settled in remote parts of the country, who had began by endeavouring to hit upon some contrivance to enable them to *get along* without sending some thousand and odd miles for the thing they wanted. If the contrivance succeeded, they generally became so fond of this offspring of their ingenuity, that they brought it to Washington for a patent.

At the secretary of state's office we were shewn autographs of all the potentates with whom the Union were in alliance; which, I believe, pretty well includes all. To the parchments bearing these royal signs manual were appended, of course, the official seals of each, enclosed in gold or silver boxes of handsome workmanship: I was amused by the manner in which one of their own, just prepared for the court of Russia, was displayed to us, and the superiority of their decorations pointed out. They were superior, and in much better taste than the rest; and I only wish that the feeling that induced this display would spread to every corner of the Union, and

mix itself with every act and with every sentiment. Let
America give a fair portion of her attention to the arts and
the graces that embellish life, and I will make her another
visit, and write another book as unlike this as possible.[4]

Among the royal signatures, the only one which much interested me were two from the hand of Napoleon. The earliest of these, when he was first consul, was a most illegible
scrawl, and, as the tradition went, was written on horseback;
but his writing improved greatly after he became an emperor, the subsequent signature being firmly and clearly
written. — I longed to steal both.

The purity of the American character, formed and founded
on the purity of the American government, was made evident to our senses by the display of all the offerings of esteem
and regard which had been presented by various sovereigns
to the different American ministers who had been sent to
their courts. The object of the law which exacted this deposit
from every individual so honoured, was, they told us, to prevent the possibility of bribery being used to corrupt any en-
voy of the Republic. I should think it would be a better way
to select for the office such men as they felt could not be
seduced by a sword or a snuff-box. But they, doubtless, know
their own business best.

The bureau for Indian affairs contains a room of great interest: the walls are entirely covered with original portraits [5]
of all the chiefs who, from time to time, have come to nego-

[4] [T5, note] This must not be done, as I have been recently informed,
till Jonathan Jefferson Whitlaw is forgotten — or the system of slavery
abolished.

[Mrs. Trollope's *The Life and Adventures of Jonathan Jefferson Whit-
law; or Scenes on the Mississippi* (1836) had created some stir in the United
States because of its attacks on slavery, though not enough to warrant an
American reprinting.]

[5] [T5, note] The beautiful engravings of these portraits, which have recently reached us, would be *perfect,* were they not quite so *good.* They convey the peculiar expression of this fast perishing and most interesting race
admirably, but give much too favourable an idea of the pictorial excellence
of the originals.

ciate with their great father, as they call the President. These portraits are by Mr. King, and, it cannot be doubted, are excellent likenesses, as are all the portraits I have ever seen from the hands of that gentleman. The countenances are full of expression, but the expression in most of them is extremely similar; or rather, I should say that they have but two sorts of expressions; the one is that of very noble and warlike daring, the other of a gentle and *naïve* simplicity, that has no mixture of folly in it, but which is inexpressibly engaging, and the more touching, perhaps, because at the moment we were looking at them, those very hearts which lent the eyes such meek and friendly softness, were wrung by a base, cruel, and most oppressive act of their *great father*.

We were at Washington at the time that the measure for chasing the last of several tribes of Indians from their forest homes, was canvassed in congress, and finally decided upon by the *fiat* of the President. If the American character may be judged by their conduct in this matter, they are most lamentably deficient in every feeling of honour and integrity. It is among themselves, and from themselves, that I have heard the statements which represent them as treacherous and false almost beyond belief in their intercourse with the unhappy Indians. Had I, during my residence in the United States, observed any single feature in their national character that could justify their eternal boast of liberality and the love of freedom, I might have respected them, however much my taste might have been offended by what was peculiar in their manners and customs. But it is impossible for any mind of common honesty not to be revolted by the contradictions in their principles and practice. They inveigh against the governments of Europe, because, as they say, they favour the powerful and oppress the weak. You may hear this declaimed upon in Congress, roared out in taverns, discussed in every drawing-room, satirized upon the stage, nay, even anathematized from the pulpit: listen to it, and then look at them at home; you will see them with one hand hoisting the cap of liberty, and with the other flogging their slaves. You will see them one hour lecturing their mob on the indefeasible rights of man, and the next driving from their homes the children of the soil, whom they have bound themselves to protect by the most solemn treaties.

In justice to those who approve not this treacherous policy, I will quote a paragraph from a New York paper, which shews that there are some among them who look with detestation on the bold bad measure decided upon at Washington in the year 1830.[6]

"We know of no subject, at the present moment, of more importance to the character of our country for justice and integrity than that which relates to the Indian tribes in Georgia and Alabama, and particularly the Cherokees in the former state. The Act passed by Congress, just at the end of the session, co-operating with the tyrannical and iniquitous statute of Georgia, strikes a formidable blow at the reputation of the United States, in respect to their faith, pledged in almost innumerable instances, in the most solemn treaties and compacts."

There were many objects of much interest shewn us at this Indian bureau; but, from the peculiar circumstances of

---

6 [DS] In 1791 the United States had made a treaty of cession with the Cherokees guaranteeing them the remainder of their territory. In 1828 and 1829 Georgia extended her laws over the Indian territory in the state and began to occupy it. The Cherokees first appealed without success to President Jackson and then submitted to the Supreme Court of the United States a bill for an injunction restraining the state of Georgia from enforcing her laws within the Cherokee Nation. The Court's majority ruling was that because the Cherokees were neither, as they maintained, a foreign nation nor, on the other hand, citizens of the United States, they could not be party to a suit in the Supreme Court.

The "bold bad measure" that Mrs. Trollope mentions was perhaps that which Congress passed in May 1830 appropriating $500,000 to be used in removing the Indians, as proposed by the President in his message of December 1829.

this most unhappy and ill-used people, it was a very painful interest.

The dresses worn by the chiefs when their portraits were taken, are many of them splendid, from the embroidery of beads and other ornaments; and the room contains many specimens of their ingenuity, and even of their taste. There is a glass case in the room, wherein are arranged specimens of worked muslin, and other needle-work, some very excellent hand-writing, and many other little productions of male and female Indians, all proving clearly that they are perfectly capable of civilization. Indeed, the circumstance which renders their expulsion from their own, their native lands, so peculiarly lamentable, is, that they were yielding rapidly to the force of example; their lives were no longer those of wandering hunters, but they were becoming agriculturists, and the tyrannical arm of brutal power has not now driven them, as formerly, only from their hunting grounds, their favourite springs, and the sacred bones of their fathers, but it has chased them from the dwellings their advancing knowledge had taught them to make comfortable; from the newly-ploughed fields of their pride; and from the crops their sweat had watered. And for what? To add some thousand acres of territory to the half-peopled wilderness which borders them.

*   *   *   *   *   *

The Potomac, on arriving at Washington, makes a beautiful sweep, which forms a sort of bay, round which the city is built. Just where it makes the turn, a wooden bridge is thrown across, connecting the shores of Maryland and Virginia. This bridge is a mile and a quarter in length, and is ugly enough.[7] The navy-yard, and arsenal, are just above it, on the Maryland side, and make a handsome appearance on

[7] [T1] It has since been washed away by the breaking up of the frost of February, 1831.

the edge of the river, following the sweep above mentioned. Near the arsenal (much too near) is the penitentiary, which, as it was just finished, and not inhabited, we examined in every part. It is built for the purpose of solitary confinement for life. A gallows is a much less nerve-shaking spectacle than one of these awful cells, and assuredly, when imprisonment therein for life is substituted for death, it is no mercy to the criminal; but if it be a greater terror to the citizen, it may answer the purpose better. I do not conceive, that out of a hundred human beings who had been thus confined for a year, one would be found at the end of it who would continue to linger on there, *certain it was for ever*, if the alternative of being hanged were offered to them. I had written a description of these horrible cells,[8] but Captain Hall's picture of a similar building is so accurate, and so clear, that it is needless to insert it.

Still following the sweep of the river, at the distance of

---

[8] [TN]   Penitentiary, Washington City

I have elsewhere mentioned, that crime often escapes punishment in America, and that, not from the mildness of the laws, but from the neglect of them; but in visiting this awful building, I ceased to wonder that such a punishment was not often inflicted. Indeed I could almost doubt that any human being who had seen it, could be found firm enough in nerve to doom his fellow being to its endurance. All I have read of the Inquisition, and its varied and subtle tortures failed to impress my mind with so profound a sense of unbearable misery as the sight of this penitentiary.

In the middle of a large high-walled court is erected a spacious lofty brick building within, perfectly isolated, and detached from the exterior one. This interior building has no windows but has very small grated iron doors with an interval of three feet between them. There are four tiers of these doors to which you ascend by strong stairs constructed between the inner and outer buildings. Before each tier of doors is a gallery of three feet with a railing before it. When these grated doors are opened, you behold a cell eight feet long, four feet wide, and seven feet high, and here such as are caught, and found guilty of capital crimes are immured for life *if they prefer it, to being hanged.* It seemed to me that there was a wanton refinement of cruelty in thus letting men be doomed to a destiny so horrible by their own choice. It was like sporting with the instinct that makes us cling to life, and seeing how far it will go. Moreover the choice can seldom be fairly made — for none who have not seen them, can conceive the dreary horror of these grave-like cells.

two miles from Washington, is George Town, formerly a
place of considerable commercial importance, and likely, I
think, to become so again, when the Ohio and Chesapeak
canal, which there mouths into the Potomac, shall be in full
action. It is a very pretty town, commanding a lovely view,
of which the noble Potomac and the almost nobler capitol,
are the great features. The country rises into a beautiful line
of hills behind Washington, which form a sort of undulating
terrace on to George Town; this terrace is almost entirely occupied by a succession of gentlemen's seats. At George Town
the Potomac suddenly contracts itself, and begins to assume
that rapid, rocky, and irregular character which marks it
afterwards, and renders its course, till it meets the Shenandoah at Harper's Ferry, a series of the most wild and romantic views that are to be found in America.

Attending the debates in Congress was, of course, one of
our great objects; and, as an English woman, I was perhaps
the more eager to avail myself of the privilege allowed. It
was repeatedly observed to me that, at least in this instance,
I must acknowledge the superior gallantry of the Americans,
and that they herein give a decided proof of surpassing the
English in a wish to honour the ladies, as they have a gallery
in the House of Representatives erected expressly for them,
while in England they are rigorously excluded from every
part of the House of Commons.

But the inference I draw from this is precisely the reverse
of that suggested. It is well known that the reason why the
House of Commons was closed against ladies was, that their
presence was found too attractive, and that so many members were tempted to neglect the business before the House,
that they might enjoy the pleasure of conversing with the
fair critics in the galleries, that it became a matter of national
importance to banish them — and they were banished. It will
be long ere the American legislature will find it necessary to
pass the same law for the same reason. A lady of Washing-

ton, however, told me an anecdote which went far to shew that a more intellectual turn in the women, would produce a change in the manners of the men. She told me, that when the Miss Wrights were in Washington, with General Lafayette,[9] they very frequently attended the debates, and that the most distinguished members were always crowding round them. For this unwonted gallantry they apologized to their beautiful countrywomen by saying, that if they took equal interest in the debates, the galleries would be always thronged by the members.

The privilege of attending these debates would be more valuable could the speakers be better heard from the gallery; but, with the most earnest attention, I could only follow one or two of the orators, whose voices were peculiarly loud and clear. This made it really a labour to listen; but the extreme beauty of the chamber was of itself a reason for going again and again. It was, however, really mortifying to see this splendid hall, fitted up in so stately and sumptuous a manner, filled with men, sitting in the most unseemly attitudes, a large majority with their hats on, and nearly all, spitting to an excess that decency forbids me to describe.

Among the crowd, who must be included in this description, a few were distinguished by not wearing their hats, and by sitting on their chairs like other human beings, without throwing their legs above their heads. Whenever I enquired the name of one of these exceptions, I was told that it was Mr. This, or Mr. That, *of Virginia.*

One day we were fortunate enough to get placed on the sofas between the pillars, on the floor of the House; the galleries being shut up, for the purpose of making some altera-

---

[9] [DS] Frances Wright and her sister Camilla accompanied General Lafayette on much of his triumphal tour of America in 1824–5. They visited the Senate with him on December 9, 1824, and the House the following day, and probably visited sessions at the Capitol on many other occasions. Lafayette was received in Washington with great acclaim; Congress voted him a gift of $200,000 and a township of 24,000 acres of land.

tions, which it was hoped might improve the hearing in that part of the House occupied by the members, and which is universally complained of, as being very defective.[10] But in our places on the sofas we found we heard very much better than up stairs, and well enough to be extremely amused by the rude eloquence of a thorough horse and alligator orator from Kentucky, who entreated the house repeatedly to "go the whole hog."

If I mistake not, every debate I listened to in the American Congress was upon one and the same subject, namely, the entire independence of each individual state, with regard to the federal government. The jealousy on this point appeared to me to be the very strangest political feeling that ever got possession of the mind of man. I do not pretend to judge the merits of this question. I speak solely of the very singular effect of seeing man after man start eagerly to his feet, to declare that the greatest injury, the basest injustice, the most obnoxious tyranny that could be practised against the state of which he was a member, would be a vote of a few million dollars for the purpose of making their roads or canals; or for drainage; or, in short, for any purpose of improvement whatsoever.[11]

During the month we were at Washington, I heard a great deal of conversation respecting a recent exclusion from Congress of a gentleman, who, by every account, was one of the most esteemed men in the house, and, I think, the father of

---

[10] [T1] As a proof of this defective hearing in the Hall of Congress, I may quote a passage from a newspaper report of a debate on improvements. It was proposed to suspend a ceiling of glass fifteen feet above the heads of the members. A member, speaking in favour of this proposal, said, "Members would then, at least, be able to understand what was the question before the House, an advantage which most of them did not now possess, respecting more than half the propositions upon which they voted."

[11] [T5, note] This strange jealousy is an illustration, *en grand*, of the democratic principle, and if pushed to its utmost perfection, would speedily dislocate every social compact, and leave each individual man as gloriously free as a bear on the unsophisticated shores of Bering's Straits.

it. The crime for which this gentleman was out-voted by his own particular friends and admirers was, that he had given his vote for a grant of public money for the purpose of draining a most lamentable and unhealthy district, called *"the dismal swamp!"*

One great boast of the country is, that they have no national debt, or that they shall have none in two years. This seems not very wonderful, considering their productive tariff, and that the income paid to their president is 6,000*l. per annum;* other government salaries being in proportion, and all internal improvements, at the expense of the government treasury, being voted unconstitutional.

The Senate-chamber is, like the Hall of Congress, a semicircle, but of very much smaller dimensions. It is most elegantly fitted up, and what is better still, the senators, generally speaking, look like gentlemen. They do not wear their hats, and the activity of youth being happily past, they do not toss their heels above their heads. I would I could add they do not spit; but, alas! "I have an oath in heaven," and may not write an untruth.

A very handsome room, opening on a noble stone balcony is fitted up as a library for the members. The collection, as far as a very cursory view could enable me to judge, was very like that of a private English gentleman, but with less Latin, Greek, and Italian. This room also is elegantly furnished; rich Brussels carpet; library tables, with portfolios of engravings; abundance of sofas, and so on. The view from it is glorious, and it looks like the abode of luxury and taste.

I can by no means attempt to describe all the apartments of this immense building, but the magnificent rotunda in the centre must not be left unnoticed. It is, indeed, a noble hall, a hundred feet in diameter, and of an imposing loftiness, lighted by an ample dome.

Almost any pictures (excepting the cartoons) would look

paltry in this room, from the immense height of the walls; but the subjects of the four pictures which are placed there, are of such high historic interest that they should certainly have a place somewhere, as national records. One represents the signing of the declaration of independence; another the resignation of the presidency by the great Washington; another the celebrated victory of General Gates at Saratoga; and the fourth . . . . I do not well remember, but I think it is some other martial scene, commemorating a victory; I rather think that of York Town.[12]

One other object in the capitol must be mentioned, though it occurs in so obscure a part of the building, that one or two members to whom I mentioned it, were not aware of its existence. The lower part of the edifice, a story below the rotunda, &c., has a variety of committee rooms, courts, and other places of business. In a hall leading to some of these rooms, the ceiling is supported by pillars, the capitals of which struck me as peculiarly beautiful. They are composed of the ears and leaves of the Indian corn, beautifully arranged, and forming as graceful an outline as the acanthus itself. This was the only instance I saw, in which America has ventured to attempt national originality; the success is perfect. A sense of fitness always enhances the effect of beauty. I will not attempt a long essay on the subject, but if America, in her vastness, her immense natural resources, and her remote grandeur, would be less imitative, she would be infinitely more picturesque and interesting.

The President has regular evening parties, every other Wednesday, which are called his *levées;* the last syllable is pronounced by every one as long as possible, being exactly the reverse of the French and English manner of pronounc-

----

[12] [DS] The fourth of John Trumbull's pictures for the rotunda does represent the surrender of Cornwallis at Yorktown. The second mentioned by Mrs. Trollope shows Washington resigning not the presidency but his commission as commander in chief of the Army.

ing the same word. The effect of this, from the very frequent repetition of the word in all companies, is very droll, and for a long time I thought people were quizzing these public days. The reception rooms are handsome, particularly the grand saloon, which is elegantly, nay, splendidly furnished; this has been done since the visit of Captain Hall, whose remarks upon the former state of this room may have hastened its decoration; but there are a few anomalies in some parts of the entertainment, which are not very courtly. The company are about as select as that of an Easter-day ball at the Mansion-house.[13]

The churches at Washington are not superb; but the Episcopalian and Catholic were filled with elegantly dressed women. I observed a greater proportion of gentlemen at church at Washington than any where else.

The Presbyterian ladies go to church three times in the day, but the general appearance of Washington on a Sunday is much less puritanical than that of most other American towns; the people walk about, and there are no chains in the streets, as at Philadelphia, to prevent their riding or driving, if they like it.

The ladies dress well, but not so splendidly as at Baltimore. I remarked that it was not very unusual at Washington for a lady to take the arm of a gentleman, who was neither her husband, her father, nor her brother. This remarkable relaxation of American decorum has been probably introduced by the foreign legations.

At about a mile from the town, on the high terrace ground

---

13 [DS] Mansion House: the official residence of the Lord Mayor of London.

Captain Hall remarks in his *Travels in North America* (1829) that he had been surprised to find the President's "ball-room . . . entirely unfinished and bare. Even the walls were left in their unpainted plaster. Here was a degree of republican simplicity beyond what I should have expected, as it seemed out of character with what I saw elsewhere."

above described, is a very pretty place, to which the proprietor has given the name of Kaleirama. It is not large, or in any way magnificent, but the view from it is charming; and it has a little wood behind, covering about two hundred acres of broken ground, that slopes down to a dark cold little river, so closely shut in by rocks and evergreens, that it might serve as a noon-day bath for Diana and her nymphs. The whole of this wood is filled with wild flowers, but such as we cherish fondly in our gardens.

A ferry at George Town crosses the Potomac, and about two miles from it, on the Virginian side, is Arlington, the seat of Mr. Custis, who is the grandson of General Washington's wife. It is a noble looking place, having a portico of stately white columns, which, as the mansion stands high, with a back ground of dark woods, forms a beautiful object in the landscape. At George Town is a nunnery, where many young ladies are educated, and at a little distance from it, a college of Jesuits for the education of young men, where, as their advertisements state, "the humanities are taught."

We attended mass at the chapel of the nunnery, where the female voices that performed the chant were very pleasing. The shadowy form of the veiled abbess in her little sacred parlour, seen through a grating and a black curtain, but rendered clearly visible by the light of a Gothic window behind her, drew a good deal of our attention; every act of genuflection, even the telling her beads, was discernible, but so mistily that it gave her, indeed, the appearance of a being who had already quitted this life, and was hovering on the confines of the world of shadows.

The convent has a considerable inclosure attached to it, where I frequently saw from the heights above it, dark figures in awfully thick black veils, walking solemnly up and down.

The American lady, who was the subject of one of Prince Hohenlohe's celebrated miracles, was pointed out to us at

Washington.[14] All the world declare that her recovery was marvellous.

＊   ＊   ＊   ＊   ＊   ＊

There appeared to be a great many foreigners at Washington, particularly French. In Paris I have often observed that it was a sort of fashion to speak of America as a new Utopia, especially among the young liberals, who, before the happy accession of Philip, fancied that a country without a king, was the land of promise; but I sometimes thought that, like many other fine things, it lost part of its brilliance when ex-

[14] [DS] Prince Leopold Alexander of Hohenlohe-Waldenburg-Schillingsfurst was a European priest who practiced miraculous cures in 1821 and a few years thereafter until he desisted, probably because of a sharp private reprimand from the Pope.

Mrs. Ann Mattingly, the "American lady" whom Mrs. Trollope refers to, suffered for six years from a tumor, which four leading physicians of Washington had pronounced incurable. The pastor of her church wrote Prince Hohenlohe asking him to pray for her. The Prince replied that he had so many similar petitions that he regularly prayed at nine o'clock in the morning on the tenth of each month for all sick persons out of Europe who had asked for his intercessions. He requested of all who wished to profit by these prayers that they fulfill certain conditions. Mrs. Mattingly complied with them. The sequel is thus reported in the *New York Statesman* for March 13, 1824:

"The letter arrived a short time since, and its contents were communicated to the Father Confessor. This day, being the 10th of the first month since its arrival, was anticipated with trembling hope and solicitude. The very hour of the day, when the miracle was to be performed, was calculated with minute accuracy, by allowing for the difference of longitude, thus knowing precisely at what time the Prince would offer up his prayers.

"In the mean time, the lady had become reduced apparently to the verge of the grave. Her nurse believed last night and early this morning, that she was dying. The consecrated host was administered to prepare her soul for its departure. She was unable to swallow, and her friends were gathered about the bed, expecting that her spirit would momently take its flight to a better world. But what was their joy and surprise, when at 10 o'clock this morning, all of a sudden, she rose from her bed of death; her tongue was loosed: she addressed her friends: she wept for joy: she burst into raptures: she fell upon her knees, and returned thanks to God. She even insisted on going out, and offering up her devotions in public; but her friends dissuaded her from this act of imprudence. Praise and thanksgiving rang through the house, which but lately resounded with lamentations and woe." Mrs. Mattingly lived until 1855, her seventy-fifth year.

XV EX PEDE HERCULEM

XVI LIVE STOCK
Virginia. 1830

amined too nearly; I overheard the following question and answer pass between two young Frenchmen, who appeared to have met for the first time.

"Eh bien, Monsieur, comment trouvez-vous la liberté et l'égalité mises en action?"

"Mais, Monsieur, je vous avoue que le beau idéal que nous autres, nous avons conçu de tout cela à Paris, avait quelque chose de plus poétique que ce que nous trouvons ici!" [15]

On another occasion I was excessively amused by the tone in which one of these young men replied to a question put to him by another Frenchman. A pretty looking woman, but exceeding deficient in *tournure*, was standing alone at a little distance from them, and close at their elbows stood a very awkward looking gentleman. "Qui est cette dame?" said the enquirer. "Monsieur," said my young *fat*, with an indescribable grimace, "c'est la femelle de ce male," indicating his neighbour by an expressive curl of his upper lip.

The theatre was not open while we were in Washington but we afterwards took advantage of our vicinity to the city, to visit it. The house is very small, and most astonishingly dirty and void of decoration, considering that it is the only place of public amusement that the city affords. I have before mentioned the want of decorum at the Cincinnati theatre, but certainly that of the capital at least rivalled it in the freedom of action and attitude; a freedom which seems to disdain the restraints of civilized manners. One man in the pit was seized with a violent fit of vomiting, which appeared not in the least to annoy or surprise his neighbours; and the happy coincidence of a physician being at that moment per‑

---

[15] [DS] " '*Eh bien*,' " etc.:

" 'Well, Monsieur, how do you like liberty and equality put into prac‑ tice?'

" 'Why, Monsieur, I confess that the lovely ideal that we conceived of all that at Paris was more poetic than what we find here.' "

In the next paragraph, the one Frenchman asks: "Who is that lady?" The young *fat* (fop) replies: "It's the female of that male."

sonated on the stage, was hailed by many of the audience as an excellent joke, of which the actor took advantage, and elicited shouts of applause by saying, "I expect my services are wanted elsewhere."

The spitting was incessant; and not one in ten of the male part of the illustrious legislative audience sat according to the usual custom of human beings; the legs were thrown sometimes over the front of the box, sometimes over the side of it; here and there a senator stretched his entire length along a bench, and in many instances the front rail was preferred as a seat.

I remarked one young man, whose handsome person, and most elaborate toilet, led me to conclude he was a first-rate personage, and so I doubt not he was; nevertheless, I saw him take from the pocket of his silk waistcoat a lump of tobacco, and daintily deposit it within his cheek.

I am inclined to think this most vile and universal habit of chewing tobacco is the cause of a remarkable peculiarity in the male physiognomy of Americans; their lips are almost uniformly thin and compressed. At first I accounted for this upon Lavater's theory, and attributed it to the arid temperament of the people; [16] but it is too universal to be so explained; whereas the habit above mentioned, which pervades all classes (excepting the literary) well accounts for it, as the act of expressing the juices of this loathsome herb, enforces exactly that position of the lips, which gives this remarkable peculiarity to the American countenance.

---

[16] [DS] Johann Kaspar Lavater (1741–1801), celebrated Swiss physiognomist, states in his *Physiognomic Fragments* (1775) that whatever is in the mind reveals itself in the mouth:

"As are the lips so is the character.

"Firm lips, firm character; weak lips, and quick in motion, weak and wavering character. . . .

"A lipless mouth, resembling a single line, denotes coldness, industry, a love of order, precision, housewifery; and if it be drawn upward at the two ends, affectation, pretension, vanity, and, which may ever be the production of cool vanity, malice."

A member of Congress died while we were at Washington, and I was surprised by the ceremony and dignity of his funeral. It seems that whenever a senator or member of Congress dies during the session, he is buried at the expense of the government, (this ceremony not coming under the head of internal improvement), and the arrangements for the funeral are not interfered with by his friends, but become matters of State. I transcribed the order of the procession as being rather grand and stately.

Chaplains of both Houses.
Physicians who attended the deceased.
Committee of arrangement.
THE BODY,
(Pall borne by six members.)
The Relations of the deceased, with the Senators and Representatives of the State to which he belonged, as
Mourners.
Sergeant at arms of the House of Representatives.
The House of Representatives,
Their Speaker and Clerk preceding.
The Senate of the United States,
The Vice-president and Secretary preceding.
THE PRESIDENT

The procession was of considerable extent, but not on foot, and the majority of the carriages were hired for the occasion. The body was interred in an open "grave yard" near the city. I did not see the monument erected on this occasion, but I presume it was in the same style as several others I had remarked in the same burying-ground, inscribed to the memory of members who had died at Washington. These were square blocks of masonry without any pretension to splendour.

CHAPTER XXI

Stonington — Great Falls of the Potomac

THE greatest pleasure I had promised myself in visiting Washington was the seeing a very old friend, who had left England many years ago, and married in America; she was now a widow, and, as I believed, settled in Washington. I soon had the mortification of finding that she was not in the city; but ere long I learnt that her residence was not more than ten miles from it. We speedily met, and it was settled that we should pass the summer with her in Maryland, and after a month devoted to Washington, we left it for Stonington.[1]

We arrived there the beginning of May, and the kindness of our reception, the interest we felt in becoming acquainted with the family of my friend, the extreme beauty of the surrounding country, and the lovely season, altogether, made our stay there a period of great enjoyment.

I wonder not that the first settlers in Virginia, with the bold Captain Smith of chivalrous memory at their head, should have fought so stoutly to dispossess the valiant father of Pocohontas of his fair domain, for I certainly never saw a more tempting territory. Stonington is about two miles from the most romantic point of the Potomac River, and Virginia

---

[1] [DS] Very little is known of Mrs. Stone, the "very old friend" with whom Mrs. Trollope was to spend the next months. Her maiden name was Garnett, and she was probably the Mrs. Anna Garrett (Garnett) Stone whom John Harry Shannon speaks of on January 26, 1919 in "The Rambler," the feature that he conducted for the Washington *Evening Star:* ". . . Stonington, a house still standing on the road which leads from the Conduit road to the village of Potomac. Stonington was built by Mrs. Anna Garrett Stone, an English woman, who came to Washington in the early part of the nineteenth century and taught school here."

spreads her wild, but beautiful, and most fertile Paradise, on the opposite shore. The Maryland side partakes of the same character, and perfectly astonished us by the profusion of her wild fruits and flowers.

We had not been long within reach of the great falls of the Potomac before a party was made for us to visit them; the walk from Stonington to these falls is through scenery that can hardly be called forest, park, or garden; but which partakes of all three. A little English girl accompanied us, who had but lately left her home; she exclaimed, "Oh! how many English ladies would glory in such a garden as this!" and in truth they might; cedars, tulip-trees, planes, shumacs, junipers, and oaks of various kinds, most of them new to us, shaded our path. Wild vines, with their rich expansive leaves, and their sweet blossom, rivalling the mignionette in fragrance, clustered round their branches. Strawberries in full bloom, violets, anemonies, heart's-ease, and wild pinks, with many other, and still lovelier flowers, which my ignorance forbids me to name, literally covered the ground. The arbor judæ, the dog-wood, in its fullest glory of star-like flowers, azalias, and wild roses, dazzled our eyes whichever way we turned them. It was the most flowery two miles I ever walked.

The sound of the falls is heard at Stonington, and the gradual increase of this sound is one of the agreeable features of this delicious walk. I know not why the rush of waters is so delightful to the ear; all other monotonous sounds are wearying, and harass the spirits, but I never met any one who did not love to listen to a water-fall. A rapid stream, called the "Branch Creek," was to be crossed ere we reached the spot where the falls are first visible. This rumbling, turbid, angry little rivulet, flows through evergreens and flowering underwood, and is crossed *à plusieures reprises*,[2] by logs thrown from rock to rock. The thundering noise of the still unseen falls suggests an idea of danger while crossing these

---

[2] [DS] "*à plusieures reprises*": "several times."

rude bridges, which hardly belongs to them; having reached the other side of the creek, we continued under the shelter of the evergreens for another quarter of a mile, and then emerged upon a sight that drew a shout of wonder and delight from us all. The rocky depths of an enormous river were opened before our eyes, and so huge are the black crags that inclose it, that the thundering torrents of water rushing through, over, and among the rocks of this awful chasm, appear lost and swallowed up in it.

The river, or rather the bed of it, is here of great width, and most frightful depth, lined on all sides with huge masses of black rock of every imaginable form. The flood that roars through them is seen only at intervals; here in a full heavy sheet of green transparent water, falling straight and unbroken; there dashing along a narrow channel, with a violence that makes one dizzy to see and hear. In one place an unfathomed pool shews a mirror of inky blackness, and as still as night; in another the tortured twisted cataract tumbles headlong in a dozen different torrents, half hid by the cloud of spray they send high into the air. Despite this uproar, the slenderest, loveliest shrubs, peep forth from among these hideous rocks, like children smiling in the midst of danger. As we stood looking at this tremendous scene, one of our friends made us remark, that the poison alder, and the poison vine, threw their graceful, but perfidious branches, over every rock, and assured us also that innumerable tribes of snakes found their dark dwellings among them.

To call this scene beautiful would be a strange abuse of terms, for it is altogether composed of sights and sounds of terror. The falls of the Potomac are awfully sublime; the dark deep gulf which yawns before you, the foaming, roaring cataract, the eddying whirlpool, and the giddy precipice, all seem to threaten life, and to appal the senses. Yet it was a great delight to sit upon a high and jutting crag, and look and listen.

I heard with pleasure that it was to the Virginian side of the Potomac that the "felicity hunters" of Washington resorted to see this fearful wonder, for I never saw a spot where I should less have liked the annoying "how d'ye," of a casual rencontre. One could not even give or receive the exciting "is it not charming," which Rousseau talks of, for if it were uttered, it could not be heard, or, if heard, would fall most earthly dull on the spirit, when rapt by the magic of such a scene. A look, or the silent pressure of the arm, is all the interchange of feeling that such a scene allows, and in the midst of my terror and my pleasure, I wished for the arm and the eye of some few from the other side of the Atlantic.

The return from such a scene is more soberly silent than the approach to it; but the cool and quiet hour, the mellowed tints of some gay blossoms, and the closed bells of others, the drowsy hum of the insects that survive the day, and the moist freshness that forbids the foot to weary in its homeward path, have all enjoyment in them, and seem to harmonize with the half wearied, half excited state of spirits, that such an excursion is sure to produce: and then the entering the cool and moonlit portico, the well-iced sangaree, or still more refreshing coffee, that awaits you, is all delightful; and if to this be added the happiness of an easy sofa, and a friend like my charming Mrs. S—, to sooth you with an hour of Mozart, the most fastidious European might allow that such a day was worth waking for.

CHAPTER XXII

Small Landed Proprietors — Slavery

I NOW, for the first time since I crossed the mountains, found myself sufficiently at leisure to look deliberately round, and mark the different aspects of men and things in a region which, though bearing the same name, and calling itself the same land, was, in many respects, as different from the one I had left, as Amsterdam from St. Petersburgh. There every man was straining, and struggling, and striving for himself (heaven knows!). Here every white man was waited upon, more or less, by a slave. There, the newly-cleared lands, rich with the vegetable manure accumulated for ages, demanded the slightest labour to return the richest produce; where the plough entered, crops the most abundant followed; but where it came not, no spot of native verdure, no native fruits, no native flowers cheered the eye; all was close, dark, stifling forest. Here the soil had long ago yielded its first fruits; much that had been cleared and cultivated for tobacco (the most exhausting of crops) by the English, required careful and laborious husbandry to produce any return; and much was left as sheep-walks. It was in these spots that the natural bounty of the soil and climate was displayed by the innumerable wild fruits and flowers which made every dingle and bushy dell seem a garden.

On entering the cottages I found also a great difference in the manner of living. Here, indeed, there were few cottages without a slave, but there were fewer still that had their beef-steak and onions for breakfast, dinner, and supper. The herrings of the bountiful Potomac supply their place. These are excellent "relish," as they call it, when salted, and, if I mistake not, are sold at a dollar and a half per thousand. Whiskey, however, flows every where at the same fatally cheap rate of twenty cents (about one shilling) the gallon, and its hideous effects are visible on the countenance of every man you meet.

The class of people the most completely unlike any existing in England, are those who, farming their own freehold estates, and often possessing several slaves, yet live with as few of the refinements, and I think I may say, with as few of the comforts of life, as the very poorest English peasant. When in Maryland, I went into the houses of several of these small proprietors, and remained long enough, and looked and listened sufficiently, to obtain a tolerably correct idea of their manner of living.

One of these families consisted of a young man, his wife, two children, a female slave, and two young lads, slaves also. The farm belonged to the wife, and, I was told, consisted of about three hundred acres of indifferent land, but all cleared. The house was built of wood, and looked as if the three slaves might have overturned it, had they pushed hard against the gable end. It contained one room, of about twelve feet square, and another adjoining it, hardly larger than a closet; this second chamber was the lodging-room of the white part of the family. Above these rooms was a loft, without windows, where I was told the "staying company" who visited them, were lodged. Near this mansion was a "shanty," a black hole, without any window, which served as kitchen and all other offices, and also as the lodging of the blacks.

We were invited to take tea with this family, and readily consented to do so. The furniture of the room was one heavy huge table, and about six wooden chairs. When we arrived the lady was in rather a dusky dishabille, but she vehemently urged us to be seated, and then retired into the closet-chamber above mentioned, whence she continued to address to us from behind the door, all kinds of "genteel country visiting talk," and at length emerged upon us in a smart new dress.

Her female slave set out the great table, and placed upon it cups of the very coarsest blue ware, a little brown sugar in one, and a tiny drop of milk in another, no butter, though the lady assured us she had a *"deary"* and two cows. Instead of butter, she "hoped we would fix a little relish with our crackers," in ancient English, eat salt meat and dry biscuits. Such was the fare, and for guests that certainly were intended to be honoured. I could not help recalling the delicious repasts which I remembered to have enjoyed at little dairy farms in England, not *possessed*, but rented, and at high rents too; where the clean, fresh-coloured, bustling mistress herself skimmed the delicious cream, herself spread the yellow butter on the delightful brown loaf, and placed her curds, and her junket, and all the delicate treasures of her dairy before us, and then, with hospitable pride, placed herself at her board, and added the more delicate "relish" of good tea and good cream. I remembered all this, and did not think the difference atoned for, by the dignity of having my cup handed to me by a slave. The lady I now visited, however, greatly surpassed my quondam friends in the refinement of her conversation. She ambled through the whole time the visit lasted, in a sort of elegantly mincing familiar style of gossip, which, I think, she was imitating from some novel, for I was told she was a great novel reader, and left all household occupations to be performed by her slaves. To say she addressed us in a tone of equality, will give no adequate idea of her manner; I am persuaded that no misgiving on the subject ever entered her head. She told us that their estate was her divi-*dend* of her father's property. She had married a first cousin, who was as fine a gentleman as she was a lady, and as idle, preferring hunting (as they call shooting) to any other occupation. The consequence was, that but a very small portion of the divi-*dend* was cultivated, and their poverty was extreme. The slaves, particularly the lads, were considerably more than half naked, but the air of dignity with which, in the midst of

all this misery, the lanky lady said to one of the young negroes, "Attend to your young master, Lycurgus," must have
been heard to be conceived in the full extent of its mock
heroic.

Another dwelling of one of these landed proprietors was a
hovel as wretched as the one above described, but there was
more industry within it. The gentleman, indeed, was himself one of the numerous tribe of regular whiskey drinkers,
and was rarely capable of any work; but he had a family of
twelve children, who, with their skeleton mother, worked
much harder than I ever saw negroes do. They were, accordingly, much less elegant and much less poor than the heiress;
yet they lived with no appearance of comfort, and with, I believe, nothing beyond the necessaries of life. One proof of
this was, that the worthless father would not suffer them to
raise, even by their own labour, any garden vegetables, and
they lived upon their fat pork, salt fish, and corn bread, summer and winter, without variation. This, I found, was frequently the case among the farmers. The luxury of whiskey
is more appreciated by the men than all the green delicacies
from the garden, and if all the ready money goes for that and
their darling chewing tobacco, none can be spent by the wife
for garden seeds; and as far as my observation extended, I
never saw any American *ménage* where the toast and no
toast question would have been decided in favour of the
lady.

There are some small farmers who hold their lands as tenants, but these are by no means numerous: they do not pay
their rent in money, but by making over a third of the produce to the owner; a mode of paying rent, considerably more advantageous to the tenant, than the landlord; but the difficulty
of obtaining *money* in payment, excepting for mere retail
articles, is very great in all American transactions. "I can pay
in pro-*duce*," is the offer which I was assured is constantly
made on all occasions, and if rejected, "Then I guess we can't

deal," is the usual rejoinder. This statement does not, of course, include the great merchants of great cities, but refers to the mass of the people scattered over the country; it has, indeed, been my object, in speaking of the customs of the people, to give an idea of what they are *generally*.

The effect produced upon English people by the sight of slavery in every direction is very new, and not very agreeable, and it is not the less painfully felt from hearing upon every breeze the mocking words, "All men are born free and equal." One must be in the heart of American slavery fully to appreciate that wonderfully fine passage in Moore's Epistle to Lord Viscount Forbes, which describes perhaps more faithfully, as well as more powerfully, the political state of America, than any thing that has ever been written upon it.[1]

> Oh! Freedom, Freedom, how I hate thy cant!
> Not eastern bombast, nor the savage rant
> Of purpled madmen, were they numbered all
> From Roman Nero, down to Russian Paul,
> Could grate upon my ear so mean, so base,
> As the rank jargon of that factious race,
> Who, poor of heart, and prodigal of words,
> Born to be slaves, and struggling to be lords,
> But pant for licence, while they spurn controul,
> And shout for rights, with rapine in their soul!
> Who can, with patience, for a moment see
> The medley mass of pride and misery,
> Of whips and charters, manacles and rights,
> Of slaving blacks, and democratic whites,
> Of all the pyebald polity that reigns

---

[1] [DS] Thomas Moore (1779–1852), wit, poet, musician, friend and biographer of Byron, made a brief tour of the Eastern cities of the United States as a young man in 1804, spending most of his time with British naval officers whose ships were in port and with wealthy Federalists, who bitterly resented Jefferson's control of the government. Moore later expressed regret for many of the sharp things he had said about America in his poems of this period; he confessed that he had been "left open too much to the influence of the feelings and prejudices of those I chiefly consorted with. . . ."

"To the Lord Viscount Forbes" has the pointed subtitle: "From the City of Washington." Moore paid a call upon the President and was shocked at the homely dress in which Jefferson received him.

In free confusion o'er Columbia's plains?
To think that man, thou just and gentle God!
Should stand before thee with a tyrant's rod,
O'er creatures like himself, with soul from thee,
Yet dare to boast of perfect liberty:
Away, away, I'd rather hold my neck
By doubtful tenure from a Sultan's beck,
In climes where liberty has scarce been named,
Nor any right, but that of ruling, claimed,
Than thus to live, where bastard freedom waves
Her fustian flag in mockery over slaves;
Where (motley laws admitting no degree
Betwixt the vilely slaved, and madly free)
Alike the bondage and the licence suit,
The brute made ruler, and the man made brute!

The condition of domestic slaves, however, does not generally appear to be bad; but the ugly feature is, that should
it be so, they have no power to change it. I have seen much
kind attention bestowed upon the health of slaves; but it is
on these occasions impossible to forget, that did this attention
fail, a valuable piece of property would be endangered. Unhappily the slaves, too, know this, and the consequence is,
that real kindly feeling very rarely can exist between the
parties. It is said that slaves born in a family are attached to
the children of it, who have grown up with them. This may
be the case where the petty acts of infant tyranny [2] have not
been sufficient to conquer the kindly feeling naturally produced by long and early association; and this sort of attach-
ment may last as long as the slave can be kept in that state
of profound ignorance which precludes reflection. The law
of Virginia has taken care of this. The State legislators may

---

[2] [T5, note] Perhaps the most disgusting part of the spectacle (except
the often recurring infliction of personal punishment) is that in which all
that is most hateful in our nature is displayed in the infant tyranny of white
children towards their slaves. I cannot even at this distance of time recal[l]
the puny bullying and well-taught ingenious insult of almost baby children
towards stalwart slaves, who raised their heads towards heaven like men,
but seemed to have lost the right of being so classed, without a feeling of
indignation that makes my heart beat painfully.

truly be said to be "wiser in their generation than the children of light," and they ensure their safety by forbidding light to enter among them. By the law of Virginia it is penal to teach any slave to read, and it is penal to be aiding and abetting in the act of instructing them. This law speaks volumes. Domestic slaves are, generally speaking, tolerably well fed, and decently clothed; and the mode in which they are lodged seems a matter of great indifference to them. They are rarely exposed to the lash, and they are carefully nursed in sickness. These are the favourable features of their situation. The sad one is, that they *may* be sent to *the south* and sold. This is the dread of all the slaves north of Louisiana. The sugar plantations, and more than all, the rice grounds of Georgia and the Carolinas, are the terror of American negroes; and well they may be, for they open an early grave to thousands; and to *avoid loss* it is needful to make their previous labour pay their value.

There is something in the system of breeding and rearing negroes in the Northern States, for the express purpose of sending them to be sold in the South, that strikes painfully against every feeling of justice, mercy, or common humanity. During my residence in America I became perfectly persuaded that the state of a domestic slave in a gentleman's family was preferable to that of a hired American "help," both because they are more cared for and valued, and because their condition being born with them, their spirits do not struggle against it with that pining discontent which seems the lot of all free servants in America. But the case is widely different with such as, in their own persons, or those of their children, "loved in vain," are exposed to the dreadful traffic above mentioned. In what is their condition better than that of the kidnapped negroes on the coast of Africa? Of the horror in which this enforced migration is held I had a strong proof during our stay in Virginia. The father of a young slave, who belonged to the lady with whom we boarded, was destined to this fate, and within an hour after it was made known to him, he sharpened the hatchet with which he had been felling timber, and with his right hand severed his left from the wrist.

But this is a subject on which I do not mean to dilate; it has been lately treated most judiciously by a far abler hand.[3] Its effects on the moral feelings and external manners of the people are all I wish to observe upon, and these are unquestionably most injurious. The same man who beards his wealthier and more educated neighbour with the bullying boast, "I'm as good as you," turns to his slave, and knocks him down, if the furrow he has ploughed, or the log he has felled, please not this stickler for equality. There is a glaring falsehood on the very surface of such a man's principles that is revolting. It is not among the higher classes that the possession of slaves produces the worst effects. Among the poorer class of landholders, who are often as profoundly ignorant as the negroes they own, the effect of this plenary power over males and females is most demoralising; and the kind of coarse, not to say brutal, authority which is exercised, furnishes the most disgusting moral spectacle I ever witnessed. In all ranks, however, it appeared to me that the greatest and best feelings of the human heart were paralyzed by the relative positions of slave and owner. The characters, the hearts of children, are irretrievably injured by it. In Virginia we boarded for some time in a family consisting of a widow and her four daughters, and I there witnessed a scene strongly indicative of the effect I have mentioned. A young female slave, about eight years of age, had found on the shelf of a cupboard a biscuit, temptingly buttered, of which she had eaten a considerable portion before she was observed. The butter had been copiously sprinkled with arsenic for the destruction of rats, and had been thus most incautiously placed by one of the young ladies of the family. As soon as the cir-

[3] [T1] See Captain Hall's Travels in America.

cumstance was known, the lady of the house came to consult me as to what had best be done for the poor child; I immediately mixed a large cup of mustard and water (the most rapid of all emetics) and got the little girl to swallow it. The desired effect was instantly produced, but the poor child, partly from nausea, and partly from the terror of hearing her death proclaimed by half a dozen voices round her, trembled so violently that I thought she would fall. I sat down in the court where we were standing, and, as a matter of course, took the little sufferer in my lap. I observed a general titter among the white members of the family, while the black stood aloof, and looked stupified. The youngest of the family, a little girl about the age of the young slave, after gazing at me for a few moments in utter astonishment, exclaimed, "My! If Mrs. Trollope has not taken her in her lap, and wiped her nasty mouth! Why I would not have touched her mouth for two hundred dollars!"

The little slave was laid on a bed, and I returned to my own apartments; some time afterwards I sent to enquire for her, and learnt that she was in great pain. I immediately went myself to enquire farther, when another young lady of the family, the one by whose imprudence the accident had occurred, met my anxious enquiries with ill-suppressed mirth — told me they had sent for the doctor — and then burst into uncontrollable laughter. The idea of really sympathising in the sufferings of a slave, appeared to them as absurd as weeping over a calf that had been slaughtered by the butcher. The daughters of my hostess were as lovely as features and complexion could make them; but the neutralizing effect of this total want of feeling upon youth and beauty, must be witnessed, to be conceived.

There seems in general a strong feeling throughout America, that none of the negro race can be trusted, and as fear, according to their notions, is the only principle by which a slave can be actuated, it is not wonderful if the imputation

be just. But I am persuaded that were a different mode of
moral treatment pursued, most important and beneficial consequences would result from it. Negroes are very sensible to
kindness, and might, I think, be rendered more profitably
obedient by the practice of it towards them, than by any
other mode of discipline whatever. To emancipate them entirely throughout the Union cannot, I conceive, be thought
of, consistently with the safety of the country; but were the
possibility of amelioration taken into the consideration of the
legislature, with all the wisdom, justice, and mercy, that
could be brought to bear upon it, the negro population of
the Union might cease to be a terror, and their situation no
longer be a subject either of indignation or of pity.

I observed every where throughout the slave states that all
articles which can be taken and consumed are constantly
locked up, and in large families where the extent of the establishment multiplies the number of keys, these are deposited
in a basket, and consigned to the care of a little negress, who
is constantly seen following her mistress's steps with this
basket on her arm, and this, not only that the keys may be
always at hand, but because should they be out of sight one
moment, that moment would infallibly be employed for purposes of plunder. It seemed to me in this instance, as in
many others, that the close personal attendance of these sable
shadows, must be very annoying; but whenever I mentioned
it, I was assured that no such feeling existed, and that use
rendered them almost unconscious of their presence.

I had, indeed, frequent opportunities of observing this
habitual indifference to the presence of their slaves. They
talk of them, of their condition, of their faculties, of their conduct, exactly as if they were incapable of hearing. I once
saw a young lady, who, when seated at table between a male
and a female, was induced by her modesty to intrude on the
chair of her female neighbour to avoid the indelicacy of
touching the elbow of *a man*. I once saw this very young lady

lacing her stays with the most perfect composure before a
negro footman. A Virginian gentleman told me that ever
since he had married, he had been accustomed to have a
negro girl sleep in the same chamber with himself and his
wife. I asked for what purpose this nocturnal attendance was
necessary? "Good heaven!" was the reply, "if I wanted a glass
of water during the night, what would become of me?" [4]

[4] [DS] Even in Mrs. Trollope's report of this dialogue, it sounds very
much as if the Virginian gentleman was quizzing the note-taking traveler.

CHAPTER XXIII

Fruits and Flowers of Maryland and Virginia — Copper-head Snake — Insects — Elections

OUR summer in Maryland, (1830,) was delightful. The thermometer stood at 94, but the heat was by no means so oppressive as what we had felt in the West. In no part of North America are the natural productions of the soil more various, or more beautiful. Strawberries of the richest flavour sprung beneath our feet; and when these past away, every grove, every lane, every field looked like a cherry orchard, offering an inexhaustible profusion of fruit to all who would take the trouble to gather it. Then followed the peaches; every hedge-row was planted with them, and though the fruit did not equal in size or flavour those ripened on our garden walls, we often found them good enough to afford a delicious refreshment on our long rambles. But it was the flowers, and the flowering shrubs that, beyond all else, rendered this region the most beautiful I had ever seen, (the Alleghany always excepted.) No description can give an idea of the variety, the profusion, the luxuriance of them. If I talk of wild roses, the English reader will fancy I mean the pale ephemeral blossoms of our bramble hedges; but the wild roses of Maryland and Virginia might be the choicest favorites of the flower garden. They are very rarely double, but the brilliant eye atones for this. They are of all shades, from the deepest crimson to the tenderest pink. The scent is rich and delicate; in size they exceed any single roses I ever saw, often measuring above four inches in diameter. The leaf greatly resembles that of the china rose; it is large, dark, firm, and brilliant. The sweet brier grows wild, and blossoms abundantly; both leaves and flowers are considerably larger than with us. The acacia, or as it is there called, the locust, blooms with great richness and profusion; I have gathered a branch less than a foot long, and counted twelve full bunches of flowers on it. The scent is equal to the orange flower. The dogwood is another of the splendid white blossoms that adorn the woods. Its lateral branches are flat, like a fan, and dotted all over with star-like blossoms, as large as those of the gum-cistus. Another pretty shrub, of smaller size, is the poison alder. It is well that its noxious qualities are very generally known, for it is most tempting to the eye by its delicate fringe-like bunches of white flowers. Even the touch of this shrub is poisonous, and produces violent swelling. The arbor judæ is abundant in every wood, and its bright and delicate pink is the earliest harbinger of the American spring. Azalias, white, yellow, and pink; kalmias of every variety, the too sweet magnolia, and the stately rhododendron, all grow in wild abundance there. The plant known in England as the Virginian creeper, is often seen climbing to the top of the highest forest trees, and bearing a large trumpet-shaped blossom of a rich scarlet. The sassafras is a beautiful shrub, and I cannot imagine why it has not been naturalized in England, for it has every appearance of being extremely hardy. The leaves grow in tufts, and every tuft contains leaves of five or six different forms. The fruit is singularly beautiful; it resembles in form a small acorn, and is jet black; the cup and stem looking as if they were made of red coral. The graceful and fantastic grapevine is a feature of great beauty, and its wandering festoons bear no more resemblance to our well-trained vines, than our stunted azalias, and tiny magnolias, to their thriving American kindred.

There is another charm that haunts the summer wanderer in America, and it is perhaps the only one found in greatest perfection in the West: but it is beautiful every where. In a bright day, during any of the summer months, your walk is through an atmosphere of butterflies, so gaudy in hue, and so varied in form, that I often thought they looked like flowers on the wing. Some of them are very large, measuring three or four inches across the wings; but many, and I think the most beautiful, are smaller than ours. Some have wings of the most dainty lavender colour, and bodies of black; others are fawn and rose colour; and others again are orange and bright blue. But pretty as they are, it is their number, even more than their beauty, that delights the eye. Their gay and noiseless movement as they glance through the air, crossing each other in chequered maze, is very beautiful. The humming-bird is another pretty summer toy; but they are not sufficiently numerous, nor do they live enough on the wing to render them so important a feature in the transatlantic show, as the rainbow-tinted butterflies. The fire-fly was a far more brilliant novelty. In moist situations, or before a storm, they are very numerous, and in the dark sultry evening of a burning day, when all employment was impossible, I have often found it a pastime to watch their glancing light, now here, now there; now seen, now gone; shooting past with the rapidity of lightning, and looking like a shower of falling stars, blown about in the breeze of evening.

*　*　*　*　*　*

In one of our excursions we encountered and slew a copper-head snake. I escaped treading on it by about three inches. While we were contemplating our conquered foe, and doubting in our ignorance if he were indeed the deadly copper-head we had so often heard described, a farmer joined us, who, as soon as he cast his eyes on our victim, exclaimed, "My! if you have not got a copper. That's right down well done, they be darnation beasts." He told us that he had once seen a copper-head bite himself to death, from being teazed by a stick, while confined in a cage where he could find no other victim. We often heard terrible accounts of the number of these desperate reptiles to be found on the rocks near the great falls of the Potomac; but not even the terror these stories inspired could prevent our repeated visits to that sublime scene; luckily our temerity was never punished by seeing any there. Lizards, long, large, and most hideously like a miniature crocodile, I frequently saw, gliding from the fissures of the rocks, and darting again under shelter, perhaps beneath the very stone I was seated upon; but every one assured us they were harmless. Animal life is so infinitely abundant, and in forms so various, and so novel to European eyes, that it is absolutely necessary to divest oneself of all the petty terrors which the crawling, creeping, hopping, and buzzing tribes can inspire, before taking an American summer ramble. It is, I conceive, quite impossible for any description to convey an idea of the sounds which assail the ears from the time the short twilight begins, until the rising sun scatters the rear of darkness, and sends the winking choristers to rest.

Be where you will (excepting in the large cities) the appalling note of the bull-frog will reach you, loud, deep, and hoarse, issuing from a thousand throats in ceaseless continuity of croak. The tree-frog adds her chirping and almost human voice; the kattiedid repeats her own name through the livelong night; the whole tribe of locusts chip, chirrup, squeak, whiz, and whistle, without allowing one instant of interval to the weary ear; and when to this the mosquito adds her threatening hum, it is wonderful that any degree of fatigue can obtain for the listener the relief of sleep. In fact, it is only in ceasing to listen that this blessing can be found. I passed many feverish nights during my first summer, literally in listening to this most astounding mixture of noises, and it was only when they became too familiar to excite attention, that I recovered my rest.

I know not by what whimsical link of association the recapitulation of this insect din suggests the recollection of other discords, at least as harsh and much more troublesome.

Even in the retirement in which we passed this summer, we were not beyond reach of the election fever which is constantly raging through the land. Had America every attraction under heaven that nature and social enjoyment can offer, this electioneering madness would make me fly it in disgust. It engrosses every conversation, it irritates every temper, it substitutes party spirit for personal esteem; and, in fact, vitiates the whole system of society.

disapprove of Am. politics

When a candidate for any office starts, his party endow him with every virtue, and with all the talents. They are all ready to peck out the eyes of those who oppose him, and in the warm and mettlesome south-western states, do literally often perform this operation: [1] but as soon as he succeeds, his virtues and his talents vanish, and, excepting those holding office under his appointment, every man Jonathan of them sets off again full gallop to elect his successor. When I first arrived in America Mr. John Quincy Adams was President, and it was impossible to doubt, even from the statement of his enemies, that he was every way calculated to do honour to the office. All I ever heard against him was, that "he was too much of a gentleman;" but a new candidate must be set up, and Mr. Adams was out-voted for no other reason, that I could learn, but because it was "best to change." "Jackson for ever!" was, therefore, screamed from the majority of mouths, both drunk and sober, till he was elected; but no sooner in his place, than the same ceaseless operation went on again, with "Clay for ever" for its war-whoop.

I was one morning paying a visit, when a party of gentle-

---

[1] [DS] Mrs. Trollope refers to "gouging," an art sometimes practiced in the Kentucky region of the United States. According to James Flint's *Letters from America* (1822), fights were often "characterized by the most savage ferocity. Gouging or putting out the antagonist's eyes by thrusting the thumbs into the sockets, is a part of the *modus operandi* . . . kicking and biting are also means used in combat; I have seen several fingers that have been deformed, also several noses and ears which have been mutilated by this canine mode of fighting."

men arrived at the same house on horseback. The one whose air proclaimed him the chief of his party, left us not long in doubt as to his business, for he said, almost in entering,

"Mr. P—, I come to ask for your vote."

"Who are you for, sir?" was the reply.

"Clay for ever!" the rejoinder; and the vote was promised.

This gentleman was candidate for a place in the state representation, whose members have a vote in the presidential election.

I was introduced to him as an English woman: he addressed me with, "Well, madam, you see we do these things openly and above-board here; you mince such matters more, I expect."

After his departure, his history and standing were discussed. "Mr. M. is highly respectable, and of very good standing; there can be no doubt of his election if he is a thorough-going Clay-man," said my host.

I asked what his station was.

The lady of the house told me that his father had been a merchant, and when this future legislator was a young man, he had been sent by him to some port in the Mediterranean as his supercargo. The youth, being a free-born high-spirited youth, appropriated the proceeds to his own uses, traded with great success upon the fund thus obtained, and returned, after an absence of twelve years, a gentleman of fortune and excellent standing. I expressed some little disapprobation of this proceeding, but was assured that Mr. M. was considered by every one as a very "honourable man."

Were I to relate one-tenth part of the dishonest transactions recounted to me by Americans, of their fellow-citizens and friends, I am confident that no English reader would give me credit for veracity; it would, therefore, be very unwise to repeat them, but I cannot refrain from expressing the opinion that nearly four years of attentive observation impressed on me, namely, that the moral sense is

on every point blunter than with us. Make an American believe that his next-door neighbour is a very worthless fellow,
and I dare say (if he were quite sure he could make nothing
by him) he would drop the acquaintance; but as to what
constitutes a worthless fellow, people differ on the opposite
sides of the Atlantic, almost by the whole decalogue. There
is, as it appeared to me, an obtusity on all points of honourable feeling.[2]

"Cervantes laughed Spain's chivalry away," but he did not
laugh away that better part of chivalry, so beautifully described by Burke as "the unbought grace of life, the cheap
defence of nations, that chastity of honour, which feels a
stain as a wound, which ennobles whatever it touches, and
by which vice itself loses half its evil, by losing all its grossness." This better part of chivalry still mixes with gentle
blood in every part of Europe, nor is it less fondly guarded
than when sword and buckler aided its defence. Perhaps this
unbought grace of life is not to be looked for where chivalry
has never been. I certainly do not lament the decadence of
knight errantry, nor wish to exchange the protection of the
laws for that of the doughtiest champion who ever set lance
in rest; but I do, in truth, believe that this knightly sensitiveness of honourable feeling is the best antidote to the petty
soul-degrading transactions of every-day life, and that the
total want of it, is one reason why this free-born race care so
very little for the vulgar virtue called probity.

---

[2] [T5, note] It is remarkable how often in re-perusing these pages, it
strikes me that since they were written, the old country has in many points
assimilated itself to the new. If my memory does not entirely fail me, there
was more attention shown to moral character formerly, and a greater necessity for those who sought advancement to stand well in public opinion as to
their worth and honour than at present.

CHAPTER XXIV

*Journey to Philadelphia — Chesapeak and Delaware Canal — City
of Philadelphia — Miss Wright's Lecture*

IN the latter part of August, 1830,[1] we paid a visit to
Philadelphia, and, notwithstanding the season, we were so
fortunate as to have both bright and temperate weather for
the expedition. The road from Washington to Baltimore,
which was our first day's journey, is interesting in summer
from the variety and luxuriance of the foliage which borders
great part of it.[2]

---

[1] [DS] Either Mrs. Trollope or her printer confused the date of this visit
to Philadelphia. It began in the latter part of June, as Mrs. Trollope's record
of the events that occurred during her stay in the city makes clear, and the
fortnight that she remained there probably carried into the early days of
July.

[2] [TN] The road from Washington to Baltimore is interesting in summer
from the marvellous variety and luxuriance of foliage which borders great
part of it. America produces many varieties of oak. I reckoned seven on this
road, and these varieties do not consist in the delicate differences that science only can discover or assuredly I should never have found them out,
but though evidently all oak, they are as little alike in general appearance
as a plane tree to a weeping willow. One has large dark shining leaves that
resemble those of the fig tree; another small light coloured & so deeply in-
dented that they look like fringe — another grows in fans of four or five
leaves radiating from a centre. This species is of a dark bright shining green
and is exquisitely beautiful. Another has leaves so enormous that I hardly
hope to escape the charge of using a traveller's license in describing them.
I have one that measured when freshly gathered $\frac{14}{19}$ inches and a half in
length and $\frac{10}{11\frac{1}{2}}$ in width. This is called the black jack oak — its botanical
name I could not learn. I must not attempt to describe all those beautiful
and capricious varieties, for I know I can give no idea of them separately
and still less of the richness, and luxuriance, the brightness, the gorgeous
splendour of the general effect. What increased this effect in the particular
region I am now speaking of is the copious growth of underwood. From
time to time some stately old trees are to be seen but by much the largest
parties have been cut down in the manner of our copses, and the growth
that follows is gigantic in its foliage. The beautiful tufts of the ever grace-

We passed the night at Baltimore, and embarked next
morning on board a steam-boat for Philadelphia. The scenery of the Elk river, upon which you enter soon after leaving the port of Baltimore, is not beautiful. We embarked at
six in the morning, and at twelve reached the Chesapeak and
Delaware canal; we then quitted the steam-boat, and walked
two or three hundred yards to the canal, where we got on
board a pretty little decked boat, sheltered by a neat awning,
and drawn by four horses. This canal cuts across the state of
Delaware, and connects the Chesapeak and Delaware rivers:
it has been a work of great expense, though the distance is
not more than thirteen miles; for a considerable part of this
distance the cutting has been very deep, and the banks are
in many parts thatched, to prevent their crumbling. At the
point where the cutting is deepest, a light bridge is thrown
across, which, from its great height, forms a striking object
to the travellers passing below it. Every boat that passes this
canal pays a toll of twenty dollars.

Nothing can be less interesting than that part of the state
of Delaware through which this cut passes, the Mississippi
hardly excepted. At one, we reached the Delaware river, at
a point nearly opposite Delaware Fort, which looks recently
built, and is very handsome.[3] Here we again changed our
vessel, and got on board another of their noble steam-boats;
both these changes were made with the greatest regularity
and dispatch.

There is nothing remarkable in the scenery of the Delaware. The stream is wide and the banks are flat; a short distance before you reach Philadelphia two large buildings of

ful sassafras and the laurel hue of the persimmon occasionally mix with this
world of oak, Magnolia- & wild rose. It surprises me that so little has been
said or written of the magnificent foliage of the U. S. or perhaps it is that
such things make but a slight impression in description; if so, it is vain to
dwell upon them, but I may fairly promise those who visit America the
pleasure of seeing the trees of the forest in a degree of perfection which
unseen they cannot imagine.

[3] [T1] This fort was destroyed by fire a few months afterwards.

singular appearance strike the eye. On enquiry I learnt that
they were erected for the purpose of sheltering two ships of
war. They are handsomely finished, with very neat roofs, and
are ventilated by many windows. The expense of these buildings must have been considerable, but, as the construction
of the vast machines they shelter was more so, it may be
good economy.

We reached Philadelphia at four o'clock in the afternoon.[4]
The approach to this city is not so striking as that to Baltimore; though much larger, it does not now shew itself so
well: it wants domes and columns: it is, nevertheless, a beautiful city. Nothing can exceed its neatness; the streets are
well paved, the foot-way, as in all the old American cities, is
of brick, like the old pantile walk at Tunbridge Wells. This
is almost entirely sheltered from the sun by the awnings,
which, in all the principal streets, are spread from the shop
windows to the edge of the pavement.

The city is built with extreme and almost wearisome regularity; the streets, which run north and south, are distinguished by numbers, from one to — I know not how many,
but I paid a visit in Twelfth Street; these are intersected at
right angles by others, which are known by the names of
various trees; Mulberry (more commonly called Arch-
street), Chesnut, and Walnut, appear the most fashionable:
in each of these there is a theatre. This mode of distinguishing the streets is commodious to strangers, from the facility it
gives of finding out whereabouts you are; if you ask for the

---

4 [TN] We were at the Philadelphia hotel in second street, a very comfortable house with large airy sitting rooms, [and] an excellent table d'hote
at a dollar a day. The company were perfectly well dressed, so I suppose
they were *of good standing*, but I did not perceive much difference between
Philadelphia & the West either in the rapidity or silence of the meals or in
the universality of the spitting abomination.

I had the pleasure of conversing repeatedly with Mr. Lea, the well
known Philadelphia publisher, and found him a very well informed man —
full of anecdote, general information and completely a man of the world.
His wife is an admirable proof that enlarged education and literary habits
are all that are wanting to make the American ladies agreeable.

United States Bank, you are told it is in Chesnut, between Third and Fourth, and as the streets are all divided from each other by equal distances, of about three hundred feet, you are sure of not missing your mark. There are many handsome houses, but none that are very splendid; they are generally of brick, and those of the better order have white marble steps, and some few, door frames of the same beautiful material; but, on the whole, there is less display of it in the private dwellings than at Baltimore.

The Americans all seem greatly to admire this city, and to give it the preference in point of beauty, to all others in the Union, but I do not agree with them. There are some very handsome buildings, but none of them so placed as to produce a striking effect, as is the case both with the Capitol and the President's house, at Washington. Notwithstanding these fine buildings, one or more of which are to be found in all the principal streets, the *coup d'œil* is every where the same. There is no Place de Louis Quinze or Carrousel, no Regent Street, or Green Park, to make one exclaim "how beautiful!" all is even, straight, uniform, and uninteresting.

There is one spot, however, about a mile from the town, which presents a lovely scene. The water-works of Philadelphia have not yet perhaps as wide extended fame as those of Marley, but they are not less deserving it. At a most beautiful point of the Schuylkill River the water has been forced up into a magnificent reservoir, ample and elevated enough to send it through the whole city. The vast yet simple machinery by which this is achieved is open to the public, who resort in such numbers to see it, that several evening stages run from Philadelphia to Fair Mount for their accommodation. But interesting and curious as this machinery is, Fair Mount would not be so attractive had it not something else to offer. It is, in truth, one of the very prettiest spots the eye can look upon. A broad wear is thrown across the Schuylkill, which produces the sound and look of a cascade. On the farther side of the river is a gentleman's seat, the beautiful lawns of which slope to the water's edge, and groups of weeping-willows and other trees throw their shadows on the stream. The works themselves are enclosed in a simple but very handsome building of freestone, which has an extended front opening upon a terrace, which overhangs the river: behind the building, and divided from it only by a lawn, rises a lofty wall of solid lime-stone rock, which has, at one or two points, been cut into, for the passage of the water into the noble reservoir above. From the crevices of this rock the catalpa was every where pushing forth, covered with its beautiful blossom. Beneath one of these trees an artificial opening in the rock gives passage to a stream of water, clear and bright as crystal, which is received in a stone basin of simple workmanship, having a cup for the service of the thirsty traveller. At another point, a portion of the water in its upward way to the reservoir, is permitted to spring forth in a perpetual *jet d'eau*, that returns in a silver shower upon the head of a marble *naïad* of snowy whiteness. The statue is not the work of Phidias, but its dark, rocky back-ground, the flowery catalpas which shadow it, and the bright shower through which it shews itself, altogether make the scene one of singular beauty; add to which, the evening on which I saw it was very sultry, and the contrast of this cool spot to all besides certainly enhanced its attractions; it was impossible not to envy the nymph her eternal shower-bath.

On returning from this excursion we saw hand-bills in all parts of the city announcing that Miss Wright was on that evening to deliver her parting address to the citizens of Philadelphia, at the Arch Street theatre, previous to her departure for Europe. I immediately determined to hear her, and did so, though not without some difficulty, from the crowds who went thither with the same intention. The house, which is a very pretty one, was filled in every part, including the stage, with a well dressed and most attentive audience. There was a larger proportion of ladies present than I ever saw on any other occasion in an American theatre. One reason for this might be, perhaps, that they were admitted gratis.

Miss Wright came on the stage surrounded by a body guard of Quaker ladies, in the full costume of their sect. She was, as she always is, startling in her theories, but powerfully eloquent, and, on the whole, was much applauded, though one passage produced great emotion, and some hissing. She stated broadly, on the authority of Jefferson, furnished by his posthumous works, that "Washington was not a Christian." One voice from the crowded pit exclaimed, in an accent of indignation, "Washington was a Christian;" but it was evident that the majority of the audience considered Mr. Jefferson's assertion as a compliment to the country's idol, for the hissing was soon triumphantly clapped down.[5] Gen-

---

[5] [DS] From the Philadelphia *Saturday Bulletin* (June 26, 1830) — a letter headed "The Farewell Address":

"Passing along Sixth street on Tuesday evening, I observed somewhat of a crowd making for Arch Street Theatre, and on inquiry learned that Miss Fanny Wright was to hold forth to 'the people.' . . . I followed the current . . . and very soon a motley crew of Miss Fanny's friends, to the number of near eighty, marched across the stage led by their queen. They looked and acted much like the witches in Macbeth, and after toiling round and round in search of seats, the priestess *took off her hat.* This was listened to with profound attention, and the lengthened operation of adjusting her curls having been minutely examined with a silence bordering on veneration, after a survey of the audience, and a shake of the head to every individual present, we were entertained with a tissue of nonsense and a farrago of wild assertion without the shadow of proof, which has no parallel in the annals of our fair city. . . . Several interruptions of claps and hisses obliged the lady to sit down. . . . [She stated, on continuing, that Washington was no Christian.]

"This was too much for the audience, and the most violent hisses obliged the defamatory priestess to say, 'I beg the audience to give way to the opposition — let them hiss — it does not proceed from Americans, but foreigners!!!!!' . . . It was so completely ridiculous that the hissing was redoubled, and a voice cried out from amidst the storm, '*Washington WAS a Christian.*' . . .

"Such, Mr. Editor, is the specious sophistry of this speculator in opinions and in negro flesh — if I were 'Governor,' I would calm her *transports* by transporting her back to old England, where I verily believe she would rot in a jail for uttering such abominations."

eral Washington himself, however, gives a somewhat different account of his own principles, for in his admirable farewell address on declining a re-election to the Presidency, I
find the following passage.

"Of all the dispositions and habits which lead to political
prosperity, religion and morality are indispensable supports.
In vain would that man claim the tribute of patriotism who
would labour to subvert these great pillars of human happiness, these firmest props of the destinies of men and citizens.
A volume could not trace all their connections with private
and public felicity. And let us with caution indulge the sup-
position that morality can be maintained without religion,
reason and experience both forbid us to expect that national
morality can prevail in exclusion of religious principle."

Whether Mr. Jefferson or himself knew best what his principles were, I will not decide, but, at least, it appears fair,
when repeating one statement, to add the other also.

XVII   ANTIQUE STATUE GALLERY

XVIII EVENING AT A BOARDING HOUSE

CHAPTER XXV

Washington Square — American Beauty — Gallery of Fine Arts —
Antiques — Theatres — Museum

OUR mornings were spent, as all travellers' mornings must be, in asking questions, and in seeing all that the answers told us it was necessary to see. Perhaps this can be done in no city with more facility than in Philadelphia; you have nothing to do but to walk up one straight street, and down another, till all the parallelograms have been threaded. In doing this you will see many things worth looking at. The United States, and Pennsylvania banks, are the most striking buildings, and are both extremely handsome, being of white marble, and built after Grecian models. The State House has nothing externally to recommend it, but the room shewn as that in which the declaration of independence was signed, and in which the estimable Lafayette was received half a century after he had shed his noble blood in aiding to obtain it, is an interesting spot. At one end of this room is a statue in wood of General Washington; on its base is the following inscription: —

FIRST IN PEACE,

FIRST IN WAR,

AND

FIRST IN THE HEARTS OF HIS COUNTRYMEN.

There is a very pretty enclosure before the Walnut Street entrance to the State House, with good well-kept gravel walks, and many of their beautiful flowering trees. It is laid down in grass, not in turf: that, indeed, is a luxury I never saw in America. Near this enclosure is another of much the same description, called Washington Square. Here there was an excellent crop of clover; but as the trees are numerous, and highly beautiful, and several commodious seats are placed beneath their shade, it is, spite of the long grass, a very agreeable retreat from heat and dust. It was rarely, however, that I saw any of these seats occupied; the Americans have either no leisure, or no inclination for these moments of *delassement* that all other people, I believe, indulge in. Even their drams, so universally taken by rich and poor, are swallowed standing, and, excepting at church, they never have the air of leisure or repose. This pretty Washington Square is surrounded by houses on three sides, but (lasso!) has a prison on the fourth; it is nevertheless the nearest approach to a London square that is to be found in Philadelphia.

One evening, while the rest of my party went to visit some object which I had before seen, I agreed to await their return in this square, and sat down under a magnificent catalpa, which threw its fragrant blossoms in all directions; the other end of the bench was occupied by a young lady, who was employed in watching the gambols of a little boy. There was something in her manner of looking at me, and exchanging a smile when her young charge performed some extraordinary feat of activity on the grass, that persuaded me she was not an American. I do not remember who spoke first, but we were presently in a full flow of conversation. She spoke English with elegant correctness, but she was a German, and with an ardour of feeling which gave her a decidedly foreign air in Philadelphia, she talked to me of her country, of all she had left, and of all she had found, or rather of all she had not found, for thus ran her lament: —

"They do not love music, Oh no! and they never amuse themselves — no; and their hearts are not warm, at least they seem not so to strangers; and they have no ease, no forgetfulness of business and of care — no, not for a moment. But I will not stay long, I think, for I should not live."

She told me that she had a brother settled there as a merchant, and that she had passed a year with him; but she was hoping soon to return to her father land.

I never so strongly felt the truth of the remark, that expression is the soul of beauty, as in looking at, and listening to this young German. She was any thing but handsome; it is true she had large eyes full of gentle expression, but every feature was irregular; but, oh! the charm of that smile, of that look of deep feeling which animated every feature when she spoke of her own Germany! The tone of her voice, the slight and graceful action which accompanied her words, all struck me as so attractive, that the half hour I passed with her was continually recurring to my memory. I had often taxed myself with feeling something like prejudice against the beautiful American women; but this half hour set my conscience at rest; it is not prejudice which causes one to feel that regularity of features is insufficient to interest, or even to please, beyond the first glance. I certainly believe the women of America to be the handsomest in the world, but as surely do I believe that they are the least attractive.

* * * * * *

We visited the nineteenth annual exhibition of the Pennsylvanian academy of the fine arts; 431 was the number of objects exhibited, which were so arranged as to fill three tolerably large rooms, and one smaller, called the director's room. There were among the number about thirty engravings, and a much larger proportion of water-colour drawings; about seventy had the P.A. (Pennsylvanian Academician) annexed to the name of the artist.

The principal historical composition was a large scripture piece by Mr. Washington Al[l]ston. This gentleman is spoken of as an artist of great merit, and I was told that his manner was much improved since this picture was painted, (it bears date, 1813). I believe it was for this picture Mr. Alston received a prize at the British Gallery.[1]

There was a portrait of a lady, which, in the catalogue, is designated as "the White Plume," which had the reputation of being the most admired in the collection, and the artist, Mr. Ingham, is said to rank highest among the portrait-painters of America. This picture is of very high finish, particularly the drapery, which is most elaborately worked, even to the pile of the velvet; the management of the light is much in the manner of Good; but the drawing is very defective, and the contour, though the face is a lovely one, hard and unfleshy. From all the conversations on painting, which I listened to in America, I found that the finish of drapery was considered as the highest excellence, and next to this, the resemblance in a portrait; I do not remember ever to have heard the words *drawing* or *composition* used in any conversation on the subject.

One of the rooms of this academy has inscribed over its door,

ANTIQUE STATUE GALLERY.

The door was open, but just within it was a screen, which prevented any objects in the room being seen from without. Upon my pausing to read this inscription, an old woman who appeared to officiate as guardian of the gallery, bustled up, and addressing me with an air of much mystery, said, "Now, ma'am, now; this is just the time for you — nobody can see you — make haste."

I stared at her with unfeigned surprise, and disengaging my arm, which she had taken apparently to hasten my movements, I very gravely asked her meaning.

---

[1] [DS] Allston's "large scripture piece" was probably his *Dead Man Revived by Touching Elisha's Bones*, which the Pennsylvania Academy of Fine Arts had purchased in 1816 for $3,500. It was first exhibited at the British Gallery in London and there received a first prize of two hundred guineas.

"Only, ma'am, that the ladies like to go into that room by themselves, when there be no gentlemen watching them."

On entering this mysterious apartment, the first thing I remarked, was a written paper, deprecating the disgusting depravity which had led some of the visitors to mark and deface the casts in a most indecent and shameless manner. This abomination has unquestionably been occasioned by the coarse-minded custom which sends alternate groups of males and females into the room. Were the antique gallery thrown open to mixed parties of ladies and gentlemen, it would soon cease. Till America has reached the degree of refinement which permits of this, the antique casts should not be exhibited to ladies at all. I never felt my delicacy shocked at the Louvre, but I was strangely tempted to resent as an affront the hint I received, that I might steal a glance at what was deemed indecent. Perhaps the arrangements for the exhibition of this room, the feelings which have led to them, and the result they have produced, furnish as good a specimen of the kind of delicacy on which the Americans pride themselves, and of the peculiarities arising from it, as can be found. The room contains about fifty casts, chiefly from the antique.

In the director's room I was amused at the means which a poet had hit upon for advertising his works, or rather HIS WORK, and not less at the elaborate notice of it.[2] His portrait

---

2 [DS] Dr. Richard Emmons was a citizen of Great Crossing, Kentucky. His Gargantuan epic, published in 1827, received scant attention from American literati, and it is understandable that he resorted to the device Mrs. Trollope mentions to bring his poem to the attention of the public. In the preface to *The Fredoniad* Emmons speaks of his long labors despite the coldness of critics:

"The poem has cost me many an aching, burning thought. For the last eight years, before the rising of the sun, have the efforts of my soul been engaged upon the subject, and the flicker of the midnight lamp found me in communion with the invisible Genius of Poesy. I feel that many are its imperfections. . . .

"It is true, in the course of my labours, I have communicated the sub-

was suspended there, and attached to the frame was a paper
inscribed thus: —

"PORTRAIT OF THE AUTHOR
of
The Fredoniad, or Independence Preserved, a political, naval,
and military poem, on the late war of 1812, in forty cantos;
the whole compressed into four volumes; each
volume averaging more than 305 pages,
By Richard Emmons,
M.D."

*   *   *   *   *   *

I went to the Chesnut Street Theatre to see Mr. Booth, formerly of Drury Lane, in the character of Lear, and a Mrs. Duff
in Cordelia; but I have seen too many Lears and Cordelias
to be easily pleased; I thought the whole performance very
bad. The theatre is of excellently moderate dimensions, and

---

ject of the poem to several citizens of the Republick eminent for their literature; — but silence was their only answer, or cold indifference, or damping
discouragement. . . . The publick must decide whether it be a lily or a
bramble; an oak, or an upas."

In the following sample from canto III of *The Fredoniad* Washington
speaks from heaven:

"But O, reveal, — is Freedom's virtue gone?
Is every sense of right and honour done?
Are all the worthies, whom I left behind,
Bent on the knee? to infamy consign'd?
Alas! the theme! — Of Jefferson, O say —
And hath his virtue gone the slippery way?
Pickering, Monroe, and worthy Madison,
Within whose veins a bold resistance run?
Floyd, Gerry, Sullivan, and Stark, and King,
Who ever to thy name did incense bring?
Scott, Carroll, Shelby, Macon, Eustis, Strong,
That shouted Liberty in choral song?
"And O, inform me of that virtuous Frank,
Who scorn'd his royal birth and join'd the rank
With those for Freedom toiling — La Fayette —
Who oft in battle made his sword-blade wet
With blood of tyranny — whose soul stood high,
To give to man his boon of Liberty."
He sat. Fredonia with sweet breath began. . . .

prettily decorated. It was not the fashionable season for the theatres, which I presume must account for the appearance of the company in the boxes, which was any thing but elegant; nor was there more decorum of demeanour than I had observed elsewhere; I saw one man in the lower tier of boxes deliberately take off his coat that he might enjoy the refreshing coolness of shirt sleeves; all the gentlemen wore their hats, and the spitting was unceasing.

On another evening we went to the Walnut Street Theatre; the chief attraction of the night was furnished by the performance of a young man who had been previously exhibited as "a living skeleton." [3] He played the part of Jeremiah Thin, and certainly looked the part well, and here I think must end my praise of the evening's performances.

The great and most striking contrast between this city and those of Europe, is perceived after sun-set; scarcely a sound is heard; hardly a voice or a wheel breaks the stillness. The streets are entirely dark, except where a stray lamp marks an hotel or the like; no shops are open, but those of the apothecary, and here and there a cook's shop; scarcely a step is heard, and for a note of music, or the sound of mirth, I listened in vain. In leaving the theatre, which I always did before the afterpiece, I saw not a single carriage; the night of Miss Wright's lecture, when I stayed to the end, I saw one.

[3] [DS] Calvin Edson, "the celebrated living skeleton," is thus described in the Philadelphia *Saturday Bulletin* (June 12, 1830):

"He was born in the year 1788, in Stafford, Conn. . . . His height when he arrived at manhood, was 5 feet 4 inches, and weight 135 pounds. [He served in the War of 1812, but soon thereafter began to lose flesh] without any apparent disease, having scarcely been sick one day, or taken any medicine, except one small dose of Lee's pills. He weighs at present but 54 lbs. He lost 7 lbs. last year, but appears to have no more flesh to spare; his appearance is that of a skeleton, animated with and performing all the actions of life, but still the mere shadow of a man, being literally speaking, but skin and bones. But what is the most remarkable, he enjoys good health, sleeps well, his appetite is good, and the digestive functions appear to be perfectly performed. . . . He has a wife and three children, the youngest a babe of only eleven months old."

This darkness, this stillness, is so great, that I almost felt it awful. As we walked home one fine moonlight evening from the Chesnut Street house, we stopped a moment before the United States Bank, to look at its white marble columns by the subdued light said to be so advantageous to them; the building did, indeed, look beautiful; the incongruous objects around were hardly visible, while the brilliant white of the building, which by day-light is dazzling, was mellowed into fainter light and softer shadow.

While pausing before this modern temple of Theseus, we remarked that we alone seemed alive in this great city; it was ten o'clock, and a most lovely cool evening, after a burning day, yet all was silence. Regent Street, Bond Street, with their blaze of gas-lit *bijouterie*, and still more the Italian Boulvard of Paris, rose in strong contrast on the memory; the light, which outshines that of day — the gay, graceful, laughing throng — the elegant saloons of Tortoni, with all their varieties of cooling nectar — were all remembered. Is it an European prejudice to deem that the solitary dram swallowed by the gentlemen on quitting an American theatre, indicates a lower and more vicious state of manners, than do the ices so sedulously offered to the ladies on leaving a French one?

*   *   *   *   *   *

The Museum contains a good collection of objects illustrative of natural history, and some very interesting specimens of Indian antiquities; both here and at Cincinnati I saw so many things resembling Egyptian relics, that I should like to see the origin of the Indian nations enquired into, more accurately than has yet been done.

The shops, of which there appeared to me to be an unusually large proportion, are very handsome; many of them in a style of European elegance. Lottery offices abound, and that species of gambling is carried to a great extent. I saw fewer carriages in Philadelphia than either at Baltimore or Washington, but in the winter I was told they were more numerous.

Many of the best families had left the city for different watering-places, and others were daily following. Long Branch is a fashionable bathing place on the Jersey shore, to which many resort, both from this place and from New York; the description given of the manner of bathing appeared to me rather extraordinary, but the account was confirmed by so many different people, that I could not doubt its correctness. The shore, it seems, is too bold to admit of bathing machines, and the ladies have, therefore, recourse to another mode for insuring the enjoyment of a sea-bath with safety. The accommodation at Long Branch is almost entirely at large boarding-houses, where all the company live at a *table d'hote*. It is customary for ladies on arriving to look round among the married gentlemen, the first time they meet at table, and to select the one her fancy leads her to prefer as a protector in her purposed visits to the realms of Neptune; she makes her request, which is always graciously received, that he would lead her to taste the briny wave; but another fair one must select the same protector, else the arrangement cannot be complete, as custom does not authorize *tête à tête* immersion.[4]

---

[4] [TN] One Long Branch anecdote amused me, and the more so as I was well acquainted with the gentleman who was the hero of it. It happened that a lady of very delicate sensibilities, ventured upon this experiment for the strengthening her nerves. Unhappily her petticoat, the most important part of her bathing costume, dropped off, when she was only knee deep in the friendly wave; but the gentleman dived — and replaced it with equal politeness and dexterity. He was an Englishman, and, as I was told, had frequently the honour of being chosen to this interesting office, often cheering the pleasing labour by singing "Hail Columbia! happy land."

CHAPTER XXVI

Quakers — Presbyterians — Itinerant Methodist Preacher —
Market —Influence of females in society

I HAD never chanced, among all my wanderings, to enter a Quaker Meeting-house; and as I thought I could no where make my first visit better than at Philadelphia, I went under the protection of a Quaker lady to the principal *orthodox* meeting of the city. The building is large, but perfectly without ornament; the men and women are separated by a rail which divides it into two equal parts; the meeting was very full on both sides, and the atmosphere almost intolerably hot. As they glided in at their different doors, I spied many pretty faces peeping from the prim head gear of the females, and as the broad-brimmed males sat down, the welcome Parney supposes prepared for them in heaven, recurred to me,

"Entre donc, et garde ton chapeau." [1]

The little bonnets and the large hats were ranged in long rows, and their stillness was for a long time so unbroken, that I could hardly persuade myself the figures they surmounted were alive. At length a grave square man arose, laid aside his ample beaver, and after another solemn interval of silence, he gave a deep groan, and as it were by the same effort uttered, "Keep thy foot." Again he was silent for many minutes, and then he continued for more than an hour to put forth one word at a time, but at such an interval from each other that I found it quite impossible to follow his meaning, if, indeed, he had any. My Quaker friend told me she

---

[1] [DS] *"Entre donc,"* etc.: "Enter, then, and guard thy hat."

knew not who he was, and that she much regretted I had heard so poor a preacher. After he had concluded, a gentle-man-like old man (a physician by profession) arose, and delivered a few moral sentences in an agreeable manner; soon after he had sat down, the whole congregation rose, I know not at what signal, and made their exit. It is a singular kind of worship, if worship it may be called, where all prayer is forbidden; yet it appeared to me, in its decent quietness, infinitely preferable to what I had witnessed at the Presbyterian and Methodist meeting-houses. A great schism had lately taken place among the Quakers of Philadelphia; many objecting to the over-strict discipline of the orthodox. Among the seceders there are again various shades of difference; I met many who called themselves Unitarian Quakers, others were Hicksites, and others again, though still wearing the Quaker habit, were said to be Deists.

We visited many churches and chapels in the city, but none that would elsewhere be called handsome, either internally or externally.

I went one evening, not a Sunday, with a party of ladies to see a Presbyterian minister inducted. The ceremony was woefully long, and the charge to the young man awfully impossible to obey, at least if he were a man, like unto other men. It was matter of astonishment to me to observe the deep attention, and the unwearied patience with which some hundreds of beautiful young girls who were assembled there, (not to mention the old ladies,) listened to the whole of this tedious ceremony; surely there is no country in the world where religion makes so large a part of the amusement and occupation of the ladies. Spain, in its most catholic days, could not exceed it: besides, in spite of the gloomy horrors of the Inquisition, gaiety and amusement were not there offered as a sacrifice by the young and lovely.

The religious severity of Philadelphian manners is in nothing more conspicuous than in the number of chains thrown across the streets on a Sunday to prevent horses and carriages from passing. Surely the Jews could not exceed this country in their external observances. What the gentlemen of Philadelphia do with themselves on a Sunday, I will not pretend to guess, but the prodigious majority of females in the churches is very remarkable. Although a large proportion of the population of this city are Quakers, the same extraordinary variety of faith exists here, as every where else in the Union, and the priests have, in some circles, the same unbounded influence which has been mentioned elsewhere.

One history reached me, which gave a terrible picture of the effect this power may produce; it was related to me by my mantua-maker; a young woman highly estimable as a wife and mother, and on whose veracity I perfectly rely. She told me that her father was a widower, and lived with his family of three daughters, at Philadelphia. A short time before she married, an itinerant preacher came to the city, who contrived to obtain an intimate footing in many respectable families. Her father's was one of these, and his influence and authority were great with all the sisters, but particularly with the youngest. The young girl's feelings for him seem to have been a curious mixture of spiritual awe and earthly affection. When she received a hint from her sisters that she ought not to give him too much encouragement till he spoke out, she shewed as much holy resentment as if they had told her not to say her prayers too devoutly. At length the father remarked the sort of covert passion that gleamed through the eyes of his godly visitor, and he saw too, the pallid anxious look which had settled on the young brow of his daughter; either this, or some rumours he had heard abroad, or both together, led him to forbid this man his house. The three girls were present when he did so, and all uttered a deprecating "Oh father!" but the old man added stoutly, "If you shew yourself here again, reverend sir, I will not only teach you the way out of my house, but out of the city also." The preacher withdrew, and was never heard of in Philadelphia afterwards; but when a few months had passed, strange whispers began to creep through the circle which had received and honoured him, and, in due course of time, no less than seven unfortunate girls produced living proofs of the wisdom of my informant's worthy father. In defence of this dreadful story I can only make the often repeated quotation, "I tell the tale as 'twas told to me;" but, in all sincerity I must add, that I have no doubt of its truth.

* * * * * *

I was particularly requested to visit the market of Philadelphia, at the hour when it presented the busiest scene; I did so, and thought few cities had any thing to shew better worth looking at; it is, indeed, the very perfection of a market, the *beau ideal* of a notable housewife, who would confide to no deputy the important office of caterer. The neatness, freshness, and entire absence of every thing disagreeable to sight or smell, must be witnessed to be believed. The stalls were spread with snow-white napkins; flowers and fruit, if not quite of Paris or London perfection, yet bright, fresh, and fragrant; with excellent vegetables in the greatest variety and abundance, were all so delightfully exhibited, that objects less pleasing were overlooked and forgotten. The dairy, the poultry-yard, the forest, the river, and the ocean, all contributed their spoil; in short, for the first time in my life, I thought a market a beautiful object. The prices of most articles were, as nearly as I could calculate between dollars and francs, about the same as at Paris; certainly much cheaper than in London, but much dearer than at Exeter.

My letters of introduction brought me acquainted with several amiable and interesting people. There is something in the tone of manners at Philadelphia that I liked; it appeared to me that there was less affectation of ton there than elsewhere. There is a quietness, a composure in a Philadelphia drawing-room, that is quite characteristic of a city founded by William Penn. The dress of the ladies, even those who are not Quakers, partakes of this; they are most elegantly neat, and there was a delicacy and good taste in the dress of the young ladies that might serve as a model to the whole Union. There can hardly be a stronger contrast in the style of dress between any two cities than may be remarked between Baltimore and Philadelphia; both are costly, but the former is distinguished by gaudy splendour, the latter by elegant simplicity.

It is said that this city has many gentlemen distinguished by their scientific pursuits; I conversed with several well-informed and intelligent men, but there is a cold dryness of manner and an apparent want of interest in the subjects they discuss, that, to my mind, robs conversation of all its charm. On one occasion I heard the character and situation of an illustrious officer discussed, who had served with renown under Napoleon, and whose high character might have obtained him favour under the Bourbons, could he have abandoned the principles which led him to dislike their government. This distinguished man had retreated to America after the death of his master, and was endeavoring to establish a sort of Polytechnic academy at New York: in speaking of him, I observed, that his devotion to the cause of freedom must prove a strong recommendation in the United States. "Not the least in the world, madam," answered a gentleman who ranked deservedly high among the *literati* of the city, "it might avail him much in England, perhaps, but here we are perfectly indifferent as to what people's principles may be."

This I believe to be exactly true, though I never before heard it avowed as a national feature.

The want of warmth, of interest, of feeling, upon all subjects which do not immediately touch their own concerns, is universal, and has a most paralysing effect upon conversation. All the enthusiasm of America is concentrated to the one point of her own emancipation and independence; on this point nothing can exceed the warmth of her feelings. She may, I think, be compared to a young bride, a sort of Mrs. Major Waddle; her independence is to her as a newly-won bridegroom; for him alone she has eyes, ears, or heart; — the honeymoon is not over yet; — when it is, America will, perhaps, learn more coquetry, and know better how to *faire l'aimable* to other nations.

I conceive that no place in the known world can furnish so striking a proof of the immense value of literary habits as the United States, not only in enlarging the mind, but what is of infinitely more importance, in purifying the manners. During my abode in the country I not only never met a literary man who was a tobacco chewer or a whiskey drinker, but I never met any who were not, that had escaped these degrading habits. On the women, the influence is, if possible, still more important; unfortunately, the instances are rare, but they are to be found. One admirable example occurs in the person of a young lady of Cincinnati: [2] surrounded by a society totally incapable of appreciating, or even of comprehending her, she holds a place among it, as simply and unaffectedly as if of the same species; young, beautiful, and gifted by nature with a mind singularly acute and discriminating, she has happily found such opportunities of cultivation as might distinguish her in any country; it is, indeed, that best of all cultivation which is only to be found in domestic habits of literature, and in that hourly education which the daughter of a man of letters receives when she is made the companion and friend of her father. This young lady is the more admirable as she contrives to unite all the

---

[2] [DS] Identified in Mrs. Trollope's notebooks as Miss Emeline Flint. According to John Ervin Kirkpatrick, biographer of Timothy Flint, she was "strong minded, but not imaginative like others of the family." In 1833 she married a General Thomas, an attorney and a man of extensive business holdings.

multifarious duties which usually devolve upon American ladies, with her intellectual pursuits. The companion and efficient assistant of her father's literary labours, the active aid in all the household cares of her mother, the tender nurse of a delicate infant sister, the skilful artificer of her own always elegant wardrobe, ever at leisure, and ever prepared to receive with the sweetest cheerfulness her numerous acquaintance, the most animated in conversation, the most indefatigable in occupation, it was impossible to know her, and study her character without feeling that such women were "the glory of all lands," and, could the race be multiplied, would speedily become the reformers of all the grossness and ignorance that now degrade her own. Is it to be imagined, that if fifty modifications of this charming young woman were to be met at a party, the men would dare to enter it reeking with whiskey, their lips blackened with tobacco, and convinced, to the very centre of their hearts and souls, that women were made for no other purpose than to fabricate sweetmeats and gingerbread, construct shirts, darn stockings, and become mothers of possible presidents? Assuredly not. Should the women of America ever discover what their power might be, and compare it with what it is, much improvement might be hoped for. While, at Philadelphia, among the handsomest, the wealthiest, and the most distinguished of the land, their comparative influence in society, with that possessed in Europe by females holding the same station, occurred forcibly to my mind.

Let me be permitted to describe the day of a Philadelphian lady of the first class, and the inference I would draw from it will be better understood.

It may be said that the most important feature in a woman's history is her maternity. It is so; but the object of the present observation is the social, and not the domestic influence of woman.

This lady shall be the wife of a senator and a lawyer in the highest repute and practice. She has a very handsome house, with white marble steps and door-posts, and a delicate silver knocker and door-handle; she has very handsome drawing-rooms, very handsomely furnished, (there is a sideboard in one of them, but it is very handsome, and has very hand-some decanters and cut glass water-jugs upon it); she has a very handsome carriage, and a very handsome free black coachman; she is always very handsomely dressed; and, moreover, she is very handsome herself.

She rises, and her first hour is spent in the scrupulously nice arrangement of her dress; she descends to her parlour neat, stiff, and silent; her breakfast is brought in by her free black footman; she eats her fried ham and her salt fish, and drinks her coffee in silence, while her husband reads one newspaper, and puts another under his elbow; and then, perhaps, she washes the cups and saucers. Her carriage is ordered at eleven; till that hour she is employed in the pastry-room, her snow-white apron protecting her mouse-coloured silk. Twenty minutes before her carriage should appear, she re-tires to her chamber, as she calls it, shakes, and folds up her still snow-white apron, smooths her rich dress, and with nice care, sets on her elegant bonnet, and all the handsome *et cætera;* then walks down stairs, just at the moment that her free black coachman announces to her free black footman that the carriage waits. She steps into it, and gives the word, "Drive to the Dorcas society." Her footman stays at home to clean the knives, but her coachman can trust his horses while he opens the carriage door, and his lady not being accus-tomed to a hand or an arm, gets out very safely without, though one of her own is occupied by a work-basket, and the other by a large roll of all those indescribable matters which ladies take as offerings to Dorcas societies. She enters the par-lour appropriated for the meeting, and finds seven other ladies, very like herself, and takes her place among them; she presents her contribution, which is accepted with a gentle circular smile, and her parings of broad cloth, her ends of ribbon, her gilt paper, and her minikin pins, are added to the parings of broad cloth, the ends of ribbon, the gilt paper, and the minikin pins with which the table is already covered; she also produces from her basket three ready-made pincushions, four ink-wipers, seven paper-matches, and a paste-board watch-case; these are welcomed with acclamations, and the youngest lady present deposits them carefully on shelves, amid a prodigious quantity of similar articles. She then produces her thimble, and asks for work; it is presented to her, and the eight ladies all stitch together for some hours. Their talk is of priests and of missions; of the profits of their last sale, of their hopes from the next; of the doubt whether young Mr. This, or young Mr. That should receive the fruits of it to fit him out for Liberia; of the very ugly bonnet seen at church on Sabbath morning, of the very handsome preacher who performed on Sabbath afternoon, and of the very large collection made on Sabbath evening. This lasts till three, when the carriage again appears, and the lady and her basket return home; she mounts to her chamber, carefully sets aside her bonnet and its appurtenances, puts on her scolloped black silk apron, walks into the kitchen to see that all is right, then into the parlour, where, having cast a careful glance over the table prepared for dinner, she sits down, work in hand, to await her spouse. He comes, shakes hands with her, spits, and dines. The conversation is not much, and ten minutes suffices for the dinner; fruit and toddy, the newspaper and the work-bag succeed. In the evening the gentleman, being a savant, goes to the Wister society,[3] and afterwards plays a snug rubber at a neighbour's. The lady receives at tea a young missionary and three members of the Dorcas society. — And so ends her day.

For some reason or other, which English people are not

---

[3] [DS] Philadelphia's Wistar Society was in 1830 a small, learned circle who assembled once a week for literary and scientific discussions.

very likely to understand, a great number of young married persons board by the year, instead of "going to house-keeping," as they call having an establishment of their own. Of course this statement does not include persons of large fortune, but it does include very many whose rank in society would make such a mode of life quite impossible with us. I can hardly imagine a contrivance more effectual for ensuring the insignificance of a woman, than marrying her at seventeen, and placing her in a boarding-house. Nor can I easily imagine a life of more uniform dulness for the lady herself; but this certainly is a matter of taste. I have heard many ladies declare that it is "just quite the perfection of comfort to have nothing to fix for oneself." Yet despite these assurances I always experienced a feeling which hovered between pity and contempt, when I contemplated their mode of existence.

How would a newly-married Englishwoman endure it, her head and her heart full of the one dear scheme —

"Well ordered home, *his* dear delight to make?"

She must rise exactly in time to reach the boarding table at the hour appointed for breakfast, or she will get a stiff bow from the lady president, cold coffee, and no egg. I have been sometimes greatly amused upon these occasions by watching a little scene in which the bye-play had much more meaning than the words uttered. The fasting, but tardy lady, looks round the table, and having ascertained that there was no egg left, says distinctly, "I will take an egg if you please." But as this is addressed to no one in particular, no one in particular answers it, unless it happen that her husband is at table before her, and then he says, "There are no eggs, my dear." Whereupon the lady president evidently cannot hear, and the greedy culprit who has swallowed two eggs (for there are always as many eggs as noses) looks pretty considerably afraid of being found out. The breakfast proceeds in sombre silence, save that sometimes a parrot, and sometimes a canary bird, ventures to utter a timid note. When it is finished, the gentlemen hurry to their occupations, and the quiet ladies mount the stairs, some to the first, some to the second, and some to the third stories, in an inverse proportion to the number of dollars paid, and ensconce themselves in their respective chambers. As to what they do there it is not very easy to say; but I believe they clear-starch a little, and iron a little, and sit in a rocking-chair, and sew a great deal. I always observed that the ladies who boarded wore more elaborately worked collars and petticoats than any one else. The plough is hardly a more blessed instrument in America than the needle. How could they live without it? But time and the needle wear through the longest morning, and happily the American morning is not very long, even though they breakfast at eight.

It is generally about two o'clock that the boarding gentlemen meet the boarding ladies at dinner. Little is spoken, except a whisper between the married pairs. Sometimes a sulky bottle of wine flanks the plate of one or two individuals, but it adds nothing to the mirth of the meeting, and seldom more than one glass to the good cheer of the owners. It is not then, and it is not there, that the gentlemen of the Union drink. Soon, very soon, the silent meal is done, and then, if you mount the stairs after them, you will find from the doors of the more affectionate and indulgent wives, a smell of cigars steam forth, which plainly indicates the felicity of the couple within. If the gentleman be a very polite husband, he will, as soon as he has done smoking and drinking his toddy, offer his arm to his wife, as far as the corner of the street, where his store, or his office is situated, and there he will leave her to turn which way she likes. As this is the hour for being full dressed, of course she turns the way she can be most seen. Perhaps she pays a few visits; perhaps she goes to chapel; or, perhaps, she enters some store where her husband deals, and ventures to order a few notions; and then she goes home again — no, not home — I will not give that name to a boarding-house, but she re-enters the cold heartless atmosphere in which she dwells, where hospitality can never enter, and where interest takes the management instead of affection. At tea they all meet again, and a little trickery is perceptible to a nice observer in the manner of partaking the pound-cake, &c. After this, those who are happy enough to have engagements, hasten to keep them; those who have not, either mount again to the solitude of their chamber, or, what appeared to me much worse, remain in the common sitting-room, in a society cemented by no tie, endeared by no connection, which choice did not bring together, and which the slightest motive would break asunder. I remarked that the gentlemen were generally obliged to go out every evening on business, and, I confess, the arrangement did not surprise me.

It is not thus that the women can obtain that influence in society which is allowed to them in Europe, and to which, both sages and men of the world have agreed in ascribing such salutary effects. It is in vain that "collegiate institutes" are formed for young ladies, or that "academic degrees" are conferred upon them. It is after marriage, and when these young attempts upon all the sciences are forgotten, that the lamentable insignificance of the American women appears, and till this be remedied, I venture to prophesy that the tone of their drawing-rooms will not improve.

Whilst I was at Philadelphia a great deal of attention was excited by the situation of two criminals, who had been convicted of robbing the Baltimore mail, and were lying under sentence of death. The rare occurrence of capital punishment in America makes it always an event of great interest; and the approaching execution was repeatedly the subject of conversation at the boarding table. One day a gentleman told us he had that morning been assured that one of the criminals had declared to the visiting clergyman that he was certain of being reprieved, and that nothing the clergyman could say to the contrary made any impression upon him. Day after day this same story was repeated, and commented upon at table, and it appeared that the report had been heard in so many quarters, that not only was the statement received as true, but it began to be conjectured that the criminal had some ground for his hope. I learnt from these daily conversations that one of the prisoners was an American, and the other an Irishman, and it was the former who was so strongly persuaded he should not be hanged. Several of the gentlemen at table, in canvassing the subject, declared, that if the one were hanged and the other spared, this hanging would be a murder, and not a legal execution.[4] In discussing this point, it was stated that very nearly all the white men who

---

[4] [DS] According to the lengthy account of the robbery and the subsequent trial given in the Philadelphia *Saturday Bulletin* (May 15, 1830), James Porter, the Irishman, was the more hardened criminal of the two. "His countenance," says the writer, "is absolutely the blackest and most fiendish we ever looked upon." Born in 1800, Porter in his "very childhood . . . exhibited symptoms of a bold, audacious and vindictively wicked disposition, which defied all advice and correction." He was a member of a gang of thieves which practiced burglary and highway robbery. Porter fled to Liverpool at the age of seventeen, with the law at his heels. From there he took ship for America. He found work as a day laborer on the Erie Canal, but soon gained a reputation for violence. He was the leader in "many of the riots among the workmen which attended the progress of that great work, some of which were sanguinary and deadly." A worker with whom he quarreled was found murdered in a gloomy and isolated thicket in the neighborhood of the canal, "his body mangled in a manner too shocking to the feelings to be here described." Porter and a crony of his had been seen coming out of the thicket only a few hours before the murder, but in the absence of additional evidence they were acquitted. For an offense not specified in the *Bulletin,* Porter was committed to the Maryland Penitentiary and there met Wilson and Poteet, another man who played a part in the robbery of the mail coach. The three of them on being discharged from prison committed various petty thefts for some time.

Becoming dissatisfied with the small returns for their efforts, however, they broke into the shop of a West Philadelphia gunsmith named Watt and stole five pistols, powder flasks, and other equipment. With these they held up the Reading mail. Porter broke one of the lamps of the coach, put out all other lights, and tied up the passengers. He then robbed them of their money and watches, passing these over to Poteet, who assisted him. Wilson took the mail from the coach, poured it out into the road, removed

had suffered death since the Declaration of Independence
had been Irishmen. What truth there may be in this general statement I have no means of ascertaining; all I know
is, that I heard it made. On this occasion, however, the Irishman was hanged, and the American was not.

---

the money, and then burned the letters.

Poteet, upon capture, turned state's evidence. The extent of his punishment is not specified. Wilson was condemned to be hanged, but President
Jackson commuted the sentence to life imprisonment, apparently because
Wilson possessed information of some sort that the government considered
valuable enough to warrant the bargain.

The trial of Wilson and Porter caused great excitement in Philadelphia.
The following account of the execution of Porter is given in the Philadelphia
American Sentinel and Mercantile Advertiser (July 3, 1830):

"THE EXECUTION

"The sentence of law was executed upon JAMES PORTER, the mail rob-
ber at about a quarter before eleven o'clock yesterday morning. — It had
been known to the public for several days, that WILSON, one of the accom-
plices of Porter, had been pardoned of the capital offence by the president
of the United States, in consequence, as was stated, of some important information which he had communicated to the post office department. The
mass of the people, however, unacquainted with the circumstances which
led to a discrimination between the two convicts, and perceiving no difference in their moral or legal guilt, were loud in the expression of their dis-
satisfaction. Hence many persons were apprehensive that the execution of
Porter would be attended with riot, if not with bloodshed. The Marshal,
therefore, took precautionary measures to enable him to carry the law into
effect. [These included special constables, the city watch, and a corps of
Marines.] But as might have been expected from the orderly habits and
correct moral feeling of this community, they were unnecessary."

CHAPTER XXVII

Return to Stonington — Thunder-storm — Emigrants — Illness —
Alexandria

A FORTNIGHT passed rapidly away in this great
city, and, doubtless, there was still much left unseen when
we quitted it, according to previous arrangement, to return
to our friends in Maryland. We came back by a different
route, going by land from Newcastle to French Town, instead of passing by the canal. We reached Baltimore in the
middle of the night, but finished our repose on board the
steam-boat, and started for Washington at five o'clock the
next morning.

Our short abode amid the heat and closeness of a city
made us enjoy more than ever the beautiful scenery around
Stonington. The autumn, which soon advanced upon us,
again clothed the woods in colours too varied and gaudy to
be conceived by those who have never quitted Europe; and
the stately maize, waving its flowing tassels, as the long
drooping blossoms are called, made every field look like a
little forest. A rainy spring had been followed by a summer
of unusual heat; and towards the autumn frequent thunder-
storms of terrific violence cleared the air, but at the same
time frightened us almost out of our wits. On one occasion I
was exposed, with my children, to the full fury of one of
these awful visitations. We suffered considerable terror during this storm, but when we were all again safe, and comfortably sheltered, we rejoiced that the accident had occurred, as it gave us the best possible opportunity of witnessing, in all its glory, a transatlantic thunder-storm. It was,
however, great imprudence that exposed us to it, for we
quitted the house, and mounted a hill at a considerable dis-

tance from it, for the express purpose of watching to advantage the extraordinary aspect of the clouds. When we reached the top of the hill half the heavens appeared hung with a heavy curtain; a sort of deep blue black seemed to colour the very air; the buzzards screamed, as with heavy wing they sought the earth. We ought, in common prudence, to have immediately retreated to the house, but the scene was too beautiful to be left. For several minutes after we reached our station, the air appeared perfectly without movement, no flash broke through the seven-fold cloud, but a flickering light was visible, darting to and fro behind it; and by degrees the thunder rolled onward, nearer and nearer, till the inky cloud burst asunder, and cataracts of light came pouring from behind it. From that moment there was no interval, no pause, the lightning did not flash, there were no claps of thunder, but the heavens blazed and bellowed above and around us, till stupor took the place of terror, and we stood utterly confounded. But we were speedily aroused, for suddenly, as if from beneath our feet, a gust arose which threatened to mix all the elements in one. Torrents of water seemed to bruise the earth by their violence; eddies of thick dust rose up to meet them; the fierce fires of heaven only blazed the brighter for the falling flood; while the blast almost out-roared the thunder. But the wind was left at last the lord of all, for after striking with wild force, now here, now there, and bringing worlds of clouds together in most hostile contact, it finished by clearing the wide heavens of all but a few soft straggling masses, whence sprung a glorious rainbow, and then retired, leaving the earth to raise her half crushed forests; and we, poor pigmies, to call back our frighted senses, and recover breath as we might.

During this gust, it would have been impossible for us to have kept our feet; we crouched down under the shelter of a heap of stones, and, as we informed each other, looked most dismally pale.

Many trees were brought to the earth before our eyes; some torn up by the roots, and some mighty stems snapt off several feet from the ground. If the West Indian hurricanes exceed this, they must be terrible indeed.

The situation of Mrs. S° ° ° °'s house was considered as remarkably healthy, and I believe justly so, for on more than one occasion, persons who were suffering from fever and ague at the distance of a mile or two, were perfectly restored by passing a week or fortnight at Stonington; but the neighbourhood of it, particularly on the side bordering the Potomac, was much otherwise, and the mortality among the labourers on the canal was frightful.

I have elsewhere stated my doubts if the labouring poor of our country mend their condition by emigrating to the United States, but it was not till the opportunity which a vicinity to the Chesapeake and Ohio canal gave me, of knowing what their situation was after making the change, that I became fully aware how little it was to be desired for them.

Of the white labourers on this canal, the great majority are Irishmen; their wages are from ten to fifteen dollars a month, with a miserable lodging, and a large allowance of whiskey. It is by means of this hateful poison that they are tempted, and indeed enabled for a time, to stand the broiling heat of the sun in a most noxious climate: for through such, close to the romantic but unwholesome Potomac, the line of the canal has hitherto run. The situation of these poor strangers, when they sink at last in *"the fever,"* which sooner or later is sure to overtake them, is dreadful. There is a strong feeling against the Irish in every part of the Union, but they will do twice as much work as a negro, and therefore they are employed. When they fall sick, they may, and must, look with envy on the slaves around them; for they are cared for; they are watched and physicked, as a valuable horse is watched and physicked: not so the Irishman; he is literally

thrown on one side, and a new comer takes his place. Details
of their sufferings, and unheeded death, too painful to dwell
upon, often reached us; on one occasion a farmer calling at
the house, told the family that a poor man, apparently in a
dying condition, was lying beside a little brook at the distance of a quarter of a mile. The spot was immediately visited by some of the family, and there in truth lay a poor creature, who was already past the power of speaking; he was
conveyed to the house, and expired during the night. By
enquiring at the canal, it was found that he was an Irish labourer, who having fallen sick, and spent his last cent, had
left the stifling shantee where he lay, in the desperate attempt of finding his way to Washington, with what hope I
know not. He did not appear above twenty, and as I looked
on his pale young face, which even in death expressed suffering, I thought that perhaps he had left a mother and a home
to seek wealth in America. I saw him buried under a
group of locust trees, his very name unknown to those who
laid him there, but the attendance of the whole family at the
grave, gave a sort of decency to his funeral which rarely, in
that country, honours the poor relics of British dust: but no
clergyman attended, no prayer was said, no bell was tolled;
these, indeed, are ceremonies unthought of, and in fact unattainable without much expence, at such a distance from a
town; had the poor youth been an American, he would have
been laid in the earth in the same unceremonious manner. But
had this poor Irish lad fallen sick in equal poverty and destitution among his own people, he would have found a blanket
to wrap his shivering limbs, and a kindred hand to close his
eyes.

The poor of great Britain whom distress, or a spirit of enterprise tempt to try another land, ought, for many reasons,
to repair to Canada; [1] there they would meet co-operation

---

[1] [T5, note] On this point also a considerable change has taken place.
The advantages of emigration to Canada have become very doubtful.

and sympathy, instead of malice, hatred, and all uncharitableness.

I frequently heard vehement complaints, and constantly met the same in the newspapers, of a practice stated to be very generally adopted in Britain of sending out cargoes of parish paupers to the United States. A Baltimore paper heads some such remarks with the words

"INFAMOUS CONDUCT!"

and then tells us of a cargo of aged paupers just arrived from England, adding, "John Bull has squeezed the orange, and now insolently casts the skin in our faces." Such being the feeling, it will be readily believed that these unfortunates are not likely to meet much kindness or sympathy in sickness, or in suffering of any kind. If these American statements be correct, and that different parishes are induced, from an excessive population, to pay the voyage and out-fit of some of their paupers across the Atlantic, why not send them to Canada?

It is certain, however, that all the enquiries I could make failed to substantiate these American statements. All I could ascertain was, that many English and Irish poor, arrived yearly in the United States, with no other resources than what their labour furnished. This, though very different from the newspaper stories, is quite enough to direct attention to the subject. It is generally acknowledged that the suffering among our labouring classes arises from the excess of our population; and it is impossible to see such a country as Canada, its extent, its fertility, its fine climate, and know that it is British ground, without feeling equal sorrow and astonishment that it is not made the means of relief. How earnestly it is to be wished that some part of that excellent feeling which is for ever at work in England to help the distressed, could be directed systematically to the object of emigration to the Canadas. Large sums are annually raised for charitable purposes, by weekly subscriptions of one penny; were only a part of the money so obtained to be devoted to this object, hundreds of families might yearly be sent to people our own land. The religious feeling, which so naturally mixes with every charitable purpose, would there find the best field for its exertions. Where could a missionary, whether Protestant or Catholic, find a holier mission than that which sent him to comfort and instruct his countrymen in the wilderness? or where could he reap a higher reward in this world, than seeing that wilderness growing into fertile fields under the hands of his flock?

*　　*　　*　　*　　*　　*

I never saw so many autumn flowers as grow in the woods and sheep-walks of Maryland; a second spring seemed to clothe the fields, but with grief and shame I confess, that of these precious blossoms I scarcely knew a single name. I think the Michaelmas daisy, in wonderful variety of form and colour, and the prickly pear, were almost my only acquaintance: let no one visit America without having first studied botany; it is an amusement, as a clever friend of mine once told me, that helps one wonderfully up and down hill, and must be superlatively valuable in America, both from the plentiful lack of other amusements, and the plentiful material for enjoyment in this; besides, if one is dying to know the name of any of these lovely strangers, it is a thousand to one against his finding any one who can tell it.

The prettiest eclipse of the moon I ever saw was that of September, of this year, (1830.) We had been passing some hours amid the solemn scenery of the Potomac falls, and just as we were preparing to quit it, the full moon arose above the black pines, with half our shadow thrown across her. The effect of her rising thus eclipsed was more strange, more striking by far, than watching the gradual obscuration; and as I turned to look at the black chasm behind me, and saw the deadly alder, and the poison-vine waving darkly on the rocks around, I thought the scene wanted nothing but the figure of a palsied crone, plucking the fatal branches to concoct some charm of mischief.

Whether some such maga dogged my steps, I know not, but many hours had not elapsed ere I again felt the noxious influence of an American autumn. This fever, "built in th' eclipse," speedily brought me very low, and though it lasted not so long as that of the preceding year, I felt persuaded I should never recover from it. Though my forebodings were not verified by the event, it was declared that change of air was necessary, and it was arranged for me, (for I was perfectly incapable of settling any thing for myself,) that I should go to Alexandria, a pretty town at the distance of about fifteen miles, which had the reputation of possessing a skilful physician.

It was not without regret that we quitted our friends at Stonington; but the prescription proved in a great degree efficacious; a few weeks' residence in Alexandria restored my strength sufficiently to enable me to walk to a beautiful little grassy terrace, perfectly out of the town, but very near it, from whence we could watch the various craft that peopled the Potomac between Alexandria and Washington. But though gradually regaining strength, I was still far from well; all plans for winter gaiety were abandoned, and finding ourselves very well accommodated, we decided upon passing the winter where we were. It proved unusually severe; the Potomac was so completely frozen as to permit considerable traffic to be carried on by carts, crossing on the ice, from Maryland. This had not occurred before for thirty years. The distance was a mile and a quarter, and we ventured to brave the cold, and walk across this bright and slippery mirror, to make a visit on the opposite shore; the fatigue of keeping our feet was by no means inconsiderable, but we were rewarded by seeing as noble a winter landscape around us as the eye could look upon.

When at length the frost gave way, the melting snow produced freshes so violent as to carry away the long bridge at Washington; large fragments of it, with the railing still erect, came floating down amidst vast blocks of ice, during many successive days, and it was curious to see the intrepidity with which the young sailors of Alexandria periled their lives to make spoil of the timber.

The solar eclipse on the 12th of February, 1831, was nearer total than any I ever saw, or ever shall see. It was completely annular at Alexandria, and the bright ring which surrounded the moon's shadow, though only 81° in breadth, gave light sufficient to read the smallest print; the darkness was considerably lessened by the snow, which, as the day was perfectly unclouded, reflected brightly all the light that was left us.

Notwithstanding the extreme cold we passed the whole time in the open air, on a rising ground near the river; in this position many beautiful effects were perceptible; the rapid approach and change of shadows, the dusky hue of the broad Potomac, that seemed to drink in the feeble light, which its snow-coloured banks gave back to the air, the gradual change of every object from the colouring of bright sunshine to one sad universal tint of dingy purple, the melancholy lowing of the cattle, and the short, but remarkable suspension of all labour, gave something of mystery and awe to the scene that we shall long remember.

During the following months I occupied myself partly in revising my notes, and arranging these pages; and partly in making myself acquainted, as much as possible, with the literature of the country.

While reading and transcribing my notes, I underwent a strict self-examination. I passed in review all I had seen, all I had felt, and scrupulously challenged every expression of disapprobation; the result was, that I omitted in transcription much that I had written, as containing unnecessary details of things which had displeased me; yet, as I did so, I felt strongly that there was no exaggeration in them; but such details, though true, might be ill-natured, and I retained no more than were necessary to convey the general impressions I received. While thus reviewing my notes, I discovered that many points, which all scribbling travellers are expected to notice, had been omitted; but a few pages of miscellaneous observations will, I think, supply all that can be expected from so idle a pen.

XIX THE TOILET

XX WALKING IN THE SNOW

CHAPTER XXVIII

American Cooking — Evening Parties — Dress — Sleighing —
Money-getting Habits — Tax-Gatherer's Notice — Indian Summer
— Anecdote of the Duke of Saxe-Weimar

IN relating all I know of America, I surely must not
omit so important a feature as the cooking. There are sundry
anomalies in the mode of serving even a first-rate table; but
as these are altogether matters of custom, they by no means
indicate either indifference or neglect in this important business; and whether castors are placed on the table or on the
side-board; whether soup, fish, patties, and salad be eaten in
orthodox order or not, signifies but little. I am hardly capable, I fear, of giving a very erudite critique on the subject;
general observations therefore must suffice. The ordinary
mode of living is abundant, but not delicate. They consume
an extraordinary quantity of bacon. Ham and beef-steaks
appear morning, noon, and night. In eating, they mix things
together with the strangest incongruity imaginable. I have
seen eggs and oysters eaten together; the sempiternal ham
with apple-sauce; beef-steak with stewed peaches; and salt
fish with onions. The bread is everywhere excellent, but they
rarely enjoy it themselves, as they insist upon eating horrible
half-baked hot rolls both morning and evening. The butter
is tolerable; but they have seldom such cream as every little
dairy produces in England; in fact, the cows are very roughly
kept, compared with our's. Common vegetables are abundant and very fine. I never saw sea-cale, or cauliflowers, and
either from the want of summer rain, or the want of care, the
harvest of green vegetables is much sooner over than with
us. They eat the Indian corn in a great variety of forms;

sometimes it is dressed green, and eaten like peas; sometimes it is broken to pieces when dry, boiled plain, and
brought to table like rice; this dish is called hominy. The
flour of it is made into at least a dozen different sorts of
cakes; but in my opinion all bad. This flour, mixed in the
proportion of one-third, with fine wheat, makes by far the
best bread I ever tasted.

I never saw turbot, salmon, or fresh cod; but the rock and
shad are excellent. There is a great want of skill in the composition of sauces; not only with fish, but with every thing.
They use very few made dishes, and I never saw any that
would be approved by our savants. They have an excellent
wild duck, called the Canvass Back, which, if delicately
served, would surpass the black cock; but the game is very
inferior to our's; they have no hares, and I never saw a pheas-
ant. They seldom indulge in second courses, with all their
ingenious temptations to the eating a second dinner; but almost every table has its dessert, (invariably pronounced
desart) which is placed on the table before the cloth is removed, and consists of pastry, preserved fruits, and creams.
They are "extravagantly fond," to use their own phrase, of
puddings, pies, and all kinds of "sweets," particularly the
ladies; but are by no means such connoisseurs in soups and
ragoûts as the gastronomes of Europe. Almost every one
drinks water at table, and by a strange contradiction, in the
country where hard drinking is more prevalent than in any
other, there is less wine taken at dinner; ladies rarely exceed
one glass, and the great majority of females never take any.
In fact, the hard drinking, so universally acknowledged, does
not take place at jovial dinners, but, to speak plain English,
in solitary dram-drinking. Coffee is not served immediately
after dinner, but makes part of the serious matter of tea-
drinking, which comes some hours later. Mixed dinner parties of ladies and gentlemen are very rare, and unless several
foreigners are present, but little conversation passes at table.

It certainly does not, in my opinion, add to the well ordering a dinner table, to set the gentlemen at one end of it, and the ladies at the other; but it is very rarely that you find it otherwise.

Their large evening parties are supremely dull; the men sometimes play cards by themselves, but if a lady plays, it must not be for money; no ecarté, no chess; very little music, and that little lamentably bad. Among the blacks, I heard some good voices, singing in tune; but I scarcely ever heard a white American, male or female, go through an air without being out of tune before the end of it; nor did I ever meet any trace of science in the singing I heard in society. To eat inconceivable quantities of cake, ice, and pickled oysters — and to shew half their revenue in silks and satins, seem to be the chief object they have in these parties.

The most agreeable meetings, I was assured by all the young people, were those to which no married women are admitted; of the truth of this statement I have not the least doubt. These exclusive meetings occur frequently, and often last to a late hour; on these occasions, I believe, they generally dance. At regular balls, married ladies are admitted, but seldom take much part in the amusement. The refreshments are always profuse and costly, but taken in a most uncomfortable manner. I have known many private balls, where every thing was on the most liberal scale of expense, where the gentlemen sat down to supper in one room, while the ladies took theirs, standing, in another.

What we call pic-nics are very rare, and when attempted, do not often succeed well. The two sexes can hardly mix for the greater part of a day without great restraint and ennui; it is quite contrary to their general habits; the favourite indulgences of the gentlemen (smoking cigars and drinking spirits), can neither be indulged in with decency, nor resigned with complacency.

The ladies have strange ways of adding to their charms.

They powder themselves immoderately, face, neck, and arms, with pulverised starch; the effect is indescribably disagreeable by day-light, and not very favourable at any time. They are also most unhappily partial to false hair, which they wear in surprising quantities; this is the more to be lamented, as they generally have very fine hair of their own. I suspect this fashion to arise from an indolent mode of making their toilet, and from accomplished ladies' maids not being very abundant; it is less trouble to append a bunch of waving curls here, there, and every where, than to keep their native tresses in perfect order.

Though the expense of the ladies' dress greatly exceeds, in proportion to their general style of living, that of the ladies of Europe, it is very far (excepting in Philadelphia) from being in good taste. They do not consult the seasons in the colours or in the style of their costume; I have often shivered at seeing a young beauty picking her way through the snow with a pale rose-coloured bonnet, set on the very top of her head: I knew one young lady whose pretty little ear was actually frost-bitten from being thus exposed. They never wear muffs or boots, and appear extremely shocked at the sight of comfortable walking shoes and cotton stockings, even when they have to step to their sleighs over ice and snow. They walk in the middle of winter with their poor little toes pinched into a miniature slipper, incapable of excluding as much moisture as might bedew a primrose. I must say in their excuse, however, that they have, almost universally, extremely pretty feet. They do not walk well, nor, in fact, do they ever appear to advantage when in movement.[1] I know not why this should be, for they have abun-

---

[1] [DS] On their part, American women did not always approve of Mrs. Trollope's walking-dress or mode of movement. The Cincinnati *Mirror and Ladies' Parterre* (August 18, 1832) says, on the "authority of a very intelligent lady of Cincinnati": "[Mrs. Trollope] might be seen ever and anon, in a green calash, and long plaid cloak draggling at her heels . . . walking with those colossean strides unattainable by any but English women."

dance of French dancing-masters among them, but somehow or other it is the fact. I fancied I could often trace a mixture of affectation and of shyness in their little mincing unsteady step, and the ever changing position of the hands. They do not dance well; perhaps I should rather say they do not look well when dancing; lovely as their faces are, they cannot, in a position that exhibits the whole person, atone for the want of *tournure*, and for the universal defect in the formation of the bust, which is rarely full, or gracefully formed.

I never saw an American man walk or stand well; notwithstanding their frequent militia drillings, they are nearly all hollow chested and round shouldered: perhaps this is occasioned by no officer daring to say to a brother free-born "hold up your head;" whatever the cause, the effect is very remarkable to a stranger. In stature, and in physiognomy, a great majority of the population, both male and female, are strikingly handsome, but they know not how to do their own honours; half as much comeliness elsewhere would produce ten times as much effect.

Nothing can exceed their activity and perseverance in all kinds of speculation, handicraft, and enterprise, which promises a profitable pecuniary result. I heard an Englishman, who had been long resident in America, declare that in following, in meeting, or in overtaking, in the street, on the road, or in the field, at the theatre, the coffee-house, or at home, he had never overheard Americans conversing without the word DOLLAR being pronouced between them. Such unity of purpose, such sympathy of feeling, can, I believe, be found nowhere else, except, perhaps, in an ants' nest. The result is exactly what might be anticipated. This sordid object, for ever before their eyes, must inevitably produce a sordid tone of mind, and, worse still, it produces a seared and blunted conscience on all questions of probity. I know not a more striking evidence of the low tone of morality which is generated by this universal pursuit of money, than the manner in which the New England States are described by Americans. All agree in saying that they present a spectacle of industry and prosperity delightful to behold, and this is the district and the population most constantly quoted as the finest specimen of their admirable country; yet I never met a single individual in any part of the Union who did not paint these New Englanders as sly, grinding, selfish, and tricking. The Yankees (as the New Englanders are called) will avow these qualities themselves with a complacent smile, and boast that no people on the earth can match them at over-reaching in a bargain.[2] I have heard them unblushingly relate stories of their cronies and friends, which, if believed among us, would banish the heroes from the fellowship of honest men for ever; and all this is uttered with a simplicity which sometimes led me to doubt if the speakers knew what honour and honesty meant. Yet the Americans declare that "they are the most moral people upon earth." Again and again I have heard this asserted, not only in conversation, and by their writings, but even from the pulpit. Such broad assumption of superior virtue demands examination, and after four years of attentive and earnest observation and enquiry, my honest conviction is, that the standard of moral character in the United States is very greatly lower than in Europe. Of their religion, as it appears outwardly, I have had occasion to speak frequently; I pretend not to judge the heart, but, without any uncharitable presumption, I must take permission to say, that both Protestant England and Catholic France[3] shew an infinitely superior religious and moral aspect to mortal observation, both as to reverend decency of external observance, and as to the inward fruit of honest dealing between man and man.

---

[2] [T5, note] Vide the exquisite personifications of "Sam Slick, the watchmaker." His "soft soder," and his "human nater" furnish an abstract and brief chronicle of the whole race.

[For further comment on Sam Slick, see note 4, page 209.]

[3] [T5, note] As well as both Catholic and Protestant Germany.

In other respects I think no one will be disappointed who visits the country, expecting to find no more than common sense might teach him to look for, namely,[4] a vast continent, by far the greater part of which is still in the state in which nature left it, and a busy, bustling, industrious population, hacking and hewing their way through it. What greatly increases the interest of this spectacle, is the wonderful facility for internal commerce, furnished by the rivers, lakes, and canals, which thread the country in every direction, producing a rapidity of progress in all commercial and agricultural speculation altogether unequalled. This remarkable feature is perceptible in every part of the Union into which the fast spreading population has hitherto found its way, and forms, I think, the most remarkable and interesting peculiarity of the country. I hardly remember a single town where vessels of some description or other may not constantly be seen in full activity.

Their carriages of every kind are very unlike ours; those belonging to private individuals seem all constructed with a

---

[4] [T5, note] It is perhaps impossible (the absolutely savage life being put out of the question) for human nature to appear under aspects more strongly contrasted than the traveller may see it in the United States and in Austria.

All that is useful and desirable in the one, is exactly what is found wanting in the other; while nothing that is objectionable in either can find a parallel in its moral and political antipodes.

The bustling, struggling, crafty, enterprising, industrious, swaggering, drinking, boasting, money-getting Yankee, who cares not who was his grandfather, and meditates on nothing, past, present, or to come, but his dollars, his produce, and his slaves, is as unlike the longsome, speculative, frank, contented, sober, tranquil, yet gay-spirited Austrian, who glories in the glories of his race, and who sings and dances through to-day, without disturbing himself about the morrow, as the square blocks of brick and mortar which constitute a transatlantic city, are to the venerable, fantastic, beautiful remains of a dozen centuries, scattered up and down the time-honoured region of Germany.

A contrast as striking might be found, too, in the comparative value and reprobation accorded to each, by those who examine and pass judgment on them; and so violent would the discrepancy of opinion be found, that an unprejudiced listener to both might be apt to doubt the value of human judgment on any subject.

view to summer use, for which they are extremely well calculated, but they are by no means comfortable in winter. The
waggons and carts are built with great strength, which is indeed necessary, from the roads they often have to encounter.
The stage-coaches are heavier and much less comfortable
than those of France; to those of England they can bear no
comparison. I never saw any harness that I could call handsome, nor any equipage which, as to horses, carriage, harness, and servants, could be considered as complete. The
sleighs are delightful, and constructed at so little expense
that I wonder we have not all got them in England, lying by,
in waiting for the snow, which often remains with us long
enough to permit their use. Sleighing is much more generally
enjoyed by night than by day, for what reason I could never
discover, unless it be, that no gentlemen are to be found
disengaged from business in the mornings. Nothing, certainly, can be more agreeable than the gliding smoothly and
rapidly along, deep sunk in soft furs, the moon shining with
almost mid-day splendour, the air of crystal brightness, and
the snow sparkling on every side, as if it were sprinkled with
diamonds. And then the noiseless movement of the horses,
so mysterious and unwonted, and the gentle tinkling of the
bells you meet and carry, all help at once to soothe and excite the spirits: in short, I had not the least objection to
sleighing by night, I only wished to sleigh by day also.

Almost every resident in the country has a carriage they
call a carryall, which name I suspect to be a corruption of
the cariole so often mentioned in the pretty Canadian story
of Emily Montagu.[5] It is clumsy enough, certainly, but extremely convenient, and admirably calculated, with its thick
roof and moveable draperies, for every kind of summer excursion.

Their steam-boats, were the social arrangements somewhat

---

[5] [DS] Frances Brooke's four-volume *The History of Emily Montague*,
a romance set in Canada, was first published in 1769.

improved, would be delightful, as a mode of travelling; but they are very seldom employed for excursions of mere amusement: nor do I remember seeing pleasure-boats, properly so called, at any of the numerous places where they might be used with so much safety and enjoyment.

How often did our homely adage recur to me, "All work and no play would make Jack a dull boy;" Jonathan is a very dull boy. We are by no means so gay as our lively neighbours on the other side of the channel, but, compared with Americans, we are whirligigs and tetotums; every day is a holyday, and every night a festival.

Perhaps if the ladies had quite their own way, a little more relaxation would be permitted; but there is one remarkable peculiarity in their manners which precludes the possibility of any dangerous out-breaking of the kind: few ladies have any command of ready money entrusted to them. I have been a hundred times present when bills for a few dollars, perhaps for one, have been brought for payment to ladies living in perfectly easy circumstances, who have declared themselves without money, and referred the claimant to their husbands for payment. On every occasion where immediate disbursement is required it is the same; even in shopping for ready cash they say, "send a bill home with the things, and my husband will give you a draft."

I think that it was during my stay at Washington, that I was informed of a government regulation, which appeared to me curious; I therefore record it here.

Every Deputy Post-Master is required to insert in his return the title of every newspaper received at his office for distribution. This return is laid before the Secretary of State, who, perfectly knowing the political character of each newspaper, is thus enabled to feel the pulse of every limb of the monster mob.[6] This is a well imagined device for getting a

_____

[6] [DS] Each postmaster was required to make such a return, stating not only the titles of newspapers and periodicals received by him but also the

peep at the politics of a country where newspapers make part of the daily food, but is it quite consistent with their entire freedom? I do not believe we have any such tricks to regulate the deposal of offices and appointments.

I believe it was in Indiana that Mr. T. met with a printed notice relative to the payment of taxes, which I preserved as a curious sample of the manner in which the free citizens are coaxed and reasoned into obeying the laws.

"LOOK OUT DELINQUENTS

"Those indebted to me for taxes, fees, notes, and accounts, are specially requested to call and pay the same on or before the 1st day of December, 1828, as no longer indulgence will be given. I have called time and again, by advertisement and otherwise, to little effect; but now the time has come when my situation requires immediate payment from all indebted to me. It is impossible for me to pay off the amount of the duplicates of taxes and my other debts without recovering the same of those from whom it is due. I am at a loss to know the reason why those charged with taxes neglect to pay; from the negligence of many it would seem that they think the money is mine, or that I have funds to discharge the taxes due to the State, and that I can wait with them until it suits their convenience to pay. The money is not mine; neither have I the funds to settle amount of the duplicate. My only resort is to collect; in doing so I should be sorry to have to resort to the authority given me by law for the recovery of the same. It should be the first object of every good citizen to pay his taxes, for it is in that way government is supported. Why are taxes assessed unless they are collected? Depend upon it I shall proceed to collect agreeably to law, so govern yourselves accordingly.

"JOHN SPENCER
"Sh'ff and Collector, D. C.

"*Nov.* 20, 1828.

"N.B. On Thursday, the 27th inst. A. St. Clair and Geo. H. Dunn, Esqrs. depart for Indianapolis; I wish as many as can pay to do so, to

---

number of copies of each title (*Laws, Instructions and Forms, for the Regulation of the Post-Office Department* [1832]). Whether or not this ruling was exploited for political purposes, it seems to have had a bona fide reason for being put into practice. The Post Office Department had been trying for some time to stop loopholes in its methods of collecting postage on newspapers (see "Newspaper Returns" in *Post-Office Laws, Instructions and Forms* [1828]).

enable me to forward as much as possible, to save the twenty-one per cent. that will be charged against me after the 8th of December next.

"J. S."

The first autumn I passed in America, I was surprised to find a great and very oppressive return of heat, accompanied with a heavy mistiness in the air, long after the summer heats were over; when this state of the atmosphere comes on, they say, "we have got to the Indian summer." On desiring to have this phrase explained, I was told that the phenomenon described as the *Indian summer* was occasioned by the Indians setting fire to the woods, which spread heat and smoke to a great distance; but I afterwards met with the following explanation, which appears to me much more reasonable. "The Indian summer is so called because, at the particular period of the year in which it obtains, the Indians break up their village communities, and go to the interior to prepare for their winter hunting. This season seems to mark a dividing line, between the heat of summer, and the cold of winter, and is from its mildness, suited to these migrations. The cause of this heat is the slow combustion of the leaves and other vegetable matter of the boundless and interminable forests. Those who at this season of the year have penetrated these forests, know all about it. To the feet the heat is quite sensible, whilst the ascending vapour warms every thing it embraces, and spreading out into the wide atmosphere, fills the circuit of the heavens with its peculiar heat and smokiness."

This unnatural heat sufficiently accounts for the sickliness of the American autumn. The effect of it is extremely distressing to the nerves, even when the general health continues good; to me, it was infinitely more disagreeable than the glowing heat of the dog-days.

A short time before we arrived in America, the Duke of Saxe-Weimar made a tour of the United States.[7] I heard

---

[7] [DS] Bernard, Duke of Saxe-Weimar, had toured the United States in 1825 and 1826. His *Travels through North America* (1828) is an interesting and valuable record of his experiences.

many persons speak of his unaffected and amiable manners, yet he could not escape the dislike which every trace of gentlemanly feeling is sure to create among the ordinary class of Americans. As an amusing instance of this, I made the following extract from a newspaper.

"A correspondent of the Charlestown Gazette tells an anecdote connected with the Duke of Saxe-Weimar's recent journey through our country, which we do not recollect to have heard before, although some such story is told of the veritable Capt. Basil Hall. The scene occurred on the route between Augusta and Milledgeville; it seems that the sagacious Duke engaged three or four, or more seats, in the regular stage, for the accommodation of himself and suite, and thought by this that he had secured the monopoly of the vehicle. Not so, however; a traveller came along, and entered his name upon the book, and secured his seat by payment of the customary charges. To the Duke's great surprise on entering the stage, he found our traveller comfortably housed in one of the most eligible seats, wrapped up in his fearnought, and snoring like a buffalo. The Duke, greatly irritated, called for the question of consideration. He demanded, in broken English, the cause of the gross intrusion, and insisted in a very princely manner, though not, it seems, in very princely language, upon the incumbent vacating the seat in which he had made himself so impudently at home. But the Duke had yet to learn his first lesson of republicanism. The driver was one of those sturdy southrons, who can always, and at a moment's warning, whip his weight in wild cats: and he as resolutely told the Duke, that the traveller was as good, if not a better man, than himself; and that no alteration of the existing arrangement could be permitted. Saxe-Weimar became violent at this opposition, so unlike any to which his education hitherto had ever subjected him, and threatened John with the application of the bamboo. This was one of those threats which in Georgia dialect would subject a man to 'a rowing up salt river;' and, accordingly, down leaped our driver from his box, and peeling himself for the combat, he leaped about the vehicle in the most wild-boar style, calling upon the prince of a five acre patch to put his threat in execution. But he of the star refused to make up issue in the way suggested, contenting himself with assuring the enraged southron of a complaint to his excellency the Governor, on arrival at the seat of government. This threat was almost as unlucky as the former, for it wrought the individual for whom it was intended into that species of fury, which, though discriminating in its madness, is nevertheless without much limit in its violence, and he swore that the Governor might go to ——, and for his part he would just as leave lick the Governor as the Duke; he'd like no better fun than to give both Duke and Governor a dressing in the same breath; could do it, he had little doubt, &c. &c.; and instigating one fist to diverge into the face of the marvelling and panic-stricken nobleman, with the other he thrust him down into a seat alongside the traveller, whose presence had been originally of such sore discomfort to his excellency, and bidding the attendants jump in with their discomfited master, he mounted his box in triumph, and went on his journey."

I fully believe that this brutal history would be as distasteful to the travelled and polished few who are to be found scattered through the Union, as it is to me; but if they do not deem the *possibility* of such a scene to be a national degradation, I differ from them. The American people, (speaking of the great mass,) have no more idea of what constitutes the difference between this "Prince of a five acre patch," and themselves, than a dray-horse has of estimating the points of the elegant victor of the race-course. Could the dray-horse speak, when expected to yield the daintiest stall to his graceful rival, he would say, "a horse is a horse;" and is it not with the same logic that the transatlantic Houynnhnm puts down all superiority with "a man is a man?"

This story justifies the reply of Talleyrand, when asked by Napoleon what he thought of the Americans, "Sire, ce sont des fiers cochons, et des cochons fiers." [8]

---

[8] [DS] *"Sire, ce sont,"* etc. A rough equivalent is "Sire, those are proud pigs, and pigs that are proud." But the nuance of the passage escapes translation.

CHAPTER XXIX

Literature — Extracts — Fine Arts — Education

THE character of the American literature is, generally speaking, pretty justly appreciated in Europe. The immense exhalation of periodical trash, which penetrates into every cot and corner of the country, and which is greedily sucked in by all ranks, is unquestionably one great cause of its inferiority. Where newspapers are the principal vehicles of the wit and wisdom of a people, the higher graces of composition can hardly be looked for.

That there are many among them who can write well, is most certain; but it is at least equally so, that they have little encouragement to exercise the power in any manner more dignified than becoming the editor of a newspaper or a magazine. As far as I could judge, their best writers are far from being the most popular. The general taste is decidedly bad; this is obvious, not only from the mass of slip-slop poured forth by the daily and weekly press, but from the inflated tone of eulogy in which their insect authors are lauded.

To an American writer, I should think it must be a flattering distinction to escape the admiration of the newspapers. Few persons of taste, I imagine, would like such notice as the following, which I copied from a New York paper, where it followed the advertisement of a partnership volume of poems by a Mr. and Mrs. Brooks; but of such, are their literary notices chiefly composed.

"The lovers of impassioned and classical numbers may promise themselves much gratification from the muse of Brooks, while the many-stringed harp of his lady, the Norna of the Courier Harp, which none but she can touch, has a chord for every heart."

Another obvious cause of inferiority in the national literature, is the very slight acquaintance with the best models of
composition, which is thought necessary for persons called
well educated. There may be reason for deprecating the lavish expense of time bestowed in England on the acquirement
of Latin and Greek, and it may be doubtful whether the
power of composing in these languages with correctness and
facility, be worth all the labour it costs; but as long as letters
shall be left on the earth, the utility of a perfect familiarity
with the exquisite models of antiquity, cannot be doubted. I
think I run no risk of contradiction, when I say that an extremely small proportion of the higher classes in America
possess this familiar acquaintance with the classics. It is vain
to suppose that translations may suffice. Noble as are the
thoughts the ancients have left us, their power of expression
is infinitely more important as a study to modern writers; and
this no translation can furnish. Nor did it appear to me that
their intimacy with modern literature was such as to assist
them much in the formation of style. What they class as modern literature seems to include little beyond the English publications of the day.

To speak of Chaucer, or even Spenser, as a modern, appears
to them inexpressibly ridiculous; and all the rich and varied
eloquence of Italy, from Dante to Monti, is about as much
known to them, as the Welsh effusions of Urien and Modred,
to us.

Rousseau, Voltaire, Diderot, &c., were read by the old federalists, but now they seem known more as naughty words,
than as great names. I am much mistaken if a hundred un-
travelled Americans could be found, who have read Boileau
or Le [sic] Fontaine. Still fewer are acquainted with that
delightful host of French female writers, whose memoirs and
letters sparkle in every page with unequalled felicity of style.
The literature of Spain and Portugal are no better known,
and as for "the wits of Queen Anne's day," they are laid *en*

masse upon a shelf, in some score of very old fashioned houses, together with Sherlock and Taylor, as much too anti-quated to suit the immensely rapid progress of mind which distinguishes America.

The most perfect examples of English writing, either of our own, or of any former day, have assuredly not been pro-duced by the imitation of any particular style; but the Fairy Queen would hardly have been written, if the Orlando had not; nor would Milton have been the perfect poet he was, had Virgil and Tasso been unknown to him. It is not that the scholar mimics in writing the phrases he has read, but that he can neither think, feel, nor express himself as he might have done, had his mental companionship been of a lower order.

They are great novel readers, but the market is chiefly fur-nished by England. They have, however, a few very good native novels. Mr. Flint's Francis Berrian is delightful.[1] There is a vigor and freshness in his writing that is exactly in ac-cordance with what one looks for, in the literature of a new country; and yet, strange to say, it is exactly what is most wanting in that of America. It appeared to me that the style of their imaginative compositions was almost always affected, and inflated. Even in treating their great national subject of romance, the Indians, they are seldom either powerful or original. A few well known general features, moral and physi-cal, are presented over and over again in all their Indian stories, till in reading them you lose all sense of individual character. Mr. Flint's History of the Mississippi Valley[2] is a

---

[1] [DS] Timothy Flint's *Francis Berrian, or the Mexican Patriot* (1826) is a tale of the Mexican Revolution in 1821. The hero is a Yankee who leads a dashing and implausible career among Comanche Indians, Spanish hidal-gos, and beautiful señoras and señoritas. The novel was criticized for its faulty plotting and characterizations, but praised for its descriptions of natu-ral scenery. It was reprinted in London in 1834.

[2] [DS] *A Condensed Geography and History of the Western States, or the Mississippi Valley* (1828). Flint republished this work with a great many additions in 1832 under the title *The History and Geography of the*

work of great interest, and information, and will, I hope, in time find its way to England, where I think it is much more likely to be appreciated than in America.

Dr. Channing [3] is a writer too well known in England to require my testimony to his great ability. As a preacher he has, perhaps, hardly a rival any where. This gentleman is an Unitarian, and I was informed by several persons well acquainted with the literary characters of the country, that nearly all their distinguished men were of this persuasion.[4]

Mr. Pierpoint is a very eloquent preacher, and a sweet poet. His works are not so well known among us as they ought to be. Mr. Everett has written some beautiful lines, and if I may judge from the specimens of his speeches, as preserved in the volumes intitled "Eloquence of the United States," I should say that he shone more as a poet than an orator. But American fame has decided otherwise.

Mr. M. Flint, of Louisiana, has published a volume of poems which ought to be naturalised here.[5] Mr. Hallock [sic],

---

Mississippi Valley. The book was widely read and passed through many subsequent editions. It is generally considered Flint's most important work.

[3] [DS] William Ellery Channing (1780–1842), famous champion of Unitarianism. In the next few paragraphs Mrs. Trollope touches very lightly upon the merits of the following American writers who are not commented upon elsewhere in the notes to this edition: John Pierpont (1789–1866), Unitarian clergyman and author of facile but rather slight poems; Edward Everett (1794–1865), orator and essayist; Fitz-Greene Halleck (1790–1867), wit and poet; William Cullen Bryant (1794–1878), who had already achieved his reputation as a poet; James Kirke Paulding (1778–1860), a very popular American humorist and politician; and Nathaniel Bowditch (1773–1838), mathematician and author of *The New American Practical Navigator* (1802), a standard work that passed through more than sixty editions.

[4] [T5, note] That this statement was perfectly correct, I have every reason to believe; nor is an obvious reason for the fact wanting. The mind of a man devoted to letters undergoes a process which renders the endurance of the crude ignorant ranting of the great majority among the various sects of American preachers intolerable; and accordingly they have taken refuge in the cold comfortless stillness of Unitarianism.

[5] [DS] Micah Peabody Flint, son of Timothy Flint, had published a thin duodecimo, *The Hunter, and Other Poems,* in 1826. Mrs. Trollope's judgment of the book is probably influenced by her liking for the Flint

of New York, has much facility of versification, and is greatly in fashion as a drawing-room poet, but I think he has somewhat too much respect for himself, and too little for his readers.

It is, I think, Mr. Bryant who ranks highest as the poet of the Union. This is too lofty an eminence for me to attack; besides "I am of another parish," and therefore, perhaps, no very fair judge.

From miscellaneous poetry I made a great many extracts, but upon returning to them for transcription I thought that ill-nature and dulness, ("oh ill-matched pair!") would be more served by their insertion, than wholesome criticism.

The massive Fredoniad of Dr. Emmons, in forty cantos, I never read; but as I did not meet a single native who had, I hope this want of poetical enterprise will be excused.

They have very few native tragedies; not more than half a dozen I believe, and those of very recent date. It would be ungenerous to fall heavily upon these; the attempt alone, nearly the most arduous a poet can make, is of itself honourable: and the success at least equal to that in any other department of literature.

Mr. Paulding is a popular writer of novels; some of his productions have been recently republished in England. Miss Sedgwick is also well known among us; her "Hope Leslie" is a beautiful story. Mr. Washington Irving and Mr. Cooper have so decidedly chosen another field, whereon to reap their laurels, that it is hardly necessary to name them here.[6]

I am not, of course, competent to form any opinion of their scientific works; but some papers which I read almost accidentally, appeared to me to be written with great clearness, and neatness of definition.

family. "The Hunter" tells of the adventures of a backwoodsman who, because of Indian outrages, turns hermit. Micah Flint died in 1830.

[6] [DS] Washington Irving was secretary of the United States legation in London (1829–32); James Fenimore Cooper was nominally United States consul at Lyon (1826–33).

It appears extraordinary that a people who loudly declare their respect for science, should be entirely without observatories. Neither at their seats of learning, nor in their cities, does any thing of the kind exist; nor did I in any direction hear of individuals, given to the study of astronomy.

I had not the pleasure of making any acquaintance with Mr. Bowditch, of Boston, but I know that this gentleman ranks very high as a Mathematician in the estimation of the scientific world of Europe.

Jefferson's posthumous works were very generally circulated whilst I was in America. They are a mighty mass of mischief. He wrote with more perspicuity than he thought, and his hot-headed democracy has done a fearful injury to his country. Hollow and unsound as his doctrines are, they are but too palatable to a people, each individual of whom would rather derive his importance from believing that none are above him, than from the consciousness that in his station he makes part of a noble whole. The social system of Mr. Jefferson, if carried into effect, would make of mankind an unamalgamated mass of grating atoms, where the darling "I'm as good as you," would soon take place of the law and the Gospel.[7] At it is, his principles, though happily not fully put in action, have yet produced most lamentable results. The assumption of equality, however empty, is sufficient to tincture the manners of the poor with brutal insolence, and subjects the rich to the paltry expediency of sanctioning the falsehood, however deep their conviction that it is such. It

---

[7] [T5, note] If the information which, as stated in a former note, I have received since my return to Europe, from a distinguished citizen of the United States, be correct, namely, that the private sentiments of Mr. Jefferson were exactly the reverse of all he published, and that he declared his conviction during his hours of social confidence, that the existence of a practical democracy was a prodigious fable, what is the judgment that must be past upon him? The United States have paid, and will long continue to pay, a grievously heavy penalty for this "great man's popularity." They are not, as a people, what they would have been had Jefferson never lived, and Washington remained their unrivalled authority.

cannot, I think, be denied that the great men of America attain to power and to fame, by eternally uttering what they
know to be untrue. American citizens are not equal. Did
Washington feel them to be so, when his word out-weighed,
(so happily for them,) the votes of thousands? Did Franklin
think that all were equal when he shouldered his way from
the printing press to the cabinet? True, he looked back in
high good humour, and with his kindest smile told the poor
devils whom he left behind, that they were all his equals; but
Franklin did not speak the truth, and he knew it. The great,
the immortal Jefferson himself, he who when past the three
score years and ten, still taught young females to obey his
nod, and so became the father of unnumbered generations of
groaning slaves,[8] what was his matin and his vesper hymn?
"All men are born free and equal?" Did the venerable father
of the gang believe it? Or did he too purchase his immortality
by a lie?

$$*\quad*\quad*\quad*\quad*\quad*$$

From the five heavy volumes of the "Eloquence of the United
States," I made a few extracts,[9] which I give more for the
sake of their political interest, than for any purpose of literary
criticism.

Mr. Hancock, (one of those venerated men who signed the

---

[8] [DS] For comment on this widely circulated canard concerning Jefferson, see note 8, page 72.

[9] [DS] Mrs. Trollope's extracts from *Eloquence of the United States,*
compiled by E. B. Williston and published in 1827, look a little better in
context. John Hancock is speaking of the evils that threaten nations that
maintain large standing armies and implies that Britain may be overrun by
hers. Richard Rush delivered his oration on the Fourth of July 1812, two
weeks after the declaration of war between the United States and England.
As for Edward Everett's oration, the sentence following the last one quoted
by Mrs. Trollope helps somewhat to bring his subject down from the airy
regions: "Henceforward we have only to strive that the practical operation
of our systems may be true to their spirit and theory." It may be worth adding that in November 1830, while the English Parliament still suffered from
the "rotten borough" method of election, the Duke of Wellington told Parliament that "no better system could be devised by the wit of man."

act of independence,) in speaking of England, thus expresses himself: "But if I was possessed of the gift of prophecy, I dare not (except by Divine command) unfold the leaves on which the destiny of that once powerful kingdom is inscribed." It is impossible not to regret that Mr. Hancock should thus have let "I dare not, wait upon I would." It would have been exceedingly edifying to have known beforehand all the terrible things the republic was about to do for us.

This prophetic orator spoke the modest, yet awful words, above quoted, nearly sixty years ago; in these latter days men are become bolder, for in a modern fourth of July oration, Mr. Rush, without waiting, I think, for divine command, gives the following amiable portrait of the British character.

"In looking at Britain, we see a harshness of individual character in the general view of it, which is perceived and acknowledged by all Europe; a spirit of unbecoming censure as regards all customs and institutions not their own; a ferocity in some of their characteristics of national manners, pervading their very pastimes, which no other modern people are endued with the blunted sensibility to bear; [10] an universally self-assumed superiority, not innocently manifesting itself in speculative sentiments among themselves, but unamiably indulged when with foreigners, of whatever description, in their own country, or when they themselves are the temporary sojourners in a foreign country; a code of criminal law that forgets to feel for human frailty, that sports with human misfortune, that has shed more blood in deliberate judicial severity for two centuries past, constantly increasing, too, in its sanguinary hue, than has ever been sanctioned by the jurisprudence of any ancient or modern nation, civilized and refined like herself; the merciless whippings in her army, peculiar to herself alone, the conspicuous commission and freest acknowledgment of vice in the upper classes; the over-

[10] [T5, note] Negro flogging is not classed as a pastime.

weening distinctions shewn to opulence and birth, so destructive of a sound moral sentiment in the nation, so baffling to virtue. These are some of the traits that rise up to a contemplation of the inhabitants of this isle."

Where is the alchymy that can extract from Captain Hall's work one thousandth part of the ill-will contained in this one passage? Yet America has resounded from shore to shore with execrations against his barbarous calumnies.

But now we will listen to another tone. Let us see how Americans can praise. Mr. Everett, in a recent fourth of July oration, speaks thus: —

"We are authorised to assert, that the era of our independence dates the establishment of the only perfect organization of government." Again, "Our government is in its theory perfect, and in its operation it is perfect also. Thus we have solved the great problem in human affairs." And again, "A frame of government perfect in its principles has been brought down from the airy regions of Utopia, and has found a local habitation and a name in our country."

Among my miscellaneous reading, I got hold of an American publication giving a detailed, and, indeed, an official account of the capture of Washington by the British, in 1814.[11] An event so long past, and of so little ultimate importance, is, perhaps, hardly worth alluding to; but there are some passages in the official documents which I thought very amusing.

At the very moment of receiving the attack of the British on the heights of Bladensburgh, there seems to have been a most curious puzzle among the American generals, as to where they were to be stationed, and what they were to do. It is stated that the British threw themselves forward in open

---

[11] [DS] Mrs. Trollope refers to (24) *Report of the Committee Appointed on the Twenty-Third of September Last to Inquire into the Causes and Particulars of the Invasion of the City of Washington, by the British Forces in the Month of August, 1814*, published in 1814. The name of the American general whom she quotes was Winder (not Winden).

order, advancing singly. The American general (Winden) goes on in his narrative to describe what followed, thus: —

"Our advanced riflemen now began to fire, and continued it for half a dozen rounds, when I observed them to run back to an orchard. They halted there, and seemed for a moment about returning to their original position, but in a few moments entirely broke and retired to the left of Stansburg's line. The advanced artillery immediately followed the riflemen.

"The first three or four rockets fired by the enemy were much above the heads of Stansburg's line; but the rockets having taken a more horizontal direction, an universal flight of the centre and left of this brigade was the consequence. The 5th regiment and the artillery still remained, and I hoped would prevent the enemy's approach, but they advancing singly, their fire annoyed the 5th considerably, when I ordered it to retire, to put it out of the reach of the enemy. This order was, however, immediately countermanded, from an aversion to retire before the necessity became stronger, and from a hope that the enemy would issue in a body, and enable us to act upon him on terms of equality. But the enemy's fire beginning to annoy the 5th still more, by wounding several of them, and a strong column passing up the road, and deploying on its left, I ordered them to retire; their retreat became a flight of absolute and total disorder."

Of Beall's regiment, the general gives the following succinct account — "It gave one or two ineffectual fires and fled."

In another place he says, piteously, — "The cavalry would do any thing but charge."

General Armstrong's gentle and metaphysical account of the business was, that — "Without all doubt the determining cause of our disasters is to be found in the love of life."

This affair at Washington, which in its result was certainly advantageous to America, inasmuch as it caused the present beautiful capitol to be built in the place of the one we burnt, was, nevertheless, considered as a national calamity at the time. In a volume of miscellaneous poems I met with one, written with the patriotic purpose of cheering the country under it; one triplet struck me as rather alarming for us, however soothing to America.

> "Supposing George's house at Kew
> Were burnt, as we intend to do,
> Would that be burning England too?"

I think I have before mentioned that no work of mere pleasantry has hitherto been found to answer; but a recent attempt of the kind has been made, with what success cannot as yet be decided. The editors are comedians belonging to the Boston company, and it is entitled "The American Comic Annual." [12] It is accompanied by etchings, somewhat in the manner, but by no means with the spirit of Cruikshank's. Among the pleasantries of this lively volume are some biting attacks upon us, particularly upon our utter incapacity of speaking English. We really must engage a few American professors, or we shall lose all trace of classic purity in our language. As a specimen, and rather a favourable one, of the work, I transcribed an extract from a little piece, entitled, "Sayings and Doings, a Fragment of a Farce." One of the personages of this farce is an English gentleman, a Captain Mandaville, and among many speeches of the same kind, I selected the following. Collins's Ode is the subject of conversation.

"A—r, A—a—a it stroiks me that that you manetion his the hode about hangger and ope and orror and revenge you know.

---

[12] [DS] *The American Comic Annual*, edited by Henry James Finn and illustrated by D. C. Johnston, was published at Boston. Mrs. Trollope quotes from "Sayings and Singings: a Fragment of a Farce," in the volume for 1831. The speaker is "Capt. Mandeville Cockaigne," who is described as "From Lunnun; a pretty-considerable Traveller; a collector of Fiction, and recollector of Fact — smiling on the Yankees here, and sneering at them at home; the personification of a steamer, upon the low-pres-sure system, that sails across the Atlantic, for the purpose of issuing smoke, in two thick volumes." This is Mrs. Trollope's friend Captain Basil Hall, of course.

I've eard Mrs. Sitdowns hencored in it at Common Garden
and Doory Lane in the ight of her poplarity you know. By the
boye, hall the hactin in Amareka is werry orrid. You're honely
in the hinfancy of the istoryonic hart you know; your performers never haspirate the haitch in sich vords for instance
as hink and hoats, and leave out the *w* in wice wanity you
know; and make nothink of homittin the *k* in somethink." [13]

There is much more in the same style, but, perhaps, this
may suffice. I have given this passage chiefly because it affords an example of the manner in which the generality of
Americans are accustomed to speak of English pronunciation
and phraseology.

It must be remembered, however, here and every where,
that this phrase, "the Americans," does not include the instructed and travelled portion of the community.

It would be absurd to swell my little volumes with extracts in proof of the veracity of their contents, but having
spoken of the taste of their lighter works, and also of the
general tone of manners, I cannot forbear inserting a page
from an American annual, (The Token), which purports to
give a scene from fashionable life. [14] It is part of a dialogue
between a young lady of the "highest standing" and her
"tutor," who is moreover her lover, though not yet acknowledged.

---

[13] [T5, note] Of the correctness of this imitation of the colloquial style
of English gentlemen, I will give no opinion; on this point every person
must judge for himself . . . but on reperusing it I am tempted to insert a
few extracts from a MS. which we brought home with us, which was the result of my having desired every member of my family to note down whatever words or phrases struck them as new to English ears — and from the
collection thus made, I composed several dialogues, some portions of which
may serve fairly enough as a *pendant* to the "Fragment of a Farce." This
pendant will be found at the end of the chapter.

[This *"pendant"* is given in Appendix A, together with the earlier — and
much different — form of it that Mrs. Trollope had set down in her notebooks under the title "Day of a Lady in the West."]

[14] [DS] Mrs. Trollope quotes from "The Ruse," by N. P. Willis, in *The
Token: a Christmas and New Year's Present* (1829).

" 'And so you won't tell me,' said she, 'what has come over you, and why you look as grave and sensible as a Dictionary, when, by general consent, even mine, "motley's the only wear?" '

" 'Am I so grave, Miss Blair?'

" 'Are you so grave, Miss Blair? One would think I had not got my lesson to-day. Pray, sir, has the black ox trod upon your toe since we parted?'

"Philip tried to laugh, but he did not succeed; he bit his lip and was silent.

" 'I am under orders to entertain you, Mr. Blondel, and if my poor brain can be made to gird this fairy isle, I shall certainly be obedient. So I begin with playing the leech. What ails you, sir?'

" 'Miss Blair!' he was going to remonstrate.

" 'Miss Blair! Now, pity, I'm a quack! for whip me, if I know whether Miss Blair is a fever or an ague. How did you catch it, sir?'

" 'Really, Miss Blair — '

" 'Nay, I see you don't like doctoring; I give over, and now I'll be sensible. It's a fine day, Mr. Blondel.'

" 'Very.'

" 'A pleasant lane, this, to walk in, if one's company were agreeable.'

" 'Does Mr. Skefton stay long?' asked Philip, abruptly.

" 'No one knows.'

" 'Indeed! are you so ignorant?'

" 'And why does your wisdom ask that question?' "

In no society in the world can the advantage of travel be so conspicuous as in America. In other countries a tone of unpretending simplicity can more than compensate for the absence of enlarged views or accurate observation; but this tone is not to be found in America, or if it be, it is only among those who, having looked at that insignificant portion of the world not included in the Union, have learnt to know how much is still unknown within the mighty part which is. For the rest, they all declare, and do in truth believe, that they only, among the sons of men, have wit and wisdom, and that one of their exclusive privileges is that of speaking English *elegantly*. There are two reasons for this latter persuasion; the one is, that the great majority have never heard any English but their own, except from the very lowest of the Irish; and the other, that those who have chanced to find themselves in the society of the few educated English who have visited America, have discovered that there is a marked difference between their phrases and accents and those to which they have been accustomed, whereupon they have, of course, decided that no Englishman can speak English.

The reviews of America contain some good clear-headed articles; but I sought in vain for the playful vivacity and the keenly-cutting satire, whose sharp edge, however painful to the patient, is of such high utility in lopping off the excrescences of bad taste, and levelling to its native clay the heavy growth of dulness. Still less could I find any trace of that graceful familiarity of learned allusion and general knowledge which mark the best European reviews, and which make one feel in such perfectly good company while perusing them. But this is a tone not to be found either in the writings or conversation of Americans; as distant from pedantry as from ignorance, it is not learning itself, but the effect of it; and so pervading and subtle is its influence that it may be traced in the festive halls and gay drawing-rooms of Europe as certainly as in the cloistered library or student's closet; it is, perhaps, the last finish of highly-finished society.

A late American quarterly has an article on a work of Dr. Von Schmidt Phiseldek, from which I made an extract,[15] as a curious sample of the dreams they love to batten on.

Dr. Von Phiseldek (not Fiddlestick), who is not only a doctor of philosophy, but a knight of Dannebrog to boot, has

---

[15] [DS] *The American Quarterly Review* for June 1831.

never been in America, but he has written a prophecy, shewing that the United States must and will govern the whole
world, because they are so very big, and have so much uncul-
tivated territory; he prophesies that an union will take place
between North and South America, which will give a death-
blow to Europe, at no distant period; though he modestly
adds that he does not pretend to designate the precise period
at which this will take place. This Danish prophecy, as may
be imagined, enchants the reviewer. He exhorts all people to
read Dr. Phiseldek's book, because "nothing but good can
come of such contemplations of the future, and because it is
eminently calculated to awaken the most lofty anticipations
of the destiny which awaits them, and will serve to impress
upon the nation the necessity of being prepared for such high
destiny." In another place the reviewer bursts out, "America,
young as she is, has become already the beacon, the patri-
arch of the struggling nations of the world;" and afterwards
adds, "It would be departing from the natural order of things,
and the ordinary operations of the great scheme of Providence, it would be shutting our ears to the voice of experience, and our eyes to the inevitable connection of causes and
their effects, were we to reject the extreme probability, not
to say *moral certainty,* that the old world is destined to receive its influences in future from the new." There are twenty
pages of this article, but I will only give one passage more; it
is an instance of the sort of reasoning by which American
citizens persuade themselves that the glory of Europe is, in
reality, her reproach. "Wrapped up in a sense of his superiority, the European reclines at home, shining in his borrowed
plumes, derived from the product of every corner of the
earth, and the industry of every portion of its inhabitants,
with which his own natural resources would never have invested him, he continues reveling in enjoyments which nature
has denied him."

The American Quarterly deservedly holds the highest place

in their periodical literature, and, therefore, may be fairly quoted as striking the keynote for the chorus of public opinion. Surely it is nationality rather than patriotism which leads it thus to speak in scorn of the successful efforts of enlightened nations to win from every corner of the earth the riches which nature has scattered over it.

*   *   *   *   *   *

The incorrectness of the press is very great: they make strange work in the reprints of French and Italian; and the Latin, I suspect, does not fare much better: I believe they do not often meddle with Greek.

With regard to the fine arts, their paintings, I think, are quite as good, or rather better, than might be expected from the patronage they receive; the wonder is that any man can be found with courage enough to devote himself to a profession in which he has so little chance of finding a maintenance. The trade of a carpenter opens an infinitely better prospect; and this is so well known, that nothing but a genuine passion for the art could beguile any one to pursue it. The entire absence of every means of improvement, and effectual study, is unquestionably the cause why those who manifest this devotion cannot advance farther. I heard of one young artist, whose circumstances did not permit his going to Europe, but who being nevertheless determined that his studies should, as nearly as possible, resemble those of the European academies, was about to commence drawing the human figure, for which purpose he had provided himself with a thin silk dress, in which to clothe his models, as no one of any station, he said, could be found who would submit to sit as a model without clothing.

It was at Alexandria that I saw what I consider as the best picture by an American artist that I met with. The subject was Hagar and Ishmael It had recently arrived from Rome, where the painter, a young man of the name of Chapman, had been studying for three years.[16] His mother told me that he was twenty-two years of age, and passionately devoted to the art; should he, on returning to his country, receive sufficient encouragement to keep his ardour and his industry alive, I think I shall hear of him again.

*   *   *   *   *   *

Much is said about the universal diffusion of education in America, and a vast deal of genuine admiration is felt and expressed at the progress of mind throughout the Union. They believe themselves in all sincerity to have surpassed, to be surpassing, and to be about to surpass, the whole earth in the intellectual race. I am aware that not a single word can be said, hinting a different opinion, which will not bring down a transatlantic anathema on my head; yet the subject is too interesting to be omitted. Before I left England I remember listening, with much admiration, to an eloquent friend, who deprecated our system of public education, as confining the various and excursive faculties of our children to one beaten path, paying little or no attention to the peculiar powers of the individual.

This objection is extremely plausible, but doubts of its intrinsic value must, I think, occur to every one who has marked the result of a different system throughout the United States.

From every enquiry I could make, and I took much pains

---

[16] [DS] John G. Chapman, born in Alexandria, Virginia, in 1808, had painted *Hagar and Ishmael Fainting in the Wilderness* while studying at Rome. The Roman *Giornall di Belle Arti* considered the picture good enough to reproduce it in November 1830 as its first example of American art. In 1831 Chapman returned to the United States and achieved a limited success. He made himself familiar to the public eye through his 1,400 drawings for the Harper's Bible, published in 1846. In 1848 Chapman returned to Rome and remained there during most of the latter half of his life. He died in 1889.

to obtain accurate information, it appeared that much is attempted, but very little beyond reading, writing, and book-keeping, is thoroughly acquired. Were we to read a prospectus of the system pursued in any of our public schools, and that of a first-rate seminary in America, we should be struck by the confined scholastic routine of the former, when compared to the varied and expansive scope of the latter; but let the examination go a little farther, and I believe it will be found that the old fashioned school discipline of England has produced something higher, and deeper too, than that which roars so loud, and thunders in the index.

They will not afford to let their young men study till two or three and twenty, and it is therefore declared, *ex cathedrâ Americanâ*, to be unnecessary. At sixteen, often much earlier, education ends, and money-making begins; the idea that more learning is necessary than can be acquired by that time, is generally ridiculed as obsolete monkish bigotry; added to which, if the seniors willed a more prolonged discipline, the juniors would refuse submission. When the money-getting begins, leisure ceases, and all of lore which can be acquired afterwards, is picked up from novels, magazines, and newspapers.

At what time can the taste be formed? How can a correct and polished style, even of speaking, be acquired? or when can the fruit of the two thousand years of past thinking be added to the native growth of American intellect? These are the tools, if I may so express myself, which our elaborate system of school discipline puts into the hands of our scholars; possessed of these, they may use them in whatever direction they please afterwards, they can never be an incumbrance.

No people appear more anxious to excite admiration and receive applause than the Americans, yet none take so little trouble, or make so few sacrifices to obtain it. This may answer among themselves, but it will not, with the rest of the world; individual sacrifices must be made, and national econ-

XXI THE PRESIDENT OF THE UNITED STATES
1831

XXII BOX AT THE THEATRE

omy enlarged, before America can compete with the old
world in taste, learning, and liberality.

The reception of General Lafayette is the one single instance in which the national pride has overcome the national
thrift; [17] and this was clearly referable to the one single feeling of enthusiasm of which they appear capable, namely, the
triumph of their successful struggle for national independence. But though this feeling will be universally acknowledged as a worthy and lawful source of triumph and of pride,
it will not serve to trade upon for ever, as a fund of glory and
high station among the nations. Their fathers were colonists;
they fought stoutly, and became an independent people. Success and admiration, even the admiration of those whose yoke
they had broken, cheered them while living, still sheds a
glory round their remote and untitled sepulchres, and will
illumine the page of their history for ever.

Their children inherit the independence; they inherit too
the honour of being the sons of brave fathers; but this will
not give them the reputation at which they aim, of being
scholars and gentlemen, nor will it enable them to sit down
for evermore to talk of their glory, while they drink mint
julap [18] and chew tobacco, swearing by the beard of Jupiter

[17] [DS] For further comment on General Lafayette's triumphal tour of
America in 1824–5, see section VIII of the Introduction and note 9, page
226.

[18] [DS] In her novel *The Old World and the New* (1849) Mrs. Trollope
at last admitted her own admiration for this popular American beverage,
and thought of it as the best restorative for her English characters, tired and
hot from inspecting land in the neighborhood of Cincinnati:

". . . it would, I truly believe, be utterly impossible for the art of man
to administer anything so likely to restore them from the overwhelming
effects of heat and fatigue, as a large glass filled to the brim with the
fragrant leaves of nerve-restoring mint, as many solid lumps of delicately pel-
lucid, crystal-looking ice, as it can conveniently contain, a proper proportion of fine white sugar, (not beet-root), and then — I would whisper it gently, if I knew how — a whole wine-glass full of whiskey poured upon it, to
find its insinuating way among the crystal rocks, and the verdant leaves, till
by gentle degrees, a beverage is produced, that must create a delicious sensation of coolness, under a tropical sun, and a revival of strength, where
strength seemed gone for ever.

(or some other oath) that they are very graceful and agreeable, and, moreover, abusing every body who does not cry out Amen!

To doubt that talent and mental power of every kind, exist in America would be absurd; why should it not? But in taste and learning they are woefully deficient; and it is this which renders them incapable of graduating a scale by which to measure themselves. Hence arises that overweening complacency and self-esteem, both national and individual, which at once renders them so extremely obnoxious to ridicule, and so peculiarly restive under it.

If they will scorn the process by which other nations have become what they avowedly intend to be, they must rest satisfied with the praise and admiration they receive from each other; and turning a deaf ear to the criticisms of the old world, consent to be their "own prodigious great reward."

*   *   *   *   *   *

Alexandria has it churches, chapels, and conventicles as abundantly, in proportion to its size, as any city in the Union. I visited most of them, and in the Episcopal and Catholic heard the services performed quietly and reverently.

The best sermon, however, that I listened to, was in a

"It really is very dreadful to be driven by a love of truth, to publish a page in praise of dram-drinking, but, at least in the case of ladies, I would only recommend it upon such a desperately fatiguing occasion as that which brought Mary and Katherine into Major Dickson's celebrated 'Eagle and Thunderbolt Hotel.' "

Thus her English family learned a lesson: ". . . never to turn lightly and unadvisedly away from any well established national practice, that carried with it the appearance of comfort.

"Now this axiom by no means includes any necessity of chewing tobacco, or of incessant smoking. Neither is it intended to imply the desirability of public and private expectoration, and persons who turn from these very flagrant abuses of the freedom of man, are not likely to turn away unadvisedly or lightly. But it does include the not turning away from mint julep! which could only be done, if done at all, lightly, unadvisedly, and most unwisely."

Methodist church, from the mouth of a Piquot Indian. It was impossible not to be touched by the simple sincerity of this poor man. He gave a picture frightfully eloquent of the decay of his people under the united influence of the avarice and intemperance of the white men. He described the effect of the religious feeling which had recently found its way among them as most salutary. The purity of his moral feeling, and the sincerity of his sympathy with his forest brethren, made it unquestionable that he must be the most valuable priest who could officiate for them. His English was very correct, and his pronunciation but slightly tinctured by native accent.

* * * * * *

While we were still in the neighbourhood of Washington, a most violent and unprecedented schism occurred in the cabinet. The four secretaries of State all resigned, leaving General Jackson to manage the queer little state barge alone.

Innumerable contradictory statements appeared upon this occasion in the papers, and many a segar was thrown aside, ere half consumed, that the disinterested politician might give breath to his cogitations on this extraordinary event; but not all the eloquence of all the smokers, nor even the ultra-diplomatic expositions which appeared from the seceding secretaries themselves, could throw any light on the mysterious business. It produced, however, the only tolerable caricature I ever saw in the country. It represents the President seated alone in his cabinet, wearing a look of much discomfiture, and making great exertions to detain one of four rats, who are running off, by placing his foot on the tail. The rats' heads bear a very sufficient resemblance to the four ex-ministers.[19] General Jackson, it seems, had requested Mr.

---

[19] [DS] The cartoon was entitled "Rats Leaving a Falling House"; it was the work of Edward Williams Clay, an English artist, as Mrs. Trollope would have been pleased to know. The political situation that it caricatures had a complicated history, with the Peggy Eaton scandal in the spotlight and

Van Buren, the Secretary of State, to remain in office till his place was supplied; this gave occasion to a *bon mot* from his son, who, being asked when his father would be in New York, replied, "When the President takes off his foot."

Calhoun's connivings against Van Buren behind scenes. Jackson was not in the pathetic plight that Mrs. Trollope describes; he stood to profit greatly from the shift of seats in his cabinet.

CHAPTER XXX

Journey to New York — Delaware River — Stage-coach — City of New York — Collegiate Institute for Young Ladies — Theatres — Public Garden — Churches — Morris Canal — Fashions — Carriages

AT length, spite of the lingering pace necessarily attending consultations, and arrangements across the Atlantic, our plans were finally settled; the coming spring was to shew us New York, and Niagara, and the early summer was to convey us home.

No sooner did the letter arrive which decided this, than we began our preparations for departure. We took our last voyage on the Potomac, we bade a last farewell to Virginia, and gave a last day to some of our kind friends near Washington.

The spring, though slow and backward, was sufficiently advanced to render the journey pleasant; and though the road from Washington to Baltimore was less brilliant in foliage than when I had seen it before, it still had much of beauty. The azalias were in full bloom, and the delicate yellow blossom of the sassafras almost rivalled its fruit in beauty.

At Baltimore we again embarked on a gigantic steam-boat, and reached Philadelphia in the middle of the night. Here we changed our boat, and found time, before starting in the morning, to take a last look at the Doric and Corinthian porticos of the two celebrated temples dedicated to Mammon.

The Delaware river, above Philadelphia, still flows through a landscape too level for beauty, but it is rendered interesting by a succession of gentlemen's seats, which, if less elaborately finished in architecture, and garden grounds, than the lovely villas on the Thames, are still beautiful objects to gaze upon as you float rapidly past on the broad silvery stream that washes their lawns. They present a picture of wealth and enjoyment that accords well with the noble city to which they are an appendage. One mansion arrested our attention, not only from its being more than usually large and splendid, but from its having the monument which marked the family resting-place, rearing itself in all the gloomy grandeur of black and white marble, exactly opposite the door of entrance.

In Virginia and Maryland we had remarked that almost every family mansion had its little grave yard, sheltered by locust and cypress trees; but this decorated dwelling of the dead seemed rather a melancholy ornament in the grounds.

We had, for a considerable distance, a view of the dwelling of Joseph Bonaparte, which is situated on the New Jersey shore, in the midst of an extensive tract of land, of which he is the proprietor.[1]

Here the ex-monarch has built several houses, which are occupied by French tenants. The country is very flat, but a terrace of two sides has been raised, commanding a fine reach of the Delaware River; at the point where this terrace forms a right angle, a lofty chapel has been erected, which looks very much like an observatory; I admired the ingenuity with which the Catholic prince has united his religion and his love of a fine terrestrial prospect. The highest part of the

---

[1] [DS] Joseph Bonaparte (1768–1844), one year older than his brother Napoleon, was not ambitious for power, although for a time he had greatness thrust upon him. He was made King of Naples in 1806 and King of Spain and the Indies in 1808. After Waterloo he fled under an assumed name to the United States on an American ship. He lived for one year at Philadelphia and then purchased his estate at Bordentown, New Jersey, where his daughters and their families joined him. While he lived at Bordentown, he was offered the crown of Mexico, but refused, saying, according to report: "I have worn two crowns; I would not take a step to wear a third." After 1832 he spent most of the remaining twelve years of his life in Europe.

building presents, in every direction, the appearance of an immense cross; the transept, if I may so express it, being formed by the projection of an ample balcony, which surrounds a tower.

A Quaker gentleman, from Philadelphia, exclaimed, as he gazed on the mansion, "There we see a monument of fallen royalty! Strange! that dethroned kings should seek and find their best strong-hold in a Republic."

There was more of philosophy than of scorn in his accent, and his countenance was the symbol of gentleness and benevolence; but I overheard many unquakerlike jokes from others, as to the comfortable assurance a would-be king must feel of a faithful alliance between his head and shoulders.

At Trenton, the capital of New Jersey, we left our smoothly-gliding comfortable boat for the most detestable stage-coach that ever Christian built to dislocate the joints of his fellow men. Ten of these torturing machines were crammed full of the passengers who left the boat with us. The change in our movement was not more remarkable than that which took place in the tempers and countenances of our fellow-travellers. Gentlemen who had lounged on sofas, and balanced themselves in chairs, all the way from Philadelphia, with all the conscious fascinations of stiff stays and neck-cloths, which, while doing to death the rash beauties who ventured to gaze, seemed but a whalebone panoply to guard the wearer, these pretty youths so guarded from without, so sweetly at peace within, now crushed beneath their armour, looked more like victims on the wheel, than dandies armed for conquest; their whalebones seemed to enter into their souls, and every face grew grim and scowling. The pretty ladies too, with their expansive bonnets, any one of which might handsomely have filled the space allotted to three, — how sad the change! I almost fancied they must have been of the race of Undine, and that it was only when they heard the splashing of water that they could smile. As

I looked into the altered eyes of my companions, I was tempted to ask, "Look I as cross as you?" Indeed, I believe that, if possible, I looked crosser still, for the roads and the vehicle together were quite too much for my philosophy.

At length, however, we found ourselves alive on board the boat which was to convey us down the Raraton River to New York.

We fully intended to have gone to bed, to heal our bones, on entering the steam-boat, but the sight of a table neatly spread, determined us to go to dinner instead. Sin and shame would it have been, indeed, to have closed our eyes upon the scene which soon opened before us. I have never seen the bay of Naples, I can therefore make no comparison, but my imagination is incapable of conceiving any thing of the kind more beautiful than the harbour of New York. Various and lovely are the objects which meet the eye on every side, but the naming them would only be to give a list of words, without conveying the faintest idea of the scene. I doubt if ever the pencil of Turner could do it justice, bright and glorious as it rose upon us. We seemed to enter the harbour of New York upon waves of liquid gold, and as we darted past the green isles which rise from its bosom, like guardian centinels of the fair city, the setting sun stretched his horizontal beams farther and farther at each moment, as if to point out to us some new glory in the landscape.

New York, indeed, appeared to us, even when we saw it by a soberer light, a lovely and a noble city. To us who had been so long travelling through half-cleared forests, and sojourning among an "I'm-as-good-as-you" population, it seemed, perhaps, more beautiful, more splendid, and more refined than it might have done, had we arrived there directly from London; but making every allowance for this, I must still declare that I think New York one of the finest cities I ever saw, and as much superior to every other in the Union, (Philadelphia not excepted,) as London to Liverpool, or Paris to Rouen. Its advantages of position are, perhaps, unequalled any where. Situated on an island, which I think it will one day cover, it rises, like Venice, from the sea, and like that fairest of cities in the days of her glory, receives into its lap tribute of all the riches of the earth.

The southern point of Manhatten [*sic*] Island divides the waters of the harbour into the north and east rivers; on this point stands the city of New York, extending from river to river, and running northward to the extent of three or four miles. I think it covers nearly as much ground as Paris, but is much less thickly peopled. The extreme point is fortified towards the sea by a battery, and forms an admirable point of defence; but in these piping days of peace, it is converted into a public promenade, and one more beautiful, I should suppose, no city could boast. From hence commences the splendid Broadway, as the fine avenue is called, which runs through the whole city. This noble street may vie with any I ever saw, for its length and breadth, its handsome shops, neat awnings, excellent *trottoir*, and well-dressed pedestrians. It has not the crowded glitter of Bond-street equipages, nor the gorgeous fronted palaces of Regent-street; but it is magnificent in its extent, and ornamented by several handsome buildings, some of them surrounded by grass and trees. The Park, in which stands the noble city-hall, is a very fine area. I never found that the most graphic description of a city could give me any feeling of being there; and even if others have the power, I am very sure I have not, of setting churches and squares, and long drawn streets, before the mind's eye. I will not, therefore, attempt a detailed description of this great metropolis of the new world, but will only say that during the seven weeks we stayed there, we always found something new to see and to admire; and were it not so very far from all the old-world things which cling about the heart of an European, I should say that I never saw a city more desirable as a residence.

The dwelling houses of the higher classes are extremely handsome, and very richly furnished. Silk or satin furniture is as often, or oftener, seen than chintz; the mirrors are as handsome as in London; the cheffoniers, slabs, and marble tables as elegant; and in addition, they have all the pretty tasteful decoration of French porcelaine, and or-molu in much greater abundance, because at a much cheaper rate. Every part of their houses is well carpeted, and the exterior finishing, such as steps, railings, and door-frames, are very superior. Almost every house has handsome green blinds on the outside; balconies are not very general, nor do the houses display, externally, so many flowers as those of Paris and London; but I saw many rooms decorated within, exactly like those of an European *petite maîtresse*.[2] Little tables, looking and smelling like flower beds, portfolios, nick-nacks, bronzes, busts, cameos, and alabaster vases, illustrated copies of lady-like rhymes bound in silk, and, in short, all the pretty coxcomalities of the drawing-room scattered about with the same profuse and studied negligence as with us.

Hudson Square [3] and its neighbourhood is, I believe, the most fashionable part of the town; the square is beautiful, excellently well planted with a great variety of trees, and only wanting our frequent and careful mowing to make it equal to any square in London. The iron railing which surrounds this enclosure is as high and as handsome as that of the Tuilleries, and it will give some idea of the care bestowed on its decoration, to know that the gravel for the walks was conveyed by barges from Boston, not as ballast, but as freight.

The great defect in the houses is their extreme uniformity — when you have seen one, you have seen all. Neither do I

[2] [DS] *"petite maîtresse"*: "foppish woman."
[3] [DS] Hudson Square, formed by Hudson, Laight, Varick, and Beach Streets, was bought by the New York Central and Hudson River Railroad in 1869, and its trees and walks were replaced by storehouses, a freight station, and a depot.

quite like the arrangement of the rooms. In nearly all the houses the dining and drawing-rooms are on the same floor, with ample folding doors between them; when thrown together they certainly make a very noble apartment; but no doors can be barrier sufficient between dining and drawing-rooms. Mixed dinner parties of ladies and gentlemen, however, are very rare, which is a great defect in the society; not only as depriving them of the most social and hospitable manner of meeting, but as leading to frequent dinner parties of gentlemen without ladies, which certainly does not conduce to refinement.

The evening parties, excepting such as are expressly for young people, are chiefly conversational; we were too late in the season for large parties, but we saw enough to convince us that there is society to be met with in New York, which would be deemed delightful any where. Cards are very seldom used; and music, from their having very little professional aid at their parties, is seldom, I believe, as good as what is heard at private concerts in London.

The Americans have certainly not the same *besoin* of being amused, as other people; they may be the wiser for this, perhaps, but it makes them less agreeable to a looker-on.

There are three theatres at New York, all of which we visited. The Park Theatre is the only one licensed by fashion, but the Bowery is infinitely superior in beauty; it is indeed as pretty a theatre as I ever entered, perfect as to size and proportion, elegantly decorated, and the scenery and machinery equal to any in London, but it is not the fashion. The Chatham is so utterly condemned by *bon ton*, that it requires some courage to decide upon going there; nor do I think my curiosity would have penetrated so far, had I not seen Miss Mitford's Rienzi advertised there. It was the first opportunity I had had of seeing it played, and spite of very indifferent acting, I was delighted. The interest must have been great, for till the curtain fell, I saw not one quarter of the queer things around me: then I observed in the front row of a dress-box a lady performing the most maternal office possible; several gentlemen without their coats, and a general air of contempt for the decencies of life, certainly more than usually revolting.

At the Park Theatre I again saw the American Roscius, Mr. Forrest. He played the part of Damon, and roared, I thought, very unlike a nightingale. I cannot admire this celebrated performer.

Another night we saw Cinderella there; [4] Mrs. Austin was the prima donna, and much admired. The piece was extremely well got up, and on this occasion we saw the Park Theatre to advantage, for it was filled with well-dressed company; but still we saw many "yet unrazored lips" polluted with the grim tinge of the hateful tobacco, and heard, without ceasing, the spitting, which of course is its consequence. [5] If their theatres had the orchestra of the Feydeau, and a choir of angels to boot, I could find but little pleasure, so long as they were followed by this running accompaniment of *thorough base*.

Whilst at New York, the prospectus of a fashionable boarding-school was presented to me. I made some extracts from

---

[4] [DS] Rossini's *La Cenerentola*, first performed at Rome in January 1817.

[5] [DS] From the New York *Constellation* (July 14, 1832):

MRS. TROLLOPE AND THE SPITTERS

Mrs. Trollope is commendably bitter
Against the filthy American spitter,
For spitting his juice all about;
While the English they (for so it is writ)
Disgustingly in their handkerchiefs spit —
Thus leaving a case of some doubt,

Which, gentle reader, I beg you will sit on,
And fairly judge 'tween the Yankee and Briton;
So render your verdict I pray:
Whether, to weigh its merits to a tittle,
You think it better to POCKET *the spittle*,
Or freely to *spit it* away?

it,[6] as a specimen of the enlarged scale of instruction proposed for young females.

Brooklyn Collegiate Institute
for Young Ladies,
Brooklyn Heights, opposite the City of
New York.

JUNIOR DEPARTMENT.
Sixth Class.

Latin Grammar, Liber Primus; Jacob's Latin Reader, (first part); Modern Geography; Intellectual and Practical Arithmetic finished; Dr. Barber's Grammar of Elocution; Writing, Spelling, Composition, and Vocal Music.

Fifth Class.

Jacob's Latin Reader, (second part); Roman Antiquities, Sallust; Clark's Introduction to the Making of Latin; Ancient and Sacred Geography; Studies of Poetry; Short Treatise on Rhetoric; Map Drawing, Composition, Spelling, and Vocal Music.

Fourth Class.

Cæsar's Commentaries; first five books of Virgil's Æneid; Mythology; Watts on the Mind; Political Geography, (Woodbridge's large work); Natural History; Treatise on the Globes; Ancient History; Studies of Poetry concluded; English Grammar, Composition, Spelling, and Vocal Music.

---

[6] [DS] Mrs. Trollope quotes from a prospectus dated 1830. The discipline of the school seems somewhat severe to a modern reader:

"COMPOSITION — Each Pupil is required to keep a *Daily Journal,* which exercise is continued throughout both Departments.

"MORALS — The Morals of the Pupils are at all times under the inspection of the Principals and Teachers; nothing being permitted to exist that may in any measure have a demoralizing tendency upon the minds of the most unwary. . . . No pupil is permitted to *receive* or *pay* visits on the Sabbath, (except in cases of necessity,) to engage in any diversions, amuse herself with unsuitable reading, or otherwise to profane the day."

J. T. Bailey, in *An Historical Sketch of the City of Brooklyn* (1840), says that the school, which was incorporated in 1829, "flourished for a few years, and gave promise of permanent utility but from want of sufficient patronage . . . has been given up."

SENIOR DEPARTMENT.

Third Class.

Virgil, (finished); Cicero's Select Orations; Modern History; Plane Geometry; Moral Philosophy; Critical Reading of Young's Poems; Perspective Drawing; Rhetoric; Logic, Composition, and Vocal Music.

Second Class.

Livy; Horace, (Odes); Natural Theology; small Compend of Ecclesiastical History; Female Biography; Algebra; Natural Philosophy, (Mechanics, Hydrostatics, Pneumatics, and Acoustics); Intellectual Philosophy; Evidences of Christianity; Composition, and Vocal Music.

First Class.

Horace, (finished); Tacitus; Natural Philosophy, (Electricity, Optics, Magnetism, Galvanism); Astronomy, Chemistry, Mineralogy, and Geology; Compend of Political Economy; Composition, and Vocal Music.

The French, Spanish, Italian, or Greek languages may be attended to, if required, at any time.

The Exchange is very handsome, and ranks about midway between the heavy gloom that hangs over our London merchants, and the light and lofty elegance which decorates the Bourse at Paris. The churches are plain, but very neat, and kept in perfect repair within and without; but I saw none which had the least pretension to splendour; the Catholic cathedral at Baltimore is the only church in America which has.

At New York, as every where else, they shew within, during the time of service, like beds of tulips, so gay, so bright, so beautiful, are the long rows of French bonnets and pretty faces; rows but rarely broken by the unribboned heads of the male population; the proportion is about the same as I have remarked elsewhere. Excepting at New York, I never saw the other side of the picture, but there I did. On the opposite side of the North River, about three miles higher up, is a place called Hoboken. A gentleman who possessed a handsome mansion and grounds there, also possessed the right of ferry, and to render this productive, he has restricted his pleasure grounds to a few beautiful acres, laying out the remainder simply and tastefully as a public walk.⁷ It is hardly possible to imagine one of greater attraction; a broad belt of light underwood and flowering shrubs, studded at intervals with lofty forest trees, runs for two miles along a cliff which overhangs the matchless Hudson; sometimes it feathers the rocks down to its very margin, and at others leaves a pebbly shore, just rude enough to break the gentle waves, and make a music which mimics softly the loud chorus of the ocean. — Through this beautiful little wood, a broad well-gravelled terrace is led by every point which can exhibit the scenery to advantage; narrower and wilder paths diverge at intervals, some into the deeper shadow of the woods, and some shelving gradually to the pretty coves below.

The price of entrance to this little Eden, is the six cents you pay at the ferry. We went there on a bright Sunday afternoon, expressly to see the humours of the place. Many thousand persons were scattered through the grounds; of these we ascertained, by repeatedly counting, that nineteen-twentieths were men. The ladies were at church. Often as the subject has pressed upon my mind, I think I never so strongly felt the conviction that the Sabbath-day, the holy day, the day on which alone the great majority of the Christian world can spend their hours as they please, is ill passed (if passed entirely) within brick walls, listening to an earth-born preacher, charm he never so wisely.⁸

⁷ [DS] This gentleman was Colonel John Stevens. He had established the first steam ferry in the world in 1811 — the *Juliana,* which plied between New York and Hoboken. Mrs. Trollope does not mention the artificial attractions of his resort, which, by 1829, included a merry-go-round, aerial ways, wax figures, a camera obscura, and a circular railway. The locomotive that operated on this railway, built in 1826, carried six or seven passengers at a rate of over twelve miles an hour; it is said to have been "the first locomotive that ever ran on a railroad in America."

⁸ [T5, note] Compare a Sunday, the greater part of which is passed in church, and the rest in rigid abstinence from every occupation which nature

"Oh! how can they renounce the boundless store
Of charms, which Nature to her vot'ries yields!
The warbling woodland, the resounding shore,
The pomp of groves, and garniture of fields,
All that the genial ray of morning gilds,
And all that echoes to the song of even,
All that the mountain's sheltering bosom yields,
And all the dread magnificence of heaven;
Oh! how can they renounce, and hope to be forgiven!"

How is it that the men of America, who are reckoned good husbands and good fathers, while they themselves enjoy sufficient freedom of spirit to permit their walking forth into the temple of the living God, can leave those they love best on earth, bound in the iron chains of a most tyrannical fanaticism? How can they breathe the balmy air, and not think of the tainted atmosphere so heavily weighing upon breasts still dearer than their own? How can they gaze upon the blossoms of the spring, and not remember the fairer cheeks of their young daughters, waxing pale, as they sit for long sultry hours, immured with hundreds of fellow victims, listening to the roaring vanities of a preacher canonized by a college of old women? They cannot think it needful to salvation, or they would not withdraw themselves. Wherefore is it? Do they fear these self-elected, self-ordained priests, and offer up their wives and daughters to propitiate them? Or do they deem their hebdomadal freedom more complete, because their wives and daughters are shut up four or five times in the day at church or chapel? It is true, that at Hoboken, as every where else, there are *reposoires*, which, as you pass them, blast the sense for a moment, by reeking forth the fumes of whiskey and tobacco, and it may be that these cannot be entered with a wife or daughter. The proprietor of the grounds, however, has contrived with great taste to render these abominations not unpleasing to the eye; there is

seems to have made congenial to the mind of man, with the simple, holy, patriarchal Sunday of Sir Walter Scott, as described in that most perfect of all existing biographies, Loc[k]hart's life of him.

one in particular, which has quite the air of a Grecian temple, and did they drink wine instead of whiskey, it might be inscribed to Bacchus; but in this particular, as in many others, the ancient and modern Republics differ.

It is impossible not to feel, after passing one Sunday in the churches and chapels of New York, and the next in the gardens of Hoboken, that the thousands of well-dressed men you see enjoying themselves at the latter, have made over the thousands of well-dressed women you saw exhibited at the former, into the hands of the priests, at least, for the day. The American people arrogate to themselves a character of superior morality and religion, but this division of their hours of leisure does not give me a favourable idea of either.

I visited all the exhibitions in New York. The Medici of the Republic must exert themselves a little more before these can become even respectable. The worst of the business is, that with the exception of about half a dozen individuals, the good citizens are more than contented, they are delighted.

The newspaper lungs of the Republic breathe forth praise and triumph, nay, almost pant with extacy in speaking of their native *chef d'œuvres*. I should be hardly believed were I to relate the instances which fell in my way, of the utter ignorance respecting pictures to be found among persons of the *first standing* in society. Often where a liberal spirit exists, and a wish to patronise the fine arts is expressed, it is joined to a profundity of ignorance on the subject almost inconceivable. A doubt as to the excellence of their artists is very nervously received, and one gentleman, with much civility, told me, that at the present era, all the world were aware that competition was pretty well at an end between our two nations, and that a little envy might naturally be expected to mix with the surprise with which the mother country beheld the distance at which her colonies were leaving her behind them.

I must, however, do the few artists with whom I became

acquainted, the justice to say, that their own pretensions are much more modest than those of their patrons for them. I have heard several confess and deplore their ignorance of drawing, and have repeatedly remarked a sensibility to the merit of European artists, though perhaps only known by engravings, and a deference to their authority, which shewed a genuine feeling for the art. In fact, I think that there is a very considerable degree of natural talent for painting in America, but it has to make its way through darkness and thick night. When an academy is founded, their first care is to hang the walls of its exhibition-room with all the unutterable trash that is offered to them. No living models are sought for; no discipline as to the manner of study is enforced. Boys who know no more of the human form, than they do of the eyes, nose, and mouth in the moon, begin painting portraits. If some of them would only throw away their palettes for a year, and learn to draw; if they would attend anatomical lectures, and take notes, not in words, but in forms, of joints and muscles, their exhibitions would soon cease to be so utterly below criticism.

The most interesting exhibition open when I was there was, decidedly, Colonel Trumbold's; [9] and how the patriots of America can permit this truly national collection to remain a profitless burden on the hands of the artist, it is difficult to understand. Many of the sketches are masterly; but like his illustrious countryman, West, his sketches are his *chef d'œuvres.*

I can imagine nothing more perfect than the interior of the public institutions of New York. There is a practical good

---

[9] [DS] Mrs. Trollope must mean the exhibition of John Trumbull (1756–1843), creator of the paintings that she had seen in the rotunda of the Capitol at Washington. On April 30, 1831 the *New-York Mirror* stated in a notice headed "The Paintings of Colonel Trumbull" that his current exhibition at New York contained "nine subjects of the American revolution, with near two hundred and fifty portraits of persons distinguished in that period. . . ."

sense in all their arrangements that must strike foreigners very forcibly. The Asylum for the Destitute offers a hint worth taking. It is dedicated to the reformation of youthful offenders of both sexes, and it is as admirable in the details of its management, as in its object. Every part of the institution is deeply interesting; but there is a difference very remarkable between the boys and the girls. The boys are, I think, the finest set of lads I ever saw brought together; bright looking, gay, active, and full of intelligence. The girls are exactly the reverse; heavy, listless, indifferent, and melancholy. In conversing with the gentleman who is the general superintendant of the establishment, I made the remark to him, and he told me, that the reality corresponded with the appearance. All of them had been detected in some act of dishonesty; but the boys, when removed from the evil influence which had led them so to use their ingenuity, rose like a spring when a pressure is withdrawn; and feeling themselves once more safe from danger, and from shame, hope and cheerfulness animated every countenance. But the poor girls, on the contrary, can hardly look up again. They are as different as an oak and a lily after a storm. The one, when the fresh breeze blows over it, shakes the raindrops from its crest, and only looks the brighter; the other, its silken leaves once soiled, shrinks from the eye, and is levelled to the earth for ever.

*   *   *   *   *   *

We spent a delightful day in New Jersey, in visiting, with a most agreeable party, the inclined planes, which are used instead of locks on the Morris canal.

This is a very interesting work; it is one among a thousand which prove the people of America to be the most enterprising in the world. I was informed that this important canal, which connects the waters of the Hudson and the Delaware, is a hundred miles long, and in this distance overcomes a variation of level amounting to sixteen hundred feet. Of this, fourteen hundred are achieved by inclined planes. The planes average about sixty feet of perpendicular lift each, and are to support about forty tons. The time consumed in passing them is twelve minutes for one hundred feet of perpendicular rise. The expense is less than a third of what locks would be for surmounting the same rise. If we set about any more canals, this may be worth attending to.

This Morris canal is certainly an extraordinary work; [10] it not only varies its level sixteen hundred feet, but at one point runs along the side of a mountain at thirty feet above the tops of the highest buildings in the town of Paterson, below; at another it crosses the falls of the Passaic in a stone aqueduct sixty feet above the water in the river. This noble work, in a great degree, owes its existence to the patriotic and scientific energy of Mr. Cadwallader Colden. [11]

There is no point in the national character of the Americans which commands so much respect as the boldness and

---

[10] [DS] The Morris Canal was the "highest climber" of all canals. "General course from New York to Easton, west: length, 101.75 miles; ascent, 915, descent, 759 feet; total rise and fall, 1674 feet; overcome by locks and inclined planes. The latter consist of apparatus for the purpose of conveying the boats from one level of the canal to another. There is a lock at each end of the plane; one at the foot, in which the boat is adjusted for its ascent, and another at the top to elevate it to the level above; when adjusted, the whole is drawn up by means of appropriate machinery, which is also used for regulating the downward passage of the boats. By means of this ingenious contrivance, which supersedes the necessity for water, as in ordinary locks, the boats are conveyed safely and expeditiously, up or down the several ascents and descents of the line. . . . 235 feet are overcome by 24 locks, and 1439 feet by 22 inclined planes, the average inclination of which is about 2 in 21; 4 guard locks; 5 dams; 30 culverts; 12 aqueducts, including one of stone at the Little Falls of Passaic, with a single arch of 80 feet span, and another of wood over the Pompton river, 236 feet in length, supported by nine stone piers; 200 bridges. Cost $3,100,000." – H. S. Tanner: *A Description of the Canals and Rail Roads of the United States* (1840).

[11] [DS] Cadwallader David Colden (1769–1834), lawyer, former mayor of New York, was an active advocate of canal-building; his most noted work in this direction was the memoir that he drew up for the city of New York in 1825 pressing the completion of canals in the state. Colden had discussed the use of inclined planes in his *Life of Robert Fulton* (1817).

energy with which public works are undertaken and carried through. Nothing stops them if a profitable result can be fairly hoped for. It is this which has made cities spring up amidst the forests with such inconceivable rapidity; and could they once be thoroughly persuaded that any point of the ocean had a hoard of dollars beneath it, I have not the slightest doubt that in about eighteen months we should see a snug covered rail-road leading direct to the spot.

*   *   *   *   *   *

I was told at New York, that in many parts of the state it was usual to pay the service of the Presbyterian ministers in the following manner. Once a year a day is fixed on which some member of every family in a congregation meet at their minister's house in the afternoon. They each bring an offering (according to their means) of articles necessary for housekeeping. The poorer members leave their contributions in a large basket, placed for the purpose, close to the door of entrance. Those of more importance, and more calculated to do honour to the piety of the donors, are carried into the room where the company is assembled. Sugar, coffee, tea, cheese, barrels of flour, pieces of Irish linen, sets of china and of glass, were among the articles mentioned to me as usually making parts of these offerings. After the party is assembled, and the business of giving and receiving is dispatched, tea, coffee, and cakes are handed round; but these are not furnished at any expense either of trouble or money to the minister, for selected ladies of the congregation take the whole arrangement upon themselves. These meetings are called spinning visits.

Another New York custom, which does not seem to have so reasonable a cause, is the changing house once a year. On the 1st of May the city of New York has the appearance of sending off a population flying from the plague, or of a town which had surrendered on condition of carrying away all their goods and chattels. Rich furniture and ragged furniture, carts, waggons, and drays, ropes, canvas, and straw, packers, porters, and draymen, white, yellow, and black, occupy the streets from east to west, from north to south, on this day. Every one I spoke to on the subject complained of this custom as most annoying, but all assured me it was unavoidable, if you inhabit a rented house. More than one of my New York friends have built or bought houses solely to avoid this annual inconvenience.

There are a great number of negroes in New York, all free; their emancipation having been completed in 1827. Not even in Philadelphia, where the anti-slavery opinions have been the most active and violent, do the blacks appear to wear an air of so much consequence as they do at New York. They have several chapels, in which negro ministers officiate; and a theatre in which none but negroes perform.[12] At this theatre a gallery is appropriated to such whites as choose to visit it; and here only are they permitted to sit; following in this, with nice etiquette, and equal justice, the arrangement of the white theatres, in all of which is a gallery appropriated solely to the use of the blacks. I have often, particularly on a Sunday, met groups of negroes, elegantly dressed; and have been sometimes amused by observing the very superior air of gallantry assumed by the men, when in attendance on their *belles*, to that of the whites in similar circumstances. On one occasion we met in Broadway a young negress in the extreme of the fashion, and accompanied by a black beau, whose toilet was equally studied; eye-glass, guard-chain, nothing was omitted; he walked beside his sable goddess uncovered, and with an air of the most tender devotion. At the window of a handsome house which they were passing, stood

---

[12] [DS] The African Company at the African Grove, corner of Bleecker and Mercer Streets, acted classic plays and comic interludes as early as 1821. See James Weldon Johnson: *Black Manhattan* (1930).

a very pretty white girl, with two gentlemen beside her; but alas! both of them had their hats on, and one was smoking!

If it were not for the peculiar manner of walking, which distinguishes all American women, Broadway might be taken for a French street, where it was the fashion for very smart ladies to promenade. The dress is entirely French; not an article (except perhaps the cotton stockings) must be English, on pain of being stigmatized as out of the fashion. Every thing English is decidedly *mauvais ton;* English materials, English fashions, English accent, English manner, are all terms of reproach; and to say that an unfortunate looks like an English woman, is the cruellest satire which can be uttered.

I remember visiting France almost immediately after we had made the most offensive invasion of her territory that can well be imagined, yet, despite the feelings which lengthened years of war must have engendered, it was the fashion to admire every thing English. I suppose family quarrels are more difficult to adjust; for fifteen years of peace have not been enough to calm the angry feelings of brother Jonathan towards the land of his fathers,

"The which he hateth passing well."

It is hardly needful to say that the most courteous amenity of manner distinguishes the reception given to foreigners by the patrician class of Americans.

Gentlemen, in the old world sense of the term, are the same every where; and an American gentleman and his family know how to do the honours of their country to strangers of every nation, as well as any people on earth. But this class, though it decidedly exists, is a very small one, and cannot, in justice, be represented as affording a specimen of the whole.

*   *   *   *   *   *

Most of the houses in New York are painted on the outside, but in a manner carefully to avoid disfiguring the material which it preserves: on the contrary, nothing can be neater. They are now using a great deal of beautiful stone called Jersey freestone; it is of a warm rich brown, and extremely ornamental to the city wherever it has been employed. They have also a grey granite of great beauty. The trottoir paving in most of the streets is extremely good, being of large flag stones, very superior to the bricks of Philadelphia.

At night the shops, which are open till very late, are brilliantly illuminated with gas, and all the population seem as much alive as in London or Paris. This makes the solemn stillness of the evening hours in Philadelphia still more remarkable.

There are a few trees in different parts of the city, and I observed many young ones planted, and guarded with much care; were they more abundant it would be extremely agreeable, for the reflected light of their fierce summer sheds intolerable day.

Ice is in profuse abundance; I do not imagine that there is a house in the city without the luxury of a piece of ice to cool the water, and harden the butter.

The hackney coaches are the best in the world,[13] but abominably dear, and it is necessary to be on the *qui vive* in making your bargain with the driver; if you do not, he has the power of charging immoderately. On my first experiment I neglected this, and was asked two dollars and a half for an excursion of twenty minutes. When I referred to the waiter of the hotel, he asked if I had made a bargain. "No." "Then I expect" (with the usual look of triumph) "that the Yankee has been too smart for you."

The private carriages of New York are infinitely handsomer and better appointed than any I saw elsewhere; the want of smart liveries destroys much of the gay effect, but,

---

13 [T5, note] Excepting those of Vienna.

on the whole, a New York summer equipage, with the pretty women and beautiful children it contains, look extremely well in Broadway, and would not be much amiss any where.

The luxury of the New York aristocracy is not confined to the city; hardly an acre of Manhatten Island but shews some pretty villa or stately mansion. The most chosen of these are on the north and east rivers, to whose margins their lawns descend. Among these, perhaps, the loveliest is one situated in the beautiful village of Bloomingdale; here, within the space of sixteen acres, almost every variety of garden scenery may be found. To describe all its diversity of hill and dale, of wood and lawn, of rock and river, would be in vain; nor can I convey an idea of it by comparison, for I never saw any thing like it. How far the elegant hospitality which reigns there may influence my impressions, I know not; but, assuredly, no spot I have ever seen dwells more freshly on my memory, nor did I ever find myself in a circle more calculated to give delight in meeting, and regret at parting, than that of Woodlawn.[14]

---

[14] [DS] The estate of Woodlawn at Bloomingdale belonged to William and Sarah Heywood. It stood between Eleventh Avenue (West End Avenue) and the Hudson River, on land that is now part of the block between 106th and 107th Streets.

CHAPTER XXXI

Reception of Captain Basil Hall's Book in the United States

HAVING now arrived nearly at the end of our travels, I am induced, ere I conclude, again to mention what I consider as one of the most remarkable traits in the national character of the Americans; namely, their exquisite sensitiveness and soreness respecting every thing said or written concerning them. Of this, perhaps, the most remarkable example I can give, is the effect produced on nearly every class of readers by the appearance of Captain Basil Hall's "Travels in North America." In fact, it was a sort of moral earthquake, and the vibration it occasioned through the nerves of the Republic, from one corner of the Union to the other, was by no means over when I left the country in July, 1831, a couple of years after the shock.

I was in Cincinnati when these volumes came out, but it was not till July, 1830, that I procured a copy of them. One bookseller to whom I applied, told me that he had had a few copies before he understood the nature of the work, but that after becoming acquainted with it, nothing should induce him to sell another. Other persons of his profession must, however, have been less scrupulous, for the book was read in city, town, village, and hamlet, steam-boat, and stage-coach, and a sort of war-whoop was sent forth perfectly unprecedented in my recollection upon any occasion whatever.

It was fortunate for me that I did not procure these volumes till I had heard them very generally spoken of, for the curiosity I felt to know the contents of a work so violently anathematised, led me to make enquiries which elicited a great deal of curious feeling.

An ardent desire for approbation, and a delicate sensitiveness under censure, have always, I believe, been considered as amiable traits of character; but the condition into which the appearance of Capt. Hall's work threw the Republic, shews plainly that these feelings, if carried to excess, produce a weakness which amounts to imbecility.

It was perfectly astonishing to hear men, who, on other subjects, were of some judgement, utter their opinions upon this. I never heard of any instance in which the common sense generally found in national criticism, was so overthrown by passion. I do not speak of the want of justice, and of fair and liberal interpretation: these, perhaps, were hardly to be expected. Other nations have been called thin-skinned, but the citizens of the Union have, apparently, no skins at all; they wince if a breeze blows over them, unless it be tempered with adulation. It was not, therefore, very surprising that the acute and forcible observations of a traveller they knew would be listened to, should be received testily. The extraordinary features of the business were, first, the excess of the rage into which they lashed themselves; and, secondly, the puerility of the inventions by which they attempted to account for the severity with which they fancied they had been treated.

Not content with declaring that the volumes contained no word of truth from beginning to end, (which is an assertion I heard made very nearly as often as they were mentioned,) the whole country set to work to discover the causes why Capt. Hall had visited the United States, and why he had published his book.

I have heard it said with as much precision and gravity as if the statement had been conveyed by an official report, that Capt. Hall had been sent out by the British government expressly for the purpose of checking the growing admiration of England for the government of the United States, — that it was by a commission from the Treasury he had come, and

that it was only in obedience to orders that he had found any
thing to object to.

I do not give this as the gossip of a coterie; I am persuaded
that it is the belief of a very considerable portion of the country. So deep is the conviction of this singular people that they
cannot be seen without being admired, that they will not
admit the possibility that any one should honestly and sincerely find aught to disapprove in them, or their country.

At Philadelphia I met with a little anonymous book,[1]
written to shew that Capt. Basil Hall was in no way to be depended on, for that he not only slandered the Americans,
but was himself, in other respects, a person of very equivocal
morals. One proof of this is given by a quotation of the following playful account of the distress occasioned by the
want of a bell. The commentator calls it an instance of
"shocking coarseness."

"One day I was rather late for breakfast, and as there was
no water in my jug, I sent off, post haste, half shaved, half
dressed, and more than half vexed, in quest of water, like a
seaman on short allowance, hunting for rivulets on some unknown coast. I went up stairs, and down stairs, and in the
course of my researches into half a dozen different apartments, might have stumbled on some lady's chamber, as the
song says, which considering the plight I was in, would have
been awkward enough."

Another indication of this moral coarseness is pointed out
in the passage where Capt. Hall says, he never saw a flirta-
tion all the time he was in the Union.

The charge of ingratitude also was echoed from mouth to
mouth. That he should himself bear testimony to the unvarying kindness of the reception he met with, and yet find
fault with the country, was declared on all hands to be a

---

[1] [DS] *Captain Hall in America, by an American.* It was published in
Philadelphia in 1830 and reprinted the same year in London under the title
A Review of Captain Basil Hall's Travels in North America. The anonymous
author was Richard Biddle, a Philadelphia lawyer.

proof of the most abominable ingratitude that it ever entered into the heart of man to conceive. I once ventured before about a dozen people to ask whether more blame would not attach to an author, if he suffered himself to be bribed by individual kindness to falsify facts, than if, despite all personal considerations, he stated them truly?

"Facts!" cried the whole circle at once, "facts! I tell you there is not a word of fact in it from beginning to end."

The American Reviews are, many of them, I believe, well known in England; I need not, therefore, quote them here, but I sometimes wondered that they, none of them, ever thought of translating Obadiah's curse into classic American; if they had done so, only placing (he, Basil Hall,) between brackets, instead of (he, Obadiah,) it would have saved them a world of trouble.

I can hardly describe the curiosity with which I sat down at length to peruse these tremendous volumes; still less can I do justice to my surprise at their contents. To say that I found not one exaggerated statement throughout the work, is by no means saying enough. It is impossible for any one who knows the country not to see that Captain Hall earnestly sought out things to admire and commend. When he praises, it is with evident pleasure, and when he finds fault, it is with evident reluctance and restraint, excepting where motives purely patriotic urge him to state roundly what it is for the benefit of his country should be known.

In fact, Captain Hall saw the country to the greatest possible advantage. Furnished, of course, with letters of introduction to the most distinguished individuals, and with the still more influential recommendation of his own reputation, he was received in full drawing-room style and state from one end of the Union to the other. He saw the country in full dress, and had little or no opportunity of judging of it un-houselled, unanointed, unannealed, with all its imperfections on its head, as I and my family too often had.

Captain Hall had certainly excellent opportunities of making himself acquainted with the form of the government and the laws; and of receiving, moreover, the best oral commentary upon them, in conversation with the most distinguished citizens. Of these opportunities he made excellent use; nothing important met his eye which did not receive that sort of analytical attention which an experienced and philosophical traveller alone can give. This has made his volumes highly interesting and valuable; but I am deeply persuaded, that were a man of equal penetration to visit the United States with no other means of becoming acquainted with the national character than the ordinary working-day intercourse of life, he would conceive an infinitely lower idea of the moral atmosphere of the country than Captain Hall appears to have done; and the internal conviction on my mind is strong, that if Captain Hall had not placed a firm restraint on himself, he must have given expression to far deeper indignation than any he has uttered against many points in the American character, with which he shews, from other circumstances, that he was well acquainted. His rule appears to have been to state just so much of the truth as would leave on the minds of his readers a correct impression, at the least cost of pain to the sensitive folks he was writing about. He states his own opinions and feelings, and leaves it to be inferred that he has good grounds for adopting them; but he spares the Americans the bitterness which a detail of the circumstances would have produced.

If any one chooses to say that some wicked antipathy to twelve millions of strangers is the origin of my opinion, I must bear it; and were the question one of mere idle speculation, I certainly would not court the abuse I must meet for stating it. But it is not so. I know that among the best, the most pious, the most benevolent of my countrymen, there are hundreds, nay, I fear thousands, who conscientiously believe

that a greater degree of political and religious liberty (such
as is possessed in America) would be beneficial for us. How
often have I wished, during my abode in the United States,
that one of these conscientious, but mistaken reasoners, fully
possessed of his country's confidence, could pass a few years
in the United States, sufficiently among the mass of the citizens to know them, and sufficiently at leisure to trace effects
to their causes. Then might we look for a statement which
would teach these mistaken philanthropists to tremble at
every symptom of democratic power among us; a statement
which would make even our sectarians shudder at the
thought of hewing down the Established Church, for they
would be taught, by fearful example, to know that it was the
bulwark which protects us from the gloomy horrors of fanatic
superstition on one side, and the still more dreadful inroads
of infidelity on the other. And more than all, such a man
would see as clear as light, that where every class is occupied
in getting money, and no class in spending it, there will neither be leisure for worshipping the theory of honesty, nor
motive strong enough to put its restrictive doctrines in practice. Where every man is engaged in driving hard bargains
with his fellows, where is the honoured class to be found into
which gentlemanlike feelings, principles, and practice, are
necessary as an introduction?

That there are men of powerful intellect, benevolent
hearts, and high moral feeling in America, I know; and I
could, if challenged to do so, name individuals surpassed by
none of any country in these qualities; but they are excellent,
despite their institutions, not in consequence of them. It is
not by such that Captain Hall's statements are called slanders,
nor is it from such that I shall meet the abuse which I well
know these pages will inevitably draw upon me; [2] and I only

---

[2] [DS] Mrs. Trollope's prophetic soul did not allow her to foresee one
ironical turn that such abuse would take. A story widely circulated had it
that *Domestic Manners* was the creation of Captain Hall masquerading in
petticoats. The story was apparently first told and started on its rounds in

trust I may be able to muster as much self-denial as my prede-
cessor, who asserts in his recently published "Fragments," [3]

---

the one-volume American edition of *Domestic Manners* published in New
York in June 1832. This edition is prefaced by "A Brief Inquiry into the
Real Name and Character of the Author of this Book, by the American
Editor." The "American Editor" develops the "hum" at great length, but
the following quotations give an idea of his tone and thesis:

"I have ascertained beyond all reasonable doubt, that the real author is
no less a person than Captain Basil Hall, or *All,* as he is called in the literary
circles of London, where he moves with such distinction. Should the reader
start at this bold annunciation, I only ask his serious attention to the proofs
I shall presently adduçe. . . .

"In the first place, gentle reader, I shall point thy attention to the positive unqualified assertion of the pretended Mrs. Trollope . . . that she
'Happens to know' that neither Captain Hall or Mrs. Hall ever entered the
ladies' cabin of the steamboat during the whole voyage.' . . . Now I would
ask how the pretended Mrs. Trollope could 'happen' to know all this?

"Secondly, the account given by the pretended Mrs. Trollope of the sensation created in the United States by the publication of the captain's logbook, furnishes another crying proof of the identity of these two persons. If
we believe the story, it was felt like the shock of an earthquake from one
extremity of the United States to the other; the earth trembled, the graves
gave up their dead, the mountains groaned, the caves *yawned* — which was
very natural, — the rivers murmured, the men swore, the women scolded,
the children cried, the calves bleated, the hens cackled, the dogs barked,
and the very dumb-fish essayed to express their indignation. . . . I would
ask, could any human being except an author whose brain had been eaten
up with self-conceit, and who mistook contemptuous indignation for fame,
have so lauded and pampered his own little logbook? . . .

"Thirdly, the various quotations introduced by the pretended Mrs. Trollope furnish additional evidence of identity in this case, by showing an intimacy with the logbook, which I verily believe has not fallen to the lot of
any human being but the captain himself. I challenge the world to produce
an instance of the captain's logbook having ever been quoted by any respectable writer, except with a view of reproving his vanity, correcting his
presumption, or establishing his ignorance. . . .

"When I listen to the garrulous foppery of the captain, I feel irresistibly
inclined to pronounce him to be Mrs. Trollope, or some such ugly old
woman in the disguise of a man; but when I ponder over the coarse delineations, the indelicate allusions, and bug and spitting stories of Mrs. Trollope,
I am as irresistibly drawn to the conviction that it is some conceited ignorant
Jack tar, breaking his forecastle jests, with a quid of tobacco in his mouth,
and his canvass hat knowingly adjusted on one side of his head. . . ."

[3] [DS] *Fragments of Voyages and Travels: Chiefly for the Use of Young
Persons,* First Series (1831). The book was primarily intended for young
men who contemplated entering upon a maritime career, but Hall admitted
in his preface that they might find some of his pages difficult and asked

XXIII INCLINED PLANE ON THE MORRIS CANAL

XXIV BLACK AND WHITE BEAUX

that he has read none of the American criticisms on his book. He did wisely, if he wished to retain an atom of his kindly feeling toward America, and he has, assuredly, lost but little on the score of information, for these criticisms, generally speaking, consist of mere downright personal abuse, or querulous complaints of his ingratitude and ill usage of them; complaints which it is quite astonishing that any persons of spirit could indulge in.

The following good-humoured paragraphs from the Fragments, must, I think, rather puzzle the Americans. Possibly they may think that Captain Hall is quizzing them, when he says he has read none of their criticisms; but I think there is in these passages internal evidence that he has not seen them. For if he had read one-fiftieth part of the vituperation of his Travels, which it has been my misfortune to peruse, he could hardly have brought himself to write what follows.

If the Americans still refuse to shake the hand proffered to them in the true old John Bull spirit, they are worse folks than even I take them for.

Captain Hall, after describing the hospitable reception he formerly met with, at a boarding-house in New York, goes on thus: — "If our hostess be still alive, I hope she will not repent of having bestowed her obliging attentions on one, who so many years afterwards made himself, he fears, less popular in her land, than he could wish to be amongst a people to whom he owes so much, and for whom he really feels so much kindness. He still anxiously hopes, however, they will believe him, when he declares, that, having said in his recent publication no more than what he conceived was due to strict truth, and to the integrity of history, as far as his observations and opinions went, he still feels, as he always has, and ever must continue to feel towards America, the heartiest good-will.

---

them to "conclude that those parts of the book may be intended for people a little further advanced."

"The Americans are perpetually repeating that the foundation-stone of their liberty is fixed on the doctrine, that every man is free to form his own opinions, and to promulgate them in candour, and in moderation. Is it meant that a foreigner is excluded from these privileges? If not, may I ask, in what respect have I passed these limitations? The Americans have surely no fair right to be offended because my views differ from their's; and yet I am told I have been rudely handled by the press of that country. If my motives are distrusted, I can only say, I am sorely belied. If I am mistaken, regret at my political blindness were surely more dignified than anger on the part of those with whom I differ; and if it shall chance that I am in the right, the best confirmation of the correctness of my views, in the opinion of indifferent persons, will perhaps be found in the soreness of those, who wince when the truth is spoken.

"Yet, after all, few things would give me more real pleasure, than to know that my friends across the water would consent to take me at my word; and, considering what I have said about them as so much public matter, which it truly is, agree to reckon me, in my absence, as they always did, when I was amongst them, and, I am sure, they would count me, if I went back again, as a private friend. I differed with them in politics, and I differ with them now as much as ever; but I sincerely wish them happiness individually; and, as a nation, I shall rejoice if they prosper. As the Persians write, 'What can I say more?' And I only hope these few words may help to make my peace with people who justly pride themselves on bearing no malice. As for myself, I have no peace to make; for I have studiously avoided reading any of the American criticisms on my book, in order that the kindly feelings I have ever entertained towards that country should not be ruffled. By this abstinence I may have lost some information, and perhaps missed many opportunities of correcting erroneous impressions. But I set so much store by the pleasing recollection of the journey itself, and of the hospitality with which my family were every where received, that whether it be right, or whether it be wrong, I cannot bring myself to read any thing which might disturb these agreeable associations. So let us part in peace! or, rather let us meet again in cordial communication; and if this little work shall find its way across the Atlantic, I hope it will be read there without reference to any thing that has passed between us; or, at all events, with reference only to those parts of our former intercourse, which are satisfactory to all parties." — *Hall's Fragments*, Vol. I. p. 200.

I really think it is impossible to read, not only this passage, but many others in these delightful little volumes, without feeling that their author is as little likely to deserve the imputation of harshness and ill-will, as any man that ever lived.

In reading Capt. Hall's volumes on America, the observation which, I think, struck me the most forcibly, and which certainly came the most completely home to my own feelings, was the following.

"In all my travels both amongst Heathens, and amongst Christians, I have never encountered any people by whom I found it nearly so difficult to make myself understood as by the Americans."

I have conversed in London and in Paris with foreigners of many nations, and often through the misty medium of an idiom imperfectly understood, but I remember no instance in which I found the same difficulty in conveying my sentiments, my impressions, and my opinions to those around me, as I did in America. Whatever faith may be given to my assertion, no one who has not visited the country can possibly conceive to what extent it is true. It is less necessary, I imagine, for the mutual understanding of persons conversing together, that the language should be the same, than that their ordinary mode of thinking, and habits of life should, in some degree, assimilate; whereas, in point of fact, there is hardly a single point of sympathy between the Americans and us; but whatever the cause, the fact is certainly as I have stated it, and herein, I think, rests the only apology for the preposterous and undignified anger felt and expressed against Capt. Hall's work. They really cannot, even if they wished it, enter into any of his views, or comprehend his most ordinary feelings; and, therefore, they cannot believe in the sincerity of the impressions he describes. The candour which he expresses, and evidently feels, they mistake for irony, or totally distrust; his unwillingness to give pain to persons from whom he has received kindness, they scornfully reject as affectation, and although they must know right well, in their own secret hearts, how infinitely more they lay at his mercy than he has chosen to betray; they pretend, even to themselves, that he has exaggerated the bad points of their character and institutions; whereas, the truth is, that he has let them off with a degree of tenderness which may be quite suitable for him to exercise, however little merited; while, at the same time, he has most industriously magnified their merits, whenever he could possibly find any thing favourable. One can perfectly well understand why Capt. Hall's avowed Tory principles should be disapproved, if in the United States, especially as (with a questionable policy in a bookselling point of view, in these reforming times) he volunteers a profession of political faith, in which, to use the Kentucky phrase, "he goes the whole hog," and bluntly avows, in his concluding chapter, that he not only holds stoutly to Church and State, but that he conceives the English House of Commons to be, if not quite perfect, at least as much so for all the required purposes of representation as it can by possibility be made in practice. Such a downright thorough-going Tory and Anti-reformer, pretending to judge of the workings of the American democratical system, was naturally held to be a monstrous abomination, and it has been visited accordingly, both in America, and as I understand, with us also. The experience

which Capt. Hall has acquired in visits to every part of the
world, during twenty or thirty years, goes for nothing with
the Radicals on either side the Atlantic: on the contrary, precisely in proportion to the value of that authority which is
the result of actual observation, are they irritated to find its
weight cast into the opposite scale. Had not Capt. Hall been
converted by what he saw in North America, from the Whig
faith he exhibited in his description of South America, his
book would have been far more popular in England during
the last two years of public excitement; [4] it may, perhaps, be
long before any justice is done to Capt. Hall's book in the
United States, but a less time will probably suffice to establish
its claim to attention at home.

---

[4] [DS] Mrs. Trollope refers to the great movement for the reform of
Parliament along more democratic lines; it was attended by much public excitement, rioting, and even secret military drill. The Reform Bill was to become law less than three months after the publication of *Domestic Manners*.
Whether Captain Hall's *Travels* or Mrs. Trollope's book would have been
more popular if the author had praised life in a democracy is a debatable
point. There was a powerful and highly literate Tory opposition. Moreover,
the Whigs, like the Americans, often read books that did not agree with
their views.

CHAPTER XXXII

Journey to Niagara — Hudson — West Point — Hyde Park —
Albany — Yankees — Trenton Falls — Rochester — Genesee Falls
— Lockport

HOW quickly weeks glide away in such a city as New York, especially when you reckon among your friends some of the most agreeable people in either hemisphere. But we had still a long journey before us, and one of the wonders of the world was to be seen.

On the 30th of May we set off for Niagara. I had heard so much of the surpassing beauty of the North River, that I expected to be disappointed, and to find reality flat after description. But it is not in the power of man to paint with a strength exceeding that of nature, in such scenes as the Hudson presents. Every mile shews some new and startling effect of the combination of rocks, trees, and water; there is no interval of flat or insipid scenery, from the moment you enter upon the river at New York, to that of quitting it at Albany, a distance of 180 miles.

For the first twenty miles, the shore of New Jersey on the left, offers almost a continued wall of trap rock, which from its perpendicular form, and lineal fissures, is called the Palisades. This wall sometimes rises to the height of a hundred and fifty feet, and sometimes sinks down to twenty. Here and there, a watercourse breaks its uniformity; and every where the brightest foliage, in all the splendour of the climate and the season, fringed and checquered the dark barrier. On the opposite shore, Manhattan Island, with its leafy coronet gemmed with villas, forms a lovely contrast to these rocky heights.

After passing Manhatten Island the eastern shore gradually assumes a wild and rocky character, but ever varying;
woods, lawns, pastures, and towering cliffs all meet the eye
in quick succession, as the giant steam-boat cleaves its swift
passage up the stream.

For several miles the voyage is one of great interest independent of its beauty, for it passes many points where important events of the revolutionary war took place.

It was not without a pang that I looked on the spot where
poor Andre was taken, and another where he was executed.[1]

Several forts, generally placed in most commanding situations, still shew by their battered ruins, where the struggle
was strongest, and I felt no lack of that moral interest so
entirely wanting in the new States, and without which no
journey can, I think, continue long without wearying the
spirits.

About forty miles from New York you enter upon the High-
lands, as a series of mountains which then flank the river on
both sides, are called. The beauty of this scenery can only be
conceived when it is seen. One might fancy that these capricious masses, with all their countless varieties of light and
shade, were thrown together to shew how passing lovely
rocks, and woods, and water could be. Sometimes a lofty
peak shoots suddenly up into the heavens, shewing in bold

---

[1] [DS] Major John Lewis André of the British Army in September 1780
came by the English ship *Vulcan* to a spot on the Hudson just south of West
Point to complete negotiations with Benedict Arnold for the betrayal of
West Point to the British. American artillery fire compelled the *Vulcan* to
fall downstream, and, having lost his means of transport, André was persuaded to attempt carrying back the treasonable papers overland in disguise. He was captured at Tarrytown by three American irregulars and
turned over to the American Army. André argued that he had gone to consult with Arnold under a flag of truce, but an American court martial decided that his changing into disguise and the nature of his mission with
Arnold made him a spy. There were official British protests, and André's
youth (he was twenty-nine) and his engaging personality aroused much
popular sympathy for him. Washington refused to intercede on his behalf,
and he was hanged on October 2, 1780, at Tappan.

relief against the sky; and then a deep ravine sinks in solemn shadow, and draws the imagination into its leafy recesses. For several miles the river appears to form a succession of lakes; you are often enclosed on all sides by rocks rising directly from the very edge of the stream, and then you turn a point, the river widens, and again woods, lawns, and villages are reflected on its bosom.

The state prison of Sing Sing is upon the edge of the water, and has no picturesque effect to atone for the painful images it suggests; the "Sleepy Hollow" of Washington Irving, just above it, restores the imagination to a better tone.

West Point, the military academy of the United States, is fifty miles from New York. The scenery around it is magnificent, and though the buildings of the establishment are constructed with the handsome and unpicturesque regularity which marks the work of governments, they are so nobly placed, and so embosomed in woods, that they look beautiful. The lengthened notes of a French horn, which I presume was attending some of their military manœuvres, sounded with deep and solemn sweetness as we passed.

About thirty miles further is Hyde Park, the magnificent seat of Dr. Hosack; here the misty summit of the distant Kaatskill begins to form the outline of the landscape; it is hardly possible to imagine any thing more beautiful than this place. We passed a day there with great enjoyment; and the following morning set forward again in one of those grand floating hotels called steam-boats. Either on this day, or the one before, we had two hundred cabin passengers on board, and they all sat down together to a table spread abundantly, and with considerable elegance. A continual succession of gentlemen's seats, many of them extremely handsome, borders the river to Albany. We arrived there late in the evening, but had no difficulty in finding excellent accommodation.

Albany is the state capital of New York, and has some very

handsome public buildings; there are also some curious relics of the old Dutch inhabitants.

The first sixteen miles from Albany we travelled in a stage, to avoid a multitude of locks at the entrance of the Erie canal; but at Scenectedy we got on board one of the canal packet-boats for Utica.

With a very delightful party, of one's own choosing, fine temperate weather, and a strong breeze to chase the mosquitos, this mode of travelling might be very agreeable, but I can hardly imagine any motive of convenience powerful enough to induce me again to imprison myself in a canal boat under ordinary circumstances. The accommodations being greatly restricted, every body, from the moment of entering the boat, acts upon a system of unshrinking egotism. The library of a dozen books, the backgammon board, the tiny berths, the shady side of the cabin, are all jostled for in a manner to make one greatly envy the power of the snail; at the moment I would willingly have given up some of my human dignity for the privilege of creeping into a shell of my own. To any one who has been accustomed in travelling, to be addressed with, "Do sit here, you will find it more comfortable," the "You must go there, I made for this place first," sounds very unmusical.

There is a great quietness about the women of America, (I speak of the exterior manner of persons casually met,) but somehow or other, I should never call it gentleness. In such trying moments as that of *fixing* themselves on board a packet-boat, the men are prompt, determined, and will compromise any body's convenience, except their own. The women are doggedly stedfast in their will, and till matters are settled, look like hedgehogs, with every quill raised, and firmly set, as if to forbid the approach of any one who might wish to rub them down. In circumstances where an English woman would look proud, and a French woman *nonchalante,* an American lady looks grim; even the youngest and the prettiest can set their lips, and knit their brows, and look as hard, and unsocial as their grandmothers.

Though not in the Yankee or New England country, we were bordering upon it sufficiently to meet in the stages and boats many delightful specimens of this most peculiar race. I like them extremely well, but I would not wish to have any business transactions with them, if I could avoid it, lest, to use their own phrase, "they should be too smart for me."

It is by no means rare to meet elsewhere, in this working-day world of our's, people who push acuteness to the verge of honesty, and sometimes, perhaps, a little bit beyond; but, I believe, the Yankee is the only one who will be found to boast of doing so. It is by no means easy to give a clear and just idea of a Yankee; if you hear his character from a Virginian, you will believe him a devil; if you listen to it from himself, you might fancy him a god — though a tricky one; Mercury turned righteous and notable. Matthews did very well, as far as "I expect," "I calculate," and "I guess;"[2] but this is only the shell; there is an immense deal within, both of sweet and bitter. In acuteness, cautiousness, industry, and perseverance, he resembles the Scotch; in habits of frugal neatness, he resembles the Dutch; in love of lucre he doth greatly resemble the sons of Abraham; but in frank admission, and superlative admiration of all his own peculiarities, he is like nothing on earth but himself.

The Quakers have been celebrated for the pertinacity with which they avoid giving a direct answer, but what Quaker could ever vie with a Yankee in this sort of fencing? Nothing, in fact, can equal their skill in evading a question, excepting that with which they set about asking one. I am afraid that in repeating a conversation which I overheard on board the Erie canal boat, I shall spoil it, by forgetting some of the

---

[2] [DS] Charles Mathews (1776–1835) was a celebrated English comedian, who had a special gift of mimicry; it enabled him to play national and regional types with what most theater-goers and critics considered a remarkable and exquisite realism.

little delicate doublings which delighted me — yet I wrote it
down immediately. Both parties were Yankees, but strangers
to each other; one of them having, by gentle degrees, made
himself pretty well acquainted with the point from which
every one on board had started, and that for which he was
bound, at last attacked his brother Reynard thus: —

"Well, now, which way may you be traveling?"

"I expect this canal runs pretty nearly west."

"Are you going far with it?"

"Well, now, I don't rightly know how many miles it may
be."

"I expect you'll be from New York?"

"Sure enough I have been at New York, often and often."

"I calculate, then, 'tis not there as you stop?"

"Business must be minded, in stopping and in stirring."

"You may say that. Well, I look then you'll be making for
the Springs?"

"Folks say as all the world is making for the Springs, and
I expect a good sight of them is."

"Do you calculate upon stopping long when you get to
your journey's end?"

" 'Tis my business must settle that, I expect."

"I guess that's true, too; but you'll be for making pleasure a
business for once, I calculate?"

"My business don't often lie in that line."

"Then, may be, it is not the Springs as takes you this line?"

"The Springs is a right elegant place, I reckon."

"It is your health, I calculate, as makes you break your
good rules?"

"My health don't trouble me much, I guess."

"No? Why that's well. How is the markets, sir? Are bread
stuffs up?"

"I a'nt just capable to say."

"A deal of money's made by just looking after the article at
the fountain's head."

"You may say that."

"Do you look to be making great dealings in produce up the country?"

"Why that, I expect, is difficult to know."

"I calculate you'll find the markets changeable these times?"

"No markets ben't very often without changing."

"Why, that's right down true. What may be your biggest article of produce?"

"I calculate, generally, that's the biggest, as I makes most by."

"You may say that. But what do you chiefly call your most particular branch?"

"Why, that's what I can't justly say."

And so they went on, without advancing or giving an inch, 'till I was weary of listening; but I left them still at it, when I stepped out to resume my station on a trunk at the bow of the boat, where I scribbled in my note-book, this specimen of Yankee conversation.

*   *   *   *   *   *

The Erie canal has cut through much solid rock, and we often passed between magnificent cliffs. The little falls of the Mohawk form a lovely scene; the rocks over which the river runs are most fantastic in form. The fall continues nearly a mile, and a beautiful village, called the Little Falls, overhangs it. As many locks occur at this point, we quitted the boat, that we might the better enjoy the scenery, which is of the wildest description. Several other passengers did so likewise, and I was much amused by one of our Yankees, who very civilly accompanied our party, pointing out to me the wild state of the country, and apologizing for it, by saying, that the property all round thereabouts had been owned by an Englishman; "and you'll excuse me, ma'am, but when the English gets a spot of wild ground like this here, they have no notions about it like us; but the Englishman have sold it, and if you was to see it five years hence, you would not know it again; I'll engage there will be by that, half a score elegant factories — 'tis a true shame to let such a privilege of water lie idle."

We reached Utica at twelve o'clock the following day, pretty well fagged by the sun by day, and a crowded cabin by night; lemon-juice and iced-water (without sugar) kept us alive. But for this delightful recipe, feather fans, and eau de Cologne, I think we should have failed altogether; the thermometer stood at 90°.

At two, we set off in a very pleasant airy carriage for Trenton Falls, a delightful drive of fourteen miles. These falls have become within the last few years only second in fame to Niagara. The West Canada Creek, which in the map shews but as a paltry stream, has found its way through three miles of rock, which, at many points, is 150 feet high. A forest of enormous cedars is on their summit; and many of that beautiful species of white cedar which droops its branches like the weeping-willow, grow in the clefts of the rock, and in some places almost dip their dark foliage in the torrent. The rock is of a dark grey limestone, and often presents a wall of unbroken surface. Near the hotel a flight of very alarming steps leads down to the bed of the stream, and on reaching it you find yourself enclosed in a deep abyss of solid rock, with no visible opening but that above your head. The torrent dashes by with inconceivable rapidity; its colour is black as night, and the dark ledge of rock on which you stand, is so treacherously level with it, that nothing warns you of danger. Within the last three years two young people, though surrounded by their friends, have stepped an inch too far, and disappeared from among them, as if by magic, never to revisit earth again. This broad flat ledge reaches but a short distance, and then the perpendicular wall appears to stop your farther progress; but there is a spirit of defiance in the mind of man; he will not be stayed either by rocks or waves. By the aid of gunpowder a sufficient quantity of the rock has been removed to afford a fearful footing round a point, which, when doubled, discloses a world of cataracts, all leaping forward together in most magnificent confusion. I suffered considerably before I reached the spot where this grand scene is visible; a chain firmly fastened to the rock serves to hang by, as you creep along the giddy verge, and this enabled me to proceed so far; but here the chain failed, and my courage with it, though the rest of the party continued for some way farther, and reported largely of still increasing sublimity. But my knees tottered, and my head swam, so while the rest crept onward, I sat down to wait their return on the floor of rock which had received us on quitting the steps.

A hundred and fifty feet of bare black rock on one side, an equal height covered with solemn cedars on the other, an unfathomed torrent roaring between them, the fresh remembrance of the ghastly legend belonging to the spot, and the idea of my children clinging to the dizzy path I had left, was altogether sombre enough; but I had not sat long before a tremendous burst of thunder shook the air; the deep chasm answered from either side, again, again, and again; I thought the rock I sat upon trembled: but the whole effect was so exceedingly grand, that I had no longer leisure to think of fear; my children immediately returned, and we enjoyed together the darkening shadows cast over the abyss, the rival clamour of the torrent and the storm, and that delightful exaltation of the spirits which sets danger at defiance. A few heavy rain drops alarmed us more than all the terrors of the spot, or rather, they recalled our senses, and we retreated by the fearful steps, reaching our hotel unwetted and unharmed. The next morning we were again early a-foot; the last night's storm had refreshed the air, and renewed our strength. We now took a different route, and instead of descending, as before, walked through the dark forest along the cliff, sufficiently near its edge to catch fearful glimpses of the scene below. After some time the path began to descend, and at length brought us to the Shantee, commemorated in Miss Sedgwick's Clarence.[3] This is by far the finest point of the falls. There is a little balcony in front of the Shantee, literally hanging over the tremendous whirlpool; though frail, it makes one fancy oneself in safety, and reminded me of the feeling with which I have stood on one side a high gate, watching a roaring bull on the other. The walls of this Shantee are literally covered with autographs, and I was inclined to join the laugh against the egotistical trifling, when one of the party discovered "Trollope, England," amidst the innumerable scrawls.[4] The well known characters were hailed with such delight, that I think I shall never again laugh at any one for leaving their name where it is possible a friend may find it.

We returned to Utica to dinner, and found that we must

---

[3] [DS] Catharine Maria Sedgwick (1789–1867) was probably the most widely read authoress in America and had a large following in Europe. Trenton Falls plays a noteworthy part in the action of *Clarence: or, a Tale of Our Own Times* (1830). Gertrude goes to view the falls by moonlight and there encounters a stranger with whom she discusses the relative beauties of Niagara and Trenton Falls. She proceeds to the summit of the lower falls, where she finds the feverish Louis Seton carrying a flute and enveloped in white garb, talking about glimpsing heaven amid these natural surroundings. She lures him away to do a moonlight picture of the falls upon a handkerchief, but he refuses because such scenes are the despair of the painter. At length Seton slips from a rock to the stream below. He is rescued by the stranger. Later Mr. Clarence agrees to meet the ladies at the shantee on the brink of the cliff above the whirlpool. From there he sees the great peril of Emilie, who dislodges some stones and drops, clutching at cedar limbs. She stops her descent by catching some fibrous twigs near a cleft in which she can place her feet. Pedrillo tries to save her, but sprains his ankle and crawls back to the shantee platform. Marion, another young man who has fallen victim to her charms, rescues her and brings her to the shantee, where she embraces him. Thereupon Pedrillo protests in rage, proclaiming that he is her fiancé. Marion exclaims: "Would to God, then, we had perished together!"

[4] [DS] Mr. Trollope and young Thomas Adolphus Trollope had paid a visit to Trenton Falls and Niagara Falls early in 1829 on their way back to England from Cincinnati. Tom recalled in his autobiography that he had "enjoyed Trenton most."

either wait till the next day for the Rochester coach, or again submit to the packet-boat. Our impatience induced us to prefer the latter, not very wisely, I think, for every annoyance seemed to increase upon us. The Oneida and the Genesee country are both extremely beautiful, but had we not returned by another route we should have known little about it. From the canal nothing is seen to advantage, and very little is seen at all. My chief amusement, I think, was derived from names. One town, consisting of a whiskey store and a warehouse, is called Port Byron. At Rome, the first name I saw over a store was Remus, doing infinite honour, I thought, to the classic lore of his godfathers and godmothers; but it would be endless to record all the drolleries of this kind which we met with. We arrived at Rochester, a distance of a hundred and forty miles, on the second morning after leaving Utica, fully determined never to enter a canal boat again, at least, not in America.

Rochester is one of the most famous of the cities built on the Jack and Bean-stalk principle. There are many splendid edifices in wood; and certainly more houses, warehouses, factories, and steam-engines than ever were collected together in the same space of time; but I was told by a fellow-traveller that the stumps of the forest are still to be found firmly rooted in the cellars.

The fall of the Genesee is close to the town, and in the course of a few months will, perhaps, be in the middle of it. It is a noble sheet of water, of a hundred and sixty feet perpendicular fall; but I looked at it through the window of a factory, and as I did not like that, I was obligingly handed to the door-way of a sawing-mill; in short, "the great water privilege" has been so ingeniously taken advantage of, that no point can be found where its voice and its movement are not mixed and confounded with those of "the admirable machinery of this flourishing city."

The Genesee fall is renowned as being the last and fatal

leap of the adventurous madman, Sam Patch; [5] he had leaped
it once before, and rose to the surface of the river in perfect
safety, but the last time he was seen to falter as he took the
leap, and was never heard of more. It seems that he had some
misgivings of his fate, for a pet bear, which he had always
taken with him on his former break-neck adventures, and
which had constantly leaped after him without injury, he on
this occasion left behind, in the care of a friend, to whom he
bequeathed him "in case of his not returning." We saw the
bear, which is kept at the principal hotel; he is a noble creature, and more completely tame than I ever saw any animal
of the species.

Our journey now became wilder every step, the unbroken
forest often skirted the road for miles, and the sight of a log-
hut was an event. Yet the road was, for the greater part of the
day, good, running along a natural ridge, just wide enough

---

[5] [DS] In the 1830's and 1840's the story of Sam Patch, his rise to vain-
glory, and his precipitous demise was the subject of newspaper squibs, anecdotes, ballads, theatrical farces, and manifold allusions. Sam performed
his first aerial feats by leaping from the roofs of factories into the Pawtucket
River at Pawtucket, Rhode Island, where he worked as a cotton spinner. He
first jumped for the public in 1827, descending from the highest cliff overlooking Passaic Falls, a leap of seventy feet. Thereafter he performed from
many bridges in New Jersey and New York until he took his most renowned
descent on October 17, 1829, at Goat Island, Niagara Falls. By this time his
name was familiar to newspaper readers throughout the United States.

On November 13 of the same year Sam made his final, fatal leap. He
had caused a scaffold twenty-five feet high to be reared above the Genesee
Falls, making the descent a total of 125 feet. After he had climbed to the
top of the scaffold, he made his last speech. Napoleon had been an eminent
man, Sam said, for he had wielded power over nations. The Duke of Wellington was a greater man, for he had conquered Napoleon. But neither of
them could jump the Genesee Falls, a feat that he, Sam Patch, alone could
perform.

According to some accounts, Sam was drunk when he made this last
leap; others say that he had had no more than a glass of brandy. In any
event, his body lost its accustomed poise as he fell, and he did not rise from
the waters. His body was not recovered until the following March, when it
was found at the mouth of the Genesee River near Lake Ontario.

For a much fuller and highly interesting recent account, see Richard M.
Dorson's "The Story of Sam Patch" in the *American Mercury* for June 1947.

for it. This ridge is a very singular elevation, and, by all the
enquiry I could make, the favourite theory concerning it is,
that it was formerly the boundary of Lake Ontario, near
which it passes. When this ridge ceased, the road ceased too,
and for the rest of the way to Lockport, we were most painfully jumbled and jolted over logs and through bogs, till every
joint was nearly dislocated.

Lockport is, beyond all comparison, the strangest looking
place I ever beheld. As fast as half a dozen trees were cut
down, a *factory* was raised up; stumps still contest the ground
with pillars, and porticos are seen to struggle with rocks. It
looks as if the demon of machinery, having invaded the
peaceful realms of nature, had fixed on Lockport as the battle-
ground on which they should strive for mastery. The fiend
insists that the streams shall go one way, though the gentle
mother had ever led their dancing steps another; nay,
the very rocks must fall before him, and take what form he
wills. The battle is lost and won. Nature is fairly routed and
driven from the field, and the rattling, crackling, hissing,
splitting demon has taken possession of Lockport for ever.

We slept there, dismally enough. I never felt more out of
humour at what the Americans call improvement; it is, in
truth, as it now stands, a most hideous place, and gladly did I
leave it behind me.

Our next stage was to Lewiston; for some miles before we
reached it, we were within sight of the British frontier; and
we made our salaams.

The monument of the brave General Brock [6] stands on an
elevated point, near Queenstown, and is visible at a great
distance.

------

[6] [DS] The British general Sir Isaac Brock, capturer of Detroit, was
killed while commanding his troops at the Battle of Queenstown, October
12, 1812. An American force of about one thousand men had invaded Canada with the purpose of capturing Queenstown, but was overpowered by superior numbers and forced to surrender. The 135-foot column in memory of
General Brock had been raised on the Heights of Queenstown in 1816.

We breakfasted at Lewiston, but felt every cup of coffee as a sin, so impatient were we, as we approached the end of our long pilgrimage, to reach the shrine, which nature seems to have placed at such a distance from her worshippers on purpose to try the strength of their devotion.

A few miles more would bring us to the high altar, but first we had to cross the ferry, for we were determined upon taking our first view from British ground. The Niagara river is very lovely here; the banks are bold, rugged, and richly coloured, both by rocks and woods; and the stream itself is bright, clear, and unspeakably green.

In crossing the ferry a fellow-passenger made many enquiries of the young boatman respecting the battle of Queenstown; he was but a lad, and could remember little about it, but he was a British lad, and his answers smacked strongly of his loyal British feeling. Among other things, the questioner asked if many American citizens had not been thrown from the heights into the river.

"Why, yes, there was a good many of them; but it was right to shew them there was water between us, and you know it might help to keep the rest of them from coming to trouble us on our own ground."

This phrase, "our own ground," gave interest to every mile, or I believe I should have shut my eyes, and tried to sleep, that I might annihilate what remained of time and space between me and Niagara.

But I was delighted to see British oaks, and British roofs, and British boys and girls. These latter, as if to impress upon us that they were not citizens, made bows and courtesies as we passed, and this little touch of long unknown civility produced great effect. "See these dear children, mamma! do they not look English? how I love them!" was the exclamation it produced.

CHAPTER XXXIII

Niagara — Arrival at Forsythes — First sight of the Falls —
Goat Island — The Rapids — Buffalo — Lake Erie —
Canandaigua — Stage-coach adventures

AT length we reached Niagara. It was the brightest day that June could give; and almost any day would have seemed bright that brought me to the object which, for years, I had languished to look upon.

We did not hear the sound of the Falls till very near the hotel, which overhangs them; as you enter the door you see beyond the hall an open space, surrounded by galleries, one above another, and in an instant you feel that from thence the wonder is visible.

I trembled like a fool, and my girls clung to me, trembling too, I believe, but with faces beaming with delight. We encountered a waiter, who had a sympathy of some sort with us, for he would not let us run through the hall to the first gallery, but ushered us up stairs, and another instant placed us where, at one glance, I saw all I had wished for, hoped for, dreamed of.

It is not for me to attempt a description of Niagara; I feel I have no powers for it.

After one long, stedfast gaze, we quitted the gallery that we might approach still nearer, and in leaving the house had the good fortune to meet an English gentleman,[1] who had

---

[1] [T1] The accomplished author of "Cyril Thornton."

[DS] Thomas Hamilton, author of the novel *Cyril Thornton* (1827), which enjoyed much popularity in its day, had come to the United States in the fall of 1830 to gather material for a book upon America. In his *Men and Manners in America* (1833) he gives his impressions of Mrs. Trollope and advances her claims for the gratitude of Cincinnati:

been introduced to us at New York; he had preceded us by a few days, and knew exactly how and where to lead us. If any man living can describe the scene we looked upon it is himself, and I trust he will do it. As for me, I can only say that wonder, terror, and delight completely overwhelmed me. I wept with a strange mixture of pleasure and of pain, and certainly was, for some time, too violently affected in the *physique* to be capable of much pleasure; but when this emotion of the senses subsided, and I had recovered some degree of composure, my enjoyment was very great indeed.

To say that I was not disappointed is but a weak expression to convey the surprise and astonishment which this long dreamed of scene produced. It has to me something beyond its vastness; there is a shadowy mystery hangs about it which neither the eye nor even the imagination can penetrate; but I dare not dwell on this, it is a dangerous subject, and any attempt to describe the sensations produced must lead direct to nonsense.

"I . . . can bear testimony to her conversation being imbued with all that grace, spirit, and vivacity, which have since delighted the world in her writings. How far Mrs. Trollope's volumes present a just picture of American society, it is not for me to decide, though I can offer willing testimony to the general fidelity of her descriptions. But her claims to the gratitude of the Cincinnatians are undoubtedly very great. Her architectural talent has beautified their city; her literary powers have given it celebrity. For nearly thirty years Cincinnati had gradually been increasing in opulence, and enjoying a vulgar and obscure prosperity. Corn had grown, and hogs had fattened; men had built houses, and women borne children; but in all the higher senses of urbane existence, Cincinnati was a nonentity. . . . There was not the glimmering of a chance that it would be mentioned twice in a twelvemonth, even on the Liverpool Exchange. But Mrs. Trollope came, and a zone of light has ever since encircled Cincinnati. Its inhabitants are no longer a race unknown to fame. Their manners, habits, virtues, tastes, vices, and pursuits, are familiar to all the world; but, strange to say, the marketplace of Cincinnati is yet unadorned by the statue of the great benefactress of the city!"

Hamilton accepted Mrs. Trollope's challenge to describe Niagara Falls and devoted seven pages to the subject. He considered the Falls a "scene of awful splendour," the first sight of which was sufficient to "extend through a lifetime" and enlarge the viewer's "sphere of thought, and influence the whole tissue of his moral being."

Exactly at the Fall, it is the Fall and nothing else you have to look upon; there are not, as at Trenton, mighty rocks and towering forests, there is only the waterfall; but it is the fall of an ocean, and were Pelion piled on Ossa on either side of it, we could not look at them.

The noise is greatly less than I expected; one can hear with perfect distinctness every thing said in an ordinary tone, when quite close to the cataract. The cause of this, I imagine to be, that it does not fall immediately among rocks, like the far noisier Potomac, but direct and unbroken, save by its own rebound. The colour of the water, before this rebound hides it in foam and mist, is of the brightest and most delicate green; the violence of the impulse sends it far over the precipice before it falls, and the effect of the ever varying light through its transparency is, I think, the loveliest thing I ever looked upon.

We descended to the edge of the gulf which receives the torrent, and thence looked at the horse-shoe fall in profile; it seems like awful daring to stand close beside it, and raise one's eyes to its immensity. I think the point the most utterly inconceivable to those who have not seen it, is the centre of the horse-shoe. The force of the torrent converges there, and as the heavy mass pours in, twisted, wreathed, and curled together, it gives an idea of irresistible power, such as no other object ever conveyed to me.

The following anecdote, which I had from good authority, may give some notion of this mighty power.

After the last American war, three of our ships, stationed on Lake Erie, were declared unfit for service, and condemned. Some of their officers obtained permission to send them over Niagara Falls. The first was torn to shivers by the rapids, and went over in fragments; the second filled with water before she reached the fall; but the third, which was in better condition, took the leap gallantly, and retained her form till it was hid in the cloud of mist below. A reward of ten dollars was

offered for the largest fragment of wood that should be found
from either wreck, five for the second, and so on. One morsel
only was ever seen, and that about a foot in length, was
mashed as by a vice, and its edges notched like the teeth of
a saw. What had become of the immense quantity of wood
which had been precipitated? What unknown whirlpool had
engulphed it, so that, contrary to the very laws of nature, no
vestige of the floating material could find its way to the
surface?

Beyond the horse-shoe is Goat Island, and beyond Goat Island the American fall, bold, straight, and chafed to snowy
whiteness by the rocks which meet it; but it does not approach, in sublimity or awful beauty, to the wondrous crescent on the other shore. There, the form of the mighty caul-
dron, into which the deluge pours, the hundred silvery
torrents congregating round its verge, the smooth and solemn movement with which it rolls its massive volume over
the rock, the liquid emerald of its long unbroken waters, the
fantastic wreaths which spring to meet it, and then, the
shadowy mist that veils the horrors of its crash below, constitute a scene almost too enormous in its features for man
to look upon. "Angels might tremble as they gazed;" and
I should deem the nerves obtuse, rather than strong, which
did not quail at the first sight of this stupendous cataract.

Minute local particulars can be of no interest to those who
have not felt their influence for pleasure or for pain. I will not
tell of giddy stairs which scale the very edge of the torrent,
nor of beetling slabs of table rock, broken and breaking, on
which, shudder as you may, you must take your stand or lose
your reputation as a tourist. All these feats were performed
again and again, even on the first day of our arrival, and most
earthly weary was I when the day was done, though I would
not lose the remembrance of it to purchase the addition of
many soft and silken ones to my existence.

By four o'clock the next morning I was again at the little

shantee, close to the horse-shoe fall, which seems reared in water rather than in air, and took an early shower-bath of spray. Much is concealed at this early hour by the heavy vapour, but there was a charm in the very obscurity; and every moment, as the light increased, cloud after cloud rolled off, till the vast wonder was again before me.

It is in the afternoon that the rainbow is visible from the British side; and it is a lovely feature in the mighty land-scape. The gay arch springs from fall to fall, a fairy bridge.

After breakfast we crossed to the American side, and ex-plored Goat Island. The passage across the Niagara, directly in face of the falls, is one of the most delightful little voyages imaginable; the boat crosses marvellously near them, and within reach of a light shower of spray. Real safety and ap-parent danger have each their share in the pleasure felt. The river is here two hundred feet deep. The passage up the rock brings you close upon the American cataract; it is a vast sheet, and has all the sublimity that height and width, and uproar can give; but it has none of the magic of its rival about it. Goat Island has, at all points, a fine view of the rapids; the furious velocity with which they rush onward to the abyss, is terrific; and the throwing a bridge across them was a work of noble daring.

Below the falls, the river runs between lofty rocks, crowned with unbroken forests; this scene forms a striking contrast to the level shores above the cataract. It appears as if the level of the river had been broken up by some volcanic force. The Niagara flows out of Lake Erie, a broad, deep river; but for several miles its course is tranquil, and its shores perfectly level. By degrees its bed begins to sink, and the glassy smoothness is disturbed by a slight ripple. The inverted trees, that before lay so softly still upon its bosom, become twisted and tortured till they lose their form, and seem madly to mix in the tumult that destroys them. The current becomes more rapid at every step, till rock after rock has chafed the stream to fury, making the green one white. This lasts for a mile, and then down sink the rocks at once, one hundred and fifty feet, and the enormous flood falls after them. God said, let there be a cataract, and it was so. When the river has reached its new level, the precipice on either side shews a terrific chasm of solid rock; some beautiful plants are clinging to its sides, and oak, ash, and cedar, in many places, clothe their terrors with rich foliage.

This violent transition from level shores to a deep ravine, seems to indicate some great convulsion as its cause, and when I heard of a burning spring close by, I fancied the volcanic power still at work, and that the wonders of the region might yet increase.

We passed four delightful days of excitement and fatigue; we drenched ourselves in spray; we cut our feet on the rocks; we blistered our faces in the sun; we looked up the cataract, and down the cataract; we perched ourselves on every pinnacle we could find; we dipped our fingers in the flood at a few yards' distance from its thundering fall; in short, we strove to fill as many inches of memory with Niagara, as possible; and I think the images will be within the power of recall for ever.

We met many groups of tourists in our walks, chiefly American, but they were, or we fancied they were, but little observant of the wonders around them.

One day we were seated on a point of the cliff, near the ferry, which commands a view of both the Falls. This, by the way, is considered as the finest general view of the scene. One of our party was employed in attempting to sketch, what, however, I believe it is impossible for any pencil to convey an idea of, to those who have not seen it. We had borrowed two or three chairs from a neighbouring cottage, and amongst us had gathered a quantity of boughs which, with the aid of

shawls and parasols, we had contrived to weave into a shelter
from the mid-day sun, so that altogether I have no doubt we
looked very cool and comfortable.

A large party who had crossed from the American side,
wound up the steep ascent from the place where the boat had
left them; in doing so their backs were turned to the cataracts,
and as they approached the summit, our party was the principal object before them. They all stood perfectly still to look
at us. This first examination was performed at the distance of
about a dozen yards from the spot we occupied, and lasted
about five minutes, by which time they had recovered breath,
and acquired courage. They then advanced in a body, and
one or two of them began to examine (wrong side upwards)
the work of the sketcher, in doing which they stood precisely
between him and his object; but of this I think it is very
probable they were not aware. Some among them next began to question us, as to how long we had been at the Falls;
whether there were much company; if we were not from the
old country, and the like. In return we learnt that they were
just arrived; yet not one of them (there were eight) ever
turned the head, even for a moment, to look at the most stupendous spectacle that nature has to shew.

The company at the hotel changed almost every day. Many
parties arrived in the morning, walked to the Falls, returned
to the hotel to dinner, and departed by the coach immediately after it. Many groups were indescribably whimsical,
both in appearance and manner. Now and then a first-rate
dandy shot in among us, like a falling star.

On one occasion, when we were in the beautiful gallery,
at the back of the hotel, which overlooks the horse-shoe fall,
we saw the booted leg of one of this graceful race protruded
from the window which commands the view, while his person
was thrown back in his chair, and his head enveloped in a
cloud of tobacco smoke.

I have repeatedly remarked, when it has happened to me

to meet any ultra fine men among the wilder and more imposing scenes of our own land, that they throw off, in a great
degree, their airs, and their "townliness," as some one cleverly
calls these *simagrées,* as if ashamed to "play their fantastic
tricks" before the god of nature, when so forcibly reminded of
his presence; and more than once on these occasions I have
been surprised to find how much intellect lurked behind the
inane mask of fashion. But in America the effect of fine
scenery upon this class of persons is different, for it is exactly
when amongst it, that the most strenuous efforts at elegant
nonchalance are perceptible among the young exquisites of
the western world. It is true that they have little leisure for
the display of grace in the daily routine of commercial activity in which their lives are passed, and this certainly offers a
satisfactory explanation of the fact above stated.

Fortunately for our enjoyment, the solemn character of the
scene was but little broken in upon by these gentry. Every
one who comes to Forsythe's Hotel (except Mrs. Bogle Corbet),[2] walks to the Shantee, writes their name in a book
which is kept there, and, for the most part, descends in the
spiral staircase which leads from the little platform before it,
to the rocks below. Here they find another Shantee, but a
few yards from the entrance of that wondrous cavern which

---

[2] [DS] In John Galt's *Mrs. Bogle Corbet; or, the Emigrants* (1831), the
heroine informs her husband, soon after they have put up at a hotel, that
there is no need for her to walk to the Falls; she has seen them already.

"'You have seen them? — when? how?'

"'The house have given us the best bed-room, and when I was up before dinner, putting my head in order, I looked out at the window.'

"'Gracious! You have seen them, and calmly eating your dinner afterwards?'

"'They were just under me, leaping, rolling, roaring, and jumping like
mad.'

"'Mrs. Bogle Corbet, what do you say?'

"'But,' she replied, 'for all that I think them, upon the whole, very neat,
and 'tis a pleasant prospect from the window.'

"'Neat! What do you say, Mrs. Corbet? — Are my ears fellows? — Neat!'

"'To be sure, but there is certainly an unaccountable and extravagant
waste of water about them.'"

is formed by the falling flood on one side, and by the mighty rock over which it pours, on the other. To this frail shelter from the wild uproar, and the blinding spray, nearly all the touring gentlemen, and even many of the pretty ladies, find their way. But here I often saw their noble daring fail, and have watched them dripping and draggled turn again to the sheltering stairs, leaving us in full possession of the awful scene we so dearly loved to gaze upon. How utterly futile must every attempt be to describe the spot! How vain every effort to convey an idea of the sensations it produces! Why is it so exquisite a pleasure to stand for hours drenched in spray, stunned by the ceaseless roar, trembling from the concussion that shakes the very rock you cling to, and breathing painfully in the moist atmosphere that seems to have less of air than water in it? Yet pleasure it is, and I almost think the greatest I ever enjoyed. We more than once approached the entrance to this appalling cavern, but I never fairly entered it, though two or three of my party did. — I lost my breath entirely; and the pain at my chest was so severe, that not all my curiosity could enable me to endure it.

What was that cavern of the winds, of which we heard of old, compared to this? A mightier spirit than Æolus reigns here.

Nor was this spot of dread and danger the only one in which we found ourselves alone. The path taken by "the company" to the Shantee, which contained the "book of names" was always the same; this wound down the steep bank from the gate of the hotel garden, and was rendered tolerably easy by its repeated doublings; but it was by no means the best calculated to manage to advantage the pleasure of the stranger in his approach to the spot. All others, however, seemed left for us alone.

During our stay we saw the commencement of another staircase, intended to rival in attraction that at present in use; it is but a few yards from it, and can in no way, I think, contribute to the convenience of the descent. The erection of the central shaft of this spiral stair was a most tremendous operation, and made me sick and giddy as I watched it. After it had been made fast at the bottom, the carpenters swung themselves off the rocks, by the means of ropes, to the beams which traversed it; and as they sat across them, in the midst of the spray and the uproar, I thought I had never seen life periled so wantonly. But the work proceeded without accident, and was nearly finished before we left the hotel.

It was a sort of pang to take what we knew must be our last look at Niagara; but "we had to do it," as the Americans say, and left it on the 10th June, for Buffalo.

The drive along the river, above the Falls, is as beautiful as a clear stream of a mile in width can make it; and the road continues close to it till you reach the ferry at Black Rock.

We welcomed, almost with a shout, the British colours which we saw, for the first time, on Commodore Barrie's pretty sloop, the *Bull Dog*, which we passed as it was towing up the river to Lake Erie, the commodore being about to make a tour of the lakes.

At Black Rock we crossed again into the United States, and a few miles of horrible jolting brought us to Buffalo.

Of all the thousand and one towns I saw in America, I think Buffalo is the queerest looking; it is not quite so wild as Lockport, but all the buildings have the appearance of having been run up in a hurry, though every thing has an air of great pretension; there are porticos, columns, domes, and colonnades, but all in wood. Every body tells you there, as in all their other new-born towns, and every body believes, that their improvement, and their progression, are more rapid, more wonderful, than the earth ever before witnessed; while to me, the only wonder is, how so many thousands, nay millions of persons, can be found, in the nineteenth century, who can be content so to live. Surely this country may be said to spread rather than to rise.

The Eagle Hotel, an immense wooden fabric, has all the pretension of a splendid establishment, but its monstrous corridors, low ceilings, and intricate chambers, gave me the feeling of a catacomb rather than a house. We arrived after the *table d'hôte* tea-drinking was over, and supped comfortably enough with a gentleman, who accompanied us from the Falls; but the next morning we breakfasted in a long, low, narrow room, with a hundred persons, and any thing less like comfort can hardly be imagined.

What can induce so many intellectual citizens to prefer these long, silent tables, scantily covered with morsels of fried ham, salt fish and liver, to a comfortable loaf of bread with their wives and children at home? How greatly should I prefer eating my daily meals with my family, in an Indian wigwam, to boarding at a *table d'hôte* in these capacious hotels; the custom, however, seems universal through the country, at least, we have met it, without a shadow of variation as to its general features, from New Orleans to Buffalo.

Lake Erie has no beauty to my eyes; it is not the sea, and it is not the river, nor has it the beautiful scenery generally found round smaller lakes. The only interest its unmeaning expanse gave me, arose from remembering that its waters, there so tame and tranquil, were destined to leap the gulf of Niagara. A dreadful road, through forests only beginning to be felled, brought us to Avon; it is a straggling, ugly little place, and not any of their "Romes, Carthages, Ithacas, or Athens," ever provoked me by their names so much. This Avon flows sweetly with nothing but whisky and tobacco juice.

The next day's journey was much more interesting, for it shewed us the lake of Canandaigua. It is about eighteen miles long, but narrow enough to bring the opposite shore, clothed with rich foliage, near to the eye; the back-ground is a ridge of mountains. Perhaps the state of the atmosphere lent an unusual charm to the scene; one of those sudden thunder-storms, so rapid in approach, and so sombre in colouring, that they change the whole aspect of things in a moment, rose over the mountains, and passed across the lake while we looked upon it. Another feature in the scene gave a living, but most sad interest to it. A glaring wooden hotel, as fine as paint and porticos can make it, overhangs the lake; beside it stands a shed for cattle. To this shed, and close by the white man's mushroom palace, two Indians had crept to seek a shelter from the storm. The one was an aged man, whose venerable head in attitude and expression indicated the profoundest melancholy: the other was a youth, and in his deep-set eye there was a quiet sadness more touching still. There they stood, the native rightful lords of the fair land, looking out upon the lovely lake which yet bore the name their fathers had given it, watching the threatening storm that brooded there; a more fearful one had already burst over them.

Though I have mentioned the lake first, the little town of Canandaigua precedes it, in returning from the West. It is as pretty a village as ever man contrived to build. Every house is surrounded by an ample garden, and at that flowery season, they were half buried in roses.

It is true these houses are of wood, but they are so neatly painted, in such perfect repair, and shew so well within their leafy setting, that it is impossible not to admire them.

Forty-six miles farther is Geneva, beautifully situated on Seneca Lake. This, too, is a lovely sheet of water, and I think the town may rival its European namesake in beauty.

We slept at Auburn, celebrated for its prison, where the highly-approved system of American discipline originated.[3] In this part of the country there is no want of churches; every

---

[3] [DS] The "silent" or "Auburn" system of confining prisoners in separate cells at night and enforcing silence in the workshops by day was first put into full practice at the Auburn prison in 1819–21. Auburn became the pattern for state prisons for the next half-century.

little village has its wooden temple, and many of them two; that the Methodists and Presbyterians may not clash.

We passed through an Indian reserve, and the untouched forests again hung close upon the road. Repeated groups of Indians passed us, and we remarked that they were much cleaner and better dressed than those we had met wandering far from their homes. The blankets which they use so gracefully as mantles, were as white as snow.

We took advantage of the loss of a horse's shoe, to leave the coach, and approach a large party of them, consisting of men, women, and children, who were regaling themselves with I know not what, but milk made a part of the repast. They could not talk to us, but they received us with smiles, and seemed to understand when we asked if they had mocassins to sell, for they shook their sable locks, and answered "no."

A beautiful grove of butternut trees was pointed out to us, as the spot where the chiefs of the six nations used to hold their senate; our informer told me that he had been present at several of their meetings, and though he knew but little of their language, the power of their eloquence was evident from the great effect it produced among themselves.

Towards the end of this day, we encountered an adventure which revived our doubts whether the invading white men, in chasing the poor Indians from their forests, have done much towards civilizing the land. For myself, I almost prefer the indigenous manner to the exotic.

The coach stopped to take in "a lady" at Vernon; she entered, and completely filled the last vacant inch of our vehicle; for "we were eight" before.

But no sooner was she seated, than *her beau* came forward with a most enormous wooden best-bonnet box. He paused for a while to meditate the possibilities — raised it, as if to place it on our laps — sunk it, as if to put it beneath our feet.

Both alike appeared impossible; when, in true Yankee style he addressed one of our party with, "If you'll just step out a minute, I guess I'll find room for it."

•"Perhaps so. But how shall I find room for myself afterwards?"

This was uttered in European accents, and in an instant half a dozen whisky drinkers stepped from before the whisky store, and took the part of *the beau.*

"That's because you'll be English travellers I expect, but we have travelled in better countries than Europe — we have travelled in America — and the box will go, I calculate."

We remonstrated on the evident injustice of the proceeding, and I ventured to say, that as we had none of us any luggage in the carriage, because the space was so very small, I thought a chance passenger could have no right so greatly to incommode us.

"Right! — there they go — that's just their way — that will do in Europe, may be; it sounds just like English tyranny, now — don't it? but it won't do here." And thereupon he began thrusting in the wooden box against our legs, with all his strength.

"No law, sir, can permit such conduct as this."

"Law!" exclaimed a gentleman very particularly drunk, "we makes our own laws, and governs our own selves."

"Law!" echoed another gentleman of Vernon, "this is a free country, *we have no laws here,* and we don't want no foreign power to tyrannize over us."

I give the words exactly. It is, however, but fair to state, that the party had evidently been drinking more than an usual portion of whiskey, but, perhaps, in whisky, as in wine, truth may come to light. At any rate the people of the Western Paradise follow the Gentiles in this, that they are a law unto themselves.

During this contest, the coachman sat upon the box without saying a word, but seemed greatly to enjoy the joke; the question of the box, however, was finally decided in our favour by the nature of the human material, which cannot be compressed beyond a certain degree.

For great part of this day we had the good fortune to have a gentleman and his daughter for our fellow-travellers, who were extremely intelligent and agreeable; but I nearly got myself into a scrape by venturing to remark upon a phrase used by the gentleman, and which had met me at every corner from the time I first entered the country. We had been talking of pictures, and I had endeavoured to adhere to the rule I had laid down for myself, of saying very little, where I could say nothing agreeable. At length he named an American artist, with whose works I was very familiar, and after having declared him equal to Lawrence, (judging by his portrait of West, now at New York), he added, "and what is more, madam, he is perfectly *self-taught.*"

I prudently took a few moments before I answered; for the equalling our immortal Lawrence to a most vile dauber stuck in my throat; I could not say Amen; so for some time I said nothing; but, at last, I remarked on the frequency with which I had heard this phrase of *self-taught* used, not as an apology, but as positive praise.

"Well, madam, can there be a higher praise?"

"Certainly not, if spoken of the individual merits of a person, without the means of instruction, but I do not understand it when applied as praise to his works."

"Not understand it, madam? Is it not attributing genius to the author, and what is teaching compared to that?"

I do not wish to repeat all my own *bons mots* in praise of study, and on the disadvantages of profound ignorance, but I would willingly, if I could, give an idea of the mixed indignation and contempt expressed by our companion at the idea that study was necessary to the formation of taste, and to the development of genius. At last, however, he closed the discussion thus, — "There is no use in disputing a point that is already settled, madam; the best judges declare that Mr. H°°°°°g's [4] portraits are equal to that of Lawrence."

"Who is it who has passed this judgment, sir?"

"The men of taste of America, madam."

I then asked him, if he thought it was going to rain?

*   *   *   *   *   *

The stages do not appear to have any regular stations at which to stop for breakfast, dinner, and supper. These necessary interludes, therefore, being generally *impromptu,* were abominably bad. We were amused by the patient manner in which our American fellow-travellers ate whatever was set before them, without uttering a word of complaint, or making any effort to improve it, but no sooner reseated in the stage, than they began their complaints — "'twas a shame" — "'twas a robbery" — "'twas poisoning folks" — and the like. I, at last, asked the reason of this, and why they did not remonstrate? "Because, madam, no American gentleman or lady that keeps an inn won't bear to be found fault with."

We reached Utica very late and very weary; but the delights of a good hotel and perfect civility sent us in good humour to bed, and we arose sufficiently refreshed to enjoy a day's journey through some of the loveliest scenery in the world.

Who is it that says America is not picturesque? I forget; [5]

---

[4] [DS] Almost certainly Chester Harding (1792–1866), who had progressed from drummer-boy in the War of 1812 to drum-maker to tavern-keeper to house-painter to sign-painter. At Paris, Kentucky, he finally established himself as a portrait-painter, charging twenty-five dollars for his works. About 1820 he removed to Boston. There he did so well that Gilbert Stuart spoke of "the Harding fever." In 1823 Harding went to England, where he became a social lion. He returned to the United States in 1826 and continued to enjoy great success, executing portraits of such celebrities as Daniel Webster, John C. Calhoun, John Marshall, and John Randolph of Roanoke.

[5] [DS] "Well might Mrs. Trollope ask, 'Who is it that says America is not picturesque?' . . . This is a severe question, for Captain Hall travelled

but surely he never travelled from Utica to Albany. I really cannot conceive that any country can furnish a drive of ninety-six miles more beautiful, or more varied in its beauty. The road follows the Mohawk River, which flows through scenes changing from fields, waving with plenty, to rocks and woods; gentle slopes, covered with cattle, are divided from each other by precipices 500 feet high. Around the little falls there is a character of beauty as singular as it is striking. Here, as I observed of many other American rivers, the stream appears to run in a much narrower channel than it once occupied, and the space which it seems formerly to have filled is now covered with bright green herbage, save that, at intervals, large masses of rock rise abruptly from the level turf; these are crowned with all such trees as love the scanty diet which a rock affords. Dwarf oak, cedars, and the mountain ash, are grouped in a hundred different ways among them; each clump you look upon is lovelier than its neighbour; I never saw so sweetly wild a spot.

I was surprised to hear a fellow-traveller say, as we passed a point of peculiar beauty, "all this neighbourhood belongs, or did belong, to Mr. Edward Ellice, an English Member of Parliament,[6] but he has sold a deal of it, and now, madam, you may see as it begins to improve;" and he pointed to a great wooden edifice, where, on the white paint, "Cash for Rags," in letters three feet high, might be seen.

I then remembered that it was near this spot that my Yankee friend had made his complaint against English indifference to "water privilege." He did not name Mr. Edward

in the very same line as Mrs. Trollope. . . . He tells us in one part of his book, that 'there are few things as fatiguing as fine scenery,' and in another, that 'the most picturesque object in every traveller's landscape is the Post Office. . . .'" — James Stuart: *Three Years in North America* (1833).

6 [DS] Edward Ellice (1781–1863), important English statesman, had inherited large estates in Canada and New York. In his early life he was engaged in the fur trade in Canada and spent much of his time colonizing his lands.

Ellice, but doubtless he was the "English, as never thought of improvement."

I have often confessed my conscious incapacity for description, but I must repeat it here to apologise for my passing so dully through this matchless valley of the Mohawk. I would that some British artist, strong in youthful daring, would take my word for it, and pass over, for a summer pilgrimage through the state of New York. In very earnest, he would do wisely, for I question if the world could furnish within the same space, and with equal facility of access, so many subjects for his pencil. Mountains, forests, rocks, lakes, rivers, cataracts, all in perfection. But he must be bold as a lion in colouring, or he will make nothing of it. There is a clearness of atmosphere, a strength of *chiaro oscuro*, a massiveness in the foliage, and a brilliance of contrast, that must make a colourist of any one who has an eye. He must have courage to dip his pencil in shadows black as night, and light that might blind an eagle. As I presume my young artist to be an enthusiast, he must first go direct to Niagara, or even in the Mohawk valley his pinioned wing may droop. If his fever run very high, he may slake his thirst at Trenton, and while there, he will not dream of any thing beyond it. Should my advice be taken, I will ask the young adventurer on his return, (when he shall have made a prodigious quantity of money by my hint), to reward me by two sketches. One shall be the lake of Canandaigua; the other the Indians' Senate Grove of Butternuts.

During our journey, I forget on which day of it, a particular spot in the forest, at some distance from the road, was pointed out to us as the scene of a true, but very romantic story. During the great and the terrible French revolution, (1792), a young nobleman escaped from the scene of horror, having with difficulty saved his head, and without the possibility of saving any thing else. He arrived at New York nearly destitute; and after passing his life, not only in splendour, but in

the splendour of the court of France, he found himself jostled
by the busy population of the New World, without a dollar
between him and starvation. In such a situation one might
almost sigh for the guillotine. The young noble strove to
labour; but who would purchase the trembling efforts of his
white hands, while the sturdy strength of many a black Hercules was in the market? He abandoned the vain attempt to
sustain himself by the aid of his fellow-men, and determined
to seek a refuge in the forest. A few shillings only remained
to him; he purchased an axe, and reached the Oneida territory. He felled a few of the slenderest trees, and made himself a shelter that Robinson Crusoe would have laughed at,
for it did not keep out the rain. Want of food, exposure to
the weather, and unwonted toil, produced the natural result;
the unfortunate young man fell sick, and stretched upon the
reeking earth, stifled, rather than sheltered, by the withering
boughs which hung over him; he lay parched with thirst, and
shivering in ague, with the one last earthly hope, that each
heavy moment would prove the last.

Near to the spot which he had chosen for his miserable rest,
but totally concealed from it by the thick forest, was the last
straggling wigwam of an Indian village. It is not known how
many days the unhappy man had lain without food, but he
was quite insensible when a young squaw, whom chance had
brought from this wigwam to his hut, entered, and found him
alive, but totally insensible. The heart of woman is, I believe,
pretty much the same every where; the young girl paused not
to think whether he were white or red, but her fleet feet rested
not till she had brought milk, rum, and blankets, and when the
sufferer recovered his senses, his head was supported on her
lap, while, with the gentle tenderness of a mother, she found
means to make him swallow the restoratives she had brought.

No black eyes in the world, be they of France, Italy, or
even of Spain, can speak more plainly of kindness, than the
large deep-set orbs of a squaw; this is a language that all

nations can understand, and the poor Frenchman read most clearly, in the anxious glance of his gentle nurse, that he should not die forsaken.

So far the story is romantic enough, and what follows is hardly less so. The squaw found means to introduce her white friend to her tribe; he was adopted as their brother, speedily acquired their language, and assumed their dress and manner of life. His gratitude to his preserver soon ripened into love, and if the chronicle spoke true, the French noble and the American savage were more than passing happy as man and wife, and it was not till he saw himself the father of many thriving children that the exile began to feel a wish of rising again from savage to civilized existence.

My historian did not explain what his project was in visiting New York, but he did so in the habit of an Indian, and learnt enough of the restored tranquillity of his country to give him hope that some of the broad lands he had left there might be restored to him.

I have made my story already too long, and must not linger upon it farther than to say that his hopes were fulfilled, and that, of a large and flourishing family, some are settled in France, and some remain in America, (one of these, I understood, was a lawyer at New York), while the hero and the heroine of the tale continue to inhabit the Oneida country, not in a wigwam, however, but in a good house, in a beautiful situation, with all the comforts of civilized life around them.

Such was the narrative we listened to, from a stage coach companion; and it appears to me sufficiently interesting to repeat, though I have no better authority to quote for its truth, than the assertion of this unknown traveller.[7]

---

[7] [DS] By 1831 the story had gained a good deal by frequent retellings. The facts are recited by Mrs. L. M. Hammond in her *History of Madison County, State of New York* (1872). Angel de Ferriere, born in 1769, a scion of the French nobility, was a member of the King's Life Guards when the palace was attacked in August 1792. He fled to Holland and embarked from there for New York the following year with some members of the Hol-

land Land Company. In New York he met Colonel John Lincklaen, with whom he went to Cazenovia, in Madison County. De Ferriere visited Cana-seraga to talk French with Lewis Dennie, the only man in the region who could speak the language. Dennie's only daughter, Polly, was "said by some to have been very beautiful, and resembling the race to which her mother belonged but little." De Ferriere married Polly Dennie and settled near Cazenovia and later at Wampsville, where his wife's brother gave him a fine farm. De Ferriere secured more land through his own industry until he was the owner of about three thousand acres. In 1817 he returned to France to claim his family's once princely estates. He came back with enough money to complete payments on his New York land. The de Ferrieres reared five children, "sending them from home to be educated." Angel de Ferriere died September 17, 1832; Polly de Ferriere lived on until March 1853.

CHAPTER XXXIV

Return to New York — Conclusion

THE comfortable Adelphi Hotel again received us at Albany, on the 14th of June, and we decided upon passing the following day there, both to see the place, and to recruit our strength, which we began to feel we had taxed severely by a very fatiguing journey, in most oppressively hot weather. It would have been difficult to find a better station for repose; the rooms were large and airy, and ice was furnished in most profuse abundance.

But notwithstanding the manifold advantages of this excellent hotel, I was surprised at the un-English arrangement communicated to me by two ladies with whom we made a speaking acquaintance, by which it appeared that they made it their permanent home. These ladies were a mother and daughter; the daughter was an extremely pretty young married woman, with two little children. Where the husbands were, or whether they were dead or alive, I know not; but they told me they had been *boarding* there above a year. They breakfasted, dined, and supped at the *table d'hôte*, with from twenty to a hundred people, as accident might decide; dressed very smart, played on the piano, in the public sitting-room, and assured me they were particularly comfortable and well accommodated. What a life!

Some parts of the town are very handsome; the Town Hall, the Chamber of Representatives, and some other public buildings, stand well on a hill that overlooks the Hudson, with ample enclosures of grass and trees around them.

Many of the shops are large, and showily set out. I was amused by a national trait which met me at one of them. I entered it to purchase some *eau de Cologne,* but finding what was offered to me extremely bad, and very cheap, I asked if they had none at a higher price, and better.

"You are a stranger, I guess," was the answer. "The Yankees want low price, that's all; they don't stand so much for goodness as the English."

Nothing could be more beautiful than our passage down the Hudson on the following day, as I thought of some of my friends in England, dear lovers of the picturesque, I could not but exclaim,

> "Que je vous plains! que je vous plains!
> Vous ne la verrez pas." [1]

Not even a moving panoramic view, gliding before their eyes for an hour together, in all the scenic splendour of Drury Lane, or Covent Garden, could give them an idea of it. They could only see one side at a time. The change, the contrast, the ceaseless variety of beauty, as you skim from side to side, the liquid smoothness of the broad mirror that reflects the scene, and most of all, the clear bright air through which you look at it; all this can only be seen and believed by crossing the Atlantic.

As we approached New York the burning heat of the day relaxed, and the long shadows of evening fell coolly on the beautiful villas we passed. I really can conceive nothing more exquisitely lovely than this approach to the city. The magnificent boldness of the Jersey shore on the one side, and the luxurious softness of the shady lawns on the other, with the vast silvery stream that flows between them, altogether form a picture which may well excuse a traveller for saying, once and again, that the Hudson river can be surpassed in beauty by none on the outside of Paradise. [2]

---

[1] [DS] *"Que je vous plains,"* etc.: "How sorry I am for you! You will not see it."

[2] [T5, note] I have since seen both the Rhine and the Danube, but I feel no inclination to retract my opinion. That both these rivers possess

It was nearly dark when we reached the city, and it was with great satisfaction that we found our comfortable apartments in Hudson Street unoccupied; and our pretty, kind (Irish) hostess willing to receive us again. We passed another fortnight there; and again we enjoyed the elegant hospitality of New York, though now it was offered from beneath the shade of their beautiful villas. In truth, were all America like this fair city, and all, no, only a small proportion of its population like the friends we left there, I should say, that the land was the fairest in the world.

But the time was come to bid it adieu! The important business of securing our homeward passage was to be performed. One must know what it is to cross the ocean before the immense importance of all the little details of accommodation can be understood. The anxious first look into the face of the captain, to ascertain if he be gentle or rough; another, scarcely less important, in that of the steward, generally a sable one, but not the less expressive; the accurate, but rapid glance of measurement thrown round the little state-rooms; another at the good or bad arrangement of the stair-case, by which you are to stumble up and stumble down, from cabin to deck, and from deck to cabin; all this, they only can understand who have felt it. At length, however, this interesting affair was settled, and most happily. The appearance promised well, and the performance bettered it. We hastened to pack up our "trumpery," as Captain Mirven unkindly calls the paraphernalia of the ladies,[3] and among the rest, my six hundred pages of griffonage. There is enough of it, yet I must add a few more lines.

---

sources of interest of which the lovely Hudson can show no trace, is certain; but with the exception of the spot immediately under the Lurleyberg on the Rhine, and that beneath the wondrous craigs of Dürrenstein on the Danube, I still think that in *natural* beauty nothing in either can equal many points of the Hudson.

[3] [DS] Captain Mirvan in Fanny Burney's novel *Evelina* (1778): "Here, Lucy, Moll, come to the fire and dry your trumpery."

I suspect that what I have written will make it evident that I do not like America. Now, as it happens that I met with individuals there whom I love and admire, far beyond the love and admiration of ordinary acquaintance, and as I declare the country to be fair to the eye, and most richly teeming with the gifts of plenty, I am led to ask myself why it is that I do not like it. I would willingly know myself, and confess to others, why it is that neither its beauty nor its abundance can suffice to neutralize, or greatly soften, the distaste which the aggregate of my recollections has left upon my mind.

I remember hearing it said, many years ago, when the advantages and disadvantages of a particular residence were being discussed, that it was the "who?" and not the "where?" that made the difference between the pleasant or unpleasant residence. The truth of the observation struck me forcibly when I heard it; and it has been recalled to my mind since, by the constantly recurring evidence of its justness. In applying this to America, I speak not of my friends, nor of my friends' friends. The small patrician band is a race apart; they live with each other, and for each other; mix wondrously little with the high matters of state, which they seem to leave rather supinely to their tailors and tinkers, and are no more to be taken as a sample of the American people, than the head of Lord Byron as a sample of the heads of the British peerage. I speak not of these, but of the population generally, as seen in town and country, among the rich and the poor, in the slave states, and the free states. I do not like them. I do not like their principles, I do not like their manners, I do not like their opinions.

Both as a woman, and as a stranger, it might be unseemly for me to say that I do not like their government, and therefore I will not say so. That it is one which pleases themselves is most certain, and this is considerably more important than pleasing all the travelling old ladies in the world. I entered the country at New Orleans, remained for more than two years west of the Alleghanies, and passed another year among the Atlantic cities, and the country around them. I conversed during this time with citizens of all orders and degrees, and I never heard from any one a single disparaging word against their government. It is not, therefore, surprising, that when the people of that country hear strangers questioning the wisdom of their institutions, and expressing disapprobation at some of their effects, they should set it down either to an incapacity of judging, or to a malicious feeling of envy and ill-will.

"How can any one in their senses doubt the excellence of a government which we have tried for half a century, and loved the better the longer we have known it?"

Such is the natural enquiry of every American when the excellence of their government is doubted; and I am inclined to answer, that no one in their senses, who has visited the country, and known the people, can doubt its fitness for them, such as they now are, or its utter unfitness for any other people.

Whether the government has made the people what they are, or whether the people have made the government what it is, to suit themselves, I know not; but if the latter, they have shewn a consummation of wisdom which the assembled world may look upon and admire.

It is matter of historical notoriety that the original stock of the white population now inhabiting the United States, were persons who had banished themselves, or were banished from the mother country. The land they found was favourable to their increase and prosperity; the colony grew and flourished. Years rolled on, and the children, the grand-children, and the great grand-children of the first settlers, replenished the land, and found it flowing with milk and honey. That they should wish to keep this milk and honey to themselves, is not very surprising. What did the mother country do for them? She sent them out gay and gallant officers to guard their frontier; the which they thought they could guard as well themselves; and then she taxed their tea. Now, this was disagreeable; and to atone for it, the distant colony had no great share in her mother's grace and glory. It was not from among them that her high and mighty were chosen; the rays which emanated from that bright sun of honour, the British throne, reached them but feebly. They knew not, they cared not, for her kings nor her heroes; their thriftiest trader was their noblest man; the holy seats of learning were but the cradles of superstition; the splendour of the aristocracy, but a leech that drew their "golden blood." The wealth, the learning, the glory of Britain, was to them nothing; the having their own way every thing.

Can any blame their wish to obtain it? Can any lament that they succeeded?

And now the day was their own, what should they do next? Their elders drew together, and said, "Let us make a government that shall suit us all; let it be rude, and rough, and noisy; let it not affect either dignity, glory, or splendour; let it interfere with no man's will, nor meddle with any man's business; let us have neither tithes nor taxes, game laws, nor poor laws; let every man have a hand in making the laws, and no man be troubled about keeping them; let not our magistrates wear purple, nor our judges ermine; if a man grow rich, let us take care that his grandson be poor, and then we shall all keep equal; let every man take care of himself, and if England should come to bother us again, why then we will fight altogether."

Could any thing be better imagined than such a government for a people so circumstanced? Or is it strange that they are contented with it? Still less is it strange that those who have lived in the repose of order, and felt secure that their country could go on very well, and its business proceed with-

out their bawling and squalling, scratching and scrambling
to help it, should bless the gods that they are not republicans.

So far all is well. That they should prefer a constitution
which suits them so admirably, to one which would not suit
them at all, is surely no cause of quarrel on our part; nor
should it be such on theirs, if we feel no inclination to exchange the institutions which have made us what we are, for
any other on the face of the earth.

But when a native of Europe visits America, a most extraordinary species of tyranny is set in action against him;
and as far as my reading and experience have enabled me to
judge, it is such as no other country has ever exercised against
strangers.

The Frenchman visits England; he is *abîmé d'ennui* at our
stately dinners; shrugs his shoulders at our *corps de ballet*,
and laughs *à gorge déployée* at our passion for driving, and
our partial affection for roast beef and plum pudding. The
Englishman returns the visit, and the first thing he does on
arriving at Paris, is to hasten to *le Théatre des Variétés*, that
he may see *"Les Anglaises pour rire,"* [4] and if among the
crowd of laughers, you hear a note of more cordial mirth than
the rest, seek out the person from whom it proceeds, and
you will find the Englishman.

The Italian comes to our green island, and groans at our
climate; he vows that the air which destroys a statue, cannot
be wholesome for man; he sighs for orange trees, and macca-
roni, and smiles at the pretensions of a nation to poetry, while
no epics are chaunted through her streets. Yet we welcome
the sensitive southern, with all kindness, listen to his complaints with interest, cultivate our little orange trees, and

---

[4] [DS] *Les Anglaises pour rire, ou la table et le logement,* a comedy in
one act by Charles Augustin Sewrin and Théophile Marion Dumersan, first
performed at Paris in 1814. As a criticism of the manners of a foreign nation, its relation to the pages of Captain Hall or Mrs. Trollope is about that
of a feather to a scalpel.

teach our children to lisp Tasso, in the hope of becoming more agreeable.

Yet we are not at all superior to the rest of Europe in our endurance of censure, nor is this wish to profit by it, at all peculiar to the English; we laugh at, and find fault with, our neighbours quite as freely as they do with us, and they join the laugh, and adopt our fashions and our customs. These mutual pleasantries produce no shadow of unkindly feeling; and as long as the governments are at peace with each other, the individuals of every nation in Europe make it a matter of pride, as well as of pleasure, to meet each other frequently, to discuss, compare, and reason upon their national varieties, and to vote it a mark of fashion and good taste to imitate each other in all the external embellishments of life.

The consequence of this is most pleasantly perceptible at the present time, in every capital of Europe. The long peace has given time for each to catch from each what was best in customs and manners, and the rapid advance of refinement and general information has been the result.

To those who have been accustomed to this state of things, the contrast upon crossing to the new world is inconceivably annoying; and it cannot be doubted that this is one great cause of the general feeling of irksomeness, and fatigue of spirit, which hangs upon the memory while recalling the hours passed in American society.

A single word indicative of doubt, that any thing, or every thing, in that country is not the very best in the world, produces an effect which must be seen and felt to be understood. If the citizens of the United States were indeed the devoted patriots they call themselves, they would surely not thus encrust themselves in the hard, dry, stubborn persuasion, that they are the first and best of the human race, that nothing is to be learnt, but what they are able to teach, and that nothing is worth having, which they do not possess.

The art of man could hardly discover a more effectual antidote to improvement, than this persuasion; and yet I never listened to any public oration, or read any work, professedly addressed to the country, in which they did not labour to impress it on the minds of the people.

To hint to the generality of Americans that the silent current of events may change their beloved government, is not the way to please them; but in truth they need be tormented with no such fear. As long as by common consent they can keep down the pre-eminence which nature has assigned to great powers, as long as they can prevent human respect and human honour from resting upon high talent, gracious manners, and exalted station, so long may they be sure of going on as they are.

I have been told, however, that there are some among them, who would gladly see a change; some, who with the wisdom of philosophers, and the fair candour of gentlemen, shrink from a profession of equality which they feel to be untrue, and believe to be impossible.

I can well believe that such there are, though to me no such opinions were communicated, and most truly should I rejoice to see power pass into such hands.

If this ever happens, if refinement once creeps in among them, if they once learn to cling to the graces, the honours, the chivalry of life, then we shall say farewell to American equality, and welcome to European fellowship one of the finest countries on the earth.

APPENDICES

&

INDEX

APPENDIX A

SELECTIONS FROM MRS. TROLLOPE'S NOTEBOOKS

AND ROUGH DRAFT [1]

I. *From the Notebooks*

AMERICAN WOMEN [2]

The women are certainly by far handsomer, speaking of them en masse, than those either of France or England. I have heard that women forgive every thing except being called ugly, and therefore I will venture after thus fully acknowledging their superiority in beauty, to express with equal freedom and sincerity my opinion on other points.

As far as I have been able to judge, they are quiet and orderly in their manners and habits [and] possess that sort of good housewifery that consists in being forever occupied about their household concerns. They are tender and attentive in the nursery, bustling and busy in the kitchen, unwearying at the needle, and beautiful in the ballroom; but in the drawing-room — they are naught. It is not that they are not blue; [3] I have seen more than one who has been dipped, and takes the dye excellently well for all purposes of business. They not only make authors but editors. It is not that they do not dress; the women, in proportion to their means, dress more, or better — but generally speaking they want intelligence. What is far worse, they want grace. They want it in sitting, they want it in standing, they want it in expression, in accent, in tone. This is felt at every moment and scene, as it were, to neutralize every charm. Were they graceful, they would, from the age of fifteen to eighteen, be beautiful creatures indeed. They marry very early; once married, they seem to drop out of sight or of court, out of all competition with the blooming race that are following them.

This, perhaps, is one reason why the drawing-room is so little attractive. From fifteen to eighteen the mind is not sufficiently developed to enable a woman to do her own honors well. Girls of that age make only a part, though a very lovely one, of the charm of society; but a flower garden possessing nothing but a bed of tulips would be no more imperfect than a salon with no other ornaments than a knot or two of these bright blossoms. The piquant observation, the lively sally,

---

[1] For a description and dating of the notebooks and rough draft, see Appendix B.

[2] Titles for passages have been supplied by the editor except where there is a statement below to the contrary.

[3] That is, "bluestockings," literary women.

the delicate coquetry, the playful yet acute remark, nay, even the abandon of enthusiasm or an elegant shadow of it, all, all meet in the varied and varying groups which form the centres round which all the stars of conversation revolve in the drawing-rooms of Europe. This cannot be where accomplishments are learnt for "a quarter," where poetry, statuary, and painting must be all *castigati* [4] before they are looked at, and where marriage draws a line of demarkation beyond which it is indiscreet to be pretty, and almost a sin to be agreeable. "They are their own exceeding great reward." Assuredly there are exceptions — ladies whom nature, or circumstances, or both combined have set apart, as it were, from their countrywomen. These are not the subjects of the foregoing observations, and they will be the last to take offence at them — for they know that they are just.

THE "FINE LADIES" OF BALTIMORE AND WASHINGTON

There is an idleness, a sauntering listlessness, that gives what we call a "creole manner" to the fine ladies of Baltimore and Washington, which, though not quite what would be most admired, is yet infinitely more a drawing-room manner than any thing to be seen in Ohio; but I did not find that the leisure obtained by the possession of slaves was in many cases employed in the improvement of the mind. The finest ladies I saw either worked muslin or did nothing. The very trifling attempts at music are rarely continued after marriage. The drawings I saw were always most ludicrously bad, though perhaps as good as the masters', and the stock of what is called general information less than I believe any one would believe possible who had not witnessed it.

DAY OF A LADY IN THE WEST [5]

(*Scene: a bedroom. Mr. and Mrs. Cob and two babies in bed. Two boys and a girl in a low bed beside them. Girl squeaks [sic].*)

MRS. COB. Hush up, daughter; don't make such a screaming. Quit, I say!

MR. COB, *waking.* What damnation noise are you after? I calculate I shall have to whip you all. Son, you must fix me a drink, that's a fact.

MASTER COB. I expect you'd better not be after whipping me. But

---

[4] Chastened.

[5] The title is Mrs. Trollope's. Mrs. Trollope decided finally that the little dramatic scene that follows was too good to waste. She incorporated it into the fifth edition of *Domestic Manners* (1839) under the title "A Fragment," the only addition that she made to the text of her book in any edition (except for the new footnotes that she supplied on many pages in the fifth edition). The scene as it appears in the fifth edition is greatly expanded, but it is also refined, with a number of the more roughly realistic details of the original scene of the notebooks omitted. Both forms are reproduced in this appendix, with Mrs. Trollope's original version given first.

I've got to fix your drink, I reckon, and I'll do it elegant. (Master Cob rises, spits, and mixes whiskey and bitters, of which he takes a little, spits again, fills up the glass, and presents it to his father.)

MR. COB. That's a fine boy. But go the whole hog, my son; give me a chew of tobacco. (Mr. Cob rises.)

MRS. COB, *looking after her child, cries,* So be it! Quit, I say! I expect we'll have no breakfast at this rate. Stir up, Angelica Clementia, stir I say. (Waking Miss Cob, who is in her bed.) Come and tend Washington Jefferson Franklin Monroe. The chintzes [6] have been mauling him all night, I expect. (Mrs. Cob rises, shakes two or three petticoats which she has on, and then goes downstairs, calling Annabella.)

ANNABELLA, *from her bed under the kitchen stairs.* Mrs. Cob, do you look for I? I is sleeping, and I guess I shan't stir yet.

MRS. COB. Annabella, when you have done sleeping, just fix them diapers, there's a fine girl.

ANNABELLA. I'll have to do it, I hear that—but you is right down bad, Mrs. Cob, to shake me so.

MRS. COB. Well, well, I am done with it. I'll just fix the things myself. (Mrs. Cob begins cutting up some onions for frying. Miss Cob comes down.)

MISS COB. Mr. George Washington is crying for you.

MRS. COB. Now, Annabella, you must be stirring, that's a fact. Torment me, we have yet to fix everything for company tonight, and I will have everything of the best. I was raised to it, and I will have it. Come, there's a fine girl, fry these onions while I go to George Washington. Just fix the coffee and make the rolls for Pa. (Exit Mrs. Cob. Annabella rises from under the kitchen stairs.)

ANNABELLA. One might as well be a neger. As soon as I have done got my silk frock paid for, you'll have no more of me, Sophy. I'll be off home and go to school.

MISS COB. We shall be in a right down unhandsome fix, I expect, if you go, Annabella. Don't tell Ma so today. She'll be so unaccountable cross.

ANNABELLA. I'll have to help her today, and it may be a day or two more, for I've not got my silk frock yet, and I don't be for going home without one. (Begins frying ham and onions.)

(Enter Mrs. Cob with George Washington in her arms.)

MRS. COB. Oh, you're stirring, Annabella. Well, that is a fine girl. Just move and fix the keeping room, for Mr. Cob will be down in a giffy for breakfast, and if it isn't all right handsome, you know who'll catch it. (Goes to the stairs and calls.) Benjamin Franklin! Come down, I say! Benjamin Franklin, my son, come down!

[6] Bedbugs.

A FRAGMENT [7]

(*Scene a bed-room. Morning. Mrs. Rapp has just got out of bed, and is shaking some part of the dress in which she had passed the night. Mr. Rapp remains in bed, and addresses two lads who are sleeping together on a low couch, which during the day is pushed under the bed occupied by their parents.*)

MR. RAPP. Come boys! up with ye! I wish I may be scorched if I don't send ye both east of sunrise if you don't jump slick.

MRS. RAPP. Benjamin Franklin! Jefferson Monro! D'ye hear dad, both of ye? You've all got to mind the market, I calculate, this day. 'Tis our quilting frolic,[8] and I must have every thing jam.

MR. RAPP. Keep cool, wife. Benjamin Franklin, my son, be a fine fellow, and bring me a stiff tumbler. Three quarters and one, may be. Quick, my hero, and you will be president, I calculate.

BENJAMIN FRANKLIN. (*Crawling slowly out of bed.*) Don't be in a lather, father, before you are shaved. I'll do your job, I expect, if you won't be in such a tarnation fuss. (*After quitting the bed, Ben. Franklin turns, and gives his brother Jefferson Monro a kick in the ribs, and says*), We are free and equal, I reckon, from Maine to Georgia, so you shan't be down while I am up, squire.

JEFFERSON MONRO. (*Starting up.*) What d'ye want with me, all of ye?

MRS. RAPP. Well! if that don't beat creation! Why, 'tis quilting frolic, my man, and lying a-bed won't convene, I calculate.

BEN. FRANKLIN. (*Goes to a table on which whiskey, water, and glasses, stand ready, and having mixed a tumbler according to order, he takes a pretty considerable sip, and exclaims in a whisper*), That's jam!

MR. RAPP. Look at him now! If he don't suck like an Ingin? [9] Fill it up, my hero, but mind which 'canter 'tis from. Come slick, boy — don't spill it. I'm as dry as a cob.

(*Benjamin Franklin presents the tumbler, and Mr. Rapp tastes it.*)

MR. RAPP. That's first rate. Now go the whole hog, and we will

---

[7] This is the form of the preceding sketch as it appears in the fifth edition of *Domestic Manners*. See the note to the title of the preceding selection.

[8] Mrs. Trollope's note: "The ladies of the Union are great workers, and, among other enterprises of ingenious industry, they frequently fabricate patchwork quilts. When the external composition of one of these is completed, it is usual to call together their neighbours and friends to witness, and assist at the *quilting*, which is the completion of this elaborate work. These assemblings are called 'quilting frolics,' and they are always solemnised with much good cheer and festivity."

[9] Mrs. Trollope's note: "In old English — Indian."

send you to Congress in no time; light a cigar for me, and you shall see if I don't smoke it.

MRS. RAPP. (Opening a door that leads to another room.) Angelina,[10] my daughter, stir! will you? Dad will be off to market in no time, and who's to fix the breakfast? I must be thinking of the quilting, and Clementina, I guess, must have her sleep out. So jump up slick, there's a fine gal.

ANGELINA. (From her bed.) How you do pother, mother. There's no reason in creation why your fine help here, that's snorting like a 'possum, shouldn't be stirring as well as me.

MRS. RAPP. My! How you do talk, Angelina! As if you did not know she'd be off, frolic or no frolic, if we did but affront her the least bit in the world.

ANGELINA. Well, I guess I shall set to, and start her, any how. She'll behave herself if I promise to loan her my poppy flowers for her hair to-night, for she is sick with longing to wear them. So here goes (screaming), Clementina!

MR. RAPP. (Rising, and slowly commencing the business of the toilet.) Well, wife, you'd best be after telling me what's to be got from market, for I shall be off like a gun. I have got no time to lose, for I must see what the slang-mongers [11] say of this new bank job.

* * * * * *

(Mrs. Rapp explains her wishes, and the whole family by degrees descend to the kitchen, when Mr. Rapp sets off for market, taking Benjamin Franklin and two large baskets with him.)

MRS. RAPP. There they go, that's jam! and now we must set to slick. I wonder that black beast Lily isn't come yet. Her missis promised to loan her to me for the day for fifty cents, and my pink waist-ribbon, and a pretty bargain I shall make of it if she don't come till doomsday. We shall be right down magged without her.

ANGELINA. That's a fact, for it won't convene for me to be mixing doe cakes and Johny cakes all day. I've got to fix my dress, I promise you, and as to Clementina she'll do just as much as she likes I expect, and no more.

CLEMENTINA. You may say that, Angelina; and where's the lady what's a white help as would do more? But if Mrs. Rapp will loan me five dollars to make up the price of my silk frock what I'm going to have, may be I'll be chirk at it, and get her through. What d'ye say, Mrs. Rapp? I guess you'd best be doing what I ask you, for you'll look streaked, I calculate, if the folks come before you're right fixed.

[10] In the notebooks, the daughter's name is clearly inscribed *Angelica Clementia.*

[11] Mrs. Trollope's note: "Newspaper writers."

MRS. RAPP. Well, now, if that don't make me crawl all over to think of it! Say no more, that's a jam gal; I'll have to loan the dollars, I expect, so be spry now, and get all the rations out ready for fixing the cakes, slick away. Don't sneak it, Clementina, but go the whole hog for me.

CLEMENTINA. Let me alone, Mrs. Rapp. Once and awhile I don't mind a spell of work, if I get what I want for it; so mind your business, and I'll mind mine; and see if I don't swiggle my way through, afore quilting time. But mind, old woman, you must not be spying after me, and sneaking about what don't concern you. If you'll be after frying the steaks and inyons [sic] for breakfast, and then fix the keeping room, I'll look after the cakes; but I won't carry 'em, mind.

MRS. RAPP. Go to the bakery, Jefferson Monro, and ask one of the young gentlemen, if he'll be so genteel as to step over about noon for the cakes for my quilting frolic.

ANGELINA. Well now, mother, I expect that you calculate upon loaning me your ringlets for to-night?

MRS. RAPP. If that don't beat all creation. How d'ye think I am to fix myself, then?

ANGELINA. Loan me the two corkscrews then, mother, just to hang behind my spit curls, and keep the short bunches for yourself.

MRS. RAPP. Well, I expect it will make muddy water between us if I say no, my daughter. But thanks be to the praise, here comes black Lily. What makes you so late, you nasty nigger varment?

LILY. Oh my missus! There was such a swod of market ladies and gentlemen, comed over in the first boat,[12] that I was 'most mashed to a slab in pushing to get in among 'em, they was all scrouging so thick one upon t'other; and after I had swiggled and swiggled, they made no bones of tossing me 'most into the water; and 'twas all I could do to streak it to dry footing.

MRS. RAPP. I calculate, Miss Lily, you gave 'em some nigger impendence, 'cause you was upon crossing to a free state.

LILY. No, my missus, I told 'em I wasn't sneaking it, but was coming to help a grand lady; and then one of 'em fetched me a clip over my shoulders, and said it was best show me my place afore I crossed.

MRS. RAPP. My! what a long jabber! 'Twas lucky you comed when you did, I tell you, for I was getting homely, that's a fact; and now set to, Miss Lily, or you'll hear of the cow-hide when you cross back again.

(Enter Jefferson Monro.)

JEFF. MONRO. The gentleman at the bakery says as you must fetch over the cakes yourself, if you wants 'em fixed, for he's got no mind that such trotting would be good for him.

---

12 Lily has probably crossed on the ferryboat that plied between Covington, Kentucky, and Cincinnati.

Mrs. Rapp. Cross crither! I should like 'peshily to see him soused in Big Muddy Creek, that's a fact. But here comes father.

(*Enter* Mr. Rapp *and* Benjamin Franklin, *from Market.*)

Mrs. Rapp. Back already, Squire? And how have you got along?

Mr. Rapp. Well now, I don't know exactly, but you must be clever, wife, and not be after putting my darder [dander?] up, by faulting me if all is not slick right.

Mrs. Rapp. Let's look it, husband. I'm all of a crawl till I see how my tea's to be.

Benjamin Franklin. (Taking off his hat, which is filled with peaches.) Well mother, here's my part of the job — that's for your dulcits — and they bean't smashed nothing to speak of, for sauce.

Mrs. Rapp. Now then, father.

Mr. Rapp. Well; there's your turkey — and a first rater — half a dollar for that; and here be your right chickens for frying. Bean't they little beauties? hardly bigger than humming birds; a dollar seventy five for they. Three fips for the hominy, a levy for the squash, and a quarter for the limes; inyons a fip, carolines a levy, green cobs ditto. And now comes the tarnation plague of the whole. I know you'll be homely, wife; but you may allot upon it if you be, you'll eventuate by getting the worst of it, for I shall be tarnation wrathy on my side.

Mrs. Rapp. Well, don't sneak it. What is it man? say.

Mr. Rapp. Well, then, I've got no pickled oysters.

Mrs. Rapp. Possible! But you needn't be looking fierce, Thomas Rapp. I'm not going to fault you, but I expect you'll convene you'd have conducted better if you hadn't obliviated what looks so 'peshly elegant on a tea-table.

Mr. Rapp. Woman, I did not obliviate. There was none to be had for money, so don't look streaked about what can't be helped; but be spry, and give me my breakfast slick.

(The family sit down to breakfast in the kitchen. Clementina eats with them, and Lily waits upon them all. Mr. Rapp then departs for his store, saying as he goes out), You need not allot upon seeing me till sundown; your dinner won't be over jam to-day, I calculate, so I shall contrive it to the hotel.

* * * * * *

(Mrs. Rapp, her daughter Angelina, her white help Clementina, and her borrowed slave Lily, labour unremittingly throughout the day to prepare for the *tea* in the best style of quilting frolic liberality. Benjamin Franklin and Jefferson Monro are employed during the whole time in running errands. By about 5 o'clock all is completed; Mrs. Rapp and her daughter are full dressed in the keeping room; whiskey, water, sugar, and tumblers, are ranged upon the sideboard; and the two boys washed, combed, and properly adorned in all respects, receive their mother's instructions for their behaviour.)

MRS. RAPP. Well now, be sure to behave yourselves both of you, and remember, above all things, to shake all the gentlemen as they come in, and to take the ladies' bonnets and their shoes if any of 'em change. We shall have a swod of company, and you must not sneak it in no way, but keep looking about you chirk and lively; and when any gentleman squints towards the sideboard, run slick and mix him some whiskey.

BENJAMIN FRANKLIN. Keep cool, mother, I know a thing or two.

MRS. RAPP. (Turning to Angelina.) Well, my daughter, I must say you look pretty considerable jam, and them corkscrews do convene, that's a fact. You are dreadful handsome, Angelina. I expect nobody can dubiate that. But you must be 'peshily spry to-night, or you may allot upon it we shall have father's darder up. I tell you he is talking from July to eternity about the quarters you have had; and you may realise that after the quilting is over, he'll be looking to you to happify the company with your accomplishments. Well! there they come across the clover lot, lock and lock together. My! what a swod of them, all in a slush! Why, here's every body about creation, that's a fact.

(Enter a great many American ladies and gentlemen.)

LACK OF "GENTLEMANLY" AND "LADYLIKE FEELING"

I caught in general conversation with ladies a thousand traits, too minute to record, but which, like the droppings of water, have left an impression. Among others it always appeared to me that there was a frequent want of what we call "gentlemanly feeling" and "ladylike feeling." If a bargain was to be made, which in the intercourse of the drawing-room may accidentally happen, the tone of the negotiating parties was exactly the reverse of what it would be with us. I heard of *repeated* instances in which ladies, when paying the school bills for the education of their daughters, urged the mistress of the school to "take off something," and that when both parties were in the very first line in their respective classes — but, as I said before, these things look trifling in narration; nay worse, they look ill natured, and yet such things are, and are not without importance in the colouring of the portrait.

AMERICAN MEN

Uncle Sam has long ago decided upon being a man of fashion. Paris and London must furnish his wardrobe. Bow and the Rue Vivienne are put in requisition for his toilet. He has therefore fairly challenged competition with the artificial refinements of the Old World and should not be offended if the Old World look out to see how he supports these pretensions.

Did the tailor altogether make the man, I should say well, very well. What can I say more? If they would make a standard for themselves, if they would say it is the fashion to be like the President or the President's son or any other person they might choose from among themselves as a model, it would be the very worst description of impertinence to enter amongst them and decry these manners and customs; but instead of that the fashionable part among them prefers to form themselves to the model of the Old World and must therefrom stand the comparison they have themselves invited. When tried by this standard, I will not say they are inferior to their models, I only say they are unlike them. The cities of Eastern America are greatly more advanced in refinement than the western country, yet as it appears to me they are ages behind Europe.

I know not whether it will be necessary for them to go through all the stages, as we of the Old World have done before them, but if it be, the next century might see them in the age of chivalry, and questionless some among them might couch a lance right manfully. Then should they have minstrels whose wandering melody might alter the rude horse and alligator of the Mississippi and smooth the calculating brow of the anxious Yankee; then would a parliament of love sit in judgement, and doom to worse than death the spitter and tobacco chewer. Then shall a loyal lover deem it no long service were he to adore his lady love for seven years before she wedded him, during the whole of which time it would be impossible for him to chew tobacco, and then the habit might be broken and many other advances in civilization would go forward that in the course of time might do much . . . [space left blank] up to the perfect gentleman.

But perhaps I have omitted the most important stage in the process, that which preceded our rudeness. For has not modern Europe before her a model, an acknowledged model antecedent in time, and superior in finish to all others? We do not disdain to confess that ancient Greece is still before us and above us in refinement, and it is the consciousness of this that has led us on so far, and that will lead us farther still. Whether a tobacco-chewing age preceded that of Anacreon, my books do not say, but if human faculties be progressive, I conceive that the joys of the grape, quaffed sparkling from the golden cup, while beauty, poetry, and music smiled around . . . [space left blank].

The age when "divine leisure" was passed in the enjoyment of all that art can win from nature; when the air was taught to breathe fragrance and the limbs in all the grace of ease stretched themselves on roses; when the juice of the bright grape was quaffed sparkling from the golden cup, first pressed by the lips of beauty; when painting, poetry, and music, like duteous handmaids ever at command, stood ready to waken the soul to rapture, or soothe it to the slumbers of the blest — this age must, I think, let the march of mind be never so rapid, be at considerable distance in point of time from that in which a glass of gin cock-tail, or egg nog, receive their highest relish from a mouthful of chewed tobacco, where the absence of the ladies is thought favourable to the enjoyment of perfect comfort, and where unrestrained spitting is the emblem of unshackled freedom.

LACK OF ORIGINALITY

Had Americans the freshness of originality, they would be something. It is this mincing affectation of Europe that makes them ridiculous. It is a country every way interesting to visit — but those who have been used to the refinements of Europe and who have the means of still enjoying them have no business to take up their residence and then abuse it. The country is a glorious country. The people are enterprising and intelligent. I do not think they are what is called amiable — but after all, that only means that they did not reach my beau ideal of agreeability. They appear to like each other.

SEPARATION OF THE SEXES

All these strongly marked differences between our national manners I attribute to the men and women not living more together. It would but bestow much tediousness upon the reader were I to follow out all the reasoning that has led me to this conclusion, but that I have arrived at it without the help of prejudice I do believe. West or East, my observations have brought me to the same point, namely that the American people will not equal the nations of Europe in refinement till women become of more importance among them.

EPITAPH FOR AN EXPECTORATING AMERICAN [13]

~~The best~~   chew
A faultless   new
The perfect husband father patriot friend
                        life but
Here ~~finds~~ shall finds his ~~sorrows~~ not his glory end
Trusting above that glory to renew
      lies
Here ~~is~~ meanwhile George Washington Spitchew.

---

[13] This is one of the two pieces of poetry that occur in the notebooks. The other, which consists of a few couplets upon Mrs. Trollope's entry into the New World by way of the Mississippi, is quoted in section IX of the Introduction. The epitaph for George Washington Spitchew seems to be Mrs. Trollope's way of saying that a tobacco-chewer would appear incongruous amid the heavenly choir. Both her first draft and her revised version are given. They are written lengthwise across one page of the notebooks.

A faultless husband, father, patriot, friend
Here finds his life, but not his glory end
Trusting above that glory to renew
With
~~Here~~ patience waits George Washington Spitchew.

AMERICANS' LOVE OF DRESS AND SPIRITS

I am aware that the great majority of the population are poor, what
we should call very poor, but the disproportionate expense of their
dress to all other expenses is surprising. Their inordinate love of spirits, I often fancied, savours a little of savage life. The Negro and the
Indian would anywhere, and at any time, barter all else for finery and
strong drink.

NATIONAL PRIDE AND SECTIONAL PREJUDICE

We have been told in every essay, review, magazine, and newspaper
that issues from the American press that "we do not understand the
American people." In all simplicity of spirit I determined to correct
this. I felt that my prejudices, my habits, my tastes might all prove so
many porcupine's quills, catching and entangling in everything I encountered, and so irritating the inward spirit as to render it incapable
of judging what things were, leaving only the consciousness of what
they were to me.

To correct this as far as I could, I made it my custom wherever I
went, by land or by water, in steamboats or stagecoaches, in hotels or
in boarding-houses, with farmers and mechanics, with members of
Congress and gentleman carpenters, with senators and erudite shoe-
makers, with priest and lawyer, with ladies of high standing, and
with ladies of no standing, with slaves and with free, with rich and
with poor, *to talk to them about themselves and their country*. What
makes this manner of obtaining information the more likely to prove
successful is that these are the only subjects that they appear to con-
verse upon with pleasure, at least with foreigners. According to my
custom, I wrote down constantly the precis of all the information I obtained, and I do not believe that any note-writing traveller in the
world ever possessed such a prodigious mass of contradictory statements as my portfolios contain.

There are some points certainly on which they all agree — namely,
that the American government is the best in the world. That America
has produced the greatest men that ever existed. That all the nations
of the earth look upon them with a mixture of wonder and envy and
that in time they will all follow their great example and have a president. This, or something like it, I heard everywhere, and as the uniform result of my enquiring, I have ventured the statement that the
Americans are all strongly attached to their government; but beyond

this all I have learnt from them goes but to confirm the truth of the sentence passed on all their English visitors. I do not understand the American people.

In Louisiana I was told that if I stayed long enough in the state, I should find the most polished society in the world. That Spain, France, and America were there blended into one delightful whole, but to the north I should be less pleased. The people were rude and little civilized, and were unfortunately very jealous of the people of the South — but the American government was the best in the world. "America has produced ——." In Tennessee I heard that if I were to place myself there I should have an opportunity of watching the progress of the finest country upon Earth — that the noble equality that reigned among the whites would not annoy me, because the black population supply the place of the servile class in Europe. That probably I might find Ohio a disagreeable residence for the want of this, but that the American government was the finest in the world.

In Indiana I was told that the slave states were abominations & some free ones not much better, but that they gave a model to the Union in the wisdom and virtue of their state laws — yet the American government was the best in the world. In Ohio they said that I might congratulate myself upon resting there for a while, for a few years more would make that the centre of the Mighty Union. The seat of the Federal government would be placed there, and the world would look on and wonder at the station they held among men. The Yankees, to be sure, were a detestable race and the Virginians worse still, and it is lucky I had not got into that hornets' nest; but yet the American government is the best in the world and ——. In Kentucky they swore that I was in the very soul of America, and that every other state was but a paltry limb, for one Kentuckian could *whip* three from any other state from Georgia to Maine. But the American government was the best in the world ——.

In Virginia I heard that I was come to the land of gentlemen. That their high spirit passed the dirty mercantile drudges of the Atlantic cities. That the progress of time would spread Virginia's feelings and Virginia's principles over the Union, and it would then become the wondered admiration of the universe, for the American government was the best in the world and America has produced ——. In Maryland I was pitied for having entered America by the back door, and they were sure I must have been sadly disgusted by all I had seen — but that I should now see what a free people could do. The American government was the best in the world and ——. In Delaware I heard that I might now judge whether plenty smiled on America. Their swamps, to be sure, were not healthy; but they possessed great and peculiar advantages, and the American government was the best in the world. In Pennsylvania they said that the slave states had shown me a country of monsters. That Yankeeland would in another manner disgust me as much, but that Pennsylvania was the paradise of the world, for besides all their other advantages the American government was the best in the world and America had produced ——. In the District of Columbia there seemed but one voice, and that was raised to the highest pitch to declare that Washington was Washington and that the American government was the best in the world.

EQUALITY

I greatly doubt if the tone of equality affected by the lower orders really produces more satisfactory feelings to themselves than it does to those of the higher classes. It constantly puts them *dans une fausse position*,[14] and they must feel it. It is not their clawing hold of a soft hand unused to labour that will spare them the necessity of continuing that which has indurated their own. Nor can their entering a drawing-room and defiling its carpet with tobacco and mud produce the slightest change in their own dwellings, unless, indeed, it should make them appear more dreary by comparison. This useless meeting of incongruities prevails all over the Union; greatly less in the Atlantic cities than in the country, and considerably less at New York[15] than in any other city — but yet something of the kind is left. You are not startled by a man reeking with work and whiskey approaching to take your hand, but that air of respect, elsewhere assumed by tradesmen, is wanting; the common courtesies of salutation are abridged, as if every one was afraid of compromising his dignity by being too condescending. All this is trifling; but human life is made up of trifles, & they may quite as well be graceful as not.

Among the really poor I am quite sure that the effect is not trifling: They are constantly kept in a state of irritation by feeling that their boasted equality is a falsehood. It is a delusion which their pride leads them to wish at while their penury goads them to hate the solid reality of inequality which exists in America exactly as much as it does elsewhere. The only inequality that does not exist is precisely that which touches a poor labouring man in no way whatever — purely that of titles. The honors emanating from the throne, and secured by those immediately surrounding it, may form a brilliant nucleus to a native splendour but can in no way prejudice the freedom or prosperity of other ranks. Unless, however, the contrary can be proved, the Englishman is in every possible meaning of the words as free and as equal as the American.

Another evil that I strongly felt arose from this fictitious equality

[14] In a false position.

[15] Mrs. Trollope must have written this passage into her first notebook long before she visited New York, perhaps resolving to check it by experience later.

(which like all other lies takes more trouble to support than the most recondite truth) was the impossibility of obliging those who served me. In countries better organized there is a feeling of mutual kindness between the serving and the served that has often been found to form one of the strongest attachments of social life. In America this cannot exist. All you can do is hardly enough to enforce civility. Gratitude is totally out of the question.

BLACKBERRIES

I am almost sure I shall be laughed at if I say that the blackberries of North America are almost the finest fruit I ever tasted of the berry kind, but so it is. They are as large as moderate-sized mulberries, and as juicy. They are less acid and the flavour is incomparably richer. As a sweetmeat they are much finer than either raspberries or straw-berries.

CLARITY OF AMERICAN ATMOSPHERE

Of all the points in which America has the advantage of England, I think the one I felt most sensibly was the clearness and brightness of the atmosphere. By day and by night this exquisite purity of air gives tenfold beauty to every object. Claude's landskips convey the best idea of it that can be given on canvass, but it makes itself felt as well as seen, and is indeed a constant source of enjoyment.

AN AMERICAN SEA CAPTAIN

Whenever I was well enough to be on deck, I greatly enjoyed the conversation of the captain. He was so truly a sailor, so truly an American sailor, which is really a very fine variety of that interesting species of which all the world know that English tars are class one, that I found him very agreeable. Our ship was his darling, his business, his plaything. To overtake and pass another ship (which happened more than once) was delightful. His bright black eyes danced in his head, and the smile that curled his lip and dimpled his cheek was the very essence of triumph and gaiety. That he could safely put the head of his idol a point nearer the wind than any other was his morning and evening hymn. I could not help thinking what a fine race we mortals should be, were we all as much in earnest in what we did and what we said, as our good captain.

BASIL HALL'S METHOD OF COMPOSING

Lea, the Philadelphian publisher, told me that Capt. Hall told him the method he pursued in the composition of his work on South America was as follows: He made copious minutes of all he saw — he brought home fifteen volumes of notes. He had them all written fair by a copier. He employed his brother & brother-in-law to read them, and to mark with a number every passage according to its value, then to select two volumes full, beginning with all the number ones and going on till they had got enough. He said these voyages had been written over five times.

MRS. TROLLOPE'S LIST OF AMERICAN PHRASES [16]

That's a fact
right good
good = *well*
bad = *ill*
right bad
right jam
right down good
right down bad
smart = *clever*
clever = *kind*
lovely = *good*
fine = *useful, good* — fine boy
elegant = *excellent*
handsome = *well written, comfortable*
unhandsome fix = *uncomfortable*
to fix = *to arrange*
I guess
I expect = *I suppose*
I calculate
I guess, I guess
I reckon
Say!
Uncle ⎫ to Negroes — everybody
Aunt ⎭
half horse, half alligator = *Kentuckian*
jab savagorous [17]
first-rate disgusting

class leader ⎫
Sister ⎬ Methodists
Brother ⎭
Gd d–n　17 times within hearing
raised = *brought up*
standing = *station in life*
representation = *portrait*
go the whole hog
hold fast
Map = *landskip*
Go it = *do it*
altogether too much, or too bad
entirely too much, or too bad
pretty considerably much
If you can't find it, ⎫ playful to
make it ⎬ Negroes
you creature you ⎭
To learn = *to teach*
Quit = *leave off*
Corn dodger　hoe cake
Johny Cakes
Waffles
Batter cakes
I did so.
Venison [?]
Rock = *bass*
Sturgeon
Shad
Squash

[16] This list appears in Notebook 1 under the title "Phrases" immediately after Henry Trollope's writings, and was probably Mrs. Trollope's first entry in her notebooks. For the sake of clarity definitions are printed in italics.

[17] In Chapter xiii of *Domestic Manners*, Mrs. Trollope tells how the dressing-room of Mrs. Drake, the actress, was visited by a Western lady who picked up the dagger that Mrs. Drake was to use in the course of the evening's performance and exclaimed with much emotion: "What! do you really jab this into yourself sevagarous?" (The word is clearly spelled *savagorous* in the notebooks.)

Lima beans
Hominy = *ground corn*
Green corn
Blackberries & cream
A drink
I've got to
I had to
Sun down
selling a Notion — Yankee
Wait a bit
This 'ere
jist
I swow [swan?] = *I vow*
hadn't ought
you'd ought

Bakery [18]
to tote = *to count*
ugly = *unamiable*
It done me no good
done deaded [?]
Them are the men what made you
  fly

from July to eternity
ornery = *ordinary*
drap = *drop*
'cute
soft
darn'd
darnation
ax [ask?]
I done it
Hop toads is little creatures what
  hop like a frog
by all means
scrouge
scrouge hard

Handsome writing
I am done with it.
He is done with that.
Too hot for anything.
Too bad for anything, etc.
Boarding — plunder   Truck
"Squash of fat" — Negro phrase

ORIGIN OF "UNCLE SAM"

Uncle Sam seems almost to have taken place of Brother Jonathan as the national cognomen of the United States. It arose from the following circumstance. During the last war a magazine of army stores was superintended by a Mr. Samuel Wilson, who was familiarly called by all the workers Uncle Sam. The casks were marked U. S., as all government stores are, but it seems that some person ignorant of this enquired of the workmen what these letters meant. A wag among them gravely replied that they were the initials of Uncle Sam, the superintendent. This valuable piece of information was speedily repeated, and so forcibly caught the fancy of the hearer that he sent it to a newspaper. The joke gained favor, and has long been recognised as a national pleasantry throughout the Union.

"LITTLE RESPONSIBILITIES"

I was amused by the new use of a word which appears to have a fair chance of being naturalized in the U. S., and for which I understand

[18] This word and the words and phrases that follow do not appear in Mrs. Trollope's collected list of phrases, but are jotted down at random places in the notebooks. Her dramatic sketch "Day of a Lady in the West," already given, is, of course, a mine of such phrases.

they are indebted to Miss Wright; children, when spoken of in reference to the duties they impose, are styled "little responsibilities."

ROBERT OWEN

When the community was first commenced at New Harmony, either from decency or discretion Mr. Owen, I am told, did not proclaim that full extent to which his liberalism extended in *domestic legislation,* which has since been declared to be the doctrine of his school. The histories I have heard of New Harmony are chiefly poor. These had been decoyed thither at its commencement and consisted chiefly of accounts of the . . . [end of passage].

CINCINNATI MORALS

It gave me no favorable idea of the tone of morals in Cincinnati to be told that it was unsafe for any woman to appear in the streets after *sun down*. Without a protector it was impossible, and even with one it was to be avoided if possible, lest sights and sounds of disorder might meet their eyes. This restraint was the more unpleasant from the heat of the climate, which made it almost impossible to leave the house when the sun was above the horizon.

CHURCH GOVERNMENT

All the power that religious institutions vest in the hands of church government where there is a national church is here thrown into the hands of individuals often of the lowest order, and the difference between the two systems is as great as there would be between a trial by jury before the appointed judges of the land, & sanctioned by the king, and a sentence passed for crime committed or imputed by a score of coal heavers on the Thames.

ROUSSEAU AND SPITTING

When Rousseau was asked for an epitaph on Fréron, he replied, *"Ce serait bientôt fait — on n'a que cracher sur son tombeau."* [19]
That exquisite answer of Rousseau when he was asked for an epitaph on a man he despised would be unintelligible here. *"On n'a ——"* would suggest no idea of contempt to the *tombeau,* but simply one of comfortable relief to the *cracheur.*

SORTIE FROM THE THEATRE [20]

A stranger contrast can hardly be imagined than between the sortie from an American theatre and from those of Paris or London — the blaze of light, the noisy throng of splendid carriages, the bustling ea-

---

[19] "That would soon be done — one needs merely spit on his tomb."
[20] Mrs. Trollope's title.

gerness of the [two words illegible] of serving men, the full dressed
groups that flit past as their high-sounding names are called, and still
amid the brilliant confusion the ever present police or *gendarmerie* to
assure safety in despite of tumult — all rushed on my recollection as
we crept through the dusty lobby and issued on the dark and silent
street.

HOPE FOR THE FUTURE

After all it is a wonderful spectacle that presents itself to the mind,
when the first effect of what is distasteful wears off. It is a wonderful
country. No very rapid traveller can do justice to the United States,
for the first impression is not agreeable. It is chiefly in superficials that
they are defective, and it takes some time to recover from the silly surprise that we are all apt to feel that this, that, and the other is not just
as we have been used to see them. The most essential things are those
to which they have first addressed their daily increasing wealth &
power. Their hospitals, their penitentiaries, their asylums, their banks
are in the very highest style of excellence. No expense has been spared
and no ability has been wanting to make them so. The great liberality
shewn by the different states in all their public works shews a universally liberal spirit which will doubtless ere many years are past lead
them to the acquirement of all that they are now deficient in.

They want taste, and they want grace — the acquirement of the latter is, I believe, the natural consequence of the diffusion of the former.
All the wealth that the nation has hitherto spent has been well spent,
and there is no reason to doubt that their yearly increasing resources
will continue to [be] well applied. If so, it follows, I think, that a
shorter time than I would venture to name will see art in all its highest branches flourishing among them. Would not Europe have had
more reason to impugn their wisdom than the new has to condemn
their want of taste, had the city of Philadelphia determined upon dip-
ping up water from the Delaware and Schuylkill and sending it in
casks round the town while the treasure she has expended on her unequalled water works had been sent off to Italy for the purchase of a
few fourth-rate pictures? or the treasure devoted to their unequalled
canals, their noble hospitals and penitentiaries as a bribe to the Pope
to let them run away with the Belvedere Apollo & the Venus di
Medicis?

When the time shall arrive that their resources without impeachment to their wisdom may be turned to the collecting of books, pictures, & statues, it is more than probable that the ambitious & striving
spirit of the people will speedily make them workers of their full share
of Earth's treasures of this kind as well as of all others — nay, it is
probable, I think, that a much larger proportion of this people will
then become patrons of art here than have ever been known else-

where; for the luxuries they have, and they are already many, are common to an infinitely greater proportion of the population than has ever been seen elsewhere.

II. *From the Rough Draft*

AN UNPUBLISHED PREFACE [21]

Two new volumes of travels is enough to produce an exclamation from writer and reader, similar to that of the Sentimentalist in the *Rejected Addresses,*

"Indeed it makes me very, very sick."

For myself, I found an antidote to the nausea attending my part of the business, in the constant excitement of having to describe scenes that amused, and objects that delighted me, and I can only hope, like all dutiful authors, that my readers may be amused and delighted, too.

My book has been altogether compiled from notes made at the moment, and can therefore pretend to little regularity of arrangement. The engravings are the work of an excellent artist and highly talented friend, who could have done himself and the subjects more justice, had he always been present with us. But as this was not the case, he could often draw only from description.[22] The best and most spirited are from the life, and may, I think, be easily distinguished.

I greatly doubt if my book contains much valuable instruction; nay, I should not be much surprised if it were called trifling; for to tell the honest truth I suspect that it is *tant soit peu,*[23] gossiping. But I have seen and heard so many queer things that wiser people may have never seen nor heard that without intending to tell one quarter of it I still may find enough respectable to fill 500 pages, and if so, I will print it. There is, in fact, so much in America that English ladies and gentlemen know nothing about; the people are so strangely like, and so strangely unlike us; the connection with us is so close, yet the disunion so entire; speaking the same language, yet having hardly a feeling in

---

[21] This strange preface, which Mrs. Trollope quite sensibly discarded, allows an unusual insight into her attitude toward her book when it was in its early stages. The preface shows, too, the openness and frankness that were characteristic of her habit of mind.

[22] Mrs. Trollope wrote Miss Mitford from New York in 1831 that Hervieu had prepared "about thirty" illustrations for her book. Probably the least effective of those that Hervieu drew "from description" were left unpublished. Certainly most of the twenty-four illustrations that appear in *Domestic Manners* were drawn from first-hand knowledge, and the rest were based upon three years' observation of American life.

[23] A very little.

common, that I am clearly of opinion there is still much untold that
is worth telling.

I really do not believe that I have any particular talent to qualify
me for the undertaking, but nobody seems to choose to visit America
who has. As to Capt. Hall, he is altogether too wise for the sort of
business I have undertaken, and to say the truth, does not appear to
have been in the very best temper in the world when he made his
North American tour. How is a man whose thoughts are fixed on the
philosophy of government to find time for such tiny observations as
my notes are filled with? And yet the world is made up of atoms, and
though I may dole them out one by one, they are still part and parcel
of the great machine we are all so fond of examining.

VOYAGE TO AMERICA [24]

We left London for New Orleans on the fourth of November 1827,
and notwithstanding the unpropitious season, we cleared the Lizard
without a fog. During the next week we saw a thousand miles, gently
and steadily, which brought us to a climate that seems incapable of
generating this worst of sea-born dangers. Nothing that I know of can
be compared to the beauty of the sea in these regions; the waves as
they lashed the side of our vessel looked, as Shelley beautifully expresses it,
          "Like light dissolved, in star-showers breaking."
The white foam, as it curled back from our prow, and broke over the
clear green sea, in endless variety of curves and angles, gave to each
wave the effect of a block of verd antique marble.[25] The bright pure
air seemed to bring every sail that passed within half its real distance,
and both our eyes and lungs confessed we were in an atmosphere such
as we had never before enjoyed.

We soon passed the Madeiras, and felt no difficulty in giving credit
to all we had heard of the healing sweetness of their air. As we advanced towards the tropics, the delicious influence of the climate, tempered as it was by the season, became more and more perceptible, and
by degrees we found ourselves obliged to walk the deck in the month
of December under the shelter of our parasols. Notwithstanding the
proverbial sameness of a sea voyage, we were constantly surrounded
by objects which to us were new and interesting. The eager delight of
the children, who felt no touch of sickness, supplied the energy that I
wanted myself, and every dolphin and flying fish, of which we made
spoil, was an object of wonder, and of pleasure. I was often suffering
from the illness that torments new sailors; but I had nevertheless in-

---

[24] Mrs. Trollope's description of her Atlantic crossing to America follows
the preface of her rough draft without title or break.

[25] A green mottled or serpentine marble.

tervals of great enjoyment. The beauty of the tropical nights has been
too often described to leave me anything to say on the subject; but
this beauty, perhaps, was never more heartily enjoyed than by the little party who assembled on the deck of the Edward to watch the
planet Venus follow the sun into the sea, and who often remained
there till midnight showed them the Southern Cross, erect.

The weather was almost uniformly fine; once only we had a gale,
and then but just enough of it to let us see that the bright blue waves
which had danced and sparkled round us for so many days could look
black and terrible. Our good-humoured Captain [26] helped to support
us on the deck, whilst we looked on what we fancied was an awful
storm, and half terrified, half delighted, we watched the foam-crested
mountains and the yawning black abyss between, till we were stunned
by the uproar, and wetted to the skin by the spray. During this hour
or two of rough weather, the ocean seemed to be throwing up all its
monsters, for the grampus, porpoise, and the huge and hideous black
fish sometimes five abreast were seen riding the tempest, and sporting
in uncouth gambols to the wild roaring of the winds.

Besides this short gale two other events only diversified the sameness of our days: The first of these was the falling in with a vessel that
had been driven out of her course, and beat about for forty days, during the last twenty of which she had been without water, or any other
provision than Malaga wine, and raisins. Our glasses soon showed that
she was much out of trim, and making every effort to come up to us.
We lay to, and she approached so closely that we saw the countenances of her pale and haggard crew. Her Captain put the speaking
trumpet to his mouth, and we all distinctly heard "twenty-one days
without water" — though the voice was faint and feeble. Our Captain
stood to hear no more, but in an instant was at the other end of the
vessel, and in shorter time than appeared possible, dispatched a hogs-
head of water, and a barrel of biscuit, accompanied by an invitation to
the Captain to come on board.

He did so, and it was not without emotion that we watched the manner of his reception; every eye beamed welcome, and not a few were
moistened as they looked on the wan and hunger-stricken countenance
of the old man. They had suffered dreadfully, and two of his crew he
said could not, he feared, recover. Every comfort that could be thought
of was sent on board her, and in return everyone, I believe, on board
the Edward received a box of their raisins — though the poor Captain
declared he loathed the sight of them so much that he almost disliked
to offer them; but the sight of the children, scrambling for the hand-
fuls our mate threw upon the deck on his return, removed his scru-

[26] Mrs. Trollope gives a further description of him in her notebooks. See
"An American Sea Captain" in section I of this appendix.

ples. We also received from him a cask or two of excellent Malaga wine.

Our next adventure was near proving a very disagreeable one: We were sitting on deck, watching as usual the setting sun, when, as darkness approached, one among us descried in the west a light that appeared like that of a beacon. We called to the Captain to tell us what it was. He looked very grave, and said, "It is a signal to us, to lie to."

"Shall you do so?" we asked. He appeared not to hear us; but we immediately heard him giving orders, which were followed by hoisting as much additional canvass as we could safely carry. He evidently kept out of our way, to avoid questions, and we saw there was something wrong, though we knew ¬ot what. The next morning, when I got on deck, I saw every glass on board pointed to a speck on the horizon.

"Is she gaining on us?" was pronounced in accents of so much anxiety by the standers-by that I became convinced something terrible was approaching. When the good Captain found that he could no longer conceal the fact, he confessed that there was every reason to believe we were chased by a pirate.

For some hours our situation was disagreeable enough: The common sailors, having less discretion than the Captain, scrupled not to assure us that they should be all barbarously murdered, and that we should be robbed, and chained down to our berths, at least, if not thrown one upon the other into the sea; the stranger sail evidently gained upon us, and terror was as evidently doing the same, when another vessel, and a right gallant one, was discovered chasing our chaser, which latter tacked, and shifted, and at length veered about, scudding away as fast as possible before the wind, with the English man of war (as she was soon discovered to be) after her. I doubt if the females on board felt at all better pleased at their escape than did the crew; it is true they knew better what the danger was than we did, and various and most ghastly were the stories with which they entertained us for many days afterward of the "water rats" that frequent these seas.

The West Indian Islands, and lastly Cuba, were passed in succession, and on Christmas day we witnessed with great delight the singular phenomenon of the mighty Mississippi, mingling its muddy mass of waters with the deep blue of the Mexican Gulf. This was the only announce[ment] of our approach to land; for the shores of this river are so utterly flat that no object upon them is perceptible at sea.

THE INDIAN AND THE NAVIGATING BEAR [27]

I must not omit to relate another anecdote connected with the Mississippi (not so ghastly as the last), which one of the passengers told us, with many assurances of its being "perfectly true." A young Indian Hunter who made a trade of selling bear skins at New Orleans had charged his light canoe for her voyage, and set forth. His faithful gun, ever loaded, and ever ready for attack or defence, lay on the skins at his feet; his more treacherous companion, the whiskey flask, flanked his right hand, equally ready for use, or abuse. Thus prepared, his steady hand rested with easy security on his paddle rudder, and gently and steadily he glided down the stream.

Suddenly his quick eye discerned a motion in a thick cane brake that darkly shaded the water's edge. With a noiseless and almost imperceptible movement, his slender prow changed its direction, and approached the spot, where he saw enough to know that a bear of no ordinary size lay crouching there. Gently, gently he drew nearer, and more near, till a large paw and, better still, a drowsy eye were visible. The gun is levelled, cocked; yet no sound has reached the half sleeping bear. Another instant, and the certain bullet had done its work, but in that instant a light breeze passed over the slender reeds, and bent them till they touched the gun, at the very moment it was discharged.

The baffled Indian had missed his aim for the first time in his life, but had no leisure to relieve his vexed spirit by any of the oaths his traffic with the Christians of New Orleans had taught him; for the bear was on his haunches, and the hunter knew he was in act to spring. One only chance was left him; could he, too, spring at the same moment with the bear, he might yet be saved. The thought and act were one. The Indian was in the brake, and his shaggy foe in the canoe. The Indian paused to mark the result; not so the bear. He had no power to pause, for his entrance into the canoe had given it an impulse that sent it from the shore into the current, and on and on it went, the wondering bear gazing wistfully from side to side in most strange dismay.

In this fashion the bear and his boat entered New Orleans, and soon every vessel on the river, and every passenger on its banks, forgot all else, to gaze at Bruin, and to wonder what, and whence, he might be. Some declared it was a savage of a nation hitherto unknown, others that it was an Indian conjuror, in one of their quaint disguises; others again (these were the travelled men) were strongly of opinion that it was an Englishman of fashion, dressed in a driving coat. Some few

---

[27] In Mrs. Trollope's rough draft this tale follows the "crocodile" story that she relates in Chapter iii of *Domestic Manners*.

ventured to differ from all the rest, and said they thought it looked very like a bear. A quiet Yankee, who had hitherto given no opinion at all, suggested that, be it what it might, they should have a better chance with it on land than in water, and proposed that a hook, attached to a cord of prudent length, should be cast in such a manner as to enable them to draw the canoe to shore. The proposal was acted upon. The prow again touched the land, and the stranger, uttering one long loud growl that speedily cleared him a passage, gave another spring that placed him high and dry upon the land, and without staying to look either to the right or to the left, he ran through the wondering throng as fast as his clumsy paws could take him, and soon found shelter in the woods.

The Indian knew the current, and knew, too, that the white men would not let his skins float away to the ocean, though guarded by the bear. The next day, therefore, brought him to New Orleans, where he found little difficulty in recovering his canoe, his skins, and his gun. Report says that when he found the whiskey flask missing he exclaimed, "The great spirit confound him! did he too learn to love it?" and then added in a gentler tone, "Poor beast! if he tasted it, how could he help it?"

APPENDIX B

DESCRIPTION AND DATING OF MRS. TROLLOPE'S
NOTEBOOKS AND ROUGH DRAFT

The notebooks and rough draft of *Domestic Manners of the Americans,*
all that remains of the book in manuscript, were formerly the property of Miss Muriel R. Trollope, great-granddaughter of Mrs. Trollope, who kindly allowed me to arrange the purchase of these materials by Indiana University so that they could be used in the preparing
of this edition. They are now in the special collections of the Indiana
University Library.

There are three notebooks, two of which bear large numbers *1* and
2 upon their covers. The first has the signature "H. Trollope" inside
the cover, and fifteen of its pages contain Henry Trollope's poems and
memoranda. Several pages, apparently occupied by Henry's copies of
his letters to one Adolphe Barzaine, have been cut out. The second
notebook has the signature "T. A. Trollope Win: Coll: Alumn: 1827"
and must have belonged originally to Thomas Adolphus Trollope; but
Tom left its pages blank, and they are now filled with his mother's
handwriting. The third notebook has what seems earlier to have been
the initials "T. A. T." (which could stand either for Thomas Adolphus
Trollope or for his father, Thomas Anthony Trollope — the initials are
not quite like those in the second notebook). The first "T" has been
written over and changed into an "F," and the "A" has been crossed
out. Beneath these initials is the date March 25, 1825. Besides part of
Frances Trollope's observations on America, the third notebook includes a nineteen-page review of Sir Walter Scott's novels. Several
pages are cut out of the book; all that remain are in Mrs. Trollope's
hand.

All together the three notebooks contain in the neighborhood of
sixty-four thousand words of material dealing with Mrs. Trollope's
American experiences. This material is in the form of isolated passages
with no discernible logic to their sequence; they range from a few
words to several hundred words each, and part are in pencil, though
the greatest number of them are in ink. The most interesting of the
brief jottings are presented in section IX of the Introduction to this
edition, where further description of the notebooks and their contents
is also given. Almost certainly Mrs. Trollope wrote the longer passages,
which run on an average somewhat under two hundred words, by piecing together and expanding notes that she had taken during her travels, probably on separate scraps of paper.

Passages in the notebooks that deal with Mrs. Trollope's experiences up to her arrival at Baltimore in March 1830 were by and large incorporated into her rough draft, where they appear in a more polished form. But the notebooks go well beyond her arrival at Baltimore (at which point the rough draft leaves off), and most, though by no means all, of the paragraphs of the printed text of *Domestic Manners* that deal with her visits to Baltimore, Philadelphia, and Washington and her residence at Stonington, Maryland, have their rougher counterparts in the notebooks. The notebooks also contain a good many passages of decided interest that Mrs. Trollope did not reproduce in either her rough draft or her printed text. Where these amplify or explain specific statements in the text, they have been given in the notes of this edition; otherwise they have been included in Appendix A.

Mrs. Trollope's rough draft contains about fifty-two thousand words. It is written in ink, except for one short passage in pencil, upon 148 large (13″ x 8″) pages of heavy paper. There are many crossings-out and emendations between the lines of the manuscript. The rough draft begins with a frank and diffident preface, followed by an account of Mrs. Trollope's Atlantic crossing to the United States, both of which items she later discarded. It carries her narrative through her visit to New Orleans, her experiences at Nashoba, her two eventful years at Cincinnati, and her journey over the Alleghenies to Baltimore, where she arrived in March 1830. It also includes a small part of her description of Baltimore and her sketch of a day in the life of a Philadelphia lady, though nothing else concerning her observations in that city. Large sections of the rough draft appear with only minor alterations in the printed text of *Domestic Manners,* but there are several passages of considerable interest that she finally decided against publishing. Where they are canceled parts of passages that appear in the printed text or where they have a direct bearing on specific passages in the text and are not cumbersomely long, they have been given in the notes to this edition. Three long selections have been included in Appendix A.

Mrs. Trollope probably composed nearly all of the 148 pages of the rough draft during her first months at Stonington in the spring of 1830. She wrote Mary Russell Mitford at the end of July that by the time of her visit to Philadelphia (which began late in June) the first volume of her book was finished "and most of the notes for the second collected." It seems likely that she was thinking of the rough draft or a large portion of it as the volume that she had already finished.

By September, when Mrs. Trollope left Stonington for Alexandria, Virginia, she must have composed nearly all the passages in the notebooks that carry her narrative beyond the rough draft, presenting her experiences and observations at Baltimore, Washington, and Philadelphia. Probably she did not complete the passages that describe her life

at Stonington until some time after her removal to Alexandria. Near
the end of Chapter xxvii of *Domestic Manners* Mrs. Trollope tells us
that early in 1831, while she was still at Alexandria, she set about
reading and revising her notes and arranging the pages of her manuscript. She "scrupulously challenged every expression of disapprobation," she says, and "omitted in transcription much that I had written,
as containing unnecessary details of things which had displeased me."
The reader of section IX of the Introduction to this edition, the notes,
and Appendix A knows that she spoke truly.

APPENDIX C

TEXTUAL NOTE

In this edition of *Domestic Manners of the Americans* the text of the first edition is reproduced without change except for correction of a few errors clearly due to oversight on the part of Mrs. Trollope or her printer. Such errors as *lon* for *long*, *grea* for *great*, *Canandaigna* for *Canandaigua*, *wo'nt* for *won't*, and omission of one of a pair of parentheses or quotation marks are pretty clearly oversights that call for correction.

Mrs. Trollope's personal habits in spelling and punctuation are another matter. She spells *chestnut* without the *t*, *julep* with an *a* instead of an *e*, and *recall* with a single *l*; she uses such archaic or individual forms as *ancles*, *skaiting*, *potatoe*, *shews*; she wavers between *Chesapeake* and *Chesapeak*, *Pitzburgh* and *Pittsburgh*, *Tuilleries* and *Tuileries*, *ours* and *our's*, *extacy* and *ecstasy*. She employs punctuation with a good feeling for the sense of her sentence but with small respect for rigid law or consistency. Such shifts and idiosyncrasies appear in her notebooks and rough draft as well as in her printed text; they are part of her book and her manner of expression. Without confusing the reader or appreciably detracting from his ease of reading, they lend character to her text. It seems best to leave them.

The second, third, and fourth editions of *Domestic Manners* [1] are identical in text with the first except that pagination varies, a few typographical errors are eliminated, and a few new errors are committed. The fifth edition, [2] published seven years after the first four editions, shows an erratic attempt to normalize Mrs. Trollope's spelling and punctuation. If the author made the alterations of this text, which seems unlikely, she worked very hurriedly and often without much care or discernment. Mrs. Trollope appended many new notes to the pages of the fifth edition. These are included among the notes of the present edition. She also added to her text "A Fragment," a dramatic sketch dealing with the life of a family in the West. This sketch, together with the original of it from her notebooks, is given in Appendix A. Her preface to the fifth edition is printed in Appendix D.

Selections from Mrs. Trollope's notebooks and rough draft have demanded a greater amount of editing than her printed text has required. She obviously intended the notebooks and rough draft for her

---

[1] The first four editions were all published by the London house of Whittaker, Treacher & Company in 1832.

[2] This edition was published at London in 1839 as part of *Bentley's Standard Library of Popular Modern Literature*.

private use and gave little attention to such matters as punctuation, spelling, capitalization, and paragraphing. There seems no value to be gained by reproducing such spellings as *triffling, confussion, french,* and *english* or presenting her many unpunctuated sentences and un-paragraphed pages without supplying some helps for the reader. The rough draft of *Domestic Manners* is somewhat more carefully written than Mrs. Trollope's notebooks, but many sentences in it would make slow and awkward reading without further punctuation and some cor-rection of her spelling. Even in the rough draft her paragraphs are of-ten of interminable length, and it seems desirable to break these on oc-casion. Where the addition of a word or part of a word is necessary to the sense of her manuscript writings, the addition is enclosed in brack-ets. In preparing passages from the notebooks and rough draft I have tried to arrive at a readable text without carrying my alterations and emendations so far as to destroy the flavor of the originals.

APPENDIX D

PREFACE TO THE FIFTH EDITION OF

DOMESTIC MANNERS OF THE AMERICANS

Six years have elapsed since this work first appeared, and very considerable changes have in that time taken place on both sides the Atlantic.

Nevertheless, while re-perusing its pages in order to prepare a new edition for the press, I have found but few points on which I have learned to alter my opinions, and fewer still in which subsequent information has led me to believe that I have misstated facts. Whenever any thing of either kind has struck me, I have acknowledged it freely in the notes subjoined.

There is, in truth, but one point on which, if the book were still to be written, I should be likely to make it greatly different from what it is at present. Had I again to travel through the Union with a view to giving an account of what I saw, I should certainly devote a much larger portion of my attention to the great national feature — negro slavery.

The tremendous exposition of the increasing horrors of this fearful enormity produced by our legislative exertions during 1835 and 1836 for its total abolition throughout all British Colonies, has not only aroused anew every Christian and every human feeling against it, but has shown with terrible clearness, that not all we can do, not all the sacrifices we can make, will avail to relieve our dark-skinned fellow-creatures from the hideous barbarities inflicted on them, so long as other countries, and the wide-spreading southern States of the Union in particular, shall continue to legalise this horrible atrocity. Not surely with any hope that the most flagrant exposure could affect the minds of people so besotted by their avarice as to be insensible to the sure approach of the vengeance which all others so plainly see approaching them, — not surely with the slightest hope of this kind would any observations on the subject be offered; but all truth on a theme so tremendously important should be uttered by every voice that can hope to make itself heard.

On other, and less important points, I have had the pleasure of receiving acknowledgments from many who at first raised their voices to contradict me, that my statements were essentially correct, and that in many cases they have been useful; nor have American voices been wanting to confirm this judgment. Were it not, indeed, for the later, and much deeper offence, *partially* given by Jonathan Jefferson Whitlaw, I should have no fear of meeting any thing but a friendly reception from the educated classes were I to revisit America. But this must not be till slavery be abolished, or, till that part of the Union which has a right to call itself free, shall separate from that whose fame and whose history rests, and will for ever rest, more on its reputation for slavery, than on its claim to freedom. Till then, indeed, the Union must be a negative one; it is life and death bound up together; and if the courage, enterprise, and industry of the Eastern and free Western States would escape the rottenness that must inevitably spread if they continue thus linked together, they must submit to the mortifying necessity of lessening the map of their Federal territory. But — when the servile vengeance preparing has done its work, the divided States may meet again and shake hands.

London, April 27, 1839.

APPENDIX E

BIBLIOGRAPHY

1. Newspapers [1]

American Sentinel (Philadelphia), 1830.
Atkinson's Saturday Evening Post (Philadelphia), 1832.
Boston Weekly Messenger and Massachusetts Journal, 1832.
Catholic Telegraph (Cincinnati), 1835.
Cincinnati Advertiser, 1825–33.
Cincinnati Chronicle and Literary Gazette, 1827–35.
Cincinnati Daily Gazette, 1829–33.
Cincinnati Journal, 1832.
Constellation (New York), 1831–2.
Daily National Intelligencer (Washington), 1824, 1830.
Daily National Journal (Washington), 1830.
Evening Gazette (Boston), 1832.
Evening Star (Washington), 1919.
Globe (Washington), 1832.
Liberty Hall and Cincinnati Gazette, 1828.
National Republican and Ohio Political Register (Cincinnati), 1828–9.
New-York American, 1832.
New-York Evening Post for the Country, 1832.
New York Standard, 1832.
New York Statesman, 1824.
Philadelphia Gazette and Daily Advertiser, 1832.
Saturday Bulletin (Philadelphia), 1830.
Sun (Philadelphia), 1832.
Washington Gazette, 1824.

2. Books, Manuscripts, and Periodicals

Abbatt, William: *The Crisis of the Revolution, Being the Story of Arnold and André* (New York, 1899).
Alexander, J. E.: *Transatlantic Sketches, Comprising Visits to the Most Interesting Scenes in North and South America and the West Indies* (Philadelphia, 1833).
American Comic Annual, The, Henry James Finn, editor, D. C. Johnston, illustrator (Boston, 1831).
American Criticisms on Mrs. Trollope's Domestic Manners of the Americans (London, 1833); also second edition with an added article (London, 1833).
"Americans and Their Detractors, The," *Edinburgh Review*, LV (1832), 479–526.

---

[1] Years significant for this edition, not complete runs, are indicated.

Anderson, Charles: "A Letter," *Miami Journal,* II (1887), 4–14.

Anstey, Christopher: *The New Bath Guide; or Memoirs of the B-N-R-D Family, in a Series of Poetical Epistles,* John Britton, editor (London, 1832).

Appleton's Cyclopædia of American Biography, James G. Wilson and John Fiske, editors (New York, 1887–9).

Atlee, S. Yorke: "Hiram Powers, the Sculptor," *Littell's Living Age,* XLII (1854), 569–71.

Bailey, J. T.: *An Historical Sketch of the City of Brooklyn, and the Surrounding Neighborhood* (brooklyn, 1840).

Bassett, John S.: *Life of Andrew Jackson* (New York, 1928).

Bellows, H. W.: "Seven Sittings with Powers the Sculptor," *Appleton's Journal of Popular Literature, Science, and Art,* I (1869), 402–4; II (1869), 54–5, 106–8.

Berger, Max: *The British Traveller in America, 1836–1860* (New York, 1943).

Bernard, Karl, Herzog von Sachsen-Weimar-Eisenach: *Travels through North America during the Years 1825 and 1826* (Philadelphia, 1828).

[Biddle, Richard:] *Captain Hall in America* (Philadelphia, 1830).

Bishop, Joseph Bucklin: *Our Political Drama; Conventions, Campaigns, Candidates* (New York, 1904).

Blunt, Edmund M.: *The Picture of New-York and Stranger's Guide to the Commercial Metropolis of the United States* (New York, 1828).

[Botsford, Mrs. Margaret:] *Adelaide: a New and Original Novel, by a Lady of Philadelphia* (Philadelphia, 1816).

[——:] *The Reign of Reform, or, Yankee Doodle Court, by a Lady* (Baltimore, 1830).

[——:] *Viola, or the Heiress of St. Valverde, An Original Poem in Five Cantos to Which is Annexed, Patriotic Songs, Sonnets, &c.* (Louisville, Kentucky, 1820).

Bradley, Cyrus P.: "Journal of Cyrus P. Bradley," *Ohio Archæological and Historical Publications,* XV (1906), 207–70.

Brandon, Edgar Ewing, compiler: *A Pilgrimage of Liberty, a Contemporary Account of the Triumphal Tour of General Lafayette through the Southern and Western States in 1825, as Reported by the Local Newspapers* (Athens, Ohio, 1944).

Bremer, Frederika: *The Homes of the New World; Impressions of America* (New York, 1854).

Brooke, Frances: *The History of Emily Montague* (London, 1769).

Brooklyn Collegiate Institute for Young Ladies [a pamphlet] (New York, 1830).

Brooks, John Graham: *As Others See Us, a Study of Progress in the United States* (New York, 1910).

Buley, R. Carlyle, and Madge E. Pickard: *The Midwest Pioneer: His Ills, Cures, & Doctors* (Crawfordsville, Indiana, 1945).

Bulfinch, Charles: *Report of Charles Bulfinch on the Subject of Penitentiaries*, February 13, 1827, in 19th Congress, 2nd Session, Report No. 98, House of Representatives.

Bullock, William: *Sketch of a Journey through the Western States of North America* (London, 1827). A review of this book appears in the *Literary Gazette* for November 10, 1827, p. 725.

Burney, Fanny (Madame D'Arblay): *Evelina; or the History of a Young Lady's Introduction to the World* (New York, 1857).

Campbell, Alexander, and Robert Owen: *Debate on the Evidences of Christianity: Containing an Examination of the Social System, and of All the Systems of Scepticism of Ancient and Modern Times* . . . (Bethany, Virginia, 1829).

Carter, Judge: *The Old Court House: Reminiscences and Anecdotes* (Cincinnati, 1880).

Chambrun, Clara Longworth de: *Cincinnati, Story of the Queen City* (New York, 1939).

——: *The Making of Nicholas Longworth* (New York, 1933).

Chevalier, Michel: *Lettres sur l'Amérique du Nord* (Paris, 1836).

Cincinnati Directory for the Year 1829 (Cincinnati, 1829).

Cincinnati Directory for 1831 (Cincinnati, 1831).

Clemens, Samuel Langhorne (Mark Twain): *Life on the Mississippi* (New York, 1944).

Coggeshall, William T.: *The Poets and Poetry of the West, with Biographical and Critical Notices* (Columbus, Ohio, 1860).

Coke, E. T.: *A Subaltern's Furlough: Descriptive of Scenes in Various Parts of the United States* . . . *and Canada* (New York, 1833).

Colden, Cadwallader D.: *The Life of Robert Fulton* (New York, 1817).

Colton, Calvin: *The Americans, by an American* (London, 1833).

Cowell, Joe: *Thirty Years Passed among the Players in England and America: Interspersed with Anecdotes and Reminiscences of a Variety of Persons* . . . (New York, 1844).

Crawford, F. Marion: "Joseph Bonaparte in Bordentown," *Century Magazine*, XLVI (1893), 81–8.

Cumings, Samuel: *The Western Pilot, Containing Charts of the Ohio River, and of the Mississippi* . . . (Cincinnati, 1829).

Darby, William: *View of the United States, Historical, Geographical, and Statistical* . . . (Philadelphia, 1828).

D'Arusmont, Frances Wright: *Views of Society and Manners in America, in a Series of Letters from That Country to a Friend in England, during the Years 1818, 1819, 1820* (London, 1821).

[De Beck, William L.:] *Murder Will Out. The First Step in Crime*

Leads to the Gallows. The Horrors of the Queen City . . . by an Old Citizen (Cincinnati, 1867).

"Description [of Mrs. Trollope's Bazaar]," *Cincinnati Mirror and Western Gazette of Literature and Science,* III (1833), 24.

Dickens, Charles: *American Notes* (London, 1842).

Dictionary of American Biography, Dumas Malone, editor (New York, 1928–36).

Dictionary of American History, James Truslow Adams and R. V. Coleman, editors (New York, 1940).

"Domestic Manners of the Americans," *Illinois Monthly Magazine,* II (1832), 505–25.

"Domestic Manners of the Americans," *Quarterly Review,* XLVII (1832), 39–80.

Dorrance, Gordan, and Clarence E. MacCartney: *The Bonapartes in America* (Philadelphia, 1939).

Dorson, Richard M.: "The Story of Sam Patch," *American Mercury,* LXIV (1947), 741–7.

Drake, B., and E. D. Mansfield: *Cincinnati in 1826* (Cincinnati, 1827).

Dumersan, Théophile Marion, and Charles Augustin Sewrin: *Les Anglaises pour rire, ou la table et le logement, comédie en un acte, mêlée de couplets* (Paris, n.d.).

Dunbar, Seymour: *A History of Travel in America* (New York, 1937).

Dunlap, William: *A History of the Rise and Progress of the Arts of Design in the United States,* Frank W. Bayley and Charles E. Goodspeed, editors (Boston, 1918).

Elliott, Maud Howe, and Laura E. Richards: *Julia Ward Howe, 1819–1910* (Boston, 1925).

Emmons, Richard: *The Fredoniad: or, Independence Preserved. An Epick Poem on the Late War of 1812* (Boston, 1827).

"England and the United States," *New-York Mirror,* IX (1831–2), 351.

Everett, Linus S.: "A New Hell," *Trumpet and Universalist Magazine,* March 14, 1829, p. 148.

Fearon, Henry Bradshaw: *Sketches of America: a Narrative of a Journey of Five Thousand Miles through the Eastern and Western States of America . . .* (London, 1819).

Ferrall, Simon Ansley: *A Ramble of Six Thousand Miles through the United States of America* (London, 1832).

Flanagan, John T.: *James Hall, Literary Pioneer of the Ohio Valley* (University of Minnesota Press, 1941).

Flint, James: *Letters from America, 1818–1820* (Edinburgh, 1822).

Flint, Micah P.: *The Hunter and Other Poems* (Boston, 1826).

Flint, Timothy: *A Condensed Geography and History of the Western States, or the Mississippi Valley* (Cincinnati, 1828). Republished as *The History and Geography of the Mississippi Valley* (Cincinnati, 1832).

Flint, Timothy: *Francis Berrian; or, The Mexican Patriot* (Boston, 1826).

——: "General Lafayette's Landing and Reception at Cincinnati, an Historical Painting. Oguest [*sic*] Jean J. Hervieu, *pinx't*. Cincinnati: 1829," *Western Monthly Review*, III (1829–30), 440–7.

——: *Recollections of the Last Ten Years, Passed in Occasional Residences and Journeyings in the Valley of the Mississippi . . . in a Series of Letters . . .* (Boston, 1826).

——: "Travellers in America," *Knickerbocker*, II (1833), 283–302.

Foote, John P.: *The Schools of Cincinnati, and Its Vicinity* (Cincinnati, 1855).

Ford, Henry A., and Mrs. Kate B. Ford: *History of Cincinnati, Ohio* (Cleveland, 1881).

Fretageot, Marie: Letters of Marie Fretageot in the collections of the Library of the Workingmen's Institute, New Harmony, Indiana.

Galt, John: *Mrs. Bogle Corbet; or The Emigrants* (London, 1831).

Goodrich, Samuel Griswold: *Cabinet of Curiosities, Natural, Artificial, and Historical . . .* (Hartford, Connecticut, 1822).

Goss, Charles Frederic: *Cincinnati, the Queen City* (Cincinnati, 1912).

Gould, S. Baring: "The Wonder-Working Prince Hohenlohe," *Gentleman's Magazine*, n.s. XXXVI (1886), 536–47.

Greve, Charles Theodore: *Centennial History of Cincinnati and Representative Citizens* (Chicago, 1904).

Grund, Francis J.: *The Americans in Their Moral, Social, and Political Relations* (London, 1837).

Hall, Basil: *Fragments of Voyages and Travels: Chiefly for the Use of Young Persons* (London, 1832).

——: *Travels in North America in the Years 1827 and 1828* (Philadelphia, 1829).

Hall, James: *Notes on the Western States; Containing Descriptive Sketches of Their Soil, Climate, Resources and Scenery* (Philadelphia, 1838).

[Hamilton, Thomas:] *Men and Manners in America* (Philadelphia, 1833).

Hammond, Mrs. L. M.: *History of Madison County, State of New York* (Syracuse, New York, 1872).

Harlow, Alvin F.: *Old Towpaths: the Story of the American Canal Era* (New York, 1926).

Hendrickson, Walter B.: "The Western Museum Society of Cincinnati," *Scientific Monthly*, LXIII (1946), 66–72.

Hepburn, A. Barton: *Artificial Waterways and Commercial Development (with a History of the Erie Canal)* (New York, 1909).

Hesse, Nicholas: *Das westliche Nord-Amerika* (Paderborn, 1838). (1 quote from the translation of William G. Bek, which is still in manuscript.)

Hingston, Edward P.: *The Genial Showman, Being Reminiscences of the Life of Artemus Ward and Pictures of a Showman's Career in the Western World* (London, 1870).

"Hiram Powers," *Western Monthly Magazine*, III (1835), 244–7.

Hobman, D. L.: "Mrs. Trollope, the Novelist's Mother," *Contemporary Review*, CLXVIII (1945), 304–8.

[Hoffman, Charles Fenno:] *A Winter in the West* (New York, 1835).

Isham, Samuel: *The History of American Painting* (New York, 1927).

Johnson, James Weldon: *Black Manhattan* (New York, 1930).

Johnston, D. C.: "Trollopania," in *Scraps, No. 4, for the Year 1833* (Boston, 1833).

Jones, Robert Ralston: *Fort Washington at Cincinnati, Ohio* (Cincinnati, 1902).

Kellogg, Elizabeth R.: "Joseph Dorfeuille and the Western Museum," *Journal of the Cincinnati Society of Natural History*, XXII (1945), 3–29.

King, Charles: *Progress of the City of New-York, during the Last Fifty Years* (New York, 1852).

Kirkpatrick, John Ervin: *Timothy Flint, Pioneer, Missionary, Author, Editor, 1780–1840* (Cleveland, Ohio, 1911).

La Mott, John Henry: *History of the Archdiocese of Cincinnati, 1821–1921* (New York, 1921).

Lavater, John Caspar: *Essays on Physiognomy*, translated by Thomas Holcroft (London and New York, n.d.).

Laws, Instructions and Forms, for the Regulation of the Post-Office Department (Washington, 1832).

Lester, Charles Edwards: *The Artists of America* (New York, 1846).

Levasseur, A.: *Lafayette in America in 1824 and 1825; or Journal of a Voyage to the United States* (Philadelphia, 1829).

Lockwood, George B.: *The New Harmony Movement* (New York, 1905).

MacCartney, Clarence E., see Dorrance, Gordan.

Mackay, Charles: *Life and Liberty in America; or, Sketches of a Tour in the United States and Canada in 1857–58* (New York, 1859).

Macklin, Charles: *Love à la Mode: an Afterpiece, in Two Acts*, in *The British Drama: a Collection of the Most Esteemed Tragedies, Comedies, Operas, and Farces, in the English Language* (Philadelphia, 1850).

Magee, James D.: *Bordentown, 1682–1932* (Bordentown, New Jersey, 1932).

Mansfield, Edward D.: *Personal Memories, Social, Political, and Literary, with Sketches of Many Noted People, 1803–1843* (Cincinnati, 1879). See also Drake, B.

Marryat, Frederick: *Diary in America, with Remarks on Its Institutions,* second series (Philadelphia, 1840).

Martineau, Harriet: *Retrospect of Western Travel* (London, 1838).

——: *Society in America* (New York, 1837).

McAllister, Anna Shannon: *In Winter We Flourish; Life and Letters of Sarah Worthington King Peter, 1800–1877* (New York, 1939).

Mesick, Jane Louise: *The English Traveller in America, 1785–1835* (New York, 1922).

Miller, James M.: *The Genesis of Western Culture, the Upper Ohio Valley, 1800–1825* (Columbus, Ohio, 1938).

Mitford, Mary Russell: *The Friendships of Mary Russell Mitford as Recorded in Letters from Her Literary Correspondents,* A. G. K. L'Estrange, editor (New York, 1882).

——: *The Life of Mary Russell Mitford, Told by Herself in Letters to Her Friends,* A. G. K. L'Estrange, editor (New York, 1870).

——: *Our Village* (London, 1824–32).

Monroe, Will S.: *History of the Pestalozzian Movement in the United States* (Syracuse, New York, 1907).

Moore, Thomas: "Poems Relating to America," in *The Poetical Works of Thomas Moore* (Boston, 1857).

Mott, Frank Luther: *Jefferson and the Press* (Louisiana State University Press, 1943).

Mott, Hopper Striker: *The New York of Yesterday, a Descriptive Narrative of Old Bloomingdale* (New York, 1908).

"Mrs. Trollope," *Niles' Weekly Register,* VII, fourth series (1833), 67.

"Mrs. Trollope and the Americans," *American Quarterly Review,* XII (1832), 109–33.

"Mrs. Trollope's 'Domestic Manners of the Americans,'" *Cincinnati Mirror and Ladies' Parterre,* I (1832), 188.

Murray, Charles Augustus: *Travels in North America during the Years 1834, 1835, & 1836* (New York, 1839).

Nevins, Allan, editor: *American Social History as Recorded by British Travellers* (New York, 1923).

——, and Frank Weitenkampf: *A Century of Political Cartoons: Caricature in the United States from 1800 to 1900* (New York, 1944).

Nichols, Thomas L.: *Forty Years of American Life* (London, 1864).

North American Tourist, The (New York, 1839).

O'Daniel, Very Rev. V. F.: *The Right Reverend Edward Dominic Fenwick, O.P.* (New York, 1920).

Odell, George: *Annals of the New York Stage* (New York, 1927–45).

O'Ferrall, Simon Ansley, see Ferrall, Simon Ansley.

"One More River to Cross [an account of the Shakers]," *Time,* L (1947), 59.

Owen, Robert: *Outline of the Rational System of Society, Founded on Demonstrable Facts* (London, 1830). See also Campbell, Alexander.

"Paintings of Colonel Trumbull, The," *New-York Mirror*, VIII (1831), 339.

Parker, Jane Marsh: *Rochester; a Story Historical* (Rochester, New York, 1884).

Perkins, A. J. G., and Theresa Wolfson: *Frances Wright, Free Enquirer; the Study of a Temperament* (New York, 1939).

Pickard, Madge E., see Buley, R. Carlyle.

Post-Office Laws, Instructions and Forms (Washington, 1828).

"Prince Pückler Muscau and Mrs. Trollope," *North American Review*, LXXVIII (1833), 1–48.

Report of the Committee . . . to Inquire into the Causes and Particulars of the Invasion of the City of Washington, by the British Forces in the Month of August, 1814 . . . (Washington, 1814).

Richards, Laura E., see Elliott, Maud Howe.

Rusk, Ralph Leslie: *The Literature of the Middle Western Frontier* (New York, 1925).

Sadleir, Michael: *Anthony Trollope, a Commentary* (Boston and New York, 1927). Revised edition entitled *Trollope, a Commentary* (New York, 1947).

Scharf, J. Thomas: *The Chronicles of Baltimore: Being a Complete History of 'Baltimore Town' and Baltimore City from the Earliest Period to the Present Time* (Baltimore, 1874).

Schlesinger, Arthur M., Jr.: *The Age of Jackson* (Boston, 1945).

Schmidt-Phiseldek, Dr. C. F. von, a review of his *Europe and America* (Copenhagen, 1820), in *American Quarterly Review*, IX (1831), 398–420.

Sedgwick, Catharine Maria: *Clarence: or, A Tale of Our Own Times* (New York, 1849).

——: *Redwood: a Tale* (New York, 1850).

Sewrin, Charles Augustin, see Dumersan, Théophile Marion.

[Shelton, Frederick William:] *The Trolloppiad; or, Travelling Gentlemen in America* (New York, 1837).

Shirreff, Patrick: *A Tour through North America* (Edinburgh, 1835).

Smith, Ophia D.: "Joseph Tosso, the Arkansaw Traveler," *Ohio State Archæological and Historical Quarterly*, LVI (1947), 16–45.

Smith, Solomon Franklin: *Theatrical Management in the West and South for Thirty Years* (New York, 1868).

Stebbins, Lucy Poate, and Richard Poate Stebbins: *The Trollopes: the Chronicle of a Writing Family* (New York, 1945).

Stuart, James: *Three Years in North America* (Edinburgh and London, 1833).

Taft, Lorado: *The History of American Sculpture* (New York, 1924).

Tanner, H. S.: *A Description of the Canals and Rail Roads of the United States* (New York, 1840).

T[hacher], B. B.: "Sketch of a Self-Made Sculptor," *Knickerbocker*, V (1835), 270–7.

Thomson, James: *The Seasons* (London, 1842).

Tocqueville, Alexis de: *Democracy in America*, Phillips Bradley, editor (New York, 1945).

Tosso, Jose: "Reminiscences of Jose Tosso," an undated newspaper clipping in the collections of the Historical and Philosophical Society of Ohio.

Trollope, Anthony: *Autobiography of Anthony Trollope* (New York, 1911).

——: *North America* (New York, 1862).

Trollope, Frances Eleanor: *Frances [Milton] Trollope, Her Life and Literary Work from George III to Victoria* (London, 1895).

Trollope, Frances Milton: *Belgium and Western Germany in 1833* (London, 1834).

——: *The Life and Adventures of Jonathan Jefferson Whitlaw; or Scenes on the Mississippi* (London, 1836).

——: *The Mother's Manual, or Illustrations of Matrimonial Economy* (London, 1833).

——: Notebooks of Mrs. Trollope for *Domestic Manners of the Americans*. See Appendix B of this edition.

——: *The Old World and the New: a Novel* (London, 1849).

——: *Paris and the Parisians in 1835* (London, 1836).

——: *Petticoat Government: a Novel* (London, 1850).

——: *The Refugee in America: a Novel* (London, 1832).

——: Rough draft of *Domestic Manners of the Americans*. See Appendix B of this edition.

——: *Tremordyn Cliff* (London, 1835).

——: *The Vicar of Wrexhill* (London, 1837).

——: *Vienna and the Austrians* (London, 1838).

——: *A Visit to Italy* (London, 1842).

Trollope, Thomas Adolphus, "Some Recollections of Hiram Powers," *Lippincott's Magazine*, XV (1875), 205–15.

——: *What I Remember* (New York, 1888).

"Trollopes," *New-York Mirror*, X (1832–3), 223.

Tuckerman, Henry T.: *America and Her Commentators, with a Critical Sketch of Travel in the United States* (New York, 1864).

Tudor, Henry: *Narrative of a Tour in North America* (London, 1834).

"Uncle Sam's Peculiarities, a Journey from New York to Philadelphia and Back," *Bentley's Miscellany*, IV (1838), 40–8.

[Vandewater, Robert J.:] *The Tourist, or Pocket Manual for Travellers on the Hudson River, the Western Canal, and Stage Road* . . . (New York, 1827).

Varle, Charles: *A Complete View of Baltimore, with a Statistical Sketch* (Baltimore, 1833).

Venable, William Henry: *Beginnings of Literary Culture in the Ohio Valley, Historical and Biographical Sketches* (Cincinnati, 1891).

———: *A Buckeye Boyhood* (Cincinnati, 1911).

Vigne, Godfrey T.: *Six Months in America* (London, 1832).

"Week in Cincinnati in 1829, A," *Knickerbocker*, IX (1837), 259–65.

Weitenkampf, Frank, see Nevins, Allan.

Wemyss, Francis Courtney: *Wemyss' Chronology of the American Stage: from 1752 to 1852* (New York, 1852).

Western Traveler's Pocket Directory and Stranger's Guide, The (Schenectady, 1834).

Williams, Stanley: *The Life of Washington Irving* (New York, 1935).

Williamson, Jefferson: *The American Hotel: an Anecdotal History* (New York, 1930).

Willis, Nathaniel P.: "The Ruse," *The Token: a Christmas and New Year's Present* (Boston, 1829), 150–75.

Williston, E. B., compiler: *Eloquence of the United States* (Middletown, Connecticut, 1827).

Winfield, Charles H.: *Hopoghan Hockingh; Hoboken, a Pleasure Resort for Old New York* (New York, 1895).

Wolfson, Theresa, see Perkins, A. J. G.

Wright, Frances, see D'Arusmont, Frances Wright.

3. Editions of *Domestic Manners of the Americans*

English and American

Domestic Manners of the Americans (London: Whittaker, Treacher & Co., 1832), 2 vols. Four editions within 1832.

Domestic Manners of the Americans (London: Printed for Whittaker, Treacher, & Co.; New York: Reprinted for the Booksellers, 1832). Four editions within 1832.[2]

Domestic Manners of the Americans (New York: Harper & Bros., 1838).[3]

Domestic Manners of the Americans, fifth English edition, Bentley's Standard Library of Popular Modern Literature, Vol. IV (London: Richard Bentley; 1839).[4] (Contains new notes by Mrs. Trollope.)

---

[2] S. Austin Allibone's *Critical Dictionary* (1882) lists as well a two-volume New York edition in 1832 and a one-volume edition entitled *Travels in America* for 1849. *American Book Prices Current*, XLIX (1942–3), 367, records the sale of a rare undated two-volume New York edition.

[3] Listed in O. A. Roorbach's *Bibliotheca Americana* (1852).

[4] *The English Catalogue of Books* (1864) lists a cheap (3s., 6d.) one-volume edition by Bentley in 1849, possibly a misprint for 1839

Domestic Manners of the Americans, with an introduction by Harry Thurston Peck (New York: Dodd, Mead & Co.; 1901).

Domestic Manners of the Americans, Unit Books, No. 6 (New York: H. W. Bell; 1904).

Domestic Manners of the Americans, with an introduction by Michael Sadleir (New York: Dodd, Mead & Co.; 1927).

In Foreign Languages

Costumbres familiares de los americanos del Norte. Obra escrita en ingles por Mistress Trollope, y traducida por Don Juan Floran . . . (Paris: Libreria de Lecointe; 1834), 2 vols.

Leben und Sitte in Nordamerika, geschildert von Mrs. Trollope. Nach den vierten Auflage aus dem Englischen, übertragen von Dr. Hermann Franz (Kiel: Universitäte Buchhandlung; 1835), 3 vols.

Mœurs domestiques des Américains, par Mistress Trollope, ouvrage traduit de l'anglais sur la quatrième édition (Paris: Librairie de Charles Gosselin; 1833), 2 vols. A third edition in one volume, same title and publisher, 1841.

Zeden, Gewoonten en Huisselijk Leven der Noord-Amerikanen, door Mistress Trollope beschreven, na een driejarig Verblijf in de Vereenigde Staten; (gevolgd naar den Vierden Engelschen Druk) (Haarlem: bij de Wed. A. Loosjes, Pz.; 1833), 2 vols.

ACKNOWLEDGMENTS

It is a pleasure to acknowledge my signal indebtedness to Professor R. Carlyle Buley of Indiana University; Professor Richard G. Lillard of the University of California at Los Angeles; Professor Gordon N. Ray of the University of Illinois; and Miss Muriel Rose Trollope, great-granddaughter of Mrs. Trollope. Other friends who have given advice and encouragement at various times during the making of this book are too numerous to name within the limits of this note, but the following must be mentioned with gratitude for special services: Mr. Morgan Blum of Indiana University; Professor Frank Davidson of Indiana University; Miss Caroline Dunn, Librarian of the William Henry Smith Memorial Library; Miss Elizabeth R. Kellogg; Dr. Robert Mitchner of Indiana University; and Professor Harry Stevens of Duke University.

A large part of the material for the Introduction and Notes to this edition was dug from the rare books and newspapers of the Historical and Philosophical Society of Ohio, to whose officers and staff, especially Mr. Virginius C. Hall, Director, and Miss Lillian Wuest, I am grateful for many kindnesses during my frequent visits to Cincinnati. I owe equally deep obligations to the librarians and officers of the Indiana University Library, my chief center of operations, and particular thanks for making the notebooks and rough draft of *Domestic Manners of the Americans* available for this edition. I am indebted also to the librarians and officers of the Cincinnati Public Library; the Harvard College Library; the Indiana Historical Society; the Library of Congress; the Miami University Library; the Newberry Library; the New York Public Library; the Ohio State Archæological and Historical Society; the Ohio State University Library; the University of Chicago Library; and the Workingmen's Institute at New Harmony, Indiana.

The Trustees and officials of Indiana University have been most kind in granting funds necessary for my researches.

Grateful acknowledgment is due to Harper & Brothers and the Trustee and the Literary Editor of the Clemens Estate for permission to quote from the suppressed passages of Mark Twain's *Life on the Mississippi;* to Professor R. Carlyle Buley for permission to quote from Madge E. Pickard and R. Carlyle Buley's *The Midwest Pioneer: His Ills, Cures, & Doctors.*

Last, and most important, there is my indebtedness to my wife, who shared with me much of the search through old books and newspapers for traces of Mrs. Trollope's life in America — a long and arduous treasure hunt, but one not without its rewarding moments.

Donald Smalley

Indiana University
December 8, 1947

INDEX

Academy of Fine Arts, Cincinnati, 64 ff.

Actors, English, popularity of, in U. S., 131–2

Adams, John Quincy, 19, 143n, 189, 255

Agriculture, see Farming

Ague, 179–80; see also Fever

Albany, New York, lx, 368–9, 396, 401–2

Alderson, Lady, lxiii

Alexandria, Virginia, lix, 294–5, 326, 330 f., 438–9

Allegheny Mountains, lii, 6, 31, 438; flowers and vegetation of, 251; Mrs. Trollope's journey over, 192–201

Alligators, 4; Mrs. Trollope's "crocodile" story and Mark Twain's comment, 21

Allston, Washington, 267–8

Almack's, 13, 51

Alms-giving, rarity of, 119

Ameling, Mrs., of Cincinnati, xxxviii

America and Her Commentators (Tuckerman), 133n

American character, see Amusements, Boastfulness, Coldness, Enterprise, Originality, Sensitiveness to criticism, etc.

American Comic Annual, The (Finn and Johnston), 321

American Dog Apollo, 66n

American Notes (Dickens), lxxi, 88n

American Quarterly Review, 94, 324–6

"Americans," Mrs. Trollope's limitation of the word, 322, 404

Americans, origins of, 405

Amusements, 137, 156, 177, 273, 298–9, 369; ball at Cincinnati, 154–5; card-playing, 299; parties at Washington, D. C., 218; at

Amusements (*continued*)
New York City, 299, 339; quilting frolic, 416; rural amusements, 177; sleighing, 304; see also Dancing, Gambling, Theaters

Amusements, general lack of, 74, 81, 118, 177, 184, 209, 218, 233, 305, 339

Anderson, Charles, xii, xxxviii, 50n

Anderson, Mrs., proprietor of hotel at Memphis, 24–6

André, Major John Lewis, 367

Anglaises pour rire, Les (Sewrin and Dumersan), 407

Anglo-American relations: great difference between English and American points of view, 363–4, 405–7, 431–2; improved transatlantic travel may better, lxxiii, 102n; see also Anti-British feeling, Sensitiveness to criticism

Anstey, Christopher, 83–4

Anti-British feeling, 101–2, 157–62, 196, 292–3, 317–22, 345, 351, 354–65, 393; as result of *Domestic Manners*, ix ff.; see also Anglo-American relations, Sensitiveness to criticism

Architecture, 35–6, 39, 204–5, 303n, 333–4, 342, 352, 368, 391; of Bazaar, xli ff.; a city of wood, 389; see also Housing

Aristocracy, salutary effects of, in Europe, 111, 156, 425

Arlington, Virginia, 231

Armstrong, General, 320

Army, American, 319–21, 367n, 378n

Arnold, Benedict, 367n

Art, 188, 206–7, 228–9, 262, 345–6, 385–6, 414; complacency of Americans regarding their artists, 394–5; exhibition at Cincinnati, 64 ff.;

Bullock, William (*continued*)
167 ff.; host to Mrs. Trollope,
xxxviii
Bulwer-Lytton, Edward George, 178
Burke, Edmund, 257
Burke, William, 143*n*
Burney, Fanny, 403*n*
Byron, George Gordon, Lord, xli,
91–2, 173, 404

Caldwell, Charles, 67–9
Calhoun, John C., 395*n*
Callender, James Thomson, 72*n*
Calomel, excessive quantities of,
prescribed for "the fever," 83–4,
178
Calvinists, 108
Camp meeting, 110, 167–75
Campbell, Alexander, his debates
with Robert Owen, 147–53
Campbell, Thomas, 149
Canada, 378*n*, 379, 396*n*; recom-
mended as haven for British poor,
291–3
Canals, 34*n*, 35, 303; canal boats,
359, 369–73, 376; Chesapeake
and Delaware, 259; Chesapeake
and Ohio, 163, 225; Erie, 286*n*,
369–73, 376; Morris, 347–8
Canandaigua, Lake, 390 f., 397
Canandaigua, New York, 391
Canaseraga, New York, 400*n*
Canova, Antonio, 173
Capital of U. S., prospect of moving
to Ohio, 424
Capital punishment, rare in U. S.,
163–6, 285
Capitol, Washington, D. C., 215–29
passim, 261, 320 f.
Captain Hall in America (Biddle),
356*n*
Caricatures, American, 96, 321*n*,
331–2
Carriages, 272, 352–3; described,
303–4
Carroll, Mary, 9 f.
Carter, Judge, of Cincinnati, 95
Catholics, *see* Roman Catholic
Church

Catskill Mountains, 368
Cazenovia, New York, 400*n*
Cervantes, 257
Channing, William Ellery, 94*n*, 314
Chapman, John G., 326–7
Charleston, Virginia, *Gazette*, 308–9
Chaucer, 92, 312
Cherokee Indians, 222
Chesapeake and Delaware Canal,
259
Chesapeake and Ohio Canal, 163,
225
Chesapeake Bay, lii, 213, 215
Chesapeake River, 259
Children: Canadian contrasted with
American, 379; at Ibbertson's
school, Baltimore, 212 f.; inde-
pendence of American, 67, 121 ff.,
213, 295, 414–20; lack of disci-
pline, 177, 213; tyranny of, over
slaves, 245
Chivalry, American failure to comprehend principle of, 257, 421
Cholera, 56, 88
Chronicles of Cannongate (Scott),
94
Churches in America, plainness of,
342
Cicero, 342
Cincinnati, liv, lvi, lxv, lxxv, 12*n*,
29*n*, 30, 193, 201, 211, 233, 272,
279, 300*n*, 329*n*, 354, 380*n*, 429,
438; Academy of Fine Arts, xx,
xxiii f., 64–7; boarding-houses, 84;
characterizations of Cincinnati,
vii, xii, xvi*n*, xix f., xxxvi f., lxxii f.;
cows in, 61–2; the fashionable of,
xlvi–ix, lxix, 51, 81, 130*n*; rapid
growth of, xliv, 43; hogs in, 38–9,
88–9, 105; hotels, 36–8, 143*n*;
lack of sanitation in, 38–40; location of, 40 f.; Letton's Museum,
xxv f., 62 f.; markets of, 60 f., 85,
417–19; Mechanics' Institute, 66*n*;
Mrs. Trollope at Cincinnati, xix–
lii, 36–181; murder in, 163–6;
Phrenological Society, 68–9; Picture Gallery, 64; reception of
President Jackson, 142–5; of La-

Hotels (*continued*)
town, Maryland, 200 f.; Lake Canandaigua, New York, 391; Lockport, New York, 378; Memphis, 24–6; a mountain inn, 196; Niagara Falls, 386–7; Philadelphia, 260n; Trenton Falls, 373; Utica, New York, 395; Washington, D. C., 216; Washington, Pennsylvania, 194; Wheeling, Virginia, 185 ff.
House of Representatives, 226–7
Houses, moving of, in streets, liv, 89
Housing: at Baltimore, 205, 261; at Cincinnati, 36, 48, 49, 84, 89 f.; at New York City, 338–9, 349–50, 352; at Philadelphia, 261, 281; of small landholders in Maryland, 241, 243; gentlemen's seats near New York City, 368; near Philadelphia, 333–4; *see also* Architecture, Boarding-houses, Hotels
Howard Society, 119
Howe, Julia Ward, 54n
Hudson River, 347, 366, 401–3
Humor, American, 209n, 233–4, 321 ff.
Hunter, The, and Other Poems (M. Flint), 314
Hyde Park, New York, 368
Hygeia, Bullock's proposed town in Kentucky, xvin, xxxviii, 50n

Ibbertson, Mr., his Infant School at Baltimore, 212 f.
Ice for relief in summer, 95, 352, 401
Illinois, 35
Immigrants: Canada recommended as haven for, 291–3; feeling against in U. S., 290–3
Inclined planes, Morris Canal, 347–8
Independence, American conception of, *see* Freedom, American conception of
Indian Affairs, Bureau of, at Washington, 220 ff.
Indian summer, cause of, 307
Indiana, 35, 42, 167, 306, 424

Indiana University Library, liv, 437
Indianapolis, Indiana, 306
Indians, 7, 35, 178, 236, 272, 307, 391–2, 398–400, 416n, 423; Bureau of Indian Affairs at Washington, 220 ff.; Delawares, 141n; Indian and bear anecdote, 435–6; portraits of, by King, 220 f.; sermon of Piquot Indian, 330 f.; unjust treatment of Cherokees by Congress, 221 ff.; weak delineations of, in American literature, 313
Infernal Regions of the Western Museum, Cincinnati, xxix–xxxiv; conceived by Mrs. Trollope, xxviii, xxxi f.; described, xxxi ff., 62 f.; executed principally by Hiram Powers, xxix; later success of, xxxiv; religious effect of, xxxiii f.
Ingham, Charles Cromwell, 268
Inns, *see* Hotels
Insects, 8, 95, 158, 176, 239, 252–4, 369, 415
Internal improvements, *see* Government, jealousy of states toward federal
Invisible Girl of the Western Museum, Cincinnati, xxvii–ix
Irish in U. S., 286, 292, 324; condition of, as canal laborers, 290 f.; feeling against, 290
Irving, Washington, 315, 368; on *Domestic Manners*, xii

Jackson, Andrew, xxv, 19, 189, 222n, 255, 286n, 331–2; visit to Cincinnati, 142–5
Jefferson, Thomas, 71–3, 141n, 244n, 263–4, 316 f.
"Jeremiah Thin," 271
Jews, 107n, 276
Johnson, James Weldon, 350n
Johnson, Miss, of Baltimore, 211n
Johnston, D. C., 96, 321n

Kaleirama, Washington, D. C., 230–1
Kean, Edmund, 130, 132

Sewrin, Charles Augustin, 407n
Sexes, segregation of, and conse-
quences, 15, 25, 47, 58, 136–7,
155 ff., 182–4, 268–9, 299, 339,
343–5, 422
Shakers, lviii, 107n, 139–41
Shakespeare, 8n, 92, 104, 129, 130n,
132
Shenandoah River, 225
Sheridan, Richard Brinsley, 130n
Sherlock, William, 313
Shippingport, Kentucky, 34n
Ships, transatlantic, lxxiii, 3, 6, 403,
426, 432–4
Shirreff, Patrick, 133n
Shops: of Albany, New York, 401–2;
of New York City, 352; of Phila-
delphia, 272
Sickness, xliv, lv, lix, 56, 88, 117,
176–80, 290 f., 294, 307; see also
Calomel, Doctors, Fever
Siddons, Sarah, 130, 322
Sing Sing, 364
"Sir Patrick Spens," 104n
Sitting, peculiar American manner
of, 134, 138–9, 162, 226, 228,
234; see also "Trollope!"
Six Months in America (Vigne),
182n
Sketch of a Journey through the
Western States (Bullock), 50n
Sketch of the Combat of Thermopy-
læ (Hervieu), xxii
Slavery, xiv, lxxi, lxvii f., 8 f., 14 f.,
52, 71–3, 157, 185–7, 194, 196,
220n, 303n, 317, 414, 424, 442–
3; domestic slaves, 245, 247–50;
effect of, on owners, 247 ff.; slave
hired by day in free territory,
417–19; teaching of slaves forbid-
den by law, 246; see also Negroes
Sleighing, 304
Smith, Captain John, 236
Smith, Seba, 209n
Snags, sawyers, and planters, 22n
Snakes, 238, 253–4
Society in America (Martineau),
53n
"Song of Steam" (Cutter), 132n

South, as section of country, 157,
186, 414, 424; see also Slavery
South Carolina, 246
Speech, peculiarities of American,
lv, lxxiii, 45, 53, 130n, 157–8,
185n, 227, 229–30, 242, 243, 298,
309, 364, 370 ff., 428 f.; Americans' belief in superiority of their
pronunciation, 321 f., 324; Mrs.
Trollope's list of words and
phrases, liv, 427–8; scene in
American dialect, 414–21; taboo
words, 136; Yankeeisms made
popular in England by Domestic
Manners, viii, lxiii
Spencer, John, 306
Spencer, Mrs., of Cincinnati, lv
Spenser, Edmund, 92, 312
"Spinning visits," 340
Spitting, lv, lxxi, 58, 86, 120, 133,
156, 184, 282, 340, 415, 421–3,
429; American poem on Mrs.
Trollope's view of, 340n; in Con-
gress, 226, 228; in theaters, 133,
234, 271; Mrs. Trollope's epitaph
for "George Washington Spit-
chew," lvi, 422
Spurzheim, Gaspar, 68
Staël, Mme de, 45n
Stafford, Connecticut, 271n
Stagecoach travel, 187, 192–203
passim, 308–9, 335–6, 369, 377–9,
389–402 passim; see also Roads
Steamboats, 22n, 23, 30 f., 34n, 35,
39, 142–4, 321n, 368; described,
15 ff., 304–5; Albany to New York
City, 366 ff., 402–3; Baltimore to
Philadelphia, 333; Baltimore to
Washington, 288; Baltimore to
Chesapeake and Delaware Canal,
259; Cincinnati to Wheeling,
180–5; Memphis to Cincinnati,
32–5; New Orleans to Memphis,
15–24; Philadelphia to Trenton,
New Jersey, 333–4; Philadelphia
to Fort Delaware, 259; Raraton
River to New York City, 336
Stevens, John, 342 ff.
Stewart, Lady Louisa, lxiii

Stone, Mrs. [probably Anna Garnett Stone; see 236n], li, liii, 236–47 *passim;* 251–7, 290, 333

Stonington, Maryland, liii–ix, 236–47, 251–7, 288–94, 438–9

Stuart, James, 395n

Swedenborgian Church, 107n, 108

"Sweets," American fondness for, 298

Swift, Jonathan, 5, 15 f., 310

Tacitus, 342

Taglioni, 135n

Talking, American fondness for, 69

Tall tales, American spinners of, 21n, 435

Talleyrand, 310

Talma, François Joseph, 132

Tanner, H. S., 348n

Tappan, New Jersey, 367n

Tarrytown, New York, 367n

Tasso, 313

Taxation, 43, 50, 117, 306

Taylor, Jeremy, 313

Tecumseh, xxvi

Tennessee, 42, 424

Texas, 147

Text of *Domestic Manners,* present edition, *see* 440–1

Theater, 190 f., 262–3, 315, 321–2; at Baltimore, 208–9; at Cincinnati, 74, 129 ff., 191, 233; at New Orleans, 14; at New York, 339–40, 350; at Philadelphia, 270–72; at Washington, D. C., 218, 233–4; scarcity of women in audiences, 263; sortie from American and European theaters contrasted, 272, 429–30

Thirty Years Passed among the Players (Cowell), xlvii f., 37n, 130n

Thompson, Pishey, 218

Thomson, James, 87

Three Years in North America (Stuart), 395n

Thunder-storms, lxiii, 87 f., 288–90, 374, 390 f.

Titles, American love of, 18 f., 32, 182

"To the Lord Viscount Forbes" (Moore), 244–5

"To the Planet Jupiter" (poem in Bristol newspaper), 103n

Tobacco, lxxi, 15 f., 18, 35, 47, 58n, 100, 117, 120, 133n, 156, 184, 192, 234, 278–80, 284, 299, 329, 340, 344, 351, 386, 390, 415, 417, 421, 422–3, 425

Token, The (American annual), 322–3

Tosso, Jose, xxviii, xxxviii

Tour through North America, A (Shirreff), 133n

Transylvania College, 68n

Travel, advantages of, for Americans, lxxiii, 323–4

Travels in North America (B. Hall), lvii–ix, lxi, 4n, 321n, 354–65

Travels in Upper and Lower Egypt (Denon), xli

Travels through North America (Saxe-Weimar), 307n

Trees, 4 f., 7 f., 19, 22, 26–7, 30, 32, 35, 42, 103, 176, 194–5, 237–9, 251, 258n, 262, 266, 288, 293, 334, 343, 352, 373, 396; *see also* Forests, Vegetation

Trenton, New Jersey, 335

Trenton Falls, 373–5, 382

Trimble, Governor of Ohio, 164n

"Trollope!" cry in theaters, ix, 133n

Trollope, Anthony, xv, xxxvi, lxvi f., lxix; beginnings of career, lxxiv; life with father at Harrow Weald, lxii; relation to novelist mother, lxxiv f.; visits Bazaar, lii

Trollope, Cecilia, xv, xvii, xxxvi, li, liii, lx, lxvi, lxviii, lxix, lxxv, 82n, 141, 379

Trollope Emily, xv, xvii, xxxvi, li, liii, lx, lxvi, lxviii, 82n, 141, 379

Trollope, Frances: characterizations of, vii, viii–xii, xiv, xvi, xxxix f., xlv, lxxv f., 300n, 359n; her attitude toward *Domestic Manners,* viii, x–xii, 106, 138n, 295–6, 357, 359, 403–5, 431–2, 442–3; voyage to U. S., xvii, lvii, 3, 6, 426, 432–

FRANCES (MILTON) TROLLOPE was born in 1780. In 1809 she married Thomas Anthony Trollope (1774-1835), a cousin of the Admiral Sir Henry Trollope who played some part in the American Revolution. In 1827-30 Mrs. Trollope visited the United States, where she was involved in her husband's disastrous scheme to start a department store in Cincinnati. In addition to her renowned report on that visit, she wrote numerous travel books— on Belgium, Paris, and Vienna—and many novels, the best-known of which were *The Vicar of Wrexhill* and *The Widow Barnaby*. Long after her husband's death (in 1855, the year of her son Anthony's first success, with his novel *The Warden*), she settled in Italy, forming one ornament of the large colony of British literati at Florence. It was in that city that she died in 1863.

DONALD ARTHUR SMALLEY was born in 1907. He received his A.B. (1929) and A.M. degrees from Indiana University, his Ph.D. (1939) from Harvard. He has been a teaching fellow at Harvard and assistant professor of English at Indiana University. During the 1948-9 and 1949-50 terms he had been visiting assistant professor of English at the University of Illinois, where he is now permanently on the English faculty. His critical edition of Robert Browning's *Essay on Chatterton* was issued in 1948 by the Harvard University Press.

THIS BOOK is set in Caledonia, a Linotype face designed by W. A. Dwiggins. Caledonia belongs to the family of printing types called "modern face" by printers—a term used to mark the change in style of type-letters that occurred about 1800. Caledonia borders on the general design of Scotch Modern, but is more freely drawn than that letter. Printed by THE MURRAY PRINTING CO., Forge Village, Mass.